# Keynes Against Capitalism

Keynes is one of the most important and influential economists who ever lived. It is almost universally believed that Keynes wrote his magnum opus, *The General Theory of Employment, Interest and Money*, to save capitalism from the socialist, communist, and fascist forces that were rising up during the Great Depression era. This book argues that this was not the case with respect to socialism.

Tracing the evolution of Keynes's views on policy from WWI until his death in 1946, Crotty argues that virtually all post-WWII "Keynesian" economists misinterpreted crucial parts of Keynes's economic theory, misunderstood many of his policy views, and failed to realize that his overarching political objective was not to save British capitalism, but rather to replace it with Liberal Socialism. This book shows how Keynes's Liberal Socialism began to take shape in his mind in the mid-1920s, evolved into a more concrete institutional form over the next decade or so, and was laid out in detail in his work on postwar economic planning at Britain's Treasury during WWII. Finally, it explains how *The General Theory* provided the rigorous economic theoretical foundation needed to support his case against capitalism in support of Liberal Socialism.

Offering an original and highly informative exposition of Keynes's work, this book should be of great interest to teachers and students of economics. It should also appeal to a general audience interested in the role the most important economist of the 20th century played in developing the case against capitalism and in support of Liberal Socialism. *Keynes Against Capitalism* is especially relevant in the context of today's global economic and political crises.

**James Crotty** is Emeritus Professor of Economics at the University of Massachusetts Amherst and Senior Research Associate at the Political Economy Research Institute. His research in theory and policy attempts to integrate the complementary analytical strengths of the Marxian and Keynesian traditions.

# Economics as Social Theory
Series edited by Tony Lawson
*University of Cambridge*

Social Theory is experiencing something of a revival within economics. Critical analyses of the particular nature of the subject matter of social studies and of the types of method, categories and modes of explanation that can legitimately be endorsed for the scientific study of social objects are re-emerging. Economists are again addressing such issues as the relationship between agency and structure, between economy and the rest of society, and between the enquirer and the object of enquiry. There is a renewed interest in elaborating basic categories such as causation, competition, culture, discrimination, evolution, money, need, order, organization, power probability, process, rationality, technology, time, truth, uncertainty, value etc.

The objective for this series is to facilitate this revival further. In contemporary economics the label "theory" has been appropriated by a group that confines itself to largely asocial, ahistorical, mathematical "modelling." Economics as Social Theory thus reclaims the "Theory" label, offering a platform for alternative rigorous, but broader and more critical conceptions of theorizing.

### 46. Knowledge, Class and Economics
Marxism without Guarantees
*Edited by Theodore Burczak, Robert Garnett and Richard McIntyre*

### 47. Markets
Perspectives from Economic and Social Theory
*William A. Jackson*

### 48. Keynes Against Capitalism
His Economic Case for Liberal Socialism
*James Crotty*

For more information about this series, please visit: www.routledge.com/Economics-as-Social-Theory/book-series/EAST

"This book is a marvel of economic narrative, with Crotty's clarity and Keynes's elegance in stunning counterpoint, from Versailles through the Depression to the war and Bretton Woods, all bringing forth the great, neglected fact that Keynes's Liberal Socialism was far more radical than modern memory would have us think."

**James K. Galbraith**, *Lloyd M. Bentsen, Jr. Chair in Government/Business Relations, University of Texas at Austin*

"James Crotty's writings have always been marked by deep thought and analysis, independence of mind, a judicious amalgamation of theory and empirical evidence and humane and realistic policies. The present volume is characterised by all these traits, it is vintage Crotty. The author makes a convincing case that Keynes since *The Economic Consequences of Peace* (1919) has been developing his ideas on liberal socialism that highlight the centrality of planning and public investment in sustaining full employment, ideas that came to full maturity in *The General Theory* and Keynes's writings and activities after its publication, in World War II and up to his death in April 1946. Crotty's arguments undermine the conventional wisdom of Keynesians and non-Keynesians alike that Keynes's aim was to save capitalism from itself and should be required reading for professional economists of all persuasions, policy makers, and concerned citizens appalled by the economic and political malaise we currently find ourselves in."

**Geoffrey Harcourt**, *Emeritus Reader in The History of Economic Theory, Cambridge, Honorary Professor UNSW, Sydney*

"This bold and brilliant work revolutionizes our understanding of Keynes' economics. Instead of reopening the often-debated topic of the essential characteristics of 'Keynesian economics,' James Crotty puts Keynes' lectures and writings into the context of both the economists and politicians with whom he interacted and of his political and policy engagements. Focusing on the moving pulse of Keynes' ideas from 1919 through his death in 1946, the author traces the evolution of his profound and extensive vision: achieving a sustainable future for capitalism cannot be left to market forces, but must be managed through public investment and of socialist planning and coordination. This book's provocative approach is perfectly timed for broad rethinking of macroeconomics that is now underway. In the density and originality of its themes, and in the integrity and depth of its scholarship, the reader is left in little doubt that this is the work of a master."

**Gary A. Dymski**, *Professor of Applied Economics, Leeds University Business School, University of Leeds*

"Regardless of whether you share Crotty's revisionist framing of Keynes' overarching vision, this smart, erudite and illuminating book is steeped in the enduring wisdom of its subject, and shines a powerful light on the fundamental differences between the economics of Keynes and practice of postwar "Keynesianism" – a distinction of pressing relevance for today's economic challenges."

*Jonathan David Kirshner*, Stephen and
Barbara Friedman Professor of International Political Economy,
Department of Government, Cornell University

"James Crotty has written an outstanding description of the evolution of Keynes's thought on the role of State involvement in a capitalism that promotes full employment and fairness. Characterisations of Keynesian economics by policy-makers and academics runs far afield from the clarity of purpose that Keynes held when describing the working of a capitalist economy. Crotty, in this clear and well written book, has surely set the record straight."

*Professor Roy Rotheim*, Skidmore College, USA

# Keynes Against Capitalism
His Economic Case for
Liberal Socialism

James Crotty

Routledge
Taylor & Francis Group

LONDON AND NEW YORK

First published 2019
by Routledge
2 Park Square, Milton Park, Abingdon, Oxon OX14 4RN

and by Routledge
52 Vanderbilt Avenue, New York, NY 10017

*Routledge is an imprint of the Taylor & Francis Group, an informa business*

© 2019 James Crotty

The right of James Crotty to be identified as author of this work has been asserted by him in accordance with sections 77 and 78 of the Copyright, Designs and Patents Act 1988.

All rights reserved. No part of this book may be reprinted or reproduced or utilised in any form or by any electronic, mechanical, or other means, now known or hereafter invented, including photocopying and recording, or in any information storage or retrieval system, without permission in writing from the publishers.

*Trademark notice*: Product or corporate names may be trademarks or registered trademarks, and are used only for identification and explanation without intent to infringe.

*British Library Cataloguing-in-Publication Data*
A catalogue record for this book is available from the British Library

*Library of Congress Cataloging-in-Publication Data*
Names: Crotty, James, 1940– author.
Title: Keynes against capitalism : his economic case
for liberal socialism / James Crotty.
Description: 1 Edition. | New York : Routledge, 2019. |
Series: Economics as social theory |
Includes bibliographical references and index.
Identifiers: LCCN 2018059994 (print) | LCCN 2019001777 (ebook) |
ISBN 9780429464911 (Ebook) | ISBN 9781138612839 (hardback : alk. paper) |
ISBN 9781138612846 (pbk. : alk. paper)
Subjects: LCSH: Keynesian economics. | Socialism. | Liberalism.
Classification: LCC HB99.7.K38 (ebook) |
LCC HB99.7.K38 C76 2019 (print) | DDC 330.15/6–dc23
LC record available at https://lccn.loc.gov/2018059994

ISBN: 978-1-138-61283-9 (hbk)
ISBN: 978-1-138-61284-6 (pbk)
ISBN: 978-0-429-46491-1 (ebk)

Typeset in Palatino
by Newgen Publishing UK
Printed by CPI Group (UK) Ltd, Croydon CR0 4YY

This book is dedicated to the hundreds of bright and highly motivated UMASS graduate students who took my course in macro theory over the four decades that I taught it. The lively discussions and debates that took place in the classroom helped me develop the interpretations of Keynes's views on economic theory and economic policy that are the subject matter of this book.

# Contents

Acknowledgments      xii

1 Introduction: was Keynes trying to save capitalism or create "Liberal Socialism?"      1

**PART I**
**From *The Economic Consequences of the Peace* to *The General Theory***      23

2 *The Economic Consequences of the Peace*: 1919      25

3 Making sense of chaos: 1919–1923      34

4 Public investment and state planning in 1924: the real Keynesian revolution begins      48

5 The return to gold in 1925: deflation, social justice, and class struggle      63

6 Three important "essays in persuasion" on the proper economic role of the state: 1925–1926      70

7 Destructive competition, corporatism, industrial policy, and the new economic role of the state: 1927–1928      84

8 *Britain's Industrial Future* and the Board of National Investment: a detailed analysis of the institutions to be used by the state to regulate capital accumulation in pursuit of full employment under Liberal Socialism      95

x  Contents

9  On the edge of the Great Depression: Keynes continues his efforts to gain political support for the radical policies in *Britain's Industrial Future*  116

10 Keynes on "insane" financial markets and the emergence of stagnation in the USA in the early 1930s  136

11 National self-sufficiency: 1933  152

**PART II**
***The General Theory*: the ultimate defense in theory of Keynes's radical policy agenda**  159

12 Methodology and ideology: Keynes versus the classicists  161

13 The priority of high-unemployment long-run equilibrium or "secular stagnation" in *The General Theory*  172

14 Upon further reflection: Keynes on secular stagnation in 1937  201

15 Keynes versus the classicists on the effects of wage and price deflation  209

16 Keynes versus the classicists on disequilibrium processes in the bond market  221

17 Chapter 12 of *The General Theory*: the "insane" stock market, capital investment, and instability  239

18 The theory of the business cycle in chapter 22: integrating the profit rate and the bond and stock markets in a theory of financial and economic instability  264

19 Are the "models" Keynes created in *The General Theory* compatible with the IS/LM interpretation of the book? A digression  269

20 Keynes's radical policy views in *The General Theory*  291

**PART III**
**State planning, public investment, and Liberal Socialism after *The General Theory***     311

21 From *The General Theory* until Britain entered WWII: 1936–1939     313

22 Keynes and government postwar economic planning for "Liberal Socialism" during the war: 1939–1945     326

23 Thoughts on the relevance of Keynes's work to solving today's economic problems: the society–economy nexus, methodology, theory, and policy     366

*References*     379
*Index*     383

# Acknowledgments

I am extremely grateful to my wife, Pam, for the encouragement and support she has given me throughout my academic career. Her willingness to take on more than her fair share of parenting and household management responsibilities allowed me to make the contributions to teaching and scholarship that appear on my record. I also wish to express my appreciation for the generous research support provided to me over the years by the Economics Department and by the Political Economy Research Institute at the University of Massachusetts Amherst campus and its co-directors, Jerry Epstein and Bob Pollin. Their support made it possible for me to work on this book while continuing to pursue my other research interests. I would like to thank Ilene Grable and Richard McIntyre for their thoughtful and detailed critical evaluation of a recent draft of the book. I am deeply indebted to my colleague and friend, Jerry Epstein, who made extensive and very helpful comments on every draft of every chapter of this book over a period of many years. Whatever its current shortcomings, the quality of this book has been substantially improved by Jerry's contributions. Thanks as well to Devika Dutt for research assistance and to Kim Weinstein for helping prepare the manuscript for publication.

# 1 Introduction
## Was Keynes trying to save capitalism or create "Liberal Socialism?"

Everyone knows that Keynes is one of the most important and influential economists who ever lived. His magnum opus, *The General Theory of Employment, Interest and Money* (hereafter *The General Theory*), was published in 1936 when much of the world was in acute economic distress and intense political turmoil in the midst of the global Great Depression. Right-wing and left-wing revolutionary forces had become powerful in many countries in Europe in the interwar years. Mussolini and Hitler were already in power, as, of course, was Stalin. Capitalism was even under assault in the USA, which experienced significant economic and political unrest in the 1930s.

*The General Theory* was an intervention in theory intended by Keynes to support a radical transformation of the institutions and practices of British political economy from those traditionally supported by the reigning classical economic theory and captured by the phrase "laissez-faire" to a system he called "Liberal Socialism." (To support my arguments about Keynes, I rely primarily on Keynes's own words as they appear in relevant volumes of *The Collected Writings of John Maynard Keynes* (hereafter CW), which were published for the Royal Economic Society by Cambridge University Press.) He believed that if Britain did not drastically reorganize its economic system, its militant working class might become a revolutionary working class. In the last chapter in the book, he summed up the situation as follows:

> It is certain that the world [i.e. the working class] *will not much longer tolerate* the unemployment which, apart from brief intervals of excitement, is associated – and, in my opinion, *inevitably associated* – with present-day capitalistic individualism. But it may be possible by a right analysis of the problem to cure the disease whilst preserving efficiency and freedom.
>
> (CW 7, p. 381, emphasis added)

It is almost universally believed that Keynes wrote *The General Theory* to save capitalism from the socialist, communist, and fascist forces that were

## 2  Introduction

rising up against it in this era. I argue in this book that this was not the case with respect to socialism. The historical record shows that Keynes wanted to replace then-current capitalism in Britain with what he referred to as "Liberal Socialism." In an interview in *The New Statesman and Nation* in January 1939, he said:

> The question is whether we are prepared to move out of the nineteenth-century <u>laissez-faire</u> state into an era of *liberal socialism*, by which I mean a system where we can act as an organised community for common purposes and to promote economic and social justice, whilst respecting and protecting the individual – his freedom of choice, his faith, his mind and its expression, his enterprise and his property.
>
> (CW 21, p. 500, emphasis added)

I shall use Keynes's term "Liberal Socialism" throughout this book to refer to the system of political economy he wanted to replace laissez-faire capitalism with.

In 1983, I published a brief article in the *Journal of Economic Literature* that could be seen as a precursor of this book. I made the case that in the interwar period Keynes was not trying to save capitalism as the conventional wisdom would have it, but to replace Britain's capitalist economy with a planned or state-guided socialist economic system built around public and semi-public control of the lion's share of large-scale capital investment. The state was to use its control over capital investment (augmented by capital controls) as the main policy tool to achieve and sustain full employment. My article opened with an outline of Keynes's 1933 article titled "National Self-Sufficiency."

> Keynes analyzed the combined domestic and international requirements for the creation of an efficient and humane economic system to replace the laissez-faire, free-trade capitalism which, he argued, had been largely responsible for the political and economic chaos of the previous twenty years. Distilled to its essentials, his program had three major aspects: first, the state would undertake primary responsibility for guiding and planning the domestic economy; second, economic intercourse with the rest of the world would be politically controlled as well as reduced in size and scope. As for capital flight, the free movement of capital across Britain's borders would be eliminated.
>
> In this essay ... Keynes argued that the two major threats facing the contemporary world – depression and the possibility of world war – were in part derivatives of existing capitalist institutions ... He pulled no punches in his indictment: "The decadent international but individualistic capitalism, in the hands of which we found ourselves after the war, is not a success. It is not intelligent, it is not beautiful, it is

not just, it is not virtuous – and it doesn't deliver the goods. In short, we dislike and are beginning to despise it" (CW 20, p. 239) ... The pursuit of peace and prosperity required the creation of additional or alternative economic institutions. Keynes proposed that Britain begin an evolutionary, trial and error, process of creating a more planned and controlled economic system at home, simultaneously instituting a system of controls over the movement of goods and especially money.

(Crotty 1983, pp. 59–60)

I went on to outline Keynes's radical policy program designed to achieve sustained full employment and domestic prosperity.

Keynes believed that the state would have to take responsibility for basic economic decisions concerning the level of investment and saving, the allocation of investment among competing uses (broadly defined), and the general distribution of income. State control of the investment process through public works, public or semi-public corporations, investment planning boards, credit allocation schemes and so forth – not monetary and fiscal policy as conventionally defined – was the cornerstone of Keynes's domestic economic policy proposals.

(Crotty 1983, p. 60)

I noted that in *The General Theory* Keynes called for a "somewhat comprehensive socialization of investment" and proposed that the state take "an ever responsibility for *directly* organizing investment" (CW 7, p. 378, emphasis added). I also argued that Keynes never changed his position on this crucial issue.

Keynes's emphasis of the use of state control of investment to stabilize the economy at full employment continued undiminished in the 1940s ... In 1943, for example, he argued that if "something like two-third to three-quarters of total investment will be under public or semi-public auspices, the amount of capital expenditures contemplated by the authorities will be the essential balancing factor ... It has nothing to do with deficit financing."

(Crotty 1983, p. 60)

This book deals with the same broad issues as my 1983 article, but it does so in rich historical detail.

When I submitted a completed draft of this book to Routledge Press for possible publication, one of the reviewers referred me to a book of essays on Keynes published in 1999 that contained a short essay by Rod O'Donnell titled "Keynes's Socialism: Conception, Strategy and Espousal." O'Donnell argued that, from 1924 through WWII, Keynes wanted to replace British capitalism with what he called Liberal Socialism. "My primary thesis is that Keynes, in his writings, advocated a kind of socialism which, to use his own term, may be called liberal socialism" (O'Donnell 1999, p. 149). He said that Keynes's commitment to socialism was "steady, durable and unwavering; he advanced his views in one form or another in virtually every year from 1924 to his death"; and it was "public and not merely private, appearing in a variety of journal articles, *The Times* newspaper, and a BBC radio broadcast" (O'Donnell 1999, pp. 163–164). O'Donnell was right about this, as this book will demonstrate in rich historical detail. Yet in spite of the historical record, O'Donnell observed:

> The suggestion that Keynes's political thought may be characterised as socialist is usually met with total skepticism. The long-standing majority view in the literature is that whatever kind of political being Keynes was, he was certainly never a socialist or even a quasi-socialist. Usually his position is depicted as either centrist liberal, right-wing liberal or even humane conservative. As the traditional account has it, his goal was to save capitalism from itself to ensure its long-term survival, not to lay the foundations for an alternative type of society.
> (O'Donnell 1999, p. 150)

As I will demonstrate in this book, virtually all post-WWII "Keynesian" economists misinterpreted crucial parts of Keynes's economic theory, misunderstood many of his most important policy views, and had no idea that his overarching political objective from 1924 until his death was not to save British capitalism, but rather to replace it with Liberal Socialism.

Keynes's Liberal Socialism began to take shape in his mind in the mid-1920s (see Chapters 4 and 6), took a more detailed institutional form with the publication of the Liberal Party's manifesto *Britain's Industrial Future* in 1928 (see Chapter 8), is argued for in the most urgent terms in 1933 in *National Self Sufficiency* (see Chapter 11), is described in outline form in *The General Theory* (see Chapter 20 of this book), and is laid out in detail in his work on postwar economic planning at Britain's Treasury during WWII (see Chapter 22).

Keynes's plans for the postwar economy were not just of academic interest. He had more influence on Britain's postwar economic planning during the war than anyone else. Most economists are aware that Keynes designed Britain's plans for financing WWII and creating a post-WWII international financial system. They also know that Keynes was Britain's chief negotiator with the USA on the latter issue. "In his narrower, and subordinate sphere, Keynes rivaled Churchill. He was, in fact, the Churchill of war finance and post-war financial planning" (Skidelsky 2002, p. xvi). It is less widely known, I think, that Keynes was also the primary architect of Britain's plans for the creation of a new political–economic system after the war (see Chapter 22). Schumpeter put the matter concisely in his 1946 survey of Keynes's contributions to economic theory and policy in the *American Economic Review*: "Everyone knows that during the war he entered the Treasury again (1940) and that his influence grew, along with Churchill, until nobody thought of challenging it" (Schumpeter 1946, p. 518). This makes his views on postwar planning of the utmost importance in understanding whether he was trying to save or to replace capitalism in Britain. And what Keynes said he was planning for over this entire period, including during WWII, was not an improved capitalism, but rather a form of socialism.

In this book, I trace the evolution of his views on policy from WWI until his death in 1946 and argue that they are qualitatively different from the policy perspective associated with what I will refer to as "Mainstream Keynesianism," the semiofficial interpretation of Keynes's theory and policy in the post-WWII era in the USA and elsewhere. I also discuss the evolution of his thinking about economic theory over this period and show how it relates to the development of his socialist policy views, with a special emphasis on *The General Theory*.

This introduction has four main parts. First, I explain why Keynes's evolving policy vision for a radically new economic system for Britain in the post-WWI era is appropriately described by him as "Liberal Socialism" rather than as "reformed capitalism." This is the main thesis of this book. Second, I present a brief overview of Keynes's critique of classical theory, the dominant theory in Britain and in the USA prior to the Keynesian "revolution" that was used to justify a laissez-faire policy regime. This is important because Keynes developed his own theory of capitalist economies partly in response to his increasing dissatisfaction with classical theory as an appropriate foundation for economic policy formation. Third, I argue that important aspects of Keynes's critique of classical theory apply with equal force to post-WWII Mainstream Keynesian theory. Mainstream Keynesian theory is not only in serious conflict with Keynes's own theory in matters of great moment; more important for our purpose, it has also inadvertently hidden his support of Liberal Socialism from several generations of economists. Fourth, I compare and contrast Keynes's preferred economic policies with those of Mainstream Keynesianism. The arguments in all four parts rely heavily on my understanding of the theory and policy presented in *The General Theory*. The discussion of the stark differences between Keynes's views on theory and policy as expressed in *The General Theory* and the theory and policy incorporated in Mainstream Keynesianism occupies about a third of this book.

The reader should be aware that, unfortunately, I am neither an economic historian nor a historian of economic thought. I would have loved to have coauthored this book with the great British economic historian, Eric Hobsbawm. Unfortunately, he died in 2012 and, to the best of my knowledge, he had never heard of me. The reader should also be aware that since this is a book about Keynes, I rely heavily on *his* interpretation of classical theory, an interpretation not universally shared by historians of economic thought.

## Keynes's Liberal Socialist economic policy agenda

Keynes's economic policy agenda was designed to create a liberal and democratic variant of a government-guided socialist economy. This government planning system did not incorporate most manufacturing and service-sector corporations; those firms that were in industries that were not oligopolistic would be left to operate in the market economy as before. The system did not involve state ownership of all productive assets as in the Soviet Union or in Labour Party manifestos. It relied instead on large publicly owned and state-influenced enterprises (such as residential construction) that together controlled the lion's share of the large-scale capital stock of the country. It also included state guidance of firms with excessive market power. The centerpiece of Keynes's new policy regime was control over major capital investment projects by "public and semi-public" institutions through a "Board of National Investment." Keynes frequently referred to the importance of "semi-public" investment projects. Investment in both residential and non-residential buildings, public transport, and public utilities are examples of semi-public investment. Some investment is semi-public because it is under the control of Britain's large number of important "public corporations." The Board would be empowered to select and prioritize the investment projects to be undertaken. To fund its projects, the Board was to receive a major share of government tax revenue and could borrow under central-government guarantee at relatively low interest rates. This is described in great detail in Chapter 8.

The primary objective of policy was to increase "public and semi-public" investment sufficiently so as to achieve and then sustain full employment over the long run, creating a dramatically improved economy *and society* in the process. This policy focus began to emerge in the mid-1920s and was sustained until Keynes's death in 1946.

Keynes could only achieve his core policy objectives if the capital stock under public and semi-public control was extremely large, which it was. In 1927, Keynes estimated that "two-thirds of the typical large-scale enterprise of this country had already been removed, mainly by Conservative and Liberal Governments, out of the category of pure private enterprise" (CW 19, pp. 695–696).[1] In 1943, while leading the group at the British Treasury responsible for post-WWII economic planning, Keynes insisted that the primary tool of postwar state economic planning was to be variations in the pace of public and semi-public investment to achieve the goal of sustained full employment. "If, as may be the case, something like two-thirds or three quarters of total investment will be under public or semi-public auspices [after the war], the amount of capital expenditures contemplated by the authorities will be the essential balancing factor" in achieving sustained full employment (CW 27, p. 352).[2]

In *The General Theory*, Keynes said:

> I expect to see the State, which is a position to calculate the marginal efficiency of [or expected return to] capital goods on long views and on the basis of the general social advantage, taking an ever greater responsibility for *directly* organising investment…
> (CW 7, p. 164, emphasis added).

The criteria for project selection were not limited to the expected rate of monetary return. They included quality-of-life issues, contributions to arts, culture, and education, priorities for working-class housing, environmental concerns, and so forth. In 1942, Keynes argued that, properly designed and implemented, state investment planning could be used to create what he called a "New Jerusalem" in Britain:

> Why should we not set aside, let us say, £50 million a year for the next twenty years to add in every substantial city of the realm the dignity of an ancient university or a European capital to our local schools and their surroundings, to our local government and its offices, and above all perhaps, to provide a local centre of refreshment and entertainment with an ample theatre, a concert hall, a dance hall, a gallery, a British restaurant, canteens, cafes and so forth. Assuredly we can afford this and much more. Anything we can actually *do* we can afford. Once done, it is *there*. Nothing can take it from us … Yet these must be only the trimmings on the more solid, urgent and necessary outgoings on housing the people, on reconstructing industry and transport and on re-planning the environment of our daily life. Not only shall we come to possess these excellent things. With a big programme carried out at a regulated pace we can hope to keep employment good for many years to come. We shall, in fact, have built our New Jerusalem out of the labour which in our former vain folly we were keeping unused and unhappy in enforced idleness.
> (CW 27, p. 270, emphasis in original)

In other words, in Liberal Socialism, the state, not the market, would make the bulk of the large-scale capital-investment decisions that are the main determinants of the economy's long-term growth path.

To prepare his readers to accept Liberal Socialism, Keynes first had to convince them that the laissez-faire capitalism in Britain after WWI was incapable of generating sustained prosperity over the long run. Contrary to the conventional wisdom that asserts that *The General Theory* deals solely with the short run, Keynes devotes considerable space in the book to an analysis of the long-run tendencies of laissez-faire capitalism. Keynes became convinced at the end of WWI that Britain and other European countries faced dismal long-run growth prospects caused by deeply rooted structural dysfunctions in the capitalisms of his time, dysfunctions that he believed were unlikely to be eliminated in the foreseeable future. He extended this analysis to the USA and much of the world in the 1930s. His very pessimistic long-run economic outlook for Europe in 1919 is discussed in the next chapter.

In the absence of unexpected fundamental change in the economic environment – such as war, system-transforming technical change, or a substantial increase in the rate of population growth – Keynes expected the rate of profit on capital to continue to be too low and the interest rate too high to maintain a pace of private investment rapid enough to sustain low unemployment under capitalism.[3] This was his version of the "secular stagnation" thesis that was popular in the 1930s and has emerged again in the wake of the global financial and economic crises that began in 2007. Keynes and Alvin Hansen of Harvard's economic department were the two non-Marxists most associated with the theory of secular stagnation in the 1930s. Keynes's version of secular stagnation theory is discussed in Chapter 16 and referred to in other chapters of *The General Theory* (see Chapter 13 of this book), in his 1937 Galton Lecture (discussed in Chapter 14 of this book), and in the next chapter.

Keynes also argued, in *The General Theory* and elsewhere, that if the state used increasing control over public and semi-public capital investment to guide the economy to sustained full employment and the foundations of stagnation remained in place, the rate of profit on capital would continue to decline and eventually fall toward zero at what we might call a point of capital saturation.[4] This had profound implications for the design of Keynes's new policy regime. The only way Liberal Socialism could succeed was if the risk-adjusted long-term rate of interest was allowed to fall toward zero along with the rate of profit on capital. To be able to force the long-term interest rate to follow a long-term downward trend required three dramatic changes in Britain's pre-WWI economic policy regime.

First, to gain control of its interest rate, Britain would have to go off the gold standard, which it did in 1931.

Second, Britain would have to enforce strict permanent capital controls to prevent capital flight as its interest rate fell below the higher rates available to investors in other countries. Keynes had been a supporter of capital controls for most of his professional life because he believed that excessive foreign lending kept the British interest rate too high to support adequate investment at home. In his role as chief negotiator for Britain in the discussions with the USA that were to determine the nature of the postwar international financial system, Keynes argued strongly in favor of mandatory, strict capital controls. If controls on outgoing funds were evaded, Keynes wanted the country receiving the funds to be obligated to return them to their country of origin. Harry Dexter White, the chief negotiator for the USA, agreed with Keynes on this issue, but powerful US financial interests successfully resisted the Keynes–White proposal. The final document gave every country the right to impose capital controls, but did not make controls mandatory. Most countries had some form of capital controls for decades after WWII ended.

Third, to sustain a policy of falling long-term interest rates, the Bank of England would have to be nationalized to end its allegiance to Britain's influential rentier class, whose major objective was high interest rates. It would also have to sever its cozy relationship with Britain's big banks, who represented rentier interests and who required free capital flows to retain their role as the center of world financial markets. Keynes believed that only a nationalized Bank of England could free itself from these class interests and support his Liberal Socialist economic agenda.

Keynes also wanted Britain to adopt a policy of "managed trade" to replace its hallowed traditional "free" trade regime (see Chapter 11). If Britain were to adopt Keynes's version of Liberal Socialism, it would grow faster than countries who remained mired in the Great Depression and would therefore run unsustainable balance of trade deficits. To avoid this fate, Britain would have to manage its imports to keep their growth in line with the growth of exports. During WWII, Keynes proposed that countries that ran persistent balance of trade surpluses should pay a fine to the International Monetary Fund (IMF), which would motivate them to grow at a faster pace, inducing more imports from deficit countries.

Clearly, the dominant role in the evolution of the economy played by state investment planning to permanently sustain full employment did not exhaust the anti-capitalist dimensions of Liberal Socialism. Consider Keynes's insistence that the risk-free rate of interest had to be driven down to zero in order to sustain adequate investment spending as the profit rate fell toward zero. When the risk-adjusted interest rate neared zero at the capital saturation point, the income flow to rentiers would be reduced to a trickle and the political power of the British rentier class would be drastically reduced. "If I am right in supposing it to be comparatively easy to make capital-goods so abundant that the marginal efficiency of [or expected rate of profit on] capital is zero, this may be the most sensible way of gradually getting rid of many of the most objectionable features of capitalism" (CW 7, p. 221).

> [This] would mean the *euthanasia of the rentier, and, consequently, the euthanasia of the cumulative oppressive power of the capitalist to exploit the scarcity value of capital* … I see, therefore, the rentier aspect of capitalism as a *transitional phase* which will disappear when it has done its work … Thus we might aim in practice … at an increase in the volume of capital until it ceases to be scarce, so that the functionless investor will no longer receive a bonus.
>
> (CW 7, p. 376, emphasis added)

Thus, a fall in the interest rate toward zero would not only reduce inequality and facilitate full employment, but also eliminate the "oppressive" and economically and politically powerful rentier class. It would be hard to get more radical than that in Britain in the mid-1930s or in the USA today.

Keynes also understood that permanent full employment brought about by a sustained high level of public investment would eliminate what Marx called the "reserve army" of unemployed. This would permanently empower workers and weaken capitalists in their economic conflicts over wages and working conditions. As Keynes put it in *The General Theory*: "Labour is not more truculent in the depression than in the boom – far from it" (CW 7, p. 9). Moreover, permanent full employment would strengthen workers and unions in their political conflicts with the capitalist class over government economic policy, including policies affecting the economic and political power of unions. This point was stressed by Michael Kalecki in his famous 1943 article explaining why capitalist-dominated governments will never permit sustained full employment (Kalecki 1943).

Reliance on public investment to generate aggregate demand (AD) would also eliminate the pressure on governments that builds up in recessions and depressions to adopt capital-friendly economic policies in the hope that these policies will tease out more investment and more jobs. In Keynes's Liberal Socialism, increased public investment could compensate for any loss in AD caused by a decline in private investment. This would dramatically decrease capital's influence on economic policy.

In the absence of capital controls, capital flight would be triggered whenever the domestic or international financial investors became dissatisfied with, or even just nervous about, the general tenor of government economic policy. This would give the rentier class effective veto power over government policy. Capital controls remove this major source of policy influence exercised by the rentier class.

Finally, Keynes supported a dramatic increase in the progressivity of taxation of income and wealth. This would increase the percentage of national income devoted to consumption spending while simultaneously weakening the economic and political influence of rentiers and big capitalists.

For all of these reasons, it is not an exaggeration to suggest that permanently sustained full employment achieved through high rates of public investment accompanied by the "euthanasia" of the rentier class, an increase in the economic and political power of labor relative to capital, radically progressive tax reform, strict capital controls, and managed trade would constitute a peaceful democratic revolution in the nature of Britain's economic system and in the structure of class power in Britain.

The conventional wisdom that Keynes wanted to save capitalism is thus either false or capitalism must be redefined to apply to any economic system in which markets, monetary incentives, and freedom of consumer choice are allowed to exist in some form, even if the most important economic decisions are determined collectively via democratic political processes before people get to choose in the marketplace. If we use the traditional definition of capitalism, it was clearly Keynes's goal to replace capitalism with a form of democratic socialism. It is my goal in this book to convince the reader that this conclusion is consistent with the historical record.

## Mr. Keynes and the "classics"[5] – and Modern Keynesians

There are two main reasons for economists to study the evolution of Keynes's thinking about macroeconomics and related theoretical issues, such as competition, industrial organization, free trade, and free capital flows (see Chapters 7 and 11). First, his long struggle to "free himself" from the hold classical orthodoxy had on his understanding of capitalism was a necessary first step in the process of creating a new and improved theory of his own.[6] Second, important aspects of his critique of classical theory are applicable as well to post-WWII Mainstream Keynesian theory, the theory that claims to be the modern embodiment of Keynes's ideas.

Keynes famously attacked the classical thesis that endogenous forces in a market economy will always force full-employment AD or spending to equal the aggregate supply (AS) of output and income at full employment. This hoary proposition is known as "Say's Law." Anyone who has taken an introductory course in macroeconomics that included Keynesian theory will be familiar with the basic argument, which I summarize here in its simplest form. The AD for or spending on goods and services is composed of consumption spending by households and investment spending by businesses. The value of the AS of goods and services, which is assumed in the simple model to equal total household income, is composed of household saving plus consumption spending. If AD equals AS at full employment, the economy will be in equilibrium because sales balance production and firms have no profit incentive to alter the level of production. If in a classical model AD or spending is smaller than AS or the value of production and income at full employment, it must be the case that investment is smaller than saving at full employment.[7]

Suppose that at some point AD falls below full-employment AS because investment spending has declined due to an increase in business pessimism about future profits. The decline in sales will create unwanted inventories of unsold goods that will force cuts in production and employment. Classical theory offers two reasons as to why the economy cannot remain in equilibrium in this situation, but must return to a full-employment equilibrium: wage and price deflation and falling interest rates.

Nominal wages will fall because unemployed workers will compete with employed workers for scarce jobs and prices will fall because firms will compete to increase sales.[8] Classical theory assumes, with little if any supporting empirical evidence according to Keynes, that the real or price-adjusted wage will fall when there is an excess supply of labor, leading firms to hire more workers. This will raise production and income. Mainstream Keynesian theory incorporates the classical view that when wages and prices are fully flexible downward, high unemployment cannot persist. Therefore, a stable equilibrium with high unemployment is possible only if strong unions refuse to accept lower money wages or if workers irrationally confuse money wages with real wages in a dysfunction referred to as "money illusion," one that is not mentioned anywhere in *The General Theory*.[9]

Keynes insisted to the contrary that if a rapid wage and price deflation set in, it could completely destabilize the economy (see chapters 2, 14, and 19 of *The General Theory* and Chapter 3 of this book). Deflation is likely to be especially destabilizing, Keynes said, in a period such as the early 1930s when both real-sector and financial-sector balance sheets were incredibly fragile due in part to the fact that the value of their assets were in a state of collapse in the severe commodity and financial asset price deflation of the period. Keynes stressed the dangers of deflation in what he called a "regime of money contract" in which the sum of all nominal legally binding commitments to pay was large relative to the size of the economy – as in the USA in the early 1930s. Deflation helped bring about the collapse of the US financial system in this period.

> It follows therefore that if labour were to respond to conditions of gradually [rising unemployment] by offering its services at a gradually diminishing money wage, this would not, as a rule, have the effect of reducing real wages and might even have the effect of increasing them ... The chief result of this policy would be to cause a great instability of prices, so violent perhaps as to make business calculations futile in an economic society functioning after the manner of that in which we live. To suppose that a flexible wage policy is a right and proper adjunct of a system which on the whole is one of *laissez-faire*, is the opposite of the truth. It is only in a highly authoritarian society, where sudden, substantial, all-around changes could be decreed that a flexible wage-policy could function with success.
> (CW 7, p. 269)

On this crucial issue of the effect of deflation on production and employment, then, both Mainstream Keynesian theory and classical theory are in direct conflict with Keynes's theory.

Second, in the basic classical model, savings out of current income were understood to be the flow demand for newly issued corporate bonds and investment the supply of newly issued corporate bonds. Thus, a sharp drop in investment spending at full employment would cause the supply of bonds to decline. This temporary excess demand for bonds would cause bond prices to rise and interest rates to fall, stimulating both investment and consumption spending.[10] Rising AD would thus match the rising level of AS caused by real-wage deflation. These disequilibrium process must continue until a full-employment equilibrium is restored.

Keynes insisted (see chapters 13–15 and 22 of *The General Theory*, his defense of *The General Theory* in the *Quarterly Journal of Economics* in 1937 and Chapters 9, 15, and 16 of this book) that the classical thesis that long-term interest rates will assuredly fall in response to a serious downturn in AD is badly mistaken. The huge jump in both nominal and real long-term interest rates in the early 1930s is only an extreme example of a process that typically occurs whenever the economy is beset by serious distress. The behavior of interest rates at the height of the recent financial crisis is another such example. In the midst of an economic and/or financial crisis, interest rates tend to rise not fall, lowering investment and consumption spending, thereby making the crisis worse.

To understand Keynes's thinking about the nature of financial markets, we must first understand the revolution he created in micro theory or the theory of agent choice, a revolution not recognized by or incorporated in Mainstream Keynesian theory or in neoclassical micro theory. Keynes built his theory of agent choice on the assumption of "fundamental," "radical," or "Keynesian" uncertainty about future states of the economy.[11] Keynes's assumption of uncertainty is different from the classical, neoclassical, and Mainstream Keynesian assumption of "risk" in which the probability distributions that determine future economic outcomes are knowable in the present and unaffected by agent choice in the current period. Keynes said of future economic conditions: "About these matters there is no scientific basis on which to form any calculable probability whatever. We simply do not know" (Keynes 1937, p. 214).

In conditions of radical uncertainty, investors in risky real and financial assets are not able to make assuredly optimal decisions in situations in which the result of their choice will not be determined until substantial time passes. In the case of long-term capital goods, this period can be measured in decades. Keynes's theory of agent choice thus requires a completely different kind of agent – a fallible and psychologically complex human being in a world of incomplete and inadequate information who knows he or she does not know the future and thus cannot possibly make assuredly optimal decisions. Classical and Mainstream Keynesian agents, to the contrary, are mathematicians who solve optimization problems under perfect probabilistic information about the future consequences of their current choice.[12]

The importance of radical uncertainty is that Keynes's agents are forced to base their financial asset acquisition decisions on fallible expectations about future security price movements formed on the basis of "conventional" or behavioral or psychological heuristics or rules of thumb that they know are not the "truth" about future security prices.

14  *Introduction*

One conventional mode of expectation formation emphasized by Keynes is through extrapolation from the behavior of the relevant variables over the recent past. If financial asset prices have been rising for a substantial period of time, investors will come to expect this trend to continue. Moreover, Keynes argued, the longer prices continue to rise, the more "confident" – his word – investors will become that their optimistic expectations are likely to be validated by future outcomes. Confidently held optimistic investor expectations can generate bubbles in which security prices eventually outpace the real-sector cash flows needed to sustain them. If an expansion lasts long enough and, in Minsky's words, the financial system becomes "fragile" because excessive borrowing by firms and households and excessive lending by financial institutions permeate the economy, panic may set in when it eventually becomes clear that security prices are substantially overvalued. This can lead to a frantic sell-off, resulting in an accelerating rate of decline in bond and stock prices. Falling bond prices mean rising interest rates that cause investment and consumption spending to fall, reinforcing the rate of decline in AD, output, and employment, which adds momentum to the process of financial asset price collapse. This is a destructive disequilibrium process absent from both classical and Modern Keynesian theories.

Keynes theory of disequilibrium dynamics is qualitatively different from the out-of-equilibrium dynamic processes assumed in both classical theory and Mainstream Keynesian theory. The former creates stability at full employment; the latter creates stability at any equilibrium level of employment. In Keynes's theory, disequilibrium dynamics can be stabilizing or destabilizing depending on conditions in the economy. The reader might be surprised to know that about forty percent of *The General Theory* is devoted to an analysis of out-of-equilibrium processes that are often destabilizing.

The outcome of the Mainstream Keynesian theory of interest rate determination lies between the positions taken by Keynes and the classicists. The reason for this is important to understand. Like classical theory, Modern Keynesian theory either assumes that the probabilistic future is knowable in the present or that the agent subjectively believes she knows the true distributions of future states of the economy. Therefore, the mathematician-agents can make assuredly optimal decisions about buying and selling real and financial assets. You cannot generate the Keynes–Minsky theory of the inherent instability of financial markets based on the Mainstream Keynesian assumption of correct expectations and the optimizing agent.

Like classical theory, Mainstream Keynesian theory concludes that the interest rate will always fall if the economy receives a negative shock to AD, an anti-Keynesian conclusion; see, for example, John Hicks's well-known IS/LM model (and Chapter 19 in this book). However, unlike classical theory, Mainstream Keynesian theory assumes that the decline in interest will always be too small to restore AD to its full-employment equilibrium.

With the assumed ability of wage deflation to raise AS blocked by strong unions and the fall in interest rates too small the push AD back to its full-employment level, Mainstream Keynesian theory can logically explain why stable high-unemployment equilibriums exist.

The systemic forces generating and reproducing the financial and economic instability of the late 1920s and 1930s or of the recent global financial crisis cannot be explained within Mainstream Keynesian theory, in part because it rejects Keynes's assumption of radical uncertainty and the fallible and psychologically complex human agent it creates. Keynes repeatedly referred to US financial markets in the 1930s as destructive, destabilizing, "insane" "gambling casinos" that not only were more likely to magnify rather than repair serious damage caused by problems in the real sector, but were also themselves capable of initiating real-sector downturns. You cannot generate such financial instability in Mainstream Keynesian theory. In an article published in *The Economic Journal* in September 1932, Keynes argued that US financial markets were inherently subject to bouts of instability. They were:

> dominated by insane gambling to get in at the bottom, just as they were dominated in the boom by insane gambling to get out at the top ... For this is no more than a vivid illustration of the disadvantages of running a country's development and enterprise as a bye-product of a casino.
> (CW 21, pp. 120–121)

In *The General Theory*, Keynes constructed a theory that, when combined with the evolution of economic and political institutions and practices over time – what he referred to as "the facts" of each historical period – could be used to explain the historical record of real-world capitalisms. This record contains periods of relatively stable economic evolution in "normal times," long periods of mostly rapid growth as in the "glorious" nineteenth century, typical business cycles, periods beset by destructive disequilibrium processes, endogenously created bouts of extreme instability in both real and financial markets in what he called "interesting times," and secular stagnation or prolonged depressions that cannot be eliminated by free-market processes and can threaten social and political stability.

Contrary to conventional wisdom, there is more than one applied economic model that can be found in *The General Theory*. In Chapter 19, I discuss five such models: (1) a long-term model of sustained high unemployment or secular stagnation; (2) a short-term model of high-unemployment equilibrium embodied in the "Keynesian" IS/LM model that is typically understood to be the sole model in the book; (3) a dynamic intermediate-run model of the business cycle that focuses on endogenously generated instability in real and financial markets; (4) a model of destructive disequilibrium processes focused on wage and price deflation and instability in financial asset prices; and (5) a short-run quasi-model or mini-model of periods or points of extreme instability, especially in financial markets. These five models contained the main arguments used in *The General Theory* to explain the facts of the interwar period and to support his core policy belief that capitalism had to be replaced by Liberal Socialism in Britain in order for long-term prosperity to be achieved.

The main contribution of the IS/LM model to our understanding of Keynes's economic theory is that it provides a clear and logical explanation of why a capitalist economy can exist in a stable high-unemployment equilibrium state in the short run. A major problem with reliance on the IS/LM model as the only model in *The General Theory* is that its policy message was understood by Modern Keynesians to be that we can save capitalism through a combination of activist monetary and fiscal policy in the context of a high average level of government spending. You cannot generate Keynes's favored Liberal Socialist policy regime from an IS/LM economic model. As we have seen, Schumpeter argued that the "pre-analytic vision" of secular stagnation permeated *The General Theory* even though, in his view, its single formal model was short run in character. He thought it could be used to create a framework for a narrative as opposed to a formal model of the causes of secular stagnation, a narrative consistent with Keynes's support for Liberal Socialism. But it has not been used for this purpose by Modern Keynesians.

In various chapters of this book, I show that Keynes used combinations of his five models to explain both the episodes of extreme economic and financial instability that took place in the interwar years and the long-term stagnation that afflicted Britain starting in the early 1920s and the USA after the late 1920s. Keynes's focus on secular stagnation somehow disappeared when Modern Keynesians adopted the short-run IS/LM model as the sole model Keynes bequeathed us. Yet as I show in Chapters 13 and 14, Keynes relied primarily on his long-run model and secondarily on the models of destructive disequilibrium processes to explain stagnation in the interwar era over and over and over again throughout *The General Theory*. These chapters also demonstrate that Keynes believed that there were no foreseeable changes on the British horizon – such as system-transforming technological progress, or faster population growth, or restoration of its dominant position in the international economy – that might return the British economy to its nineteenth-century prosperity or the US economy to its pre-1930s prosperity. He concluded that only Liberal Socialism could bring sustained prosperity to Britain or the USA and simultaneously preserve the democratic nature of their political systems.

The IS/LM model thus cleansed Keynes's work of many of its most serious criticisms of the nature of capitalism, including its potential for secular stagnation, its destructive disequilibrium processes, the "insane" behavior of lightly regulated financial markets, and its endogenous creation of instability. When the profession accepted and propagated the view that the IS/LM model incorporated all of Keynes's important contributions in *The General Theory*, the reasons for his persistent commitment to Liberal Socialism got lost in translation.

## The Mainstream Keynesian policy regime and Keynes's Liberal Socialism

Sustained high unemployment in the 1930s and inadequate or nonexistent government unemployment compensation and family income-support programs were important reasons for the growth of the mass movements against capitalism that arose in this period. The belief that capitalism inevitably created high unemployment and widespread poverty and that socialism, communism, or fascism might solve these problems became widely held. FDR's New Deal saved American capitalism from potential self-destruction in the 1930s, but even as late as 1939 the US unemployment rate was 17%. We cannot know how long stagnation might have lasted if there had not been a world war. It took a huge increase in US military spending, a government-planned war economy, and a sharp decline in the available domestic labor force during WWII to finally achieve low unemployment. The size of US armed forces rose from about 300,000 to 12,200,000 between 1939 and 1945, or from 0.2 to 8.7 percent of the population. Most Americans and Britons believed that WWII proved that the state could achieve full employment if it was determined to do so, and politicians in both countries were fearful of the political consequences of a postwar return to high unemployment.

After the war, Modern Keynesian theory eventually replaced classical theory as the dominant mode of understanding the strengths and weaknesses of capitalism, and the Modern Keynesian activist approach of countercyclical macroeconomic policy eventually replaced laissez-faire. Keynes's main conclusion about the flaws in laissez-faire capitalism as interpreted by Mainstream Keynesians is that stable high-unemployment equilibriums are possible. Therefore, some agent outside the private capitalist economy must be empowered to regulate AD. The government is the only agent that can do this job. Mainstream Keynesian growth models conclude that capitalist market economies will perform well over the long run and that the long-term growth path is not affected by short-term business cycles. But what is to prevent a high-unemployment equilibrium from persisting for many years, as occurred in the 1930s? To shorten the length and depth of recessions, the government can increase the money supply (to lower the interest rate), increase government spending, and/ or lower business or household taxes. Thus, the conventional wisdom among Mainstream Keynesians after WWII was that appropriate government macroeconomic policy can prevent episodes of sustained high unemployment and that government social welfare policies can prevent excessive inequality and poverty. There is thus no case for socialism because a reformed capitalism can achieve long-term *widely shared* prosperity.

The dramatic changes in the government's role in the economy that took place in the early decades of the postwar political economy of the USA do bear a resemblance of sorts to Keynes's Liberal Socialism, which included support for a generous social welfare state.[13] The post-WWII era saw an enormous increase in the peacetime economic role of the state. Net federal government spending as a proportion of GDP was 3 percent in 1929 and 17–20 percent from 1952 through the present. The "insane" US gambling casinos of the late 1920s and early 1930s were initially replaced by tightly regulated financial markets that were relatively stable, though political pressure to deregulate financial markets began to gather steam rather quickly after the war. Moreover, most countries used capital controls for several decades after the war and international trade was initially modest.

However, the early postwar economic structure and policy regime was neither Keynes's Liberal Socialism nor the preferred Mainstream Keynesian political–economic structure. It was not Liberal Socialism for several reasons. There was no commitment to sustained full employment. That was made clear when Congress refused to pass a 1945 bill mandating the pursuit of full employment as the main policy objective. It enacted in its place in 1946 a law that set as its goal a level of unemployment consistent with stable prices achieved through a process that would "promote free competitive enterprise," a goal that eventually became embedded in the theory of the "natural rate of unemployment." Though public investment was substantial in the immediate postwar period, there was no commitment to reliance on large-scale public and semi-public investment as the chief economic policy tool and no National Board of Investment to plan, fund, and implement this policy. Moreover, rejecting Keynes's belief that long periods of stagnation are possible in a capitalist economy, Mainstream Keynesian theory taught that capitalism always functioned well in the long run if countercyclical macro-policy is managed sensibly.

But the early postwar US economy did not reflect the preferred Mainstream Keynesian political economic structure either. Mainstream Keynesians opposed capital controls and managed trade in principle and argued that unrestricted global economic and financial integration is the best of all possible economic worlds. They promoted the radical deregulation of US financial markets, which accelerated after the 1970s because they taught that lightly regulated financial markets were "efficient" and thus could neither initiate instability nor magnify instability initiated in the real sector. In other words, Mainstream Keynesians supported the neoliberal regime that eventuated in the global economic and financial crisis that began in 2007.

Keynes, as we have seen, vehemently opposed almost all elements of the global neoliberal regime. This does not mean Keynes was right and Mainstream Keynesians wrong about the character of the financialized global neoliberal capitalism within which we currently live, though my personal opinion was that he was right about most of this. But it does mean that Mainstream Keynesians badly misunderstood Keynes's economic theory and the policy regime associated with it, and therefore mislead several generations of students about Keynes's views on these crucial issues.

It might be fitting to end this introductory chapter by asking whether the post-WWII conventional wisdom that capitalism was permanently rescued from the threat of socialism, fascism, or communism by embedding it within a Modern Keynesian regime and an adequate social welfare system is still valid. The new postwar Mainstream Keynesian policy regime did help create the "Golden Age" of modern capitalism from WWII through the mid-1970s, an era in which confidence in the belief that modern capitalism had permanently resolved all of the problems that bedeviled capitalism in the interwar years became ever stronger. However, the belief that the Golden Age of modern capitalism was eternal has been weakening since then, an almost four-decade period during which growth has slowed in the USA and in many other developed countries, and within-country inequality has risen substantially in most countries. Confidence that capitalism guided by a Modern Keynesian policy regime will permanently sustain a widely shared prosperity hit rock bottom after the recent global financial crisis, a crisis that was not foreseen by mainstream economists and cannot be explained within their theoretical paradigm. The global financial crisis was met in most developed countries either by austerity macro policies or by macro policy stimulus too weak to eliminate high unemployment and by cuts in social services and attacks on organized labor – the kinds of policies Keynes opposed in the 1930s and during WWII. This further eroded public faith in the belief that capitalism plus Mainstream Keynesian policies can deliver sustained widespread prosperity. There has even been a revival of interest in theories of secular stagnation by respected economists such as Robert Gordon, Paul Krugman, and Lawrence Summers.[14]

Meanwhile, seemingly incurable economic crises amidst high inequality have ignited a firestorm of political attacks on the economic status quo, most of which are reactionary, authoritarian, and nationalistic, though some seek a socialist remedy. The election of Donald Trump as President of the USA in 2016 is but one example of this process. In response to the question of what the eventual outcome of these political and economic struggles are likely to be, we might echo Keynes and say: "About such matters we simply do not know."

The next chapter will defend the proposition that the true Keynesian "revolution" in policy and theory began not with the publication of *The*

*General Theory* and other writings in the 1930s, but rather with the publication of his 1919 book, *The Economic Consequences of the Peace*.[15] In this book, Keynes explained why Europe faced a future of long-term stagnation and possibly a new world war unless it radically restructured its economic institutions and policies.

## Notes

1. The British historian Sidney Pollard said that a "large share of industry and transport was, even in the 1920s, not controlled by private enterprise at all, but by various types of public or non-profit-making organisations, and their growth is one of the most significant aspects of the period" (Pollard 1983, pp. 99–100).
2. Keynes added: "It has nothing whatever to do with deficit financing."
3. Keynes's 1919 book on post-WWI economic prospects in Europe, *The Economic Consequences of the Peace* (discussed in the next chapter), did express concern that war in Europe might break out again in the intermediate future. But he believed this would bring economic disaster, not prosperity.
4. When the economy approached the point of capital saturation, Keynes wanted to use progressive redistributive tax changes to raise the mpc and thereby increase the investment "multiplier." This would raise AD or total spending at all levels of investment.
5. Apologies to J.R. Hicks for borrowing the title of his influential 1937 publication.
6. In the preface to *The General Theory*, Keynes described this struggle to free himself from classical ideas: "The composition of this book has been for the author a long struggle of escape ... from habitual modes of thought and expression ... The difficulty lies, not in the new ideas, but in escaping from the old ones, which ramify, for those brought up as most of us have been, into every corner of our minds" (CW 7, p. xxiii).
7. If $AS = C + S$ and $AD = C + I$ (where C = consumption, S = savings, and I = investment), when AD is less than AS, S must be smaller than I.
8. In the standard neoclassical Walrasian General Equilibrium model, prices actually rise when AD is less than AS, an empirically repugnant proposition that ensures that real wages will decline.
9. New Keynesian theory relies on various market imperfections to explain wage and price rigidities.
10. Both investment and consumption are assumed to be positive functions of income and negative functions of the interest rate.
11. See Crotty (1994) for a detailed analysis of this issue. See also Chapters 17 and 18 of this book and chapters 11–15 and 22 of *The General Theory*.
12. In New Classical theory, the agent is assumed to know the true distributions of future outcomes and future outcomes are assumed to be unaffected by current agent choice, assumptions that are literally absurd. In neoclassical theory, agents generate distributions of expected future outcomes through a "subjective" process that agents understand cannot lead to knowledge of the "truth" about future economic outcomes. The assumed rational agents in this theory are then assumed to make their choices as if their subjective expectations of future economic outcomes were the truth about the future. These two assumptions are logically incompatible.

13 Keynes enthusiastically supported the vast expansion of Britain's postwar social welfare system proposed by Sir William Beveridge during WWII (see Chapter 22). In other words, his view of Liberal Socialism incorporated a generous social welfare system.
14 See, for example, Gordon (2016).
15 The book was first published in 1919, but all quotations used here are from the 1920 version.

# Part I

# From *The Economic Consequences of the Peace* to *The General Theory*

# 2 *The Economic Consequences of the Peace*: 1919

The true Keynesian "revolution" in theory and policy began not with *The General Theory* and other writings in the 1930s, but rather with the publication of his book *The Economic Consequences of the Peace* (Keynes 1920). In this book, which first brought him to the attention of the general public, he explained why Europe faced a future of long-term stagnation. His concern with secular stagnation continued until his death in 1946.

In *The Economic Consequences of the Peace*, Keynes argued that the halcyon days of what he often referred to as "the glorious nineteenth century" had ended and that a healthy economy could not be recreated without fundamental changes in the structure of Britain's economic system. He believed that Britain faced long-term decline, with chronically high unemployment that threatened the social and political order.

Though only 35 years old at the time, Keynes was the chief representative of the British Treasury Department and an advisor to Prime Minister Lloyd George at the Paris Peace Conference of 1919. The purpose of the Conference was to decide on the conditions of the treaty that would end WWI. The *Economic Consequences of the Peace* was written to warn the North American, European, and British public that if the provisions of the Treaty of Versailles were enforced, the world would face the prospect of economic stagnation, financial crises, rising social and political unrest, and, in some countries, violent revolution. The transfer of real resources from vanquished to victor, the crippling system of financial reparations from losers to winners, and loan repayments among the Allies would make the restoration of peace and prosperity impossible, Keynes argued. Implementation of the provisions of the Treaty, in his view, could well lead to a future world war, which, of course, it did.

Keynes also used this occasion to make public for the first time his belief that Europe stood at the interstices between two epochs of economic history, one known and the other yet to be determined. WWI accelerated the dissolution of the old order to be sure, and the Treaty threatened to make a peaceful and relatively smooth transition to a new socioeconomic structure impossible, but Keynes clearly believed that the old order was going to crumble even without these particular problems. The war simply accelerated the process of dissolution.

Keynes's main argument about the inevitable passing of the old order was that the conditions that made the high growth rate in Europe in the nineteenth century possible were inherently transitory. He listed four foundations for the prosperity of the era: a rapidly rising population; declining costs of imported food and raw materials to sustain a growing labor force; increasing global economic integration facilitated by unprecedented free trade, migration, and capital flows in the context of stable exchange rates and "security of property and person everywhere"[1]; and a symbiotic economic relation between the old world and the new, in which Europe sent abroad the money capital, physical capital, and skilled labor that helped make possible the surplus food production in the new world that sustained a growing European population. The old order thus had much to recommend it, Keynes argued:

> In this economic Eldorado, in this economic utopia, as the earlier economists would have deemed it, most of us were brought up ... What an extraordinary episode in the economic progress of man that age was that came to an end in August 1914.
> (Keynes 1920, pp. 10–11)[2]

Most importantly, unique and inherently transitory conditions in the nineteenth century made it possible for Britain and other European countries to achieve the exceptionally high rate of growth of the capital stock that was the driving force behind its prosperity. "Europe was so organized socially and economically as to secure the maximum accumulation of capital" (Keynes 1920, p. 18). When the old order passed away, the conditions necessary to sustain rapid growth in the capital stock ended with them. The rate of return on real capital was sufficiently high on average in the nineteenth century that real and financial investors in Britain came to believe that this high-profit era was permanent, so that it made sense to invest in large-scale, long-term capital projects even in uncertain economic conditions. As Keynes later expressed this idea: "prosperity is cumulative." In *The General Theory*, he argued that the British entrepreneurial class of the nineteenth century "embarked on business as a way of life, not relying on a precise calculation of prospective profit" (Keynes 1920, p. 150).

But Keynes believed the long-term foundation that sustained the high profit rate of the nineteenth century had now eroded. A good deal of space in this book is devoted to presenting Keynes's evolving theory of long-run or secular stagnation. The conventional wisdom among economists that *The General Theory* deals exclusively with short-run models is simply not true. For Keynes, as for Marx, slow long-term growth is a "tendency" of mature capitalist economies, though not a "law" that applies in all times and all economies. There are various countertendencies – such as rapid population growth, system-transforming technical change, wars, the integration of new areas of the globe into the international capitalist system, and, in Britain, disproportionate control over international trade and finance – that can generate high rates of investment and employment for extended periods of time. But there is, in his view, no law that says that these countertendencies will always be strong enough to overcome the tendency of the rate of profit on capital investment to fall over time. When he was writing *The General Theory* in the early to mid-1930s, Keynes believed there were no endogenous economic forces strong enough to create sustained full employment in Britain or to end the global depression. However, as it became increasingly clear in the late 1930s that Britain had to prepare itself for a major war, Keynes understood that stagnation was nearing its end. I discuss this transition in Chapters 21 and 22.

According to the economic historian and macroeconomist Barry Eichengreen, the interwar British economy did in fact suffer from investment stagnation as Keynes claimed. Levels of investment spending were much too low to generate anything near full employment. Britain "was hardly a high-investment economy in the 1920s and 1930s – to the contrary, the failure to sustain a higher investment rate is frequently cited as one of its shortcomings ... [and] there was no guarantee that Britain would again display respectable rates of capital investment in the future..." (Eichengreen 2004, p. 316).

Since the savings rate was also high in the nineteenth century, financial capital was affordable and available on a long-term basis to accumulating firms even when the pace of investment was rapid. Moderate interest rates in turn depended on a transitory combination of economic and social conditions. One was a very unequal distribution of income and wealth. The wealthy classes saved a high proportion of their income and were content to hold their financial wealth in the form of long-term gilt-edged bonds and, later, preferred stock at reasonable rates of interest. Moderate interest rates combined with high profit rates on capital investment facilitated the high economic growth rates that eventually, in the latter part of the nineteenth century, made life for the expanding working class at least tolerable.[3] "It was precisely the inequality of the distribution of wealth which made possible those vast accumulations of fixed wealth and of capital improvements which distinguished that age from all others" (Keynes 1920, p. 18). Keynes continued:

> I seek only to point out that the principle of accumulation based on inequality was a vital part of the pre-war order of Society and of progress ... and to emphasize that this principle depended on unstable psychological conditions which it may be impossible to recreate.
> (Keynes 1920, p. 21)

All of this had now changed, and Keynes believed the changes were likely to be permanent. One reason as to why wealthy Britons were willing to hold much of their financial wealth in the form of long-term bonds in the nineteenth century was the absence of serious capital value-eroding inflation after the Napoleonic Wars. As explained in Chapter 4, the rentier class was devastated by the very high inflation of WWI, which continued at a slower pace for a few years after the war ended. This led to huge losses in the value of long-term bonds in the war and immediate postwar periods. Not only did investors suffer capital losses on their bonds, but also their faith that long-term bonds were a safe investment was completely shattered. This caused an investor flight from bonds to short-term liquid assets that were less vulnerable to inflation. Keynes would refer to this flight in *The General Theory* as a spike in "liquidity preference." He would state just a few years later: "Nor can it be doubted that this experience must modify social psychology towards the practice of saving and investment" (CW 9, p. 67). Britain thus faced a triple long-term squeeze on AD in the interwar years: high long-term interest rates; a low propensity to consume caused by a very unequal distribution of income and wealth; and a fall in the profit rate on capital goods.[4]

The war, of course, disrupted many important aspects of the prewar economic order. It "has so shaken this system as to endanger the life of Europe altogether" (Keynes 1920, p. 25). Several of the major impediments to the reconstitution of the old order pointed to by Keynes turned out to be persistent. First, the era of cheap imported food was over. Therefore, further population growth would reduce living standards. Yet when population growth slows, the incentive to invest declines. Keynes constantly stressed that the sharp drop in the rate of population growth in Britain would weigh heavily on the rate of growth of the capital stock; see, for example, his 1937 Galton Lecture on secular stagnation reviewed in Chapter 15 of this book.

Second, the system was now heavily burdened with excessive debt of all kinds, public and private. Here is an early statement by Keynes of his belief in the crucial role played by the condition of the balance sheets of governments and real-sector and financial firms in the determination of economic conditions. It is an anticipation of what Hyman Minsky later called the "financial fragility" thesis. Keynes's concern about the dangers embedded in fragile balance sheets reappeared in his discussion of financial instability in the USA in the late 1920s and early 1930s, as described in Chapter 10 of this book.

> The war has ended with everyone owing everyone else immense sums of money. Germany owes a large sum to the Allies; the Allies owe a large sum to Great Britain; and Great Britain owes a large sum to the United States. The holders of war loans in every country are owed a large sum by the State; and the State in its turn is owed a large

sum by these and other taxpayers. The whole position is in the highest degree artificial, misleading and vexatious. We shall never be able to move again, unless we can free our limbs from these paper shackles. A general bonfire is so great a necessity that unless we can make of it an orderly and good-tempered affair in which no serious injustice is done to anyone, it will, when it comes at last, grow into a conflagration that may destroy much else as well.

(Keynes 1920, p. 280)

Keynes pleaded with the ruling elites to eliminate the internal government debt of all the major countries in Europe by a very large one-time capital levy (or wealth tax) and greatly reduce the external debt through international negotiations, a plea that ultimately went unheeded. "I am one of those who believe that a capital levy for the extinction of the [internal] debt is an absolute prerequisite of sound finance in every one of the European belligerent countries" (Keynes 1920, p. 280).

Third, the prewar system of international economic and financial exchange had broken down.

There are ... three separate obstacles to the revival of trade: a maladjustment between internal prices and international prices, a lack of individual credit ... to buy the raw materials needed to secure the working capital and to re-start the circle of exchange, and a disordered [international] currency system which renders credit operations hazardous or impossible quite apart from the ordinary risks of commerce.

(Keynes 1920. pp. 243–244)

The first of these problems would continue to plague the system and occupy Keynes's attention for much of the interwar period. Britain would go back on the fixed exchange rate gold standard in 1925 at a highly overvalued pound.[5] To prepare for the return of the gold standard, the Bank of England kept interest rates excessively high in the years leading up to 1925, a practice that continued right through 1931 when Britain left the gold standard. The fact that Britain had already lost much of its previous dominance in important segments of trade reinforced the upward pressure on interest rates that lowered the pace of capital investment.

Finally, Keynes feared the consequences of war-generated inflation. Prices had remained reasonably stable for most of the period between the Napoleonic War and WWI, though in the period from 1896 to 1914 they had risen substantially. They then rose dramatically over the five years ending in 1920 at an average rate of about 20 percent per year. "The inflationism of the currency systems of Europe has proceeded to extraordinary lengths" (Keynes 1920, p. 238).

Keynes railed against the evils of inflation and the need to eliminate the policies that reproduced it. He incorrectly attributed to Lenin the idea that "the best way to destroy the Capitalist System was to debauch the currency" (Keynes 1920, p. 235). Inflation arbitrarily redistributes wealth, he said, and thus violates canons of social justice that were very important to him, and it exacerbates uncertainty about the future to such a degree that business calculations become precarious if not futile. Uncertainty over future financial- and real-sector variables would become a centerpiece of *The General Theory*. Unpredictable inflation turns the entrepreneur into a speculator, he argued, and destroys the foundation of the financial system.[6]

> As inflation proceeds and the real value of the currency fluctuates wildly ... all permanent relations between debtors and creditors, which form the ultimate foundation of capitalism, become so utterly disordered as to be almost meaningless; and the process of wealth-getting degenerates into a gamble and a lottery.
> (Keynes 1920, p. 235)

In his 1923 *Tract on Monetary Reform* (see Chapter 3), Keynes argued that a *"regime of monetary contract"* in which the total value of all legal commitments to make nominal payments is large relative to the size of the economy is inherently financially fragile. A serious deflation can trigger a cascade of defaults, leading to a financial crisis.[7]

For all of these reasons, Keynes concluded that the current severe problems in the economies of Europe were not just the result of a temporary adjustment in the transition from a war footing to a return to a peacetime economy. Rather, they were caused by deep-seated, long-term economic problems that were likely to result in sustained low growth and sustained high unemployment over the coming decades.

Thus, the conventional wisdom that Keynes first became concerned about serious structural flaws in capitalism when the Great Depression erupted in the early 1930s is not correct. He came to that conclusion more than a decade earlier. And, as we will demonstrate, he sustained his belief that capitalism was fundamentally or structurally flawed until he died in 1946.

The British economic historian Eric Hobsbawm opened his book *Industry and Empire* with yet another structural or long-run reason as to why the economic future of Britain looked especially gloomy after WWI. Britain had economically dominated the rest of Europe and, indeed, the rest of the world from the mid-eighteenth century through the nineteenth century. Much of its economic success in this era derived from this dominance. But its superiority was inherently transitory, based on conditions that could not possibly be sustained in the long run.

> The Industrial Revolution marks the most fundamental transformation of human life in the history of the world recorded in written

documents. For a brief period it coincided with the history of a single country, Great Britain. An entire world economy was thus built on, or rather around, Britain, and this country temporarily rose to a position of global influence and power unparalleled by any state of its relative size before or since, and unlikely to be paralleled by any state in the foreseeable future. There was a moment in the world's history when Britain can be described, if we are not too pedantic, as its only workshop, its only massive importer and exporter, its only carrier, its only imperialist, almost its only foreign investor; and for that reason its only naval power and the only one that had a genuine world policy. Much of this monopoly was simply due to the loneliness of the pioneer, monarch of all he surveys because of the absence of other surveyors. When other countries industrialized, it ended automatically, though the apparatus of world economic transfers constructed by, and in terms of, Britain remained indispensable to the rest of the world for a while longer. Nevertheless, for most of the world the "British" era of industrialization was merely a phase, – the initial, or an early phase – of contemporary history.

(Hobsbawm 1969, p. 13)

Keynes drew the following conclusion from all this. "England is in a state of transition, and her economic problems are serious. We may be on the eve of great changes in her social and industrial structure" (1920, p. 253).

The most serious problems for England have been brought to a head by the war, but are in their origins more fundamental. The forces of the nineteenth century have run their course and are exhausted. The economic motives and ideals of that generation no longer satisfy us: we must find a new way and must suffer again the *malaise*, and finally the pangs, of a new industrial birth.

(Keynes 1920, p. 254, emphasis in original)

Schumpeter (1946) wrote eloquently about the centrality and depth of Keynes's commitment to the "vision" of secular stagnation and emphasized that this "vision" from 1919 was the foundation of *The General Theory*. Before undertaking his analysis of *The Economic Consequences of the Peace*, Schumpeter said:

Keynes drew a sketch of the economic and social background of the political events he was about to survey. With but slight alterations of phrasing, this sketch may be summed up like this: *Laissez-faire* capitalism, that "extraordinary episode," had come to an end in August, 1914. The conditions were passing in which entrepreneurial leadership was able to secure success after success, propelled as it had been by rapid growth of populations and by abundant opportunities to

> invest that were incessantly recreated by technological improvements and by a series of conquest of new sources of food and raw materials. Under these conditions, there had been no difficulty in absorbing the savings of a *bourgeoisie* that kept on baking cakes "in order not to eat them."[8] But now (1920) those impulses were giving out, the spirit of enterprise was flagging, investment opportunities were vanishing, and bourgeois savings had, therefore, lost their social function; their persistence actually made things worse.
>   Here, then, we have the origin of the mainstream stagnation thesis – as distinguished from the one which we may, if we choose, find in Ricardo. And here we also have the embryo of the *General Theory*. Every comprehensive "theory" of an economic state of society consists of two complementary but essentially distinct elements. There is, first, the theorist's view about the basic features of that state of society, about what is and what is not important in order to understand its life at a given time. Let us call this his vision. And there is, second, the theorist's technique, and apparatus by which he conceptualizes his vision and which turns the vision into concrete propositions or "theories." In those pages of the *Economic Consequences of the Peace* we find nothing of the theoretical apparatus of the *General Theory*. But we find the whole of the vision of things social and economic of which that apparatus is the technical complement. The *General Theory* is the final result of a long struggle to make that vision of our age analytically operative.
> 
> (Schumpeter 1946, pp. 500–501, emphasis in original)

Schumpeter argued that the secular stagnation thesis at the center of the *Economic Consequences of the Peace* was also the central pre-analytic "vision" that underpinned the economic theory and the suggested policies to fix the broken economic system presented in *The General Theory* 17 years later. *The General Theory* represents Keynes's ultimate theoretical foundation to support his "vision" of 1919.

> The social vision first revealed in the *Economic Consequences of the Peace*, the vision of an economic process in which investment opportunity flags and [high] savings habits nevertheless persist, is theoretically implemented in the *General Theory of Employment, Interest and Money*, by means of the three schedule concepts: the consumption function, the [marginal] efficiency of [or expected rate of profit on] capital function, and the liquidity-preference [or demand to hold money as an asset] function.
>
> (Schumpeter 1946, p. 510)

Schumpeter is arguing here that while the sole formal model in *The General Theory* is a short-run model such as the one formalized by Hicks as an IS/

LM model, the same formal model can be used to capture the outline of Keynes's "vision" of secular stagnation.

The old order had perished, but the appropriate structure of the new order was as yet unclear. Keynes's life work, as he saw it, was to help create a new economic order that would ensure full employment and social justice and would be brought about by evolutionary democratic processes rather than through violent revolutions such as those that shook Europe in the interwar years and would ultimately lead to WWII. He would call his proposed new economic order "Liberal Socialism." We will trace his efforts to create Liberal Socialism in Britain throughout the rest of the book.

## Notes

1 "These factors of order, security and uniformity … prepared the way for the organization of that vast mechanism of transport, coal distribution, and foreign trade which made possible an industrial order of life in the dense urban centers of new population" (Keynes 1920, p. 16).
2 The British working class did not get to participate in this prosperity until the latter part of the century.
3 In the eighteenth century and much of the nineteenth century, the condition of the emerging working class both in the factories and at home was deplorable.
4 Moreover, Keynes knew that Britain's pre-WWI dominance in important areas of international trade had also evaporated.
5 Keynes famously attacked the decision to return to gold at its prewar par in his 1925 essay "The Economic Consequences of Mr. Churchill," which is discussed in Chapter 5.
6 Data on the decline of the wealth of ruling elites at this time through war and inflation can be found in Piketty (2014).
7 Inflation ended by 1921 to be followed by three years of sharp deflation, then 12 years of moderate deflation. Keynes would argue in the early 1930s that deflation in the context of fragile balance sheets everywhere is even more destructive than inflation. Problems caused by inflation and deflation are discussed in Chapters 3 and 5.
8 This was an analogy Keynes used to express the idea that the wealthy consumed a relatively low percentage of their income.

# 3 Making sense of chaos: 1919–1923

The economic events of the immediate postwar years did nothing to weaken the view Keynes so forcefully expressed in *The Economic Consequences of the Peace* in 1919 that Europe had seen the end of the institutional foundation of the old era of prosperity and now confronted the daunting challenge of constructing a new economic regime that could operate successfully in the changed environment. The rapid inflation of the war years that so concerned him in 1919 continued through 1920; wholesale prices almost tripled from 1914 through 1920. This period was immediately followed by a powerful deflation that reduced prices by almost half in the next two years and continued at a slower pace into the mid-1930s. Such wrenching price instability wreaked havoc on financial markets, as Keynes had warned it would. It created huge speculative gains for businessmen and stock-market gamblers, as well as staggering rentier losses on the upswing, followed by crushing business and debtor losses on the downswing. And deflation worsened the heavy burden of the war debt, further tightening the "paper shackles" that gripped Europe (Keynes 1920, p. 280). Meanwhile, insured unemployment, which was negligible in 1918 and only 4 percent in 1920, jumped to 17 percent in 1921 before decreasing to just over 10 percent by 1924. It fluctuated between 10 and 12 percent for the remainder of the 1920s, then peaked at 22 percent in 1932 in the depths of the global depression (Garside 1990, p. 5). The concern that Keynes had expressed in 1919 about the dissolution of the old order was now reinforced by a collapse of production and employment followed by an era of sustained high unemployment. His fear that Britain had entered an era of stagnation grew stronger.

From 1919 through most of 1922, Keynes was energetically engaged in efforts to more rationally implement the peace treaties, make possible the rebuilding of the war-torn economies of Europe, and eliminate the severe impediment to the reconstruction and reconstitution of a viable system of international finance and trade represented by reparations and war debts.

Starting in late 1922, however, Keynes increasingly turned his attention toward domestic economic problems and domestic policy. Four lectures delivered to the Institute of Bankers in November and December provide insight into the status of his thinking at a time when the economy had hit its trough. Much of the substance of these lectures would reappear in his 1923 *Tract on Monetary Reform*, though in 1922 he had yet to come to the firm policy conclusion expressed in that manuscript.

Keynes focused on the expected return to the gold standard at the prewar par of $4.86 per pound. Appalled by the damage done to the domestic economy by the severe price instability of the recent past, Keynes at this point considered domestic price stability, not a return to gold, to be the sine qua non of a regime of persistent full employment. An expert on the mechanics of both the international and domestic banking systems, he believed that the monetary authorities now had both the tools and, for the first time, the knowledge (in part gained by the necessity to manage the value of sterling over the past few years) to enable them to control the cost and availability of credit. Deliberate control of the credit cycle in turn could be the means to permanent domestic price stability if that were to become the primary objective of monetary policy. But since 1920, both monetary and fiscal policy had been used not to pursue domestic price stability, but rather to pursue and achieve a savage deflation intended to slash wages and prices in order to improve Britain's trade balance as a precondition for a return to gold at prewar par.

With sterling still well below par, monetary policy would have to exert additional deflationary pressure by substantially raising interest rates. This would create a serious impediment to the restoration of full employment and, Keynes believed, would strike a blow to distributive justice as well. In the lectures, Keynes argued that while the continental countries were in no condition to go back on the gold standard at prewar par or at any fixed rate of exchange, Britain could probably do so, but only if the rate was well below prewar par, as it had been two years earlier when the value of the pound was below $3.50. A key problem with higher interest rates and more deflation in the depth of the postwar depression was that prices were so low they had destroyed entrepreneurs' incentive to expand production. Firms would not accept the risk involved in expanding production and employment until they were sure deflation had ended.

> [T]rade will never go ahead until people are certain [that prices] have touched bottom. They will never be certain that they have touched bottom until they see them going up a little; so that I am in favor of a moderate rise in prices as the only way of getting out of the present period of depression.
>
> (CW 19-I, p. 65)

Further deflation, he argued, would also raise the burden of an already devastating internal, primarily war-induced debt shouldered by the British taxpayer. Keynes put the current yearly debt service at about 40 percent of total government spending, or 70 percent as large as all government spending other than debt service (CW 19-I, p. 63). As on many other occasions, he insisted here that the proper way to handle this kind of problem was through a substantial, one-time, progressive "capital levy" or wealth tax, which, when applied in an appropriate and timely way, is "the justest [sic] and wisest instrument, because you can make the burden fall in the right place" (CW 19-I, p. 48).[1]

A return to gold at par would perhaps require an additional 7 percent decline in British prices when what was needed for a revival of the domestic economy was a price rise of about 15–20 percent, Keynes said. The standard way to push the pound up to par would be to use monetary policy to raise interest rates in order to "keep money in London for a very long period very dear – decidedly dearer than in New York" (CW 19-I, p. 71). Higher interest rates would be needed to reduce domestic demand by enough and for long enough to force domestic prices down, thereby eventually improving the trade balance, which would raise the value of sterling. But this would injure British industry "enormously" because it would increase unemployment and excess capacity.

Keynes understood that organized labor had become much more powerful in Britain during and after the war and would fiercely resist any significant cut in nominal wages. He made an argument here that he would make throughout the interwar era: the attempt to force nominal wage deflation would not succeed in achieving a major reduction in *real* wages in the traditional export sectors. He estimated that the real hourly wage had risen about 20 percent from its prewar level in spite of the depression. However: "The business of forcing down certain levels of wages ... into equilibrium is almost hopeless, or it will take a long time" (CW 19-I, p. 66).

Experience during this period thus led Keynes to reject a cornerstone of classical theory – that flexible money wages can be relied on to restore full employment in the event of a recession or depression. He continued until his death to attack the idea that market disequilibrium adjustment processes such as wage and price deflation could be relied on to cure unemployment. Chapters 2 and 19 of *The General Theory* were designed to demonstrate that deflation actually worsens unemployment. As Skidelsky put it:

> Money wages had fallen by a third during the slump – the last example in British economic history of downward flexibility. Yet they had not fallen enough to restore equilibrium and for the rest of the 1920s remained rigid, despite further deflationary pressure ... Keynes and the financial establishment drew different lessons from this experience. Keynes concluded that the deflation of 1920–1 had brought Britain to the 'verge of revolution,' and that, as a working assumption, wage rates should now be regarded as too rigid in the short period to adjust to the 'ebb and flow of international gold credit'

> ... We have in these lectures an early clue as to what Keynes was to be saying in the years ahead. Wages were 'stickier' than prices. This observation was not novel. More novel was the conclusion that, as a practical matter, the price level and exchange rate should be adjusted to the going wage rate, rather than the other way round.
>
> (Skidelsky 1992, p. 134)

In stressing this point about wages, Keynes merely hints at (though he does not clearly theorize here) a contradiction between a return to the gold standard at *any* fixed rate and sustained full employment at home. If inflation is unjust and corrosive of thrift and deflation is economically disastrous, then the domestic and international requirements for monetary policy will frequently be in contradiction.

The general point is this: the severity of the disequilibrium deflationary processes of the past four years had convinced Keynes that, though many of the old verities may have remained true in some abstract, theoretical long run, the process of attempting to move between long-run equilibriums under modern conditions could be long, path dependent, and enormously costly. The dysfunctional effects of supposedly short-run disequilibrium dynamics could affect the intermediate-run and even the long-run path of the economy, a point not acknowledged by supporters of the return to gold at par. They spent the entire interwar period arguing that the only long-run solution to Britain's unemployment was to deflate her way back to her prewar domination of export markets. They disdained short-run policies designed to directly raise domestic demand and lower unemployment, claiming that they only made the process of adjustment to the long-run solutions longer and costlier.

In reviewing these issues one year later in the *Tract on Monetary Reform*, Keynes made his oft-cited and oft-misunderstood observation that, in seriously troubled times, policy must focus on short- to intermediate-run problems or the hoped-for long-run return to full-employment equilibrium will never come. This was not the good old days of the nineteenth century. Britain had entered a new and more dangerous economic milieu.

> But this *long run* is a misleading guide to current affairs. *In the long run we are all dead.* Economists set themselves too easy, too useless a task if in tempestuous seasons they can only tell us that when the storm is long past the ocean is flat again.
>
> (CW 4, p. 65, emphasis in original)[2]

But the flexible exchange rate policy that Keynes now supported had its own problem, one that Keynes, as an inveterate foreign-exchange market gambler, knew all too well. With no assured center of gravity predetermined by policy, unregulated or fully flexible exchange rates can easily become the object of heavy speculation. This can transform moderate exchange rate cycles into periods of substantial instability. If there were to be flexible exchange rates, they would have to be managed by the government.[3]

In July of 1923, the Bank of England raised the interest rate it charged to commercial banks from 3 to 4 percent. The contradiction between domestic and international priorities in the use of monetary policy had now become clear to Keynes, and he had made up his mind about the direction in which the contradiction should be resolved. High domestic production and employment must be the new objectives of monetary policy replacing exchange rate and trade balance targets.

> The raising of the Bank rate to 4 per cent is one of the most misguided movements of that indicator which have ever occurred. Trade is discouraged and declining; prices are falling slightly; employment is very bad; and the political situation is such as to damp down enterprise and hold back everyone from entering into new business ... There is *no necessary* reason why disturbances on the Continent need cause a million or two of Englishmen to stand idle ... Our job is to do our best to free ourselves from the psychological reactions of foreign politics ... and resolutely to keep our own business going as best we can ... What is the explanation? ... There is not much doubt that the explanation is to be found in the fall of the dollar exchange (not at all unusual at this time of year) ... That is to say, the Bank of England thinks it more important to raise the dollar exchange a few points than to encourage flagging [domestic] trade.
> (CW 19-I, pp. 100–101, emphasis in original)[4]

Though Keynes remained unsure about precisely how to solve all of the serious problems confronting Britain at this point in time, he was quite clear that there would have to be a qualitative increase in the economic responsibilities and powers of the state in the postwar era. In January 1923, in the introduction to the last segment of an influential series of articles on European reconstruction published in the *Manchester Guardian*, he made the following observation, cited by Skidelsky:

> In our present confusion of aims, is there enough clear-sighted public spirit left to preserve the balance and complicated organisation by which we live? Communism is discredited by events; socialism [as embodied in the Soviet-style plans of the Labour Party], in its old-fashioned interpretation, no longer interests the world; capitalism has lost its self-confidence. Unless men are united by a common aim or moved by objective principles, each one's hand will be against the rest and the unregulated pursuit of individual advantage may soon destroy the whole.
> (Skidelsky 1992, p. 121)

Skidelsky notes that, at this point, "Keynesianism is already a gleam in his eye – not as an economic theory, but as the vision of an enlightened Middle Way" (Skidelsky 1992, p. 122).

## A Tract on Monetary Reform (1923)

Many important theoretical ideas and concepts we associate with the mature Keynes of *The General Theory* played an important role in the *Tract*. They include the central role given to uncertainty, expectations, conventions, business "psychology" as a key influence on production and investment, and the *"regime of money contract"* (CW 4, p. 33). The regime of money contract refers to a crucial characteristic of post-WWI capitalism. The total value of contractual obligations (mostly credit contracts) stated in nominal terms was so large relative to the size of the economy that substantial deflation could trigger a wave of defaults and even a financial crisis. To use Hyman Minsky's famous phrase, a "regime of money contract" is subject to "financial fragility." In such a regime, the condition of balance sheets can have a huge impact on economic performance. This insight would have a profound influence on Keynes's understanding of the causes of the Great Depression of the 1930s, though, surprisingly, it is mentioned – see chapters 19 and 22 – but not consistently stressed in *The General Theory*. For Keynes in the interwar years, the state of balance sheets is a crucial determinant of economic performance: balance sheets matter.

Keynes argued that stabilization of the aggregate price level was the key to reducing uncertainty and preventing expectations from becoming dysfunctional. Though his theory of "aggregate demand" was not yet fully developed, Keynes made the argument that excessive instability of the general or economy-wide price level (as distinguished from relative prices) reduced economy-wide spending, raised unemployment, and maldistributed income. Capitalist markets:

> cannot work properly if the money, which [individual savers and businessmen] assume as a stable measuring rod, is undependable. Unemployment, the precarious life of the worker, the disappointment of expectation, the sudden loss of savings, the excessive windfalls to individuals, the speculator, the profiteer – all proceed, in large measure, from the instability of the standard of value ... [R]isk ... is one of the heaviest, and the perhaps the most avoidable, burden on production. This element of risk is greatly aggravated by the instability of the standard of value.
>
> (CW 4, p. xiv)

The first chapter of the book dealt with the economic and social consequences of price instability. The term "social" is very important because Keynes is thinking here, as in *The Economic Consequences of the Peace*, in terms of the broad sweep of events taking place in the twentieth century as they relate to the social, cultural, institutional, and political preconditions for the efficient functioning of domestic and global capitalism. Though known as the most influential macroeconomist in history, Keynes, as we will see, also emphasized the influence of micro and meso (or industry) conditions as well as the psychology of individuals and groups on macroeconomic outcomes.

He began the book by restating one of his 1919 themes: that unstable price movements since 1914 had destroyed many of the preconditions for the successful reproduction of the prewar system.

> The fluctuations in the value of money since 1914 have been on a scale so great as to constitute, with all that they involve, one of the most significant events in the economic history of the modern world. The fluctuation of the standard ... has not only been of unprecedented violence, but has been visited on a society of which the economic organisation is more dependent than that of any earlier epoch on the assumption that the standard of value would be moderately stable.
> (CW 4, pp. 1–2)

Changes of this magnitude "are producing now the vastest social consequences" (CW 4, p. 1).

His first point is that over the nineteenth century there evolved a separation of "the management of property from its ownership," with fixed-income securities – "mortgages, bonds, debentures, and preference shares" – becoming increasingly important sources of financial capital (CW 4, p. 5).[5] In this historically specific form of capitalism, the high savings of the affluent rentier class were provided to the entrepreneurs of the day without substantial managerial interference, to be converted almost automatically into capital accumulation because the return on capital was high and because in this prosperous environment businessmen invested not on the basis of a careful calculation of expected profits, but almost as "a way of life" (CW 7, p. 150). The system was very successful, but such a rentier-based "regime of money contract" could not have persisted without the unusual price stability that occurred between the Napoleonic Wars (1803–1815) and the start of WWI.[6]

> For a hundred years the system worked, throughout Europe, with an extraordinary success and facilitated the growth of wealth on an unprecedented scale ... The morals, the politics, the literature, and the religion of the age joined in a grand conspiracy for the promotion of saving ... But amidst the general enjoyment of ease and progress, the extent to which the system depended on the stability of the money to

which the investing classes had committed their fortunes was generally overlooked.

(CW 4, p. 6)

Anticipating the stress placed on "conventional" expectation formation in *The General Theory*, Keynes noted that belief in the permanent stability of the value of money was not rooted in any careful study of the broad sweep of history, for such a study would have shown recurrent outbursts of instability around a long-run trend of moderately rising prices. There existed, rather, merely a *"conventional belief* in the stability and safety of a money contract" (CW 4, p. 7, emphasis added). "Custom and favourable experience had acquired for such investments an unimpeachable reputation for security" (CW 4, p. 12). Thus, the enormous inflation of prices during the war and for two years thereafter mortally injured the old system connecting rentiers and businessmen – or saving and the demand for capital investment – by nearly destroying the European rentier class itself and by making the conventional belief in price stability untenable. A system substantially based on a large volume of long-term nominal debt contracts was simply incompatible with substantial price instability.

> The monetary events which have accompanied and have followed the war have taken from [rentiers] about one-half their real value in England, seven-tenths in France, eleven-twelfths in Italy, and virtually the whole in Germany and the succession states of Austria-Hungary and Russia ... Nor can it be doubted that this experience must modify social psychology towards the practice of saving and investing.
>
> (CW 4, pp. 12, 16)

The theory Keynes presented to explain why and how price instability caused production and employment to fluctuate is as follows: "It has long been recognized, by the business world and economists alike, that a period of rising prices acts as a stimulus to enterprise and is beneficial to business men" – and vice versa (CW 4, p. 17). Since output prices tend to respond more quickly to changes in final demand than input prices (including wages), rising prices bring what Keynes called "windfall profits" to the businessman. Inflation helps him in two ways. First, it reduces the burden of his existing debt, and since, in Keynes's view, nominal interest rates rarely catch up to the pace of inflation, it lowers the cost of new credit as well. Second, since production and marketing take time, inflation raises his selling price relative to the prices paid for inputs. This stimulates output and employment. In a deflationary period, everything works in reverse. The burden of debt is increased, and not only for business borrowings: "in these days of huge national debts ... the burden of taxation becomes intolerable on the productive classes of the community" (CW 4, p. 30). In current conditions, Keynes argued, the market system left to itself is incapable of preventing destabilizing, large-scale price movements that raise unemployment. Therefore, the state must take direct responsibility for the maintenance of domestic price stability. There is also the suggestion that the destructive influence of uncertainty (here called risk) on economic instability *through the medium of expectations* is becoming stronger as economic relations grow more complex and the time between the decision to undertake production and the receipt of revenues from production lengthens.[7] The causes of this problem arise:

> to a certain extent out of the character of the social organisation described above, but [are] aggravated by the technical methods of present-day productive processes. With the development of international trade, involving great distances between the place of original production and the place of final consumption, and with the increased complication of the technical processes of manufacturing, the amount of *risk* which attaches to the undertaking of production and the length of time through which this risk must be carried are much greater than they would be in a comparatively small self-contained community.
> (CW 4, p. 32, emphasis in original)

Keynes believed that this problem of uncertainty was both increasingly dangerous and very difficult to resolve. "The provision of adequate facilities for the carrying of this risk at a moderate cost is one of the greatest of the problems of modern economic life, and one of those which so far have been least satisfactorily solved" (CW 4, p. 33). His main insight here is that as the average time involved in the processes of production and distribution lengthens, production becomes increasingly and inherently speculative, a problem that will eventually be dominated in his thinking by a focus on the *inherently* speculative nature of the process of capital investment. Unexpected changes in relative prices are one part of the problem, but unexpected changes in the average price level are more dangerous yet, especially if they are large. The latter concern is incompatible with the classical dictum that changes in the average price level that leave relative prices unaffected have no impact on the economy.

> A considerable part of the risk arises out of fluctuations in the *relative* value of a commodity compared with that of commodities in general during the interval which must elapse between the commencement of production and the time of consumption ... But there is also a considerable risk directly arising out of instability in the value of money. During the lengthy process of production the business world is incurring outgoings in terms of *money* – paying out in money for wages

and other expenses of production – in the expectation of recouping this outlay by disposing of the product for *money* at a later date. That is to say, the business world as a whole must always be in a position where it stands to gain by a rise of price and to lose by a fall of price. Whether he likes it or not, the technique of production under a regime of money contract forces the business world to carry a big speculative position; and if it is reluctant to carry this position, the productive process must be slackened.

(CW 4, p. 33, emphasis in original)[8]

Keynes seemed to be suggesting in this chapter not only that production and employment have become increasingly elastic with respect to absolute price instability, but also that increasing uncertainty about future price movements itself was adversely affecting the incentive to save and the incentive to accumulate real capital. That is, not only has the amplitude and length of the production–employment cycle been affected by institutional change and price instability, but the trend around which this cycle takes place may have been impacted as well.[9]

Finally, Keynes argues that the inflation–deflation cycle of the past decade has had profound social and political as well as economic consequences. His main concern is that price instability of this magnitude violates social justice as he defines it by creating an arbitrary and undeserved substantial redistribution of income and wealth among and within the three great classes of society: rentiers, businessmen, and workers.[10] It has often been said that Keynes did not concern himself with the issue of social justice, but this assertion is at best misleading.

On average, rentiers were devastated by inflation, while businessmen and workers were enriched. "Throughout the continent the pre-war savings of the middle class, so far as they were invested in bonds, mortgages, or bank deposits, have been largely or entirely wiped out" (CW 4, p. 16). During the inflation phase, businessmen reaped large, speculative, and undeserved gains, and many sectors of labor were able to use the greater bargaining power they achieved during the war "to take advantage of the situation not only to obtain money wages equivalent to what they had before, but to secure a real improvement [and] to combine this with a diminution in their hours of work" (CW 4, p. 26). Since no important aspect of this substantial redistribution reflected changes in the economic contributions to society of the classes, its "most striking consequence is its injustice," especially to middle-class savers (CW 4, p. 29). Deflation, on the other hand:

> means impoverishment to labour and to enterprise by leading entrepreneurs to restrict production, in their endeavour to avoid loss to themselves; and is therefore disastrous to employment ... Of the two perhaps deflation is ... the worse, because it is worse, in an

impoverished world, to provoke unemployment than to disappoint the rentier.

(CW 4, pp. 35–36)

Keynes finds this cycle of redistribution through inflation–deflation to be not only morally repugnant, but economically and politically dangerous because it destroys belief in the efficiency and fairness of economic institutions, a precondition for economic and social stability. In particular, it changes the image of the businessman from creative entrepreneur to speculator and "profiteer," destroys the incentive to save in the inflation phase, and causes depression and financial distress in the deflation stage.

Keynes's policy conclusion is simple: either the state must be given unprecedented responsibility for maintaining a relatively stable domestic aggregate price index in an environment of managed but flexible exchange rates or the conditions under which savings are made available for capital accumulation can no longer be left to individuals and the market but must be ceded to the state.

In a speech summarizing the key points made in the *Tract* at the time of its publication, Keynes stressed the seriousness of the consequences that would follow from rejection of his advice and a continuation of the economic policies appropriate to the prewar regime. It reflects a consistent theme in his attempts to sway elite public opinion to his approach to policy: *my reforms will not look so radical and unattractive, he argues, if you compare them with the disastrous alternative.*[11]

> But I should like to warn the gentlemen of the City and of High Finance that if they do not listen in time to the voice of reason their days may be numbered. I speak to this great City as Jonah spoke to Nineveh that great city. I prophesy that unless they embrace Wisdom in good time, the system upon which they live will work so very ill that they will be overwhelmed by irresistible things which they hate much more that the mild and limited remedies offered them now.
>
> (CW 19-I, p. 162)

Skidelsky ended his discussion of the *Tract* with the following observation (keep in mind that Skidelsky tended to underemphasize the radical nature of Keynes's policies):

> Beneath both the technical and the ironic drapery of the *Tract* were a series of connected propositions which were to inspire Keynes's economic work for the rest of his life. Economic health was too important to be left *to laissez-faire*. Economic management, which had already started, must become part of the modern science of government, not the tool of vested interests. The war had vastly increased the dangers of social upheaval. To preserve the core of

an individualist society from revolutionary danger some of the outerworks had to be sacrificed.

(Skidelsky 1992, p. 160, emphasis in original)

It may be helpful at this point to recapitulate the anti-classical policy conclusion Keynes developed by 1923: Britain should switch from the gold standard to managed flexibility in the exchange rate and devote monetary policy to controlling the creation of credit in pursuit of stability and thus predictability in the domestic price level rather than in defense of the fixed value of the exchange rate under the gold standard.

The cumulative effect of Keynes's shifts in theoretical perspective in these few years is impressive. By 1923, Keynes had uncovered many flaws in classical theory as it applied to modern capitalism and had developed intuitions about many of the building blocks he would later use to construct *The General Theory*. Institutional rigidities had developed in the postwar economy that are absent from the assumption set of classical theory. One is a lack of downward flexibility in the nominal wage in the face of high unemployment, especially in Britain. This removed one of the two main disequilibrium processes in classical theory that eliminate unemployment. In a direct attack on classical theory, Keynes argued that unemployment would rise, not fall, under serious wage and price deflation.[12] Therefore, as he argued in *The General Theory*, downward rigidity in nominal wages is actually a good thing.[13] Another is the "regime of money contract": bankruptcies may erupt and financial markets may even implode in the face of serious deflation if firm and bank balance sheets are fragile. This problem is also unaccounted for in classical theory. Keynes suggested that the decisions that determine the proportions of society's income that were saved and that were invested in capital goods in the nineteenth century depended on "unstable psychological conditions" that had not carried over to the interwar period (CW 4, p. 21). He also emphasized the increasing importance of uncertainty in modern economies and therefore the importance of expectations formation under uncertainty in determining the economic trajectory of the country. Since, *ceteris paribus*, increasing risk or uncertainty would permanently lower the level of capital investment, it would, of necessity, reinforce Keynes's emerging belief that Britain had entered an era of permanently sluggish growth. Keynes also hinted at an incipient theory of expectations formation based on social and behavioral heuristics or, as he put it, on "conventions." This obviously foreshadows the centrality of uncertainty and the necessity of a behavioral theory of conventional expectations formation that is at the heart of *The General Theory*.

Finally, Keynes insisted that movements in the average price level cause movements in economic activity that the market economy by itself cannot prevent. Cycles of inflation and deflation are related to cycles of credit creation and cause economic and social instability. Keynes clearly had begun the struggle that culminated in the 1930s with the theory of the effect of "aggregate demand" on income and employment with which he is associated.

## Notes

1. See also his discussion of the capital levy on pages 62–64.
2. The "In the long run we are all dead" part of this quotation is almost always taken out of context and interpreted to mean that Keynes was not interested in the long run. Nothing could be further from the truth.
3. Keynes was especially concerned that the seasonal nature of much of Britain's trade in food and raw materials would, in an unregulated system, inevitably cause seasonal exchange-rate fluctuations that would be magnified by speculation.
4. Keynes put the argument that Britain should be prepared to control its economic destiny relatively independently of the performance of the rest of Europe in a more provocative from in his important 1933 article "National Self-Sufficiency," discussed in Chapter 11.
5. The issue of common stocks was not an important source of funding for capital investment in the nineteenth century.
6. Trouble for the rentier class had actually begun before the war. "Between 1896 and 1914 ... the capital value of [an] annuity had fallen by about a third" (CW 4, p. 14). But this decline merely gave up gains achieved in the previous decade or so.
7. He will return to this idea in chapters 3 and 5 of *The General Theory*.
8. In an earlier version of this discussion about the problems caused by time and uncertainty in a regime of money contract (published in *The Nation* in August 1923), Keynes argued that when individuals and businesses expect falling prices, "They put off their purchases, not because they lack purchasing power, but because their demand is capable of postponement and may, they think, be satisfied at a lower price later on. It is these postponements which are at the root of remediable unemployment" (CW 19-I, pp. 115–116). Keynes would later make this a central distinction between a "cooperative" or barter economy and a "money-wage or entrepreneur economy." In the latter but not the former, agents can flee commodities and flock to money in times of uncertainty or of certain deflation; thus, Say's Law is invalid in a money-wage economy. This general argument also appears in chapter 19 of *The General Theory*.
9. A similar argument is made in *The General Theory* where the culprit is volatile expectations of the profit rate.
10. Keynes believed that any change in the class distribution of income not associated with a similar change in the economic contributions of the classes to the production of national output was unjust.
11. As we will see, this is the position Keynes also took in the final chapter of *The General Theory*. In that chapter, he first listed a series of very radical proposals for changing Britain's political economy. He then suggested that his policy proposals were really not as radical as they might appear to be in order not to scare his more conservative readers. But he exited the chapter with this warning to Britain's elites. If you – the economists, government officials, and

influential bankers and businessmen who control British politics – do not adopt the program I have developed in this book, all hell will break loose. "It is certain the world will not much longer tolerate the unemployment which, apart from brief periods of excitement, is associated – and in my opinion inevitably associated – with present day capitalistic individualism" (CW 7, p. 381). In other words, join my policy revolution or the working class will undertake a revolution of their own that you will not like at all.

12  He would later argue that even when money wages are downwardly flexible, as in the USA in the early 1930s, the real wage will not fall because prices can fall by as much as or more than wages; see chapters 2 and 19 in *The General Theory*, in which Keynes insists that wage and price deflation are destructive processes.

13  "The chief result of [flexible wages] would be to cause a great instability of prices, so violent perhaps as to make business calculations futile in an economic society functioning after the manner of that in which we live. To suppose that a flexible wage policy is a right and proper adjunct of a system which on the whole is *laissez-faire*, is the opposite of the truth" (CW 7, p. 269).

# 4 Public investment and state planning in 1924

## The real Keynesian revolution begins

On May 24, 1924, Keynes published an article titled "Does Unemployment Need a Drastic Remedy?" in *The Nation and Athenaeum*, the Liberal Party journal. The piece was stimulated by policy proposals made by David Lloyd George, the Liberal candidate for Prime Minister.[1] The Liberal Party had made reduction of unemployment the focus of their Fall 1923 election campaign. (The election was won by the Labour Party, which took power under Prime Minister Ramsay MacDonald in January 1924). Lloyd George had used the pages of *The Nation* in April to argue that the country needed not only expansionary monetary policy to return to full employment, but the fiscal stimulus of large public investment expenditure as well. A debate on Lloyd George's proposal in the pages of *The Nation* ensued, with Keynes having the final word.

We examine this article in detail because it contains Keynes's initial presentation and defense of public investment as the key policy tool to be used to restore and sustain full employment in a current economic system otherwise incapable of this objective. This is a policy position he perfected and fought for, in one form or another, until his death in 1946. Though the theoretical defense of this policy position would not be fully formed until the publication of *The General Theory*, the broad outline of his perspective on this question was clearly and permanently established in this 1924 debate. According to Skidelsky:

> The years 1924 and 1925 were more obviously watershed years than 1923 ... Events and the processes of his own thought radicalised him, so that he emerged the self-conscious champion of a new economic and political order ... New ideas came flooding in, and demanded expression. From 1924 Keynes knew what he wanted to do and, in very broad terms, why.
>
> (Skidelsky 1992, p. 173)

It has been argued that Keynes neglected the effects of structural factors, especially the substantial decline of exports in industries in which Britain had been dominant before the war, on the high unemployment rate of the 1920s. Indeed, the accusation the Keynes neglected the problem of structural unemployment has been made so often that it is almost universally believed that he was guilty as charged. But Keynes here *stressed* structural causes of unemployment. He estimated the current male unemployment at about 8 percent, compared to 12 percent in early 1923 and 14 percent in early 1922. Much of the male unemployment, he said, is structural.

> If the figures be analysed we find a great concentration of unemployment in the shipbuilding and engineering industries (i.e., nearly four times the percentage elsewhere). Outside these industries, unemployment amongst adult males does not now exceed much more than 4 per cent of the employable population.
>
> (CW 19-I, p. 219)

The report stated that the unemployment rates for all unionized workers (largely though not exclusively male) were 15.2, 11.3, and 8.1 percent, respectively, in 1922, 1923, and 1924 (Mitchell and Deane 1962, p. 67).[2] But the Engineering, Metal and Shipbuilding Unions reported unemployment rates of 27, 20.6, and 13.8 percent in those years. Since the all-unions number includes these high-unemployment industries, Keynes's estimate may not have been too far off the mark. The unemployment rate for all insured nonagricultural workers was 10.9 percent in 1924 (CW 19-I, p. 67).

But although progress had been made, Keynes believed that Britain was stuck in a temporary equilibrium with unemployment still too high. In retrospect, it is clear that the unemployment rate had stopped falling; the rate in the first half of 1924 had reached what would prove to be its interwar-period low.

> Business is weighed down by timidity. It lacks conviction that anything good will continue for long. It watches anxiously for the signs of retrogression; and as soon as the army wavers, individuals bolt. No one is ready to plant seeds which only a long summer can bring to fruit.
>
> (CW 19-I, p. 221)

Keynes suggested that full employment, or a "sustainable minimum" unemployment rate, was about 3 percent unemployment.[3] Given the significance of structural unemployment, he argued that a transition to full employment required a combination of macroeconomic stimulus and industrial policies – large-scale public investment to create jobs on the one hand and targeted industrial and labor market policy on the other. Most economists are unaware that Keynes emphasized sub-macro conditions throughout the interwar years.

> Part of [the unemployment] is due to the immobility of labour as between industries; part to the fault of trade unions; and part to a disparity of wages between what are called the sheltered and the unsheltered [or traded goods] industries.[4] But we cannot cure these ills by the pressure of starvation, or by breaking the power for evil, and perhaps for good also, of the trade unions, or by reducing wages in the sheltered industries to the level of the unsheltered. From these thoughts the mind must be averted, for from such directions help will not come. Rather, we must seek to submerge the rocks in a rising sea, – not forcing labour out of what is depressed, but attracting it into what is prosperous; not crushing the blind strength of organised labour, but relieving its fears, not abating wages where they are high, but raising them where they are low.
>
> (CW 19-I, p. 221)

Thus, the way to get to full employment was not through a direct attack on unions and wages in the depressed export industries as called for by the conventional wisdom. Rather, the structurally unemployed must instead be induced to move into newly created jobs generated by more rapid macroeconomic growth through public investment assisted by industrial policy.

Keynes proposed that the state should commit itself to increasing public investment by a substantial amount for a long period of time to stimulate an increase in general employment large enough to solve the jobs problem centered in the export sector. He argued that Britain "must look for succour to the principle that *prosperity is cumulative*. We have become stuck in a rut. We need an impulse, a jolt, an acceleration" (CW 19-I, p. 220, emphasis in original). The idea that "prosperity is cumulative" represented Keynes's initial attempt to link large-scale public investment with some vague form of the multiplier concept. For this reason, it might be understood to be the starting point of the real Keynesian revolution in the theory of economic policy.[5]

Keynes's concrete proposal was for the Treasury to initiate and finance "expenditures up to (say) £100,000,000 a year" – or about 2.6 percent of 1924 GDP – "on the construction of capital works at home, enlisting in various ways the aid of private genius, temperament, and skill" (CW 19-I, p. 222).

He did not hazard a guess in this article as to the number of jobs that might be created by public investment of £100,000,000 a year, but he did suggest, in an article published in July 1925, that such a sum would be "enough to make good the wastage of nearly 500,000 men in unemployment" (CW 19-I, p. 427). The implicit assumption that each worker creates a net output of £200 is quite close to the figure of £220 used most often in the more careful calculations of the job-creating power of public investment made by Keynes and the Liberal Party starting in 1929, when the multiplier concept and its role in the theory of AD first became consciously incorporated into his analysis.

It is important to understand that Keynes almost always used the concept of the multiplier coupled with a proposal for an increase in public investment. The role played by the multiplier in Keynes's decades-long effort to make public investment the centerpiece of Britain's economic policy was to show that every dollar of new public investment will raise output by two to three dollars. This means that full employment can be reached by achievable and sustainable increases in public investment. That is its role in chapter 10 of *The General Theory*, which is where the multiplier concept is introduced. In chapter 10, the examples he used of the effect of the multiplier all refer to the impact of public investment on output and employment.

Since insured unemployment was about 1.2 million in 1924, a reduction of half a million (among the insured unemployed) would have cut the unemployment rate from 10.3 to about 6 percent (Garside 1990, p. 5). This was clearly designed to be neither a modest nor a short-term program. Though the use of "public works" to help temporarily employ some of those without jobs had long been advocated by various political and economic commentators in interwar Britain, no *long-term* program of this magnitude had ever been proposed by someone of Keynes's gravitas.[6]

The funds for the program were to be diverted from current contributions to the government's "sinking fund," which collected taxes to pre-fund interest and principal payments on the vast pubic debt generated in WWI. Keynes wanted to use these revenues to finance a sharp rise in public investment. Since every pound spent on public investment initially resulted in one additional pound of debt outstanding, the investment was, in effect, debt financed. In this way, Keynes explained in a metaphor he often used, the government could replace "unproductive debt with productive debt" (CW 19-I, p. 222).

What kinds of projects should the government fund? Consistent with his general position on such questions, Keynes insisted that expert advice must be sought on this crucial issue. "It is for the technicians of building, engineering, and transport to tell us in what direction the most fruitful new improvements are awaiting us" (CW 19I, p. 222). But he did mention three projects that "are already known to everyone in a general way." Each of these projects could involve huge investment expenditures over a very long time period:

> a national scheme for the mass production of [working class] houses which would supplement the normal activities of the building industry and make up in five or ten years the deficiency with which the latter has proved unable to deal. The adaptation of road-building to the needs of motor transport ... The development of economical means for the transmission of electrical power in this country. Unaided

> private enterprise is not capable of dealing with any of these projects, even when their technical soundness is beyond doubt.
>
> (CW 19-I, pp. 222–223)

Keynes's argument reflects his belief that Britain had entered a period of stagnation. He said that previous eras of long-term prosperity in Britain had some powerful semi-exogenous engine of capital accumulation that had helped start and sustain the rapid growth process. His implicit assumption was that long eras of prosperity in capitalism require some great secular wave of transformative infrastructural, technological, and/or market-expanding investment, carried on year after year without regard to short-run fluctuations in profitability and capable of creating a powerful ripple effect of induced capital accumulation across important sectors of the economy.

> British prosperity in the nineteenth century owed very much to the railway boom in its first half, beginning at home and extending abroad, and to the immense building activity of its latter half ... The boom in motors and in building combined, no doubt, with many favourable attendant circumstances, has carried the United States to an unprecedented standard of living.
>
> (CW 19-I, p. 221)

The reference to the "railway boom" is especially instructive. More than three decades long, the construction of the British railway system totally transformed the British economy. It induced an era of high non-rail investment because it not only created widespread profitable investment opportunities by expanding and integrating markets and creating preconditions for huge economies of scale, but also stimulated a surge in optimism and confidence among British capitalists in this period as well – prosperity is "cumulative." The potential for stagnation arises because there is no guarantee that the economy will always generate system-transforming innovations capable of generating rapid long-term growth.

Keynes's argument is that private firms operating solely through ordinary market incentives cannot, in the current era, carry on the long-term, large-scale capital projects required to accelerate long-term growth. It is thus left to the public sector to step in and help create an engine of long-term capital accumulation that can pull the economy out of its distress and keep it buoyant. Note that Keynes's stated long-run objective is to create the "true socialism of the future."

> Is there not a chance that we can best achieve [prosperity] by recreating the mood and conditions in which great works of construction, requiring large capital outlays, can again be set on foot? Current savings are already available on a sufficient scale – savings which

from a lack of outlet at home, are now drifting abroad to destinations from which we as a society shall gain the least advantage. Private enterprise unaided cannot stop this flow. The policy of preventing public utilities from yielding more than a modest profit has gone so far that it is no longer worth the while of private enterprise to run risk in a field where the gain is limited and the loss unlimited.[7] We are in danger, therefore, of interfering with private initiative, yet substituting nothing for it. The advances under the Trade Facilities Act, begun for a temporary emergency and on a small scale, point the way, perhaps to a new method of administering an important part of the saving of the public. The next developments of politico-economic evolution may be found in co-operation between private initiative and the public exchequer. The *true socialism* of the future will emerge, I think, from endless experiments directed towards discovering the respective appropriate spheres of the individual and the social, and the terms of fruitful alliance between these sister instincts.

(CW 19-I, p. 222, emphasis added)[8]

His concern about capital flight or British savings "drifting abroad" with little advantage to the domestic economy was not new, nor would it prove to be merely temporary.[9] Indeed, it would receive increased emphasis in Keynes's work over the coming years.

It is worth noting that the ideas Keynes espoused here constituted heresy on a grand scale. It was not the line about "true socialism" that was heretical, for Keynes and many other radical Liberals thought of themselves as liberal socialists (to be distinguished from the "State Socialists" of the Labour Party), and they referred to themselves as such. Rather, it is the fact that Keynes here added to his previous acts of sacrilege – rejection of the gold standard and support for discretionary regulation of the credit system in pursuit of domestic objectives – his growing concern that Britain's current form of capitalism may be incapable of generating sustained full employment even under optimal monetary policy. This implied that the state might have to take upon itself *direct* control of a substantial part of the capital accumulation process in addition to its exercise of indirect influence through control of the cost and availability of credit. To complete his list of sins against orthodox belief, he will, in the course of debate in *The Nation*, argue in favor of permanent controls over the movement of financial capital out of Britain, something he had supported since his days as a student.

Keynes concluded this article by stressing three key points. First, a combination of expansionary monetary policy and a program of state-guided investment is needed to achieve full employment. Second, public investment on this scale combined with capital controls will help divert the flow of British financial capital away from largely unproductive foreign investment to domestic investment. Third, carefully selected large-scale public investments will not just increase employment in general; they can also be used as industrial policies to reduce structural unemployment.

> I look, then, for the ultimate cure of unemployment, and for the stimulus which shall initiate a cumulative prosperity, to monetary reform – which will remove fear – and to the diversion of national savings from relatively barren foreign investment into state-encouraged constructive enterprises at home – which will inspire confidence. That part of our recent unemployment, which is not attributable to an ill-controlled credit cycle, has been largely due to a slump in our constructional industries. By conducting the national wealth into capital developments at home, we may restore the balance of our economy. Let us experiment with boldness on such lines – even though some of the schemes may turn out to be failures, which is very likely.
> (CW 19-I, p. 223)

Keynes fleshed out these ideas in response to attacks by his critics. His main defense of his views appeared in a second *Nation* article in June 1924 called "A Drastic Remedy for Unemployment: Reply to Critics." In this defense, he put more stress than in the original article on: (1) the problem of excess saving – the balance between saving and investment that played such an important role in *The General Theory* had moved closer to the center of his thinking; (2) the problem of free capital mobility, which, under then-current conditions, led primarily to what he called "the flight of foreign capital"; and (3) the rigidity or lack of flexibility of the modern, postwar British economic system.

He reminded the reader that since the sinking fund throws up to £100 million a year on the capital market, it is essential that thought be given to "the supply of alternative investments" that might absorb such a sum. "At first, Local [government] Loans, home, municipal, and industrial debentures partly filled the bill. But with the advent of deflation, the Geddes Axe, and industrial depression, the supply [of new securities] has dried up" (CW 19-I. p. 226).[10] Later on, Keynes would describe a situation like this as one in which savings at full employment exceeded investment at full employment by a large amount, causing the economy to be in a high-unemployment equilibrium.

Meanwhile, the rate of interest on foreign bonds floated in London had fallen about 1 per cent below the rate for similar bonds in New York. As a result: "We are lending too cheaply resources we can ill spare. Our traditional attitude toward foreign investment demands reconsideration; it is high time to give it a bad name and call it 'the flight of capital'" (CW 19-I, p. 227). His main concern was that outward capital flows in excess of net exports (inclusive of returns on previously invested capital) would exert downward pressure on the pound, which must continue until exports rise by enough to restore the payments balance. But Keynes argued that world demand for British exports had become relatively price inelastic, so that the required depreciation was potentially quite large. This created serious problems in his view because the postwar British economy did not have the elasticity, fluidity, or easy mobility of either capital or labor that would be required for the real economy to smoothly and quickly adjust to such severe exchange rate changes. It did not resemble the flexible economy constructed in Classical theory.

> [T]here may be violent resistances to the process of adjustment. The fall of the exchange tends to raise the "cost of living," and the "sheltered" industries may struggle to avoid the reduction of real wages which this entails. Our economic structure is far from elastic, and much time may elapse and indirect loss result from the strains set up and the breakages incurred. Meanwhile, resources may lie idle and labour may be out of employment.
>
> (CW 19-I, p. 228)

Skidelsky pointed out that Keynes's new argument amounted to the proposition that the British industrial system was so inflexible that, even with the exchange rate free to float downwards, British unemployment – concentrated in the export trades – could be alleviated only by public works (Skidelsky 1992, p. 187). This emphasis on the downward rigidity of nominal wages would continue to characterize Keynes's thinking for the next two decades.[11]

The degree of resource flexibility required for either laissez-faire or the gold standard to operate effectively may have been present in the old regime, Keynes acknowledged, but it is not present in the new one.

> The old principle of *laissez-faire* was to ignore these strains and to assume that capital and labour were fluid; it also assumed that, if investors choose to send their money abroad at 5 per cent, this must mean that there is nothing at home worth doing at 5 per cent. Fifty years ago this may have been a closer approximation to the truth than it is now. With the existing rigidity of the trade-union organisation of labour, with the undue preferences which the City organisation of new issues and the Trustee Acts afford to overseas investment, and with the caution which for many reasons, some good and some bad, now oppresses the undertaking of new capital investment at home, it does not work.
>
> (CW 19-I, p. 228)[12]

In August, he would estimate that in 1923 "we invested abroad about two-thirds of what passed through the investment markets, and probably between half and a third of total savings" (CW 19-I, p. 284). In two months, he would tell readers of *The Nation* that "The Treasury should use its power of license to ... strictly ration overseas borrowers" (CW 19-I, p. 282).

The second prong is positive: stimulate the domestic demand for money-capital through a major program of large-scale government investment. There is a wealth of large-scale investment projects that are economically efficient and socially productive to undertake: "Surely [critics] cannot maintain that England is a finished job, and that there is nothing worth doing on a 5 per cent basis" (CW 19-I, p. 228). But private capitalists cannot undertake them because while the downside risk of loss is limited only by the size of the financial commitment, the potential gains today are – in contrast to the nineteenth century – exceedingly modest, about what could be earned by investing in a safe security.[13]

> Is it worth the while, or within the power, of anyone to organise a new project costing £20,000,000 with the expectation of a return of 5 per cent? These persons "exercising foresight" about new, costly, moderately remunerative projects do not exist. If there was no Manchester Ship Canal, does [anyone] suppose that a syndicate of private persons would spring up today to construct it?
>
> (CW 19-I, p. 230)

Keynes made the point several times that regulatory constraints on the profits of those firms operating in the industries designated as public utilities would not and should not be removed – "There is no going back on this." He does not explain at this point why there is no going back on this, but, as discussed in detail below, he later presented a theoretical and empirical defense of this proposition. The defense is based partly on the rise of economies of scale and scope in crucial industries that led to monopoly and oligopoly market structures across Britain. These industries could not possibly be left unregulated – and they weren't. The defense is also based on the destructive nature of competition in old export industries like cotton and coal with their large numbers of small firms, a phenomenon I discuss in Chapter 7.

Where, then, is the domestic investment demand to come from?

> In considering how to [raise the rate of capital accumulation], we are brought to my heresy – if it is a heresy. I bring in the State; I abandon *laissez-faire*, – not enthusiastically, not from contempt of that good old doctrine, but because, whether we like it or not, the conditions for its success have disappeared. It was a double doctrine, – it entrusted the public weal to private enterprise *unchecked* and *unaided*. Private enterprise is no longer unchecked, it is checked and threatened in many ways. There is no going back on this. The forces which press us may be blind, but they exist and are strong ... [T]he next developments of politico-economic evolution will emerge from new experiments

directed towards determining the appropriate spheres of individual and government action. And to proceed to particulars, I suggest that the state encouragement of new capital undertakings, by employing the best technical advice to lay the foundations of great schemes, and by lending the credit and the guarantee of the Treasury to finance them more boldly than hitherto, *is becoming an inevitable policy.*

(CW 19-I, pp. 228–229, emphasis in original)

While testifying before the government Committee on National Debt and Taxation in early October of 1924, a committee member asked Keynes about his call for £100 million a year of publicly initiated and publicly financed capital investment. He responded as follows.

Owing to the control of profits and rates, and so forth, which is now popular, an investment in a public utility is very unlikely to yield the investor any unusual gains; he will never be allowed to obtain more than a certain rate of interest. On the other hand, he is not secured against losses. The result is that the inducement to the investment of money in large public utility enterprises is very much less than it was, for example, during the period of the railway boom, when our railways were built ... I am, therefore, very doubtful whether, in present conditions, the railway system of England could be built by unaided private enterprise. I believe that considerations of this sort stand in the way at this moment of the development of our ports, of our transport system, and of our power system, and that the policy of leaving these to unaided private enterprise is a thing which is no longer practicable. As to the forms in which the state can help, I think there ought to be a great variety.

(CW 19-I, p. 322)

A statement Keynes made to the Committee on Industry and Trade in July 1925, after the election victory of the Conservatives in late October of 1924 and following Churchill's momentous announcement of the return to gold at par in April 1925, which Keynes vigorously opposed, might serve as a brief summary of his position at this time.[14] It linked his call for public investment to what he saw as the *permanent* erosion of Britain's traditional export markets and placed enormous stress on the structural imbalance in labor markets this created. Large-scale public investment, he argued, would increase the general demand for labor in the country and, simultaneously, create employment for export industry workers whose old jobs could not be saved.

[O]wing to changes in the external world ... probably our export trades will be permanently on a lower scale in relation to population than they were in pre-war days. And I think we should do well to have

> a transference of labour to some extent from the export trades to non-export trades, and balance our reduction of exports by investing less capital abroad and more capital at home ... So that my long-period policy would be the gradual transference of labour from export industries and a large programme of capital expenditures at home, which would absorb the savings which had previously found an outlet abroad ... If we had any of the great schemes that have been proposed for capital development at home, that would certainly stimulate the employment of labour in the coal industry and in the iron and steel industry because they would require the products of those industries ... [I]f there is an intake for labour the business of transfer is not an insuperable difficulty. What I think is so extraordinarily difficult is to absorb labour out of industries when the other industries are not wanting any labour. You must first of all create a condition of demand for labour in other industries.
>
> (CW 19-I, pp. 409–410)

Why did Keynes make this permanent radical left turn in mid-1924? Skidelsky notes that the economic upturn stopped and the economy stabilized in 1923. "As unemployment, despite the trade revival, remained obstinately stuck at 10 per cent of the insured workforce, his mind turned to 'drastic remedies'" (Skidelsky 1992, p. 184). Keynes feared that fiscal policy was unlikely to be used to reduce unemployment. The government's budget had moved into surplus, the war debt was in the process of being paid down, and the new Labour government was more orthodox than the Conservatives on budgetary matters.

> To many [government officials], high spending was as bad as budget deficits. "It is no part of my job as [Labour] Chancellor of the Exchequer" stated Snowden in 1924, "to put before the House of Commons proposals for the expenditure of public money. The function of the Chancellor of the Exchequer, as I understand it, is to resist all demands for expenditure made by his colleagues and, when he can no longer resist, to limit the concession to the barest minimum of acceptance."
>
> (Aldcroft 1986, p. 105)[15]

Both Labour and the Conservatives had pledged to return to gold at par at some point, and the embargo on gold exports was to expire at the end of 1925. Such thinking pointed toward monetary policy- or interest rate-induced deflation. From the middle of 1924 on, the authorities began to push up the exchange rate of the pound to a level that would make free convertibility possible. London rates of interest were raised substantially above those ruling in New York, and funds began to flow in. The belief that an attempt would be made to restore the pound to its old parity in the course of 1925, before inconvertibility would automatically lapse, attracted further funds. By April 1925, the pound had virtually reached its prewar parity with the dollar. Not only were interest rates expected to remain permanently high in defense of the pound, but, as Keynes repeatedly pointed out, the pound at parity would be 10–15 percent overvalued with respect to the US dollar. This would lead to constant trade deficits that had to be met with constantly high interest rates in order to attract foreign capital. Moreover, Keynes consistently argued that British wages and therefore British prices were downwardly rigid, which meant that the Bank of England would be under strong pressure to keep interest rates very high in a deliberate attempt to keep unemployment high enough to break through this rigidity and force wages down – a disastrous and futile policy.[16]

The British historian Sidney Pollard observed that the decision to return to gold at the old parity "called forth a large volume of criticism, among the most intelligent and far-sighted of which was that associated with the name of J.M. Keynes" (Pollard 1983, p. 137). He cited not only Keynes's famous essay "The Economic Consequences of Mr. Churchill," published after the return to gold, but also the *Tract on Monetary Reform*, published in 1923. Pollard made the important point that the decision to return to gold at prewar parity would obviously do substantial damage to both businesses and workers in the real sector of the economy while benefitting finance capital.

> The decision to return had taken appalling risks with British industry. It was a City [London financial center] decision, emphatically not a decision of the industrialists: had their views been given as much weight as those of the City, it is unlikely that the change would ever have been made.
> (Pollard 1983, p. 138)[17]

> In retrospect, it seems impossible to deny that the preparations and the return to gold at too high a rate contributed to the depressed conditions of British industry in 1925–9, at a time when much of the rest of the world enjoyed a prolific boom, just as the removal of the handicap in 1931 was responsible for the sudden spurt of British exports relative to other countries.
> (Pollard 1983, p. 139)

Keynes's economic analysis and policy proposals at this juncture reflected his increasingly radical economic and *political* perspective, and they were perceived as such by those private interests including, of course, the "City" – the largest private banks and the Bank of England, plus the rentier class they represented – and the big industrialists who feared the political as much as the economic consequences of transferring such unprecedented power from economic elites and institutions to the state. They opposed most of Keynes's policy proposals throughout the interwar period.

W.R. Garside explained the main reason why Keynes's proposals for publicly controlled capital accumulation raised such fierce opposition.

> There is no doubt, however, that to the majority of contemporary politicians, civil servants, city financiers and industrialists, a policy of deliberately unbalancing the budget in the hope of expanding employment was a fearful prospect, not least in its potential for encouraging repeated demands for yet further increases in public expenditures … The other barrier to the adoption of a more positive public works policy was the fear of state intervention. The rules of "sound finance" were, as one writer pointed out, a defense not only against economic catastrophe but *also against state socialism*. Indeed, in calling for a more drastic remedy for unemployment via loan-financed public works, Keynes remarked in May 1924 that "the next development of politico-economic evolution will emerge from new experiments directed towards determining the appropriate spheres of individual and of government action." And behind the Treasury's notorious rejection of increased government expenditure for such purposes lay the powerful conviction that it would undermine the democratic structure of local government and *threaten private property rights*. What worried contemporary politicians (not least within the Labour Party) about the development programmes of Lloyd George and Oswald Mosley was their implicit assumption of a powerful executive, their rejection of the inherent efficacy of market forces in favour of some form of "managed capitalism," and a suggested timetable of action which smacked of bureaucratic dictatorship.
>
> (Garside, 1990, pp. 551–552, emphasis added)

## Notes

1 David Lloyd George was Chancellor of the Exchequer from 1908 to 1915 and Prime Minister of the wartime coalition government from 1916 to 1922. His central role at the Versailles Peace Conference in 1919 was mentioned earlier. Lloyd George was an avid supporter of the creation of an early version of the modern welfare state.

2 The unemployment rate for union members was always higher than the rate for all workers because above-average unemployment was concentrated in the highly unionized sectors that traditionally dominated exports.

3 In *The General Theory*, Keynes defined full employment in two different ways. One was the standard definition – the level of employment at which the supply of labor equals the demand for labor. The other was the level of employment at which an increase in AD led only to rising prices and not to

additional employment. The latter definition is most compatible with his estimate here that sustainable full employment is reached at an unemployment rate of 3 percent.
4  Note that these are three of the "rigidities" Keynes referred to in the *Tract*.
5  This cumulative or multiplied effect of an initial increase in public investment is consistent with Keynes's belief that long periods of prosperity create a general rise in what Keynes in *The General Theory* would call businessmen's "animal spirits" – in the willingness of the business class to take risks and undertake investments *independently of short-run economic conditions*. If public investment can create a large enough jolt or acceleration of economic growth that lasted long enough, it could induce a rise in animal spirits that would reinforce and extend the multiplier effect.
6  Aldcroft notes that "the use of government-financed public works for employment purposes already had a reputable lineage going back to at least Elizabethan times," but that "such works were to be employed [only] sporadically during the interwar years" (Aldcroft 1986, p. 23).
7  This reference to public utilities, which have to be regulated by the state because they are natural monopolies, is an incomplete explanation for the absence of a strong incentive to invest. We will deal with the causes of this inadequate incentive for long-term investment below.
8  The Trade Facilities Act to which Keynes refers was designed to provide credit at below-market interest rates to export-oriented firms.
9  In a 1922 article in defense of free trade (against the call for protectionism from Conservative Prime Minister Stanley Baldwin), Keynes expressed a similar worry. Capital is drifting abroad that is needed at home, in part because financial markets are biased in favor of foreign loans. "Now, if we are to interfere at all with the natural course of trade, surely it should be with the object of keeping capital at home, not of driving it abroad. With our shortage of housing and the need of factories and equipment to render efficient our growing supply of labour, we need to keep more capital at home ... There is already, in my opinion, too much encouragement to the export of our capital" (CW 19-I, pp. 148–149). And, he stressed, Britain gets little benefit from this outflow of capital, at least in the short run. Indeed, to the extent that foreign loans are used by her competitors to finance infrastructural or industrial investment, they will eventually worsen Britain's trade balance.
10  A report calling for sharp public spending cuts in the midst of a stagnant economy was generated by a Parliamentary Committee under the chairmanship of Eric Geddes and was referred to as the Geddes Axe.
11  "He tried to explain why a modern industrial society could not stand a policy of *laissez-faire*. He developed an imagery of fluids and sticky masses to explain the contrast between old and new forms of industrial life, and to pinpoint the need for a new type of statesmanship. The building of an economic theory was much more difficult. He came to realise that the economics he had been taught simply assumed away the *Sturm und Drang* of actual economic life" (Skidelsky 1994, pp. 173–174).
12  "The Trustee Acts restricted the type of investments which could be made by trustees of estates or charities to a 'trustee list' which included all British and colonial government bonds, but excluded practically all shares of private

companies" (Skidelsky 1994, p. 183). See Crotty (1983) on Keynes's consistent commitment to capital controls.

13  The main problem here is the effect of the onset of secular stagnation caused by a chronically depressed expected rate of profit on capital accumulation. This point is stressed in *The General Theory*.

14  See "The Economic Consequences of Mr. Churchill" (CW 9). Britain had already suffered the consequences of the run-up to the return to gold, during which interest rates had been pushed up to attract additional gold to add to Britain's meager current holdings.

15  Though the Labour Party supported a revolutionary change from current-day capitalism to Soviet-style planning as their ultimate objective, they also believed that until this revolution was accomplished, the British government should, even under Labour Party leadership, adopt the conservative policies supported by British industry and, especially, finance.

16  In the end, it proved impossible to slash wages: "wages in 1929 stood at 99.5 (1924 = 100)" (Pollard 1983, p. 141). The deflation brought on by the return to gold also increased the burden of Britain's huge WWI debt and thus pressured the government to maintain high taxes even in a sluggish economy.

17  This is one reason why Keynes called for the "euthanasia of the rentier" in the final chapter of *The General Theory*.

# 5 The return to gold in 1925
## Deflation, social justice, and class struggle

The government announced the return to gold at prewar par on April 28, 1925. Keynes believed this policy to be profoundly ill-conceived. His most famous intervention in the debate on this issue was "The Economic Consequences of Mr. Churchill," a pamphlet based on three articles that appeared in the *Evening Standard* newspaper in July 1925.[1] The pamphlet contains a number of arguments of interest.

After stressing the fact that the rising value of sterling did not create, but only aggravated, the long-term unemployment problem – "we were not free from trouble a year ago" – Keynes reiterated his belief that Britain's export industries, which had dominated world trade for most of the nineteenth century, now suffered from permanently high excess capacity. They had to shrink substantially before they could return to full capacity and profitability. Britain could only return to prosperity, he argued, by a large increase in public investment that would create jobs for the workers displaced from the shrinking export industries. His position was heretical in that the ruling elites were determined to weaken labor and drive down costs in these industries by so much that export dominance would be restored.

> It was also probable that certain of our export industries were overstocked both with plant and with labour, and that some transference of capital and men into home industries was desirable and, in the long run, even inevitable.[2] Thus we already had an awkward problem; and one of the arguments against raising the international value of sterling was the fact that it greatly aggravated, instead of mitigating, an existing disparity between internal and external values, and that, by committing us to a period of deflation, it necessarily postponed active measures of capital expansion at home, such as might facilitate the transference of labour into the home trades.
> (CW 9, pp. 210–211)

Keynes thought that the main problem with a $4.86 pound was that it created a mismatch with "relative prices here and abroad" that would take a general real-wage reduction of some 10–12 percent to eliminate (CW 9, p. 207). The only way available under the gold standard and laissez-faire to lower costs by 10 percent in the export industries was to initiate a lengthy, costly, unjust, and potentially disastrous dynamic disequilibrium process whose end result was supposed to be lower real wages.

Keynes's main objective in this pamphlet was to critically evaluate these disequilibrium dynamics so as to make them transparent and, therefore, abhorrent to the public. His analysis of the processes by which the effects of an overvalued pound became "diffused" throughout the economy achieves a level of theoretical sophistication not yet evident in the *Tract*. He focused on the disastrous disequilibrium processes associated with wage and price deflation and criticized classical theory for its unrealistic treatment of the costs of adjustment.

Keynes made four main points about the serious problems that infected deflationary disequilibrium dynamics in the current British economy. First, the mobility of labor across industries and regions had diminished substantially since the nineteenth century. Among the causes of this change were: the rise of strong unions (which interfere with the "freedom" of unemployed workers to bid down wages); the existence of the "dole"; and the inability of workers to secure adequate housing outside the area in which they currently live. As a result of these changes, it would take much higher unemployment over a much longer period to force a cut in money wages of the required magnitude.

Second, these institutional changes would have significantly raised the adjustment costs involved in the return to gold at par, even if the economy was growing rapidly. But, as we have seen, Keynes believed that Britain had entered a period in which the normal rate of growth was sluggish. Thus, rapid growth in the rest of the economy was not available to absorb the long-term unemployed in the export industries as well as new entrants to the labor market. It is the combination of institutional rigidities plus a sluggish growth trajectory that made a return to gold at par so dangerous.

His testimony before the Committee on Industry and Trade in Parliament in July 1925 included the following statement:

> [D]*uring a considerable part of the nineteenth century we were increasing at a rapid rate: everything was on a general crescendo, just as in the United States now*; everything was increasing at the rate of three per cent per annum or something of that kind. That meant that when a given industry was too large and another too small you did not force a man out of the industry that had too much labour into the other, but you just stopped taking new men in for a certain period of time, and with the rapid general progress going on, the slack would be taken up not so much by driving men out of the industry as by simply stopping the intake for a bit. Then it was very much easier to bring your industry into equilibrium by just not taking on new hands – *which you can do*

*when the whole economic machine is stepping forward at a great pace* – than by actually discharging men ... [S]acking men ... is much more difficult both practically and humanly than stopping new men coming into the industry. So that the old [classical] assumption about the mobility of labour and about the way in which a fall of wages in one trade would be reflected in others, in my opinion, only holds good in the very long run.

(CW 19-I, pp. 396–397, emphasis added)

Third, the necessary process of deflation would distribute reductions in nominal and real incomes in a manner that violated norms of social justice that required that the distribution of income among the classes reflect their relative contributions to economic output. Therefore, if a deflationary policy is adopted by the state, the state must, in the name of social justice, simultaneously institute an equitable incomes policy. This leads to the last major point.

Fourth, the disequilibrium processes inherent in defense of the pound at par will involve economic and social costs so high they might trigger economic and political class warfare.

We begin with the first problem. The gold standard has no automatic and no equitable process to achieve a new equilibrium at par, Keynes said. This process exists only in "the imaginary academic world, peopled by City editors, members of the Cunliffe and Currency Committees ... where the necessary adjustments follow 'automatically' from a 'sound' policy by the Bank of England" (CW 9, pp. 214–215). The actual adjustment process is initiated by an increase in the interest rate that causes a rise in the value of sterling. This triggers a "depression in the export industries." This depression and the requisite tightening of credit to attract and keep foreign money in Britain are supposed to "*diffuse* themselves evenly and fairly rapidly throughout the whole community. But the professors who defend this theory do not tell us in plain language how the diffusion takes place" (CW 9, p. 214, emphasis in original). Keynes suggested an explanation in the following plain language:

To begin with, there will be a great depression in the export industries. This, in itself, will be helpful, since it will produce an atmosphere favourable to the reduction of wages. The cost of living will fall somewhat. This will be helpful too, because it will give you a good argument in favour of reducing wages. Nevertheless, the cost of living will not fall sufficiently and, consequently, the export industries will not be able to reduce their prices sufficiently, until wages have fallen in the sheltered industries [that produce non-tradable goods]. Now, wages will not fall in the sheltered industries, merely because there is unemployment in the unsheltered industries. Therefore, you will have to see to it that there is unemployment in the unsheltered industries

> also. The way to do this is by credit restriction. By means of the restriction of credit by the Bank of England, you can deliberately intensify unemployment to any required degree, until wages *do* fall ... We ought to warn you ... that it will not be safe politically to admit that you are intensifying unemployment deliberately in order to reduce wages. Thus you will have to ascribe what is happening to every conceivable cause except the true one.
>
> (CW 9, pp. 214–215, emphasis in original)

The "great question now before the country is by what process of adjustment the sheltered prices can be brought down to the level of the unsheltered prices" (CW 19-I, p. 385). The rise in the pound itself will create unemployment in the export industries and in those industries that must compete with imports whose prices are lowered by the appreciation of sterling. But these industries, on average, buy most of their inputs from industries that are sheltered from the direct effects of trade and therefore are under no pressure to lower their prices, and workers in unsheltered industries buy a high percentage of their consumption goods from sheltered industries as well. Trade-sector costs will not be reduced by nearly as much as their prices have been cut. Therefore, it becomes essential that the authorities use tight money to deliberately create unemployment and excess capacity in the sheltered industries as well in order to force down their prices, which will then be transmitted as lower costs to the unsheltered industries.[3]

The key assumption of supporters of the return to gold at par is that "labour is free to move from industry to industry and place to place, and that an unemployed man can get himself occupation by offering to work for a lower wage than the standard wage in one of the prosperous industries" (CW 19-I, p. 385). Keynes used the problems in the declining coal industry to show how out of touch with current reality this assumption is.

> That theory has no relation to the facts at all, however. It is impossible of course for a collier to offer himself as a baker below the standard wages of bakers, that cannot in fact happen, partly because of the power of the trade unions in preventing the cutting of rates by competition of unemployed labour from other industries, partly because the dole has reduced the extreme pressure to find employment elsewhere, and partly because labour for two reasons is very much less mobile between places and industries. The reason it is less mobile between places is due partly to the condition of housing. A man has a house in the place where he has been employed, and it is a rash and dangerous thing for him to give up that house to go and seek employment in another part of the country where very likely he will not be able to get a house.
>
> (CW 19-I, p. 396)

Keynes said that actual disequilibrium adjustment processes in current-day Britain are an inefficient and destructive kind of "war" in which the economically and politically strong can protect themselves while the weak are beaten down and the economy flounders. His argument here anticipated key insights into these disequilibrium dynamics of wage and price deflation in *The General Theory*. The adjustment process creates:

> a struggle with each separate group in turn, with no prospect that the final result will be fair, and no guarantee that the stronger groups will not gain at the expense of the weaker. The working classes cannot be expected to understand better than Cabinet Ministers what is happening. Those who are attacked first are faced with a depression in their standard of life, because the cost of living will not fall until all the others have been successfully attacked too; and, therefore, they are justified in defending themselves. Nor can the classes, which are first subjected to a reduction of money wages, be guaranteed that this will be compensated later by a corresponding fall in the cost of living, and will not accrue to the benefit of some other class. *Therefore, they are bound to resist so long as they can; and it must be war, until those who are economically weakest are beaten to the ground.*
> (CW 9, p. 211, emphasis added)[4]

Keynes positions on these issues led him to side with the coal miners in their desperate effort to protect themselves from vicious attacks by mine owners and the government in the general strike in 1926. This war on the miners to deliberately drive down their wages, Keynes believed, had to be opposed not only because it was economically inefficient, but also because it violated a core principal of social justice.

> On grounds of social justice no case can be made out for reducing the wages of the miners. They are the victims of the economic juggernaut. They represent in the flesh the "fundamental adjustments" engineered by the Treasury and the Bank of England to satisfy the impatience of the City fathers to bridge the "moderate gap" between $4.40 and $4.86.
> (CW 9, p. 223)

If it is unjust to force the miners to submit to mass unemployment in order to force their wages down in defense of the return to gold at par, then the whole policy is unjust because most workers will eventually be placed in a similar position. So long as the gold standard requires domestic deflation to sustain itself, it is a policy of class warfare waged by the "City" and the rentier class against the working class. Keynes clearly sees the process of out-of-equilibrium adjustments as one of class warfare. "The gold standard," Keynes argued, "with its dependence on pure chance, its faith in 'automatic adjustments', and its general regardlessness of social detail, is an essential emblem and idol of those who sit in the top tier of the machine" (CW 9, p. 224). Even the disparity of its effects within the working class is repugnant. "For the method of economic pressure, since it bears most hardly on the weaker industries where wages are already relatively low, tends to increase the existing disparities between the wages of different industrial groups" (CW 9, pp. 224–225). What, then, should be done? The only sensible choice would be to go off gold once again: "it is impossible to recommend any truly satisfactory course except its reversal" (CW 9, p. 224). Since this was obviously not in the cards, the next best solution would be the implementation of an incomes policy that would distribute the economic costs of the return to gold more equitably. The government should explain to the labor movement that a reduction of all money wages of some 10 percent is needed (under then-current international prices and exchange rates) and to ask for labor's cooperation in an attempt to attain this reduction in a fair and equitable manner – one that would not substantially change relative incomes. "If there were any machinery by which you could reduce all wages simultaneously the objections to the policy that I have been outlining would not be very serious" (19-I, p. 393). Therefore, if a deflation was to be deliberately caused by state policy – and that would be a mistake – the state was obligated to create new administrative "machinery" to see that it was done efficiently and equitably.

Keynes is here insisting that any policy involving significant deflation must, in the name of social justice, be accompanied by the implementation of what he elsewhere called a "Great National Treaty." Keynes suggested that Prime Minister Baldwin make the following proposal to labor:

> Can we not agree, therefore, to have a uniform initial reduction of money wages throughout the whole range of employment, including government and municipal workers, of (say) 5 per cent, which reduction shall not hold good unless after an interval it has been compensated by a fall in the cost of living?
>
> (CW 9, p. 228)

Labor would respond, Keynes suggested, by asking Baldwin "what he intended to do about money payments other than wages – rents, profits, and interest" (CW 9, p. 228). Keynes noted that rentier incomes are the hardest issue to deal with because "it is of the essence of any policy to lower prices that it benefits the receivers of interest at the expense of the rest of the community; this consequence of deflation is deeply embedded in our system of money contracts" (CW 9, p. 229). The only equitable solution is to use the tax system to ensure that non-wage-money income fell in proportion to wages.

> On the whole, I do not see how labour's objective can be met except by the rough-and-ready expediency of levying an additional income

tax of 1s in the £ [or 10 percent] on all income other than from employments, which should continue until real wages had recovered to their previous level.

(CW 9, p. 229).

Keynes understood that powerful class interests would never allow such an incomes policy to be implemented. He believed that the economic costs of the return to gold at par would be heavy and would be borne mostly by workers. He also believed that workers might not tolerate these costs for long. In October 1925, he wrote:

> I sympathize with the working classes in resisting a general reduction in real wages. I am sure that no material reduction is possible without engaging in a social struggle of which no one could foretell the outcome ... Indeed another five years of this policy might bring us to the edge of revolution, if revolution is even possible in this country.
> (CW 19-I, pp. 444–445)

## Notes

1 Many of the arguments in this pamphlet are presented in even greater detail in Keynes's testimony before the Committee on Industry and Trade on July 9, 1925 (see CW 19-I, pp. 383–416).
2 The phrase "over-stocked" with plant suggests one reason why the profit rate on capital and thus the incentive to invest in large-scale projects in these industries was so low in the post-WWI era due to excess capacity.
3 Here, Keynes adds that if the politicians told the truth about this process to the electorate, they would not be able to successfully implement it. "The question is how far public opinion will allow such a policy to go. It would be politically impossible for the Government to admit that it was deliberately intensifying unemployment" (CW 9, p. 225).
4 The idea that the needed adjustments can only be achieved through the deliberate application of force is reflected in the following comment: "We are depending for the reduction of wages on the pressure of unemployment and of strikes and lockouts; and in order to make sure of the result we are deliberately intensifying the unemployment" (CW 9, p. 220).

## 6 Three important "essays in persuasion" on the proper economic role of the state: 1925–1926

Continued high unemployment and the high-interest rate policy associated with the return to gold at par forced Keynes to elaborate on his increasingly radical vision of political economy in a series of articles published in 1925 and 1926. Three of these are especially important: "The End of Laissez-Faire," "Am I A Liberal?" and "Liberalism and Labour."[1] While he continued to refine the details of the policies and programs needed to implement his vision over the next two decades, the broad outlines of his thinking about the new order represented in these essays never underwent substantial revision. The ideas presented here "served him well right down to 1946" (Moggridge 1992, p. 454). Indeed, when the onset of the world slump in the 1930s added an enormous sense of urgency to Keynes's struggle for a new order, he reissued these articles in 1931 in *Essays in Persuasion*. The essays remain essential for understanding not only the true nature of Keynes's attempted revolution in economic and policy analysis, but also to appreciate the huge difference between the real Keynesian revolution and what Joan Robinson called "Bastard Keynesianism" (and that I refer to as Mainstream Keynesianism), the dominant macro theory and policy paradigm of the post-WWII era.

"The End of Laissez-Faire" was first delivered as the prestigious Sidney Ball Lecture at Oxford in November 1924, not long after the debate over "Does Unemployment Need a Drastic Remedy?" The general topic is the total inadequacy of the "individualism and *laissez-faire*" associated with classical theory as a "disposition towards public policy" in the postwar era (CW 9, p. 272). In this context, laissez-faire stands for severe limitations on government domestic economic intervention, free trade (which he supported until the end of the 1920s), and free capital flows in the international sector (which he always opposed) in the context of the gold standard. While acknowledging, as he always did, the efficacy of laissez-faire as a crude guide to both domestic and international economic policy formation in the unique circumstances of the nineteenth century, Keynes unleashed a diatribe against the use of the associated theory of government policy under the conditions of modern capitalism.

The essay is an all-out attack on classical theory – the theoretical foundation of laissez-faire policy – built on a scathing criticism of its methodology. In sharp contrast with the dominant positivist methodology used in both classical theory and today's economics profession, Keynes insisted that *the realism and completeness of the assumption set that is the foundation of a theory is a crucial determinant of the empirical validity of its derived hypotheses*. And he showed that classical theory was built on an assumption set that was in sharp conflict with the "facts" that described the interwar British economy. On the opening page of *The General Theory*, before he did anything else, Keynes made this core methodological point. It is intended to frame his project.

> I shall argue that the postulates of the classical theory are applicable to a special case only and not to the general case, the situation which it assumes being a limiting point of the possible positions of equilibrium. Moreover, the characteristics of the special case assumed by the classical theory happen not to be the those of the economic society in which we actually live, with the result that its teaching is misleading and disastrous if we attempt to apply it to the facts of experience.
> (CW 7, p. 3)

Though the conventional wisdom has it that Keynes did not think much about competition and generally accepted the assumption set of perfect competition, the truth is quite the opposite. One important part of Keynes's attack here focused on the theory of "perfect competition." He argued that this theory fails to consider the destructive dimensions of intense competition, especially under conditions of chronic excess capacity such as existed in the staple export industries in this era. This was important to him because, as is explained in Chapter 7, destructive dimensions of competition in these crucial industries prevented them from downsizing in response to chronic excess capacity. This added to the destructive disequilibrium dynamics caused by the "rigidities" mentioned above and thus helped keep unemployment high.

Keynes attributed the benign view of intense competition to the emergence of a complex set of developments in politics, philosophy, and economics in the eighteenth and nineteenth centuries. Among these were the undeniable failures of state economic interventions and the economic success of private initiative. He noted, "Almost everything which the State did in the eighteenth century in excess of its minimum functions was, or seemed, injurious or unsuccessful." Thus, it appeared that "material progress between 1750 and 1850 came from individual initiative, and owed almost nothing to the directive influence of organised society as a whole"

(CW 9, p. 275).[2] The increasing influence of Darwin's theory of evolution reinforced belief in laissez-faire. "The economists were teaching that wealth, commerce, and machinery were the children of competition – that free competition built London. But the Darwinians could go one better than that – free competition had built man" (CW 9, p. 276). These historical developments helped explain why "we feel such a strong bias in favour of *laissez-faire*," and why there had been such strong resistance to Keynes's recent policy proposals in support of "state action to regulate the value of money, [and] the course of investment" (CW 9, p. 277).

A key reason for this unfortunate situation lay in the misuse or misunderstanding of the methodology appropriate to economics. It is reasonable, Keynes said, for economists to begin their analysis with an assumption set that does not fully reflect in a realistic way all aspects of the economy they wish to study or incorporate all of the key "facts" about it. Rather, they choose the one that "is the simplest, not [the one that] is the nearest to the facts" (CW 9, p. 282). In particular, they begin with a model of the economy constructed to show that ruthless or perfect or Darwinian competition in pursuit of "unlimited private money-making as an incentive to maximum effort" (CW 9, p. 283) leads to maximum economic efficiency. The problem is that they neglect the crucial second step in the legitimate use of this method of abstraction in which assumptions are added or substituted that are more realistic reflections of the most important institutions and facts in the economy.[3]

Keynes began his analysis with the theory of competition because it is a centerpiece of conservative thinking and, he argued, because the theory of perfect competition that is the sine qua non of laissez-faire theory and policy is fatally flawed. Its flaws destroy the claims to efficiency of disequilibrium dynamics in free-market economies, a point often referred to here in part because it is rarely referred to in more traditional accounts of Keynes's economics. The concept of competition used in classical theory assumes that:

> there must be no mercy or protection for those who embark their capital or their labour in the wrong direction. It is a method of bringing the most successful profit-makers to the top by a ruthless struggle for survival, which selects the most efficient by the bankruptcy of the less efficient. *It does not count the cost of the struggle*, but only looks to the benefits of the final result, which are assumed to be permanent.
> (CW 9, pp. 282–283, emphasis added)

Orthodox theory requires the assumption of an ongoing process of "ruthless" competition, but it incorporates only one of the two key dimensions of the competitive struggle – the benevolent state of its claimed final equilibrium position. It ignores competition as a perpetual process that has destructive as well as constructive dimensions. "It does not count the cost of the struggle," Keynes said. Keynes here implicitly allied himself with Karl Marx, who believed that competition had both positive and negative dimensions, the latter of which create the economic crises and depressions observed in the historical record. He also prefigured Joseph Schumpeter in this regard. Schumpeter emphasized capitalism's endogenously generated "gales of creative destruction."[4]

Moreover, Keynes continued, the wonderful orthodox conclusions about laissez-faire are based on "an incomplete hypothesis introduced, presumably for the sake of simplicity ... [that] depends on a variety of unreal assumptions" (CW 9, p. 284). He began by arguing that orthodoxy requires two general assumptions: that "the processes of production and consumption are in no way organic" (CW 9, p. 284); and that "there exists a sufficient foreknowledge of conditions and requirements, and that there are adequate opportunities of obtaining this foreknowledge" (CW 9, p. 284). The first assumption refers to the organic–atomistic debate stressed in the *Treatise on Probability* and continued by interpreters of Keynes even today. The second refers to the axiomatic elimination of fundamental or "Keynesian" uncertainty from orthodox theory. Of course, by the time he published *The General Theory*, fundamental uncertainty had become a cornerstone of his macro theory.

Keynes then listed six important conditions that had to be omitted from the orthodox assumption set in order to arrive at its preordained economic and policy conclusions. These crucial omissions, he argued, rendered the derived hypotheses from classical theory useless. Good economists, he said, reserve for a later stage of their argument the inclusion of the following important assumptions needed to generate a usable theory – but they must eventually include them or their theory cannot provide useful guidance to policy-makers:

> (1) when the efficient units of production are large relative to the units of consumption, (2) when overhead costs or joint costs are present, (3) when internal economies tend to the aggregation of production, (4) when the time required for adjustments is long, (5) when ignorance prevails over knowledge, and (6) when monopolies and combination interfere with equality in bargaining – they reserve, that is to say, for a later stage of their analysis the actual facts.
> (CW 9, pp. 284–285)

The first, third, and sixth conditions deal with the effects of large economies of scale in production relative to the size of the market as a precondition for oligopoly and monopoly and to the damage these cause to classical theory. The fourth and fifth conditions point to problems caused by the existence of fundamental – later Keynesian – uncertainty. If the assumption set is expanded to include these important "actual facts," orthodox laissez-faire conclusions cannot possibly be sustained.[5]

But this is not the whole problem. We must now add to the analysis the costs of the destructive dimensions of the disequilibrium dynamics of the competitive process. As we have seen, Keynes had already devoted considerable effort to an attack on the disequilibrium dynamics used by classical economists to defend the return to gold at par. In this essay, he added a powerful new weapon to this war on orthodoxy. To make his point, he referred to a Darwinian story about competition among giraffes for access to leaves at the top of trees. We must "bring into the calculation the cost and character of the competitive struggle itself, and the tendency for wealth to be distributed where it is not appreciated" (CW 9, p. 285). We cannot leave out of our cost–benefit calculations, he insisted, the "sufferings" of those defeated in the struggle "who are starved out," or the loss of the productive resources destroyed in the process (for example, in the staple export industries), or the maldistribution of income and wealth that results (the "overfeeding" of the winners), or the "evil look of anxiety" on the faces of the losers, or the "struggling greediness" of the winners (CW 9, p. 285).

Keynes argued that if we take all of these important dimensions of real-world competition – including uncertainty about the future, economies of scale (which were growing rapidly), the increasing market power of monopolies and oligopolies, the large costs or losses involved in disequilibrium processes (including the plight of the poor and unemployed), and the maldistribution of income and wealth – it is impossible to make a convincing argument in support of laissez-faire in the current era.

Keynes believed that a key reason as to why classical theory had become the conventional wisdom among elites in spite of its obvious flaws was that it reflected the perceived material interests of ruling elites. Individualism and laissez-faire "could not ... have secured their lasting hold over the conduct of public affairs, if it had not been for their conformity with the needs and wishes of the business world of the day" (CW 9, p. 286).

Keynes summarized his general perspective on laissez-faire as follows:

> It is not true that individuals possess a prescriptive "natural liberty" in their economic activities. There is *no* "compact" conferring perpetual rights on those who Have or those who Acquire. The world is *not* so governed from above that private and social interest always coincide. It is *not* so managed here below that in practice they coincide. It is *not* a correct deduction from the principles of economics that enlightened self-interest always operates in the public interest. Nor is it true that self-interest generally *is* enlightened; more often individuals acting separately to promote their own ends are too ignorant or too weak to attain even these. Experience does *not* show that individuals, when

they make up a social unit, are always less clear-sighted than when they act separately.

(CW 9, pp. 287–288, emphasis in original)

Therefore, the central task of the moment is:

> to determine what the State ought to take upon itself to direct by the public wisdom, and what it ought to leave to individual exertion ... Perhaps the chief task of economists at this hour is to distinguish afresh the *Agenda* of government from the *Non-Agenda*; and the companion task of politics is to devise forms of government within a democracy which shall be capable of accomplishing the *Agenda*.
>
> (CW 9, p. 288)

Keynes first addressed the latter question: what are the appropriate institutional forms in a democracy for the creation and implementation of an unprecedented degree of government economic influence and control in a capitalist system? He believed that the institutions that will design and implement the details of economic planning must be free of political interference in their day-to-day operations. These should be the exclusive province of experts and technicians. But the general objectives and relative priorities of planning are to be under democratic political control, the sole province of the elected authorities. "Semi-autonomy within the state" – as in Britain's "public corporations" – is the key concept here.

> I believe that in many cases the ideal size for the unit of control and organisation lies somewhere between the individual and the modern State. I suggest, therefore, that progress lies in the growth and the recognition of *semi-autonomous bodies within the State* – bodies whose criterion of action within their own field is solely the public good as they understand it, and *from whose deliberations motives of private advantage are excluded*, though some place it may still be necessary to leave, until the ambit of men's altruism grows wider, to the separate advantage of particular groups, classes, of faculties – bodies which in the ordinary course of affairs are mainly autonomous within their prescribed limitations, but are *subject in the last resort to Parliament*.
>
> I propose a return, it might be said, towards medieval conceptions of separate autonomies. But, in England at any rate, *[public] corporations* are a mode of government which has never ceased to be important and is sympathetic to our institutions. It is easy to give examples, from what already exists, of separate autonomies which have attained or are approaching the mode I designate – the universities, the Bank of England, the Port of London Authority, even perhaps the railway companies. In Germany there are doubtless analogous instances.
>
> (CW 9, pp. 288–289, emphasis added)[6]

Keynes then argued that an increasing percentage of the country's largest and most important private economic institutions were evolving toward a status that is, or could easily be made to be, equivalent for planning purposes to that of a public corporation. Such companies are very large, are in important industries, often act in coordination with other large firms to influence if not control their markets, and operate independently of their stockholders – for example, "a big railway or big public utility, but also a big bank or insurance company" (CW 9, p. 289). A "public corporation" was a corporation under the ultimate control of Parliament but free to operate as its management believed appropriate in its normal day-to-day operations. Public corporations had grown to be quite important by the mid-1920s. Keynes believed that *"the public concern might become the typical unit of industrial organization" in Britain*, an eventuality about which he was quite positive (Skidelsky 1992, p. 267, emphasis added). The public corporation became a cornerstone of the new political economy he envisioned for Britain.

Keynes believed that "a new partnership had to be established between the government and the private sector to match the growing corporatism of industry" (Skidelsky 1992, p. 231). Keynes would have more to say in support of corporatism soon, but here he called attention to:

> the trend of joint stock institutions, when they have reached a certain age and size, to approximate to the status of public corporations rather than individualistic private enterprises. One of the most interesting and unnoticed developments of recent decades has been the tendency of big enterprise to socialize itself. A point arrives in the growth of a big institution – particularly a big railway or big public utility, but also a big bank or a big insurance company – at which ... the shareholders, are almost entirely disassociated from the management, with the result that the direct personal interest of the latter in the making of profit becomes quite secondary [and] the direct interest of the management often consists in avoiding criticism from the public and from the customers of the concern. This is particularly the case if their great size or semi-monopolistic position renders them conspicuous in the public eye and vulnerable to public attack.
>
> (CW 9, p. 290)

Given the dominance of giant firms operating cooperatively to avoid destabilizing competition, a vast new wave of industry nationalization was not a precondition for effective national economic planning, Keynes argued. His approach to the issue of nationalization was always pragmatic and case by case. He believed there was still a good case for nationalizing "many big undertakings, particularly public utilities enterprises and other businesses requiring a large fixed capital" (CW 9, p. 290). But he was opposed to an ideologically driven commitment to the creation of a detailed central plan based on a general nationalization of the entire economy, one that gave central planners quantitative control over all microeconomic aspects of accumulation, production, and distribution as envisioned in what Keynes called the "doctrinaire State Socialism" of the Labour Party.

Once the more macro-oriented decisions – such as the determination of national income, the levels of investment and saving, the proportion of savings invested at home versus abroad, and the allocation of investment across broad industrial categories – were under government control, there would be no reason to nationalize most firms. Public corporations and private firms in consultation with and under the ultimate control of government planners could then make the more detailed micro-oriented decisions.[7] *Note how the opening sentence suggests Keynes is a socialist speaking to other socialists.*

> The battle of Socialism against unlimited private profit is [already] being won in detail hour by hour ... We must take full advantage of the natural tendencies of the day, and we must probably prefer semi-autonomous corporations to organs of the central government for which ministers of State are directly responsible. I criticize doctrinaire State Socialism, not because it seeks to engage men's altruistic impulses in the service of society, or because it departs from *laissez-faire*, or because it takes away from man's natural liberty to make a million, or because it has the courage for bold experiments. All these things I applaud. I criticize it because it misses the significance of what is actually happening.
>
> (CW 9, p. 290)

Keynes would soon (1927) present data to support the assertion that the sum total of the capital controlled by socialized, semi-socialized, state-regulated, not-for-profit, and cooperative enterprises was on the order of *"two-thirds of the total capital of large-scale enterprises in this country"* (CW 27, p. 352, emphasis added). Thus, with two-thirds of large-scale capital already under public, semi-public, or not-for-profit control, and with important segments of private industry organized as oligopolies that could be induced or forced to cooperate with state economic planners, *effective state regulation of the main contours of economic life was already realistically within reach.*

Keynes's main example of important economic problems that require a collective solution related to saving and investment. He argued that the broad outlines of the saving and investment decisions of the community would have to come under central control, as would the amount of savings allowed to flow abroad.

> I believe that some coordinated act of intelligent judgement is required as to the scale on which it is desirable that the community as a whole should save, the scale on which these savings should go abroad in the form of foreign investments, and whether the present organisation of the investment market distributes savings along the most nationally productive lines.
>
> (CW 9, p. 292)

These were extraordinarily powerful economic functions to propose to allocate to the British state in the 1920s. The state was to choose: the percentage of national income to be saved; the balance between foreign and domestic financial investment (a cause he was obsessed with, one that necessitated the use of capital controls); the allocation of domestic investment across competing uses broadly defined; and, by implication, the level of national income itself. And, as we have seen, Keynes believed that the government should itself organize and finance a long-term program of capital accumulation whose main goal would be to sustain full employment.

This really was heresy. Keynes understood that, however thoughtful and academic his tone, he was calling for a revolution in the organization of British economic life, in the power relations between the central government and the private sector, and in the relation between the state and the capitalist class. He understood as well that his proposals would be vehemently opposed by the most powerful elements of British society – especially by the City and the rentiers it represented – as radically irresponsible and the first step towards Bolshevism.

It has often been observed that Keynes's overarching policy objective in the interwar years was to "save" the capitalist economic system in an era of anti-capitalist revolution. Logically, one cannot agree or disagree with this claim until a definition of capitalism is provided. However, as noted in the Introduction, by the definition of capitalism commonly used in economic theory this claim is incorrect. What Keynes wanted to preserve was an economic system that would sustain Britain's existing social, cultural, and political way of life. Looking over his writings on economic and social questions, it is clear that Keynes was enthusiastic about changes in the structure and organization of the capitalism of his day that were so radical they would shock liberals and social democrats in the West if proposed today. In 1926, Keynes wrote:

> I am sure that I am less conservative than the average Labour voter; I fancy that I have played in my mind with the possibilities of greater social changes than come within the present philosophies of [socialists] Mr. Sidney Webb, Mr. Thomas, or Mr. Wheatley. The republic of my imagination lies to the extreme left of celestial space.
>
> (CW 9, p. 309)

But he remained unalterably opposed to any change that would create impediments to the existence of democracy and of the way of life of the British intellectual and cultural, though not the economic, elite. In "The End of Laissez-Faire," Keynes clarified his position on this central issue. Note that he used an elastic definition of capitalism here – any economic system that depended heavily on material incentives is, apparently, capitalistic enough for Keynes. Skidelsky said that Keynes "defines capitalism as a spirit, not as a social system" (Skidelsky 1992, p. 236). In interpreting the following quotation from Keynes, keep in mind that communism and fascism were on the march.

> These reflections have been directed towards possible improvements in the technique of modern capitalism by the agency of collective action. There is nothing in them which is seriously incompatible with what seems to me to be *the essential characteristic of capitalism, namely the dependence upon an intense appeal to the money-making and money-loving* instincts of individuals as the main motive force of the economic machine ... [T]he fiercest contests and the most deeply felt divisions of opinion [on the proper economic role of the state] are likely to be waged ... not round technical questions, where the arguments on either side are mainly economic, but round those which, for want of better words, may be called psychological or, perhaps, moral ... Many people, who are really objecting to capitalism as a way of life, argue as though they were objecting to it on the grounds of its inefficiency in obtaining its own objectives. Contrariwise, devotees of capitalism are often unduly conservative, and reject reforms in its technique ... which might really strengthen and preserve it, for fear that they may prove to be first steps away from capitalism itself ... Nevertheless, a time may be coming when we shall get clearer than at present as to when we are talking about capitalism as an efficient or inefficient technique, and when we are talking about it as desirable or objectionable in and of itself. For my part I think that capitalism [defined here as any economy that relies heavily on material incentives], wisely managed, can probably be made more efficient for attaining economic ends than any alternative system yet in sight, but that in itself it is in many ways extremely objectionable. *Our problem is to work out a social organisation which shall be as efficient as possible without offending our notions of a satisfactory way of life.*
>
> (CW 9, p. 293, emphasis added)

Ironically, one of capitalism's most socially and morally objectionable characteristics to Keynes is also its defining economic characteristic – dependence on the love of money as its main motive force.

In "Liberalism and Labour" (1926), Keynes turned again to this question of the distinction between capitalism as an economic system and capitalism as a way of life.

> The political problem of mankind is to combine three things: economic efficiency, social justice, and individual liberty. The first needs criticism, precaution, and technical knowledge; the second, an unselfish and enthusiastic spirit, which loves the ordinary man; the third, tolerance, breadth, appreciation of the excellencies of variety and independence, which prefers, above all else, unhindered opportunity to the exceptional and to the aspiring.
>
> (CW 9, p. 311)

The source of efficiency, of technical expertise and constructive criticism, would be provided by Keynes, his close associates in the Liberal Party, the non-communist wing of the Labour Party ("educated, humane, socialistic reformers"), and the left wing of the Tories ("educated, humane, Conservative free traders" (CW 9, p. 300). The Labour Party would provide the thirst for social justice and the love of the ordinary man. Though it is not clear to me that Keynes himself ever was close friends with an "ordinary man," he did support what he considered to be the responsible segment of the union movement and had many influential acolytes in the Labour Party (Durbin 1985).

The third point underlines Keynes's emphasis on the non-technical, non-economic aspects of the great problems of the age. It embodies his insistence that he would not support any economic transformation that threatened Britain's cherished "way of life." "Appreciation of the excellencies of variety and independence" and "Above all else, unhindered opportunity to the exceptional and to the aspiring" were non-negotiable for Keynes. The "exceptional" and the "aspiring," it is reasonable to presume, included Keynes and his friends and associates in the worlds of education, culture, and politics.

"Am I A Liberal?" published in August 1925 after the return to the gold standard, is devoted primarily to an analysis of the strengths and weaknesses of the three major parties as potential political vehicles for the implementation of his proposed revolution in the economic role of the state. All three are found wanting, though for different reasons. He concluded that an alliance between the Labour and Liberal parties was most promising, a hoary proposition in Liberal Party thinking. The Labour Party would provide the "heart" of the alliance as well as the bulk of its electoral strength. The Liberal Party would contribute what Keynes believed it to be so rich in – intelligence, experience, and coolness of temperament; it was the party best able, in his view, to provide the requisite analytical skills and the emotional detachment needed to resist what he saw as Labour's propensity to turn to dangerous electoral appeals to workers' emotions and to foment class conflict.

Most important for our purposes, the essay underscored Keynes's core belief that the West had entered a completely new historical era in which the institutions and policies currently used to regulate economic life were totally inappropriate. He associated himself with the American institutionalist economist John R. Commons's view that Europe and America were currently in transition to a new historical epoch in which the main task was to create a new "regime which deliberately aims at controlling and directing economic forces." Commons "distinguishes three epochs," Keynes told us, "three economic orders, upon the third of which we are entering."

> The first is the era of scarcity ... In such a period "there is the minimum of individual liberty and the maximum of communistic, feudalistic or governmental control through physical coercion." This was ... the normal economic state of the world up to (say) the fifteenth or sixteenth century. Next comes the era of abundance. "In a period of abundance there is the maximum of individual liberty, the minimum of coercive control through government, and individual bargaining takes the place of rationing." ... [I]n the nineteenth century this epoch culminated gloriously in the victories of *laissez-faire* and historic Liberalism. It is not surprising or discreditable that the veterans of the party cast backward glances on that easier age. But we are now entering on a third era, which Professor Commons calls the period of stabilisation, and truly characterises as *"the actual alternative to Marx's communism."* In this period, he said, "there is a diminution of individual liberty, enforced in part by governmental sanctions, but mainly by economic sanctions through concerted actions, whether secret, semi-open, open, or arbitrational, of associations, corporations, unions, and other collective movements ..." The abuses of this epoch in the realms of government are Fascism on the one side and Bolshevism on the other. [State] Socialism offers no middle course ... The transition from economic anarchy to a *regime which deliberately aims at controlling and directing economic forces* in the interests of social justice and social stability, will present enormous difficulties both technical and political. I suggest, nevertheless, that the true destiny of the New Liberalism is to seek their solution.
> (CW 9, pp. 304–305, emphasis added)

The central message in these three essays is unmistakable. Laissez-faire as a defensible economic theory and as a guide to policy is dead. Continued support for its domestic and international policies will reproduce economic stagnation and foster social and political unrest, and perhaps even revolution in Britain. The new epoch requires a qualitative increase in the power of the state to "control and direct economic forces," a "middle-way" revolution in economic and political organization that avoids the stupidity of laissez-faire as well as the political dangers of fascism and communism. "Capitalism ... is a technique which, from having been experimental is now perhaps in danger of becoming obsolescent" (CW 19-I, p. 441), and its reliance on "money-loving" as the motive force of economics is morally repugnant.[8] What he is determined to preserve is the "way of life" that values democracy and intellectual, political, and artistic meritocracy. Fascism and Bolshevism must be rejected as models, but not because they are inherently economically inefficient. Keynes thought they had the potential to become very economically efficient. They had to be rejected because they are authoritarian and incompatible with personal freedom.[9]

"The next step forward," Keynes concluded, "must come, not from political agitation or from premature experiments, but from thought" (CW 9, p. 294). To the Liberals he argued that while there could be no blueprint for planning at this embryonic stage, the party must think through as carefully as possible its approach to the central issue of the economic role of the state in the new "epoch." "A party programme must be developed in its details, day by day, under the pressure and stimulus of actual events" (CW 9, p. 306). In July 1926, Lloyd George put up the money to finance the "Liberal Industrial Inquiry," precisely the kind of careful, well-researched policy study Keynes thought necessary. He worked hard on the project in 1926–1927. It resulted in the publication of *Britain's Industrial Future* (the Liberal Party's "Yellow Book") in early 1928, which served as the Liberal Party's election platform.

## Notes

1 Keynes gave two lectures in Moscow in September 1925 that are in the same category; they follow fairly closely the themes of "Am I a Liberal?" (see CW 19-I, pp. 434–442).
2 This statement is in fact grossly inaccurate. Britain's crucial cotton industry was built on its imperial system. See, for example, Sven Beckert (2015).
3 Keynes is not arguing against the necessity of abstraction in economic theory. But he does claim that the assumption set must eventually incorporate, even if in simplified form, all of the relevant characteristics of the aspect of the economy under investigation. He consistently supported the fundamental principle that the realism of assumptions matters to the assessment of the usefulness or empirical validity of a theory, a proposition contested by modern neoclassical economists who subscribe to Friedman's positivism. See Crotty (2013) for an analysis and evaluation of this debate.
4 For the core of Schumpeter's theory of competition, see Schumpeter (1942, chapters 6–8).
5 Keynes's analysis here prefigures much of the modern criticism of Walrasian general equilibrium theory.

6 See the Appendix to Chapter 8 on the importance of "public corporations" in this period.
7 Moggridge explained Keynes's views on these matters as follows. "Here there were questions of whether the Post Office or the telephone system should be run as a department of state under a Minister or as a public corporation, ultimately subject to Parliament but autonomous in its day-to-day operations. Similar considerations arose in connection with municipal enterprises. In all these cases, Keynes came down on the side of autonomy and professionalism, even at the cost of some centralisation, to provide varied, wide-ranging careers for the employees. Under a related heading came the matter of the organisation of the private sector, where he observed a tendency towards large units of operation, the separation of ownership from control, cartels, trade agreements and monopolies. Here Keynes put his faith in greater publicity in general and regulation in particular to protect investors and the general public. He was not averse to bigness itself: in many cases he argued it was inevitable" (Moggridge 1992, pp. 456–457).
8 In 1925, in a statement he would often repeat, Keynes denounced the love of money as immoral, even though he considered the pursuit of money to be a defining characteristic of capitalism. "[I]t seems clearer to me every day that the moral problem of our age is concerned with the love of money, with the habitual appeal to the money motive in nine-tenths of the activities of life, with ... the social approbation of money as the measure of constructive success, and with the social appeal to the hoarding instinct as the foundation of the necessary provision for the family and for the future" (CW 9, pp. 268–269).
9 In September, he observed in Moscow that the "experimental technique [of Leninism] is necessarily a matter of most high interest. We in the West will watch what you do with sympathy and lively attention, in the hope that we may find something which we can learn from you" (CW 19-I, pp. 441–442).

# 7 Destructive competition, corporatism, industrial policy, and the new economic role of the state: 1927–1928

From 1926 through the publication of *Britain's Industrial Future* by the Liberal [Party] Industrial Inquiry in 1928, Keynes was deeply engrossed in a detailed study of the structural and competitive impediments to the achievement of sustained full employment and industrial efficiency in Britain. As already noted, he emphasized on many occasions that much unemployment was structural in nature and centered in the traditional export sectors. He also believed that no solution to structural unemployment would be possible until the economy as a whole was put on a much higher growth path by his proposed macro policies of managed credit and public investment. And he had a great deal to say about how industry-level problems should be addressed: Keynes and the Liberal Party had both an industrial policy as well as a macroeconomic program of state planning. For Keynes, industrial policy and macro policy went hand in hand.[1] I will cite Volume 19 of the *Collected Writings* many times in this chapter. Volume 19 is titled *Activities 1922–1929: The Return to Gold and Industrial Policy*. Yet Keynes's writings on competition and industrial policy in this period are virtually unknown; certainly modern "Keynesian" macro theorists rarely if ever mention them.

His writings on the failures of unregulated competition in this era are of two kinds. The first kind consists of concrete studies of the troubled coal and cotton industries, which had been such important exporters before the war. These industries were populated by large numbers of small firms. Keynes emphasized the destructive nature of intense competition in such industries. "The day of the small unit is over," he said (CW 19-II, p. 642). The second kind represents an analysis of major industries dominated by a small number of giant firms in an era of increasing returns to scale and the rise of monopoly or oligopoly capitalism. For Keynes, the era in which the forces of competition could be allowed to guide and organize industries dominated by either a large number of small firms or a small number of large firms had passed. The key policy issue was: what should replace unregulated competition?

He addressed these issues in a speech to Liberal Party candidates in January 1927 called "Liberalism and Industry." The subject of the lecture is "the arrival of a new industrial revolution, a new economic transition," which needs guidance by the state if it is to lead to "an economically efficient and just society" (CW 19-II, p. 638).

Keynes situated his analysis in the context of Britain's long-term structural economic malaise. He emphasized the effect of stagnation on the buoyancy of business confidence or "animal spirits." We have seen that Keynes believed that "prosperity is cumulative" – an extended period of prosperity creates confidence in the economic future, which in turn makes future prosperity more likely. Here, he warned us that stagnation is also cumulative, and politically and economically dangerous as well because the working class had grown increasingly restless in this period.

> The optimistic Zeitgeist of the nineteenth century has given way to a pessimistic Zeitgeist. The spirit of the age is not as optimistic as it used to be. We are disappointed with the results of our existing method of carrying on. We used to think that private ambition and compound interest would between them carry us on to paradise. Our material conditions seemed to be steadily on the upgrade [in the nineteenth century]. Now we are fully content if we can prevent them from deteriorating; which means the working classes no longer have sufficient hopes in the general trend of things to divert their attention from other grievances. We no longer have sufficient confidence in the future to be satisfied with the present.
> 
> (CW 19-II, p. 641)

One of the central failings of "free" competition in the context of the 1920s, Keynes said, was that it was incapable of efficiently coordinating the downsizing of Britain's declining export industries that suffered from chronically large excess capacity. Though in decline, they still collectively generated the lion's share of Britain's exports.

> Methods which were well adapted to continually expanding business are ill adapted to stationary or declining industries. You can increase the scale of industries by small additions arranged by individuals. If there comes a need to shift from one industry to another, to curtail particular industries by small decrements, just as they have been expanded by small increments, no corresponding method is available to isolated, unorganised, individual effort.
>
> (CW 19-II, pp. 642–643)

> Combination in the business world, just as much as in the labour world, is the order of the day; it would be useless as well as foolish to try to combat it. Our task is to take advantage of it, to regulate it, to turn it into the right channels.
>
> (CW 19-II, p. 643)

British industry needed more combination, cartelization, and amalgamation. Keynes told a story about how very few guards are needed to control a large number of "dangerous lunatics" in an asylum because "lunatics never combine" (CW 19-II, p. 643).

Keynes argued that it is the responsibility of the government to try to assist those industries that suffer from excessive competition to create collusion and cooperation under government regulation. The "remedy," as he argued in "Liberalism and Labour," is to move "onwards toward order, towards society taking intelligent control of its own affairs" (CW 19-II, p. 643). What is needed is neither cut-throat competition nor the detailed central planning favored by the Labour Party, but "regulated competition" (CW 19-II, p. 643).

The government:

> must also be prepared to experiment with all kinds of new sorts of partnership between the state and private enterprise. The solution lies neither with nationalisation nor with unregulated private competition; it lies in a variety of experiments, of attempts to get the best of both worlds. In England there have been made already without due recognition a good many experiments in that direction ... The Government must recognise the trend of soundly run business toward trusts and combines. It must be prepared to recognise their existence as beneficent institutions in right conditions; and it must adopt an attitude towards them at the same time of encouragement and regulation.
>
> (CW 19-II, p. 645)

The Liberal Party had historically been associated with strong opposition to trusts and combinations. But this is:

> a wrong policy in modern conditions. It should be not discouragement, but encouragement for [trusts and combines] to live and exist in right conditions conducive to the general welfare. So far from there being any natural incompatibility between [combination and the general welfare], I believe that these great concerns run by salaried persons with a sufficient degree of decentralisation may, if they are handled by politicians and statesmen in the right manner, become a pattern and model of the way in which the world of the future will get the best both of large units and of the advantages that might be expected of nationalisation, whilst maintaining the advantages of private enterprise and decentralised control.
>
> (CW 19-II, p. 649)

The regulation of monopolies, oligopolies, and industry associations, though it represented an enormous increase in the economic role of government, was far from the only additional state responsibility in the new era. The state must also: regulate wages, hours, and working conditions; oversee labor education and training; arrange the transfer of labor from industries and areas where it is in surplus to those where it is needed; and allocate credit to high-priority uses. Keynes's enthusiastic and consistent support for state control of most large-scale capital investment is not the only "radical" policy position overlooked by mainstream "Keynesian" economists; his support of detailed industrial and labor-market policy has escaped their attention as well.

> It is not only in the direction of the regulation of capital that the state must be prepared for new functions. It must be prepared to regard the regulation of wages of great industrial groups as being not merely of private concern, and it must quite deliberately in its wages and hours policy treat the gradual betterment of the workers as the first charge on the national wealth ... The problem of the education and the mobility of labour is going to be at least as important ... It is not so much that there is no work to be done, but that men drop into occupations with no knowledge, by mere accident of circumstance and parentage and locality, often finding themselves in the wrong market, trained for something for which there is no demand, or not trained at all. There is no remedy for that by unregulated private action. It must be the concern of the state to know and have a policy as to where labour is required, what sort of training is wanted; and then where there are maladjustments, as there are in the coal industry, to work out plans for the transfer of labour from localities and trades where there is not demand to localities and other trades which are expanding and not declining. That is one example of the general policy which the Government has to be prepared for – namely, the deliberate regulation from the centre in all kinds of spheres of action where the individual is absolutely powerless left to himself ... I have given several examples of that, and as the machinery gets built up and the policy is developed, not a year will pass without an important addition to [these] spheres.
> (CW 19-II, pp. 646–647)

Keynes was so committed to this new direction that he threatened to leave the Liberal Party if it failed to support his ambitious policy initiatives. Unless the Liberal Party is willing to undertake this task, Keynes said, he and others will not be able to sustain "any live interest in party politics." Fortunately, "an attempt is now being made to work out some first outlines of such a policy by the Liberal Industrial Committee, initiated by the Liberal Summer School and encouraged and supported by Mr. Lloyd George" (CW 19-II, p. 647).

A brief description of labor–management–state relations in the coal industry would be useful background to a discussion of the problems that faced the industry in the mid-1920s. The General Strike of May 1926 sheds light on important aspects of Keynes's approach to the economics and politics of labor relations in this era.

There had been bitter conflict in the depressed coal mining industry between owners and the miners' union for several years over how to restore prosperity to the industry. This conflict was put on hold in 1925 via wage and profit subsidies while a Royal Commission studied the problem, but the subsidies were allowed to expire in April 1926. The owners locked out the miners on May 1, leading to the ill-fated General Strike from May 3 to May 12, a strike that was met with a ferocious response by both mine owners and the armed might of the state. The miners stayed out after the General Strike collapsed, but in the fall, "starvation forced them back on the owners' terms" (Skidelsky 1992, p. 251).

These events created a split in the Liberal Party between Lloyd George, who sympathized with the miners, and Lord Asquith and others, who believed that the workers' movement had committed treason and "feared that a General Strike would pave the way to revolution" (Skidelsky 1992, p. 252). Keynes supported the Lloyd George faction. The "split has come about in such a way that any radical, who is not ready to subordinate his political ideas entirely to personalities, has absolutely no choice," Keynes wrote to his sister. "I find a unanimous – astonishingly unanimous – feeling that this is so amongst every single leftish Liberal whom I have spoken to this week" (Skidelsky 1992, p. 255). Keynes believed that the miners were forced into their position by events they neither understood nor controlled.

> The strikers are not red revolutionaries; they are not seeking to overturn Parliament; they are not executing the first movement of a calculated political manoeuvre. They are caught in a coil, not entirely of their own weaving, in which behaviour, which is futile and may greatly injure themselves and their neighbors, is nevertheless the only way which seems to them to be open for expressing their feelings and sympathies and for maintaining comradeship and keeping faith … But my feelings, as distinct from my judgment, are with the workers. I cannot be stirred so as to feel the T.U.C. [Trades Union Congress] as deliberate enemies of the community, who must be crushed before they are spoken with.
>
> (CW 19-II, p. 532)

Keynes wrote a number of articles dealing with the crisis in coal. The industry had permanently lost a large part of its prewar market and was now burdened with substantial excess capacity, an excessive labor force, and uneconomical mines – problems exacerbated by the return to gold at par. He believed that these problems could never be sorted out by unregulated competition, which could only lead to overproduction and perpetually depressed prices. "I should, therefore, put the formation of a cartel of

British coal-exporters in the forefront of the remedies" (CW 19-II, pp. 535–536). But "in the absence of a pool or any other concerted action, this overproduction has resulted in a cut-throat competition which has driven down prices, mainly in the export trade, to a level that cannot yield a living wage." Therefore, "the urgent problems of the trade are ... to transfer men out of the industry, to curtail production and to raise export prices," and to arrange for "the closing down, temporarily or permanently, of a not inappreciable number of less efficient collieries" through combination and collusion (CW 19-II, p. 536). He suggested that if the owners refused to set up "a pool" through which "a scheme of quotas, of standard prices, and of penalties is drawn up, the industry must disappear or it must accept nationalisation" (CW 19-II, pp. 528–529).

However, if we want to fully understand Keynes's views on industrial policy and the role of state planning in the 1920s, we must turn from coal to the cotton industry, for he was intimately and intensely involved in efforts to create a cartel in the American (or low-grade) section of the British cotton industry centered in Lancashire from late 1926 through 1928.

The American section of the industry was divided among "over 300 fiercely competing family firms," some of which were loosely associated through the Federation of Master Cotton Spinners (Skidelsky 1992, p. 261). Keynes became an adviser to and spokesman for a group of mill owners who were attempting to turn the industry into a tightly knit cartel called the Cotton Yarn Association.

Cotton had lost 30 to 40 percent of its prewar export volume. During WWI, many of its former customers had engaged in substantial import substitution, sometimes under the protection of tariffs, and Japan had become a major competitor in coarse cotton, actually surpassing Britain in output in 1926. The industry reacted to the collapse in demand through half-hearted, incomplete, and ineffective cooperation rather than the well-coordinated collusion required to solve the industry's problems. It was a pale reflection of the successful industry "rationalization" movement led by Germany that was sweeping across Europe. In Keynes's view, the reactions of both coal and cotton:

> are founded on a belief that, if only the industries hang on, "normal" times will return when they may again hope to employ all their existing plant and labour on profitable terms. Neither industry has attempted what the Germans are calling "rationalization," that is to say, the concentration of demand on the most efficient plants, which are worked at full stretch and the rest closed down.
> (CW 19-II, p. 579)

While coal had engaged in massive overproduction and price cutting, cotton had "ruined itself by organised short-term [working hours] extending over five years," which drastically underutilized capital (the spindles) and thus substantially raised production costs (CW 19-II, p. 578). What is needed, Keynes believed, is an industry cartel – a " 'rationalisation' process designed to cut down overhead costs by the amalgamation, grouping or elimination of mills" (CW 19-II, p. 584).[2]

Keynes's writings on Lancashire cotton contain his clearest concrete or empirical observations about the costs of competition, about the myriad ways in which disequilibrium competitive processes, which may take years or even decades to work themselves out, can reproduce or even exacerbate structural unemployment and reproduce, rather than eliminate, economic inefficiencies. The clear implication is that such processes are not only costly and lengthy, they are also path dependent: they affect the new equilibrium position.

The entry point to his argument is the assumption that real capital accumulation is a substantially irreversible process. This assumption dramatically changes the character of theory. Modern neoclassical theory typically assumes that capital investment is a reversible process; if investment projects fail, you can resell the capital goods for what you paid minus depreciation. You can then repay any debt involved out of the sale proceeds. This makes capital accumulation a relatively safe investment, one subject to minimal risk. But in the real world, once a firm or industry has been built, the current system "includes no provision whatever for reversing the process, except the slow and dragging cure which time brings at last by decay and obsolescence" (CW 19-II, p. 590). Once financial capital is transformed into a concrete industrial plant and equipment and put in place in a specific production process in a specific plant in a specific location, it normally cannot be reconverted back into money form without substantial loss if and when it becomes unprofitable. Irreversible investment is a key component of what I have called destructive competition.[3]

Suppose that, after industry capacity is built to a high level, there is a permanent drop in demand that creates a condition of substantial excess capacity. Each firm will be forced to cut prices in an attempt to maintain some reasonable degree of capacity utilization so that fixed cost per unit and therefore total cost per unit are minimized. Given no substantial increase in industry demand in depressed markets, competition will drive prices down until they hit variable cost, leaving little if any revenue to cover fixed costs.

> What will happen in an unorganised industry? Competition between the owners ... will drive down prices towards the point at which no contribution at all is left towards overhead [i.e. fixed] expenses. Each individual will accept not the price which yields him a normal return, but the price which is preferable to abandoning his plant altogether and closing down his organisation.
> 
> (CW 19-II, p. 590)

Economists usually assume that in a price war, the least efficient producers are the first to be driven out of business, but this will often not be the case in what Keynes, in the *Tract*, referred to as the modern "regime of money contract." It may be the most financially fragile or indebted firms – not the least technically efficient ones – that are first into bankruptcy, for debt is often incurred to finance new capital equipment designed to put a firm on the cutting edge in terms of cost structure. "If this [price war] goes on for long, the mills which are financially weaker, though not perhaps technically inefficient, will become bankrupt."

> But even bankruptcy will not necessarily solve the problem of excess capacity [and thus will not eliminate the downward price pressure] because the firms still in business [who hope to survive until the price war is over and profits are normal again] will buy the spindles from the bankrupt firms when the price is low enough. Thus, the spindles of the bankrupt mills will not cease to exist. They will be sold at a low price and thus transferred into stronger hands on terms which will enable the competition to persist in conditions too severe for other businesses to earn their interest charges. And so the losses will continue until the gradual growth of demand over a long period or the obsolescence of the older mills restores the equilibrium at last.
> (CW 19-II, p. 590)

The problems created by "the forces of disorganised and beggar-my-neighbor competition" are, to again borrow Keynes's characterization of prosperity, cumulative (CW 19-II, p. 593). The drive to stay in business on the part of these family firms led them to finance losses through new debt and the run-down of working capital, which put them in yet more desperate straits. Though not stressed here, the same destructive dimensions of competition in periods of inadequate demand, as Schumpeter (1942) demonstrated, afflict industries dominated by a small number of very large firms.[4]

> Excessive competition, resulting from excess capacity, has, in many cases, brought down the level of profits below that of interest charges and other unavoidable outgoings. The resulting losses have been provided out of bank loans and other resources which ought only have used as current working capital. The consequence is that the normal borrowing capacity of the industry has been exhausted in meeting losses, and is not available for new capital. In short, the spinners as a class, are frightfully hard-up, which leads to the pest of what is known as "weak selling" [in which the need to pay back the bank plus the need to get revenue just to obtain new raw materials] carries the trouble a stage further and leads to prices which are worse than closing down.
> (CW 19-II, pp. 597–598)

Keynes argued that this "involuntary selling by financially necessitous mills" carries competitive pressure on price to totally irrational and destructive levels.

> What then should be done? *Disempower destructive competition and "rationalize" industry through inter-firm cooperation guided by the state.* The only rational solution to the problem of secular excess capacity and the need to shift production from the less efficient to the more efficient mills, especially in a debt-laden industry organized anarchically, is: the cartel, the holding company, and the amalgamation ... By these means, and by these means only, can the surplus capacity be withdrawn from competition and held in reserve against future requirements, so that the rest of the industry can return normal profits meanwhile.
> (CW 19-II, p. 591, emphasis added)

The detailed history of the failed attempt to create the Cotton Yarn Association discussed by Keynes need not concern us.[5] His advice was that all such firms should join an industry association so that collective decisions could be taken about minimum prices, production quotas, the elimination of "weak selling," the redistribution of production from weak to strong mills (through the sale of quotas), a collective "organisation for marketing and merchanting," collective purchasing of raw materials, perhaps even a collective approach to borrowing ("cooperative credit"), and so forth (CW 19-II, p. 621).

In spite of Keynes's many interventions over two years on its behalf, the Cotton Yarn Association, which at one point included about 70 percent of the mills, eventually collapsed under the twin burdens of declining demand and free-rider problems. The Bank of England belatedly stepped in to provide assistance to struggling firms, but their actions were too halfhearted and too late to do much good.

We might summarize the most important analytical points stressed by Keynes in his discussion of the coal and cotton industries in the 1920s as follows: he rejected classical theory because its assumption set was so at odds with the new reality that it was a catastrophic guide to policy. In particular, he attacked its assertion that intense or perfect competition will generate economic efficiency and full employment. He again argued that under then-current institutional and economic conditions, disequilibrium processes were destabilizing, of long duration, and path dependent. To the growing list of institutional impediments to efficient disequilibrium processes, Keynes here added the irreversibility both of capital investment and of labor to show that the cutthroat competition celebrated in classical theory can be tremendously destructive, especially in a regime of money contract. It made the adjustment to a new equilibrium in the major export industries very long and very inefficient. The process itself loaded the firms with debt (and the banks with bad debt) that pushed them further away from normal profitability.

As noted above, Keynes's attack on unregulated competition was not limited to industries populated by large numbers of small firms. As we saw in his three *Essays in Persuasion*, he also argued that economies of scale and scope were already large and getting larger in many important industries, causing oligopoly to become their normal and potentially most efficient state.

The giant firms that dominated these industries, Keynes argued, must operate, to use Schumpeter's word, "corespectively"; they should cooperate as well as compete, and at all costs avoid cutthroat price competition. They obviously cannot be efficiently regulated through perfect competition (see Schumpeter 1942, chapters 6–8). Where there are large economies of scale, there are large fixed costs per unit produced, marginal cost is everywhere below total cost per unit, and the gap between the two widens as capacity utilization declines and fixed cost per unit rises. Marginal cost pricing, a hallmark of "perfect" or super-intense competition, would therefore destroy the industry. Firms in such industries have to cooperate to keep price well above marginal cost and must regulate capital investment to avoid the disastrous effects of large excess capacity. Keynes argued that the state should actively help these crucial industries form organized cartels, trusts, and associations to help them efficiently self-regulate. But the state would also have to regulate these industries to prevent them from using their oligopoly power in harmful ways. The fact that many such industries had already implemented procedures for self-regulation would make it easier for the state to control and integrate them into a coherent overall government planning regime designed to create and sustain full employment. This new proposed economic policy regime is presented in some detail in the Liberal Party's book *Britain's Industrial Future* published in 1928, which is the subject of the next chapter.

## Notes

1 In the 1930s, his interests naturally focused more heavily on how to respond to the British and global depression – a mostly macro issue and, later, how to prepare for war.
2 One reason why this had not happened (in addition to the industry's anarchic structure) was that the banks who had loaned money to the now-unprofitable mills, especially in the speculative bubble of 1919–1920, had a vested interest in seeing that they remained in operation, even at a loss, in order to keep some portion of the interest payments flowing to the banks.
3 Chapters 9–11 of Crotty (2017) explain this process and show that it operated in important global industries in the neoliberal era.

4 Once a giant firm has purchased and put into place its vast array of fixed capital goods, it is likely not to exit its business lines even when times are bad because it stands to lose a large proportion of the money it spent on capital when it exits. If bad times look like they may last for many years, there will be little demand to buy these industry-specific capital goods. The firm will thus suffer large losses upon exit. The expected value of remaining in the industry in hard times, but then earning the profit that will be available once good times return, may well exceed the losses sure to be experienced upon exit. For a more detailed treatment of this issue, see Crotty (2017, pp. 244–271).
5 See CW 19-II, chapter 7.

# 8 *Britain's Industrial Future* and the Board of National Investment

A detailed analysis of the institutions to be used by the state to regulate capital accumulation in pursuit of full employment under Liberal Socialism

As mentioned above, Lloyd George put up the money to finance the "Liberal Industrial Inquiry" in July 1926. The purpose of this Inquiry was to provide the thoughtful research necessary to support a detailed new economic policy position for the Liberal Party. Keynes worked diligently on the Inquiry in 1926–1927. The outcome of this research culminated in the publication of *Britain's Industrial Future* (hereafter BIF) in early 1928. It served as the Party's election platform.

In August 1927, Keynes, as was his practice, addressed the Liberal Party Summer School. He was heavily involved at this time with the Liberal Industrial Inquiry. The subject of Keynes's talk was "The Public and the Private Concern." Keynes opened his remarks with the statement that, on the one hand, all sensible people regard "a great deal of public enterprise as unavoidable, necessary, and even desirable," while, on the other hand, "there is an enormous field of private enterprise which no one but a lunatic would seek to nationalize" (CW 19-II, p. 695). He then went on to discuss "what actually exists" with respect to capital assets held by public, semi-public, and not-for profit institutions.

> The capital of all these contributed to the stupendous total of three hundred thousand five hundred millions, which was *two-thirds of the total capital of large-scale undertakings in this country. This is the first fact to bear in mind – that two-thirds of the typical large-scale enterprise of this country had already been removed, mainly by Conservative and Liberal Governments, out of the category of pure private enterprise* ... I suggest that we should give up pretending that there are no public concerns. We should take a good look at that great body of public concerns which we already have and learn how to handle them wisely and efficiently. Then it will be time enough to consider whether we ought to add widely to the scope and field of their operations.
> (CW 19-II, pp. 695–696, emphasis added)

This fact – "that two-thirds of the typical large-scale enterprise of this country had already been removed, mainly by Conservative and Liberal Governments, out of the category of pure private enterprise" – became the foundation of his defense of the proposition that state control of the lion's share of capital assets was a politically and economically feasible task that required no substantial additional nationalization of for-profit industries.

In February 1928, the Liberal Party's Industrial Inquiry group published BIF, the end product of an 18-month study of the economic problems troubling the country. This is the most important document of the 1920s for those who wish to understand precisely how Keynes envisioned the public and private institutions and policies that could be used to restructure British industry and use state control of most large-scale capital investment to restore long-term prosperity.

The major contribution to our understanding of the evolution of Keynes's thinking about state direct and indirect control of capital investment in BIF is a detailed description of his proposed *Board of National Investment*, a permanent body that would both gather the necessary sources of finance and allocate them to pay for economically and socially efficient investment projects in a manner calculated to ensure the full employment of labor over the long run. This was not just about using public investment to "kick-start" the economy and let private enterprise take over once again. As we will see, Keynes expressed support for state control of most large-scale capital spending as the main instrument of government economic policy in many places in *The General Theory*, but he did not tell us in detail how this could be accomplished, either in that book or in any other place that I am aware of. *This is why BIF is crucial to the defense of the main policy thesis of this manuscript. It is, so to speak, the "smoking gun" of the argument.*[1]

Keynes was a member of the Inquiry's Executive Committee, along with such influential party figures as Lloyd George and Ramsey Muir. The historical record is unclear about the precise role played by Keynes and others in the collective work, but it is clear that he was a – and probably the – major force behind it. According to Harrod:

> Keynes' contributions were of central importance. He was able to get endorsement for his ideas on currency management, the stimulation of domestic investment programmes, *a public investment board*, which would also have regard to the scale of foreign investment, an Economic General Staff, greater publicity for the finance of companies, and *the encouragement of the semi-public concern as an agency of industrial operation intermediate between the state and private enterprise*.
> (Harrod 1951, pp. 392–393, emphasis added)

We do know that he was primarily responsible for Book 2 – according to Moggridge he drafted most of it – and Book 5, along with several other chapters, and that he coauthored the chapters on taxation as well as the

"Summary and Conclusions." He also went over the text as a whole before it was published.

It is thus hard to be completely sure where Keynes is presenting his own ideas in the book, where his influence is negligible, and where his more radical ideas (for he certainly was one of the most radical of the Liberals) may have been muted in response to opposition from more conservative members. Moggridge reported an important instance of muzzling by conservative voices. Robert Brand, an investment banker who was very influential in the Liberal Party, objected to Keynes's emphasis on the centrality of the state-regulated public corporation, as well as his stress on the need to "rationalize" or cartelize industries under government guidance and regulation as discussed in the previous section. According to Skidelsky, Brand's "Liberalism" was distinctly more right-wing than Keynes's. Brand had written a pamphlet titled "Why I Am Not a Socialist" in 1925.

> Brand's objections proved decisive. Most of Keynes's evolutionary speculations were omitted from Book II; a strong section on the virtues of individualism was inserted; *Keynes's insistence that the public concern should become the typical unit of industrial organisation* was dropped from that Book; and proposals for reorganising business structure largely limited to making the existing forms of public concerns more "lively and efficient."
> (Skidelsky 1992, p. 267, emphasis added)

I consider BIF to be a crucial stage in the evolution of Keynes's plans for the construction of Liberal Socialism in Britain for reasons I discuss in this section. Moggridge, on the other hand, apparently thought it to be of such little significance that he devoted only a page and a half to it in his 800-plus page "economist's biography" of Keynes.

It seems fair to conclude that: (1) Keynes influenced much of the book and was probably in general sympathy with most of the opinions expressed therein; and (2) opinions expressed in the sections of the book most closely associated with Keynes – especially Book 2 – though quite radical, may have been more conservative than he would have preferred, with more emphasis on the economic benefits of individualism and markets.

The book is surprisingly long for its intended role as a political intervention at almost 500 pages, and it contains an astounding amount of institutional detail about many aspects of the British economy and the economic role of the state. In a letter to his wife, Keynes noted that "The Liberal Inquiry has had a rather bad press." But he also said that the book:

> deserves it. Long-winded, speaking when it had nothing to say, as well as when it does … It would have been much better at half the

length, speaking only what is new and interesting and important. As it is, *any* reader must be discouraged.

(CW 19-II, p. 735, emphasis in original)

The book draws on the institutional and policy experience of many European countries in dealing with the economic dislocations of the interwar years. It looks to new experiments with the economic role of the state in Germany, Italy, France, and other countries. Reflecting important developments in Europe in the 1920s usually referred to as the "rationalization movement," BIF is a very corporatist document. Several sections discuss the importance of uniting all of the key actors in an industry – firms, labor, and the public – into a governing board that can make key industry decisions cooperatively. Such boards could then be integrated into a national decision-making body. The corporatist language on industrial relations is clearest and most administratively concrete, but other aspects of industry decisions are to be made through cooperation, amalgamation, or combination.

The potentially destructive force of class antagonism in industry receives careful attention. In addition to labor representation on industry-wide industrial relations boards, the book proposes a more egalitarian distribution of both private wealth and public services to reduce class distinctions and class tensions, as well as mandatory reporting of business costs and profits so that unions would know to what extent companies were treating them fairly. It also proposed profit-sharing and the evolutionary buildup of worker ownership of the companies that employ them, though it opposed direct worker control.

For our purposes, the most interesting aspects of the book are: (1) it supported the proposal by Keynes and Lloyd George in 1924 for reliance on public investment as the foundation of macro policy in pursuit of sustained full employment and provided for the first time supporting institutional detail for the implementation of this policy centered around a "national board of investment"; and (2) it reflected Keynes's multidimensional approach to the solution of Britain's economic problems in this period, relying not only on public investment and capital controls, but also on state-guided industrial policies and a redistribution of wealth.

BIF argued that high unemployment was primarily the result of long-term structural problems in key export industries aggravated by deflationary government policies related to the return to gold at par.[2] The solution, then, must address these industry-level problems through the kind of state-guided industrial policy Keynes had been expounding for the past two years.

But, as Keynes often argued, the transfer of labor out of the depressed industries and areas into new industries and areas would not take place even given sensible industry restructuring without a long-term macroeconomic stimulus to overall economic growth provided by a large-scale program of state-controlled public investment. Chapter XXI, which fleshed out the details of such a program under the guidance of a central government Board of National Investment, opened with an emphasis on this balanced approach, listing a few of the most important industries that could benefit from a large increase in investment.

> We put therefore, in the forefront of our proposals a vigorous policy of national reconstruction embracing within its scope, *inter alia*, the rehabilitation of agriculture, still the largest of our national industries; an extensive programme of highway development; afforestation, reclamation, and drainage; electrification, slum clearance and town planning, and the development of canals, docks, and harbours.
> (BIF, pp. 280–281)

Book 1 summarized the general condition of British industry. It stressed the great changes that had taken place in Britain's crucial export sector since the turn of the century and, especially, since the start of the WWI.

> When the War ended and the short-lived post-war boom was over, Great Britain found herself faced not merely with internal dislocation, but with her pre-war international difficulties so gravely increased as to create a completely new situation. The War had produced not only in Europe but even in far-distant countries a condition of extreme economic isolation. Our customers in the Empire, the East, and elsewhere had been compelled to provide, either at home or from some alternative source, the goods and services we had formerly provided.
> (BIF, p. 10)

> The decline in the volume of exports and the consequent stagnation of the industries which are mainly associated with export is the principal explanation of our formidable post-war unemployment. Coal, iron and steel, engineering, shipbuilding, cotton and wool, are our great exporting industries, and [represent] a large proportion of our unemployment.
> (BIF, p. 23)

Solving the unemployment problem in the export trades was made especially difficult by the fact that the capital employed there was substantially immobile, a problem assumed away in classical and neoclassical theory. We discussed this problem earlier. But, Keynes observed, labor is also burdened by irreversibility. Jobs are location-specific and skill-specific, and housing is location-specific and may plummet in value when a dominant local industry such as mining or ship-building or steel production goes into depression. Workers and their families are also part of social networks that are central to their well-being. This was not, in other words, a situation in which the decline in some particular industry is easily resolved by the free movement of redundant labor and capital from declining into expanding industries. These export industries:

> represent a very high degree of specialisation of plant and skill. They are concentrated very largely in particular localities ... It would be impossible to view their decline with the same comparative equanimity with which we have been able in the past to view the decline of other industries against whom the tide of fashion or economic opportunity had turned ... But it is only necessary to ask to what alternative purposes a coal-mine or blast furnace could be converted in order to realise that the decline of our basic industries would confront us with an altogether formidable problem.
>
> (BIF, p. 40)

Book 1 pointed to the two kinds of solutions that are stressed in the rest of the work. First, "there is in some cases a certain amount of remediable inefficiency within the industries themselves," especially in coal, textiles, and steel (BIF, p. 42). Second, on a more macro level, help can be found by following Keynes's persistent advice to restrict foreign financial investment and channel more of British savings into "a large expenditure of capital at home," "the setting up of new industries, the modernisation of old ones, the revolution in the modes of transport and in forms of power, the need to house our increased population, and to rebuild a part of our towns" (BIF, p. 44).

> It seems to us, therefore, that the time is now ripe for a bolder programme of home development which will absorb and employ the national resources of capital and labour in new ways. Such a programme, which we develop in Book 4, seems to us to be not only recommended in the national interest as a means of exploiting the technical developments of the modern age, but also as the best available method to break the vicious circle of unemployment.
>
> (BIF, p. 46)

The crucial macro dimensions of the policy proposals of BIF are contained primarily in Book 2, written by Keynes, and Book 4, overseen by Lloyd George. Book 2 is central to understanding Keynes's commitment to public investment as the core of macroeconomic policy. It lists in great detail the various categories of public, semi-public, and not-for-profit concerns, documenting their immense size and significance. The demonstration that, even with no additional nationalization, there were enormous capital assets already under the direct control or the guidance of the state had become a crucial part of his general line of argument. Book 2 also contained Keynes's first detailed public proposal for a powerful

"Board of National Investment" – *one central authority capable of selecting, overseeing, coordinating, and financing all public investment programs at every level of government.* Finally, this section supported and augmented William Beveridge's proposal for the creation of an "Economic General Staff" – "a thinking department within the Administration, at the elbow of the inner ring of the Cabinet, which shall warn Ministers of what is ahead and advise them on all broad questions of economic policy" (BIF, p. 116).

Book 2 began with a forthright rejection of what it called the "comprehensive State socialism" of the Labour Party. It stressed several advantages of decentralized enterprise decision-making, as well as the inefficiency that direct central-state control of companies can inflict. On the other hand, the chapter also acknowledged that "the pooling of knowledge, the elimination of the wastes of competition (which are very great), [and] the deliberate aiming at the general advantage ... are real advantages in central control and ownership" (BIF, p. 65). *Keynes vigorously defended the concept of public management of large-scale business enterprises*, rejecting the assumption that "the unrestricted private-profit motive" is the only way to motivate effort and efficiency in business decision-making.

> The notion that the only way to get enough effort out of the brain-worker is to offer him unfettered opportunities of making an unlimited fortune is as baseless as the companion notion that the only way of getting enough effort out of the manual worker is to hold over him the perpetual threat of starvation and misery for himself and those he loves. It has never been even supposed to be true, at all events in England, of the soldier, the statesman, the civil servant, the teacher, the scientist, the technical expert.
>
> (BIF, p. 66)

Since most managers of large private firms receive "a certain salary, plus the hope of promotion or a bonus" for their efforts, this is what managers and directors of public concerns should expect: "the performance of functions by Public Concerns in place of privately owned Companies and Corporations would make but little difference to the ordinary man" (BIF, p. 66).

As a general rule, the following kinds of private enterprises should be brought under public control: firms of great national importance that require large amounts of capital but may fail to obtain adequate private financing; large firms with monopoly or collective oligopoly power that make unregulated private enterprise dangerous to the public; or firms in which "the private shareholder has ceased to perform a useful function" (BIF, p. 75). The last criterion is of special interest because Keynes is on the record as believing that most large firms had evolved to a position of managerial as opposed to stockholder control.

Keynes's next task is crucial: to demonstrate that the public concerns over which the state already has direct or indirect control are, in the aggregate, so large that no substantial increment through nationalization is required to give the state potential control of the national capital-accumulation process. Section 2 of chapter VI ("The Public Concern") is called a "Survey of Existing Public Concerns." A Public Concern is "a form of organization which departs in one way or another from the principles of unrestricted private profit, and is operated or regulated in the public interest" (BIF, p. 63). Chapter VI organized the socialized or semi-socialized firms into various groups and presented crude estimates of the amount of capital controlled by each. "We think that most readers will be astonished by their magnitude" (BIF, p. 66). It is useful to recall here Moggridge's statement that only the heated objections of conservative voices such as Robert Brand's prevented Keynes from arguing that the Public Concern might become the "typical unit of industrial organisation" in Britain (BIF, p. 267).

The list of Public Concerns begins with the "nationalised" enterprises under the direct, day-to-day control of Government Departments. Keynes called them "few in number"; the leading examples referred to are the Post Office, the Telegraph, and the Telephone. Next came "National Undertakings operated by officially appointed *ad hoc* Bodies," of which the leading examples are the British Broadcasting Company and the Central Electricity Board. Then came "Local Undertakings operated by the Local Authority itself." These include locally owned gas, electricity, transportation, and water companies, as well as housing. They are followed by "Local Undertakings operated by officially appointed *ad hoc* Authorities" or Boards, including docks and harbors (of which the Port of London is the largest), Water Boards, and Public Authorities in London.

The list then moves on to the all-important residential construction industry with its large cooperative lending sector. Keynes believed that if the Board of National Investment lent money to the industry at low long-term interest rates, it could induce substantial growth in the level of residential construction. We "now come to another category, where profit enters in, but either not on the usual capitalistic lines (e.g. Co-operative Societies) or not without some measure of regulation or restriction of profit" (BIF, p. 70). The most important of these were the Building Societies that cooperatively financed home building and non-residential construction. They grew rapidly over the 1920s, helping finance Britain's substantial housing boom. "These societies are now administering something like *ten per cent of the total savings of the country,*" and they finance domestic rather than foreign capital accumulation (BIF, p. 71, emphasis added).

The penultimate category is "Parliamentary Companies," the leading categories of which were railways, tramways, and gas, water, and electricity companies. Railways, gas, and electricity had very large capital stocks. They were subject to tight restrictions "on profits to be earned and rates to be charged" (BIF, p. 73). Finally, reference is made to "Independent Undertakings not run for Profit," consisting of the "Ecclesiastical Commission," the Universities, Schools, City Companies, and Charities.

Keynes conclusion about the cumulative size of these concerns and their implication for state planning is of the utmost importance. His use of the term "Socialism" here refers specifically to the program of the Labour Party, which supported, in principle if not in practice, Soviet-type planning with state control of all productive property.

> Thus productive undertakings, mainly transport and public utilities, representing a capital in the neighborhood of £2,750,000,000 or £4,000,000,000 if we include roads, are already administered according to a variety of methods, all of which depart in some respect from the principles of private capitalism and unrestricted individualism. *The transportation undertakings and public utilities included in this total, measured by the amount of capital involved, must comprise at least two-thirds of what could be called the large-scale undertakings of this country,* though it would be a smaller proportion, measured in terms of the number of workmen employed ... This formidable total – amounting to over £4,000,000,000 under all heads – demonstrates what we have said above as to the unreal character of the supposed antithesis between Socialism and Individualism. What does the [Labour Party] Socialist think he could gain by assimilating all this valuable diversity, developed by experience to meet real problems and actual situations, to a single theoretical model? Are not the abuses of private capitalism and unrestricted individualism capable of being reformed, in so far as they are still to be found in these mixed types, by a further evolution along the lines already set? On the other hand, is the individualist really prepared to scrap all this elaborate special legislation by Governments of every political complexion under pressure of actual circumstances, and hand over the vast capital of our public utilities and railway system to the operation of uncontrolled individualism? If not, then there is no question of principle at stake but only on of degree, of expediency, of method.
>
> (BIF, pp. 74–75, emphasis added)

When the capital investment and financing decisions related to this huge and diverse set of undertakings is brought under the coordination of a Board of National Investment, the ability to achieve sustained or long-term full employment would be within reach. The Board would regulate public capital investment in pursuit of the goal of sustained full employment, thus defeating the destructive forces of both secular stagnation and dysfunctional disequilibrium processes. If the Board was successful, the smaller private sector would also prosper. Expectations of future sales and profits would rise substantially and uncertainty about future demand substantially would lower, increasing the incentive to invest.

Chapter IX of Book 2 ("The National Savings") introduced Keynes's proposal for the creation of a Board of National Investment. The emphasis in this chapter is on the Board's control over the flow of national savings that will provide much of the financing for the investment projects the Board decides to undertake. Lloyd George's Book 4 dealt with the question of what kinds of investments the Board should support.

The introduction to Book 4 stressed the fact that there were vast unmet economic and social needs that could be efficiently addressed by an ambitious program of public investment, and that there was a "great reservoir of unemployed labor [and] the necessary financial resources" (BIF, p. 285) to carry out this program under the guidance of the Board of National Investment. It noted that "many foreign countries have set us an example of what might be done in this kind of way," including Germany, Italy, and France (BIF, p. 285).

The book laid out an incredibly ambitious set of possible investment projects capable collectively of moving the country from stagnation to prosperity while greatly improving the quality of public and private life. In 1942, Keynes would argue that a vigorous program of wisely chosen public investment in economically and socially useful projects carried out for a substantial time could create a "New Jerusalem" in Britain, a biblical reference to the heaven that awaits the faithful at the end of time. The reference was meant to stress the incredible potential of the Board of National Investment.

Book 4 described a vast and detailed menu of productive investments and explained why each type of investment was well worth undertaking. This menu occupies 140 pages of the 502-page book.

How will these investments be paid for? The annual flow of new savings is estimated to be about £500 million, of which about £100 million currently passes through central and local governments. *Keynes suggested that about half of the funds that currently flow abroad should now be allocated to the Board via capital controls to be spent on domestic investment.* "[I]t would be to the advantage of the country if (say) £50,000,000 less were lent each year to public bodies abroad and £50,000,000 more were devoted to the development of the national resources and equipment at home" (BIF, p. 111).

It is imperative, Keynes argued, that the revenue flows to and the capital expenditures by government agencies be consolidated under a single authority. A unified national "Budget of Capital Expenditure" needed to be prepared, similar to that prepared for the government of India. "With this object in view, we propose that there be established a Board of National Investment" as a subordinate department of the Treasury under the authority of the Chancellor of the Exchequer, "who should make periodic statements to Parliament and give opportunities for discussion" (BIF, p. 111).

"All capital resources accruing in the hands of Government Departments should be pooled in the hands of this Board" (BIF, p. 111). The Board could also borrow on its own account, at the low interest rate made possible by central-government backing. It would be empowered to substitute its own debt for cash as payment from the Sinking Fund to holders of existing government debt, thus converting, as Keynes put it, unproductive into productive debt. The Board "should also be authorised to issue, when necessary, either for cash subscription or in substitution for existing Dead-weight Debt, National Investment Bonds (as they might be called) having a government guarantee" (BIF, p. 112). Since interest payments plus amortization of the National Debt is estimated later in the book to cost about 10 percent of national income (or about £800 million per year), the ability to substitute National Investment Bonds for cash repayments could provide a huge potential source of funding for the Board.

The funds generated by the Board would be used to finance "new capital expenditures by all central, local, or *ad hoc* bodies [i.e. all Public Concerns], by means of advances precisely on the lines of those now made from the Local Loans Fund" (BIF, p. 112).[3] The interest rate charged by the Board would generally be slightly above the rate the Board itself had to pay. Since this is government debt, the interest rate charged by the Board would be lower than that paid by even large profitable private corporations. The scope of lending available to the Board would be quite wide. Lending to private companies for approved investment projects that were congruent with Board objectives was specifically authorized.

> The Board should also be authorized to advance funds for new capital improvements to railways or other Parliamentary companies on terms to be mutually agreed, and also ... to any other Public Company, on the lines of the Trade Facilities Act.
>
> (BIF, p. 113)

The Trade Facilities Act made loans "for approved purposes on behalf of private concerns but with the guarantee of the Government" (BIF, p. 103). Keynes had mentioned on several occasions that the purpose of the Trade Facilities Act – to give private concerns with investment projects considered to be in the national interest government backing for its loans – was quite sensible, but that its scope had been too limited.[4]

Keynes addressed the question of how to ensure that the management of Public Concerns would operate efficiently in great detail.

> The best method of conducting large undertakings owned by the government and run in the public interest is by means of an *ad hoc* Public

Board analogous to a Joint Stock Company, in which the capital is owned and the directors appointed by the State.

(BIF, p. 457)

There is no inherent reason "why such Boards ... need be any less efficient than the Boards of large public companies, which are managed by salaried directors and officials subject to no real or effective control by their shareholders" (BIF, p. 77). He stressed the need to create a kind of Civil Service of highly trained managers and skilled directors to run the growing number of public corporations, "a class of officials for running them as capable as the General Managers of great industrial companies" (BIF, p. 81).

We need to build up an attractive career for business administration of this type open to all the talents. A regular service should be recruited for Public Concerns with a cadre and a pension scheme, with room for the rapid promotion of exceptional officials and with satisfactory prizes for those who reach the top.

(BIF, p. 80)

Keynes and the Liberals clearly had high hopes for the scale and the potential economic impact of the Board's operations. Keynes estimated that it would be able to allocate about £150 million annually to begin with and up to £300 million in the foreseeable future. "In the course of time the annual installments of repayments for loans previously made would double this sum" (BIF, p. 114).

To oversee and coordinate all the diverse regulatory and control functions proposed for the state, Keynes called for the "creation of what, following Sir William Beveridge, we may call an Economic General Staff" (BIF, p. 117). It was his belief that the Prime Minister and the Cabinet had no adequate source of skilled economic advice, yet the proposed expansions in the economic role of the state would confront government with economic responsibilities of unprecedented peacetime dimensions.

It is, therefore, a vital need for a modern State to create a thinking department within the Administration, at the elbow of the inner ring of the Cabinet, which shall warn Ministers of what is ahead and advise them on all broad questions of economic policy.

(BIF, p. 116)

In particular, it would be the duty of the Economic General Staff: "To suggest to the Government plans for solving fundamental economic difficulties, such, for instance, as measures for stabilising trade conditions, avoiding unemployment, and developing national resources" (BIF, p. 118).

Continuing the military analogy, Keynes proposed that there be a Chief of the Economic General Staff, whose "position would be of such power and importance" that it would be comparable to that of the "First Sea Lord or the Chief of the Imperial General Staff" in time of war (BIF, p. 118). The members of the General Staff would include, in addition to the Chief, the Permanent Secretary of the Treasury and the permanent heads of the Board of Trade and the Ministries of Labour, Health, and Agriculture. Finally, Keynes envisioned a Committee of Economic Policy that would be a Standing Committee of the Cabinet under the chairmanship of the Prime Minister to which the Chief of the Economic General Staff would act as Secretary. This committee would consist of the Prime Minister, the Chancellor of the Exchequer, the President of the Board of Trade, and the Ministers of Labour, Health, and Agriculture. Ultimately, the new and more powerful economic regulatory and control authority granted to Government would be the responsibility of Government's most powerful administrators.

In Book 2, Keynes addressed the more micro-oriented issues of industrial policy that concerned him in his writings on the need for rationalization in the coal and cotton industries. "In no country is an obstinate prejudice to what is called 'rationalisation' stronger than in Britain" (BIF, p. 128). He discussed the problems caused by "individualism instead of cooperation" in coal, steel, and flour-milling by way of example. The solution to such problems cannot be left to anarchic competition among large numbers of firms in unregulated markets. It:

> is not to be secured these days by mere attempts to restore the old conditions of competition, which often involve waste and effort, the uneconomical duplication of plant or equipment, and the impossibility of adopting the full advantages of large-scale production.
> (BIF, p. 93)

BIF argued that Britain had entered an era in which large economies of scale in production and in distribution were quite common. In this era, the only rational and efficient way to harness these scale economies – at least until firms were so large they needed to become a Public Corporations or Public Concern[5] – was through cooperative decision-making by industry associations and cartels. But, since such monopolistic institutions could easily operate in ways that did not serve the public good, the state would have to play a key role in regulating their activities.

> In modern conditions a tendency towards some degree of monopoly in an ever-increasing number of industries is, in our opinion, inevitable and even, quite often, desirable in the interests of efficiency.[6] It is, therefore, no longer useful to treat cartels, combinations, holding companies, and trade associations as inexpedient abnormalities in the economic system to be prevented, checked and harried. The progression from purely private individualistic enterprises to the Public Concern is one of endless gradations and intermediate stages. We believe that

> there is still room at one of these intermediate stages for large-scale enterprises of a semi-monopolistic character which are run for private profit and controlled by individuals. We must find a place for such enterprises within our national economic system and create an environment for them in which they can function to the public advantage.
>
> (BIF, p. 94)

Keynes and the Liberals had yet to develop a detailed and complete vision of the precise structures and functions of the state organs charged with regulating individual semi-monopolistic industries and coordinating their diverse activities. Keynes understood that it would take a great deal of experience and experimentation to finally arrive at an efficient system. He placed his hope in open-minded experimentation by the state and by private industry with various different kinds of structures and policies. That is, the shift from old system of laissez-faire to the new system of managed capitalism would take time and would require more information and experience. Given the radical nature of this shift, the need for time and experimentations is hardly surprising.

> In conclusion, we would reiterate the idea which has been running through this and the preceding chapter, namely, that the divorce between responsibility and ownership worked out by the growth of Joint Stock Companies, an event which has occurred since the dogmatic ideas of [Labour Party] Socialists took shape, together with the prominence of legitimate tendencies towards combinations, cartels, and Trade Associations, provide one of the clues to the future. Private enterprise has been trying during the past fifty years to solve for itself the essential problem, which the Socialists in their day were trying to solve, mainly, how to establish an efficient system of production in which management and responsibility are in different hands from those which provide the capital, run the risk, and reap the profit, and where the usual safeguards of unfettered competition are partially ineffective. Private Enterprise has had the great advantage over theoretical Socialism of being able to put forth a considerable range and variety of systems to put them into practice ... Private Enterprise by itself has, indeed, far from succeeded in finding an entirely satisfactory solution, but, in combination with the hand of the State (which has slipped in much more often than either theorists or the general public have recognised), it has provided us with a fine laboratory and many experiments, the results of which, for good and, sometimes, for evil, we are just beginning to reap. The task of modern statesmanship is to take full advantage of what has been going on, and to discern in the light of these manifold experiments which ideas are profitable and which unprofitable.
>
> (BIF, p. 100)

Thus, in the Board of National Investment, Keynes believed he had proposed a concrete government body capable of efficiently organizing and implementing the public engine of capital accumulation that, he had argued in 1924 (in his essay "Does Unemployment Need a Drastic Remedy?"), was needed to solve Britain's seemingly intractable unemployment problem. The overriding goal of the Board was very ambitious indeed – *to help recreate long-term boom conditions similar in vigor to those of the nineteenth century through public investment planning*. This definitely was not a short-term government stimulus program designed to "kick-start" a temporarily sluggish economy and then let free enterprise take over. In chapter IX, Keynes argued that the Board could be:

> with the least possible disturbance, an instrument of great power for the development of the national wealth and the provision of employment. An era of rapid progress in equipping the country with all the material adjuncts of modern civilisation might be inaugurated, *which would rival the great Railway Age of the nineteenth century.*
> (BIF, p. 114, emphasis added)

From *The Economic Consequences of the Peace* in 1919 and throughout the 1920s, Keynes had consistently argued that the Golden Age of economic progress experienced in the nineteenth century was over and could not be resuscitated using nineteenth-century institutions, practices, policies, and economic theories. He believed that without radical restructuring of the economic machine, Britain faced a perpetually stagnant economy and a potential revolt by the working class. The industrial and macro policies laid out in BIF constituted the most detailed radical program to put Britain on the path to long-term prosperity associated with Keynes in the interwar period.

To sum up: through his contribution to BIF, Keynes made a major effort to implement a peaceful economic revolution in Britain's economy in the face of bitter opposition from finance, industry, government, conservatives, some members of the Liberal Party, and most of the wealthy.

Upon publication of BIF in early 1928, Keynes argued that its proposed public investment plans would, over the longer haul, be substantially self-financing. In February 1928, he wrote that "a large number of things which we propose would involve only capital expenditure, and that of a remunerative kind, so that they would bring no burden on the Budget proper" (CW 19-II, p. 733). In spite of the almost universal belief among post-WWII commentators that the essence of Keynes's policy program was budget deficits to eliminate unemployment, the truth is that Keynes never proposed that the state incur *long-term* deficits. It was budget-neutral public investment over the long term, not deficit-augmenting tax cuts and transfer payments that was the core of Keynes's policy revolution.

In preparation for the 1929 election, the Liberal Party published a short version of BIF called *The Orange Book* as its economic platform. In March 1929, Keynes wrote a newspaper article in its support. *The Orange Book* proposed an initial public investment program of £250 million over two years, or about 3 percent of GDP each year. Keynes addressed the standard criticism that such spending will not lead to enough new jobs to make a serious dent in the unemployment problem in a newspaper article. Keynes's use of a "multiplier" concept here represented a theoretical and rhetorical breakthrough for him.

> Would the demand for labour resulting from a practicable programme of capital development make an appreciable impression on the existing unemployment? It is reasonable to suppose that an investment of £250, in types of capital production which do not depend heavily on imports, will provide wages to employ the equivalent of at least one man for a year, after meeting outgoings other than wages, and that man, in spending his wages, will set further miscellaneous productive activity moving. Thus it is a conservative estimate, in my opinion, to assume that each £1,000,000 of the kind of investment contemplated by Mr Lloyd George's programme will reduce unemployment by at least 5,000 to 6,000 men, and perhaps by more. For, once the impulse to prosperity has been started the effect will be cumulative. Accordingly, an investment programme of £100,000,000 might be expected to break the back of abnormal unemployment.
>
> (CW 19-II, p. 807)

On Keynes's reasoning, a public investment program of the modest size proposed in *The Orange Book* would lower unemployment by between 625,000 and 750,000 people. Since total unemployment in 1929 was 1.5 million, or 8 percent of the total labor force, he was, in effect, shooting to lower the total unemployment rate to between 4 and 5 percent.[7]

## Appendix

*Were Keynes's assumptions about the size of publicly controlled capital, the centrality of "Public Corporations" and the rise of market power in the private sector in Britain's interwar economy consistent with the historical record?*

In *The Development of the British Economy: 1914–1980* (Pollard 1983), the eminent British historian Sidney Pollard provided evidence broadly consistent with Keynes's interpretation of two key trends in British industry. First, public and semi-public organizations and non-profits did indeed control a very large percentage of British capital. Second, administrative substitutes for unrestrained private-sector competition were the order of the day in private industry in the interwar years.

Pollard argued:

> A large share of industry and transport was, even in the 1920s, not controlled by private enterprise at all, but by various types of public or non-profit-making organisations, and *their growth is one of the most significant aspects of the period*. Among the most important of them were the co-operative societies, registered under the Industrial and Provident Societies Act, and the building societies, registered under the Buildings Societies Act; enterprises administered by charitable, educational and similar bodies; local authorities, administering over one-third of the gas works, two-thirds of electricity supplies, four-fifths of water supplies and of tramway mileage, virtually all the trolley-bus systems as well as a large proportion of omnibus and other services. There were, further, *ad hoc* authorities such as dock and harbour boards, including those of London, Liverpool and Glasgow, and the Metropolitan Water Board, established in 1902; companies established by Act of Parliament, mainly in the public utilities field, including the railways; enterprises administered directly by the State, including the Post Office, the dockyards, and the Crown Lands; and the Public Corporations. In 1928 the Liberal Industrial Inquiry found that the capital administered by these authorities came to about £4 billion (including £1.3 billion for roads and £1.15 billion for railways) and was thus of *the same order of magnitude as the aggregate capital of all joint-stock companies*.[8]
>
> (Pollard 1983, pp. 99–100, emphasis added)

Pollard explained that it took experience and experimentation for Britain to create an acceptable and efficient way to regulate those key industries that eventually became Public Corporations.

> The country groped its way to through to a new and significant form of organization, the Public Corporation. Public Corporations had been pioneered by Dock and Harbour Boards before 1914. Between the wars the most important new authorities were the Forestry Commission (1919), the Central Electricity Board (1926), the British Broadcasting Corporation (1926), the London Passenger Transport Board (1933) and the British Overseas Airways Corporation (1939). In addition, the Post Office was modelled more closely on that of a Public Corporation … The Public Corporation was an attempt to cope with the problem of the administration of large or nationally important industries, mostly requiring large public sums, a secure control of their market and a strong interest in general or social, as distinct from sectional, welfare. It was a compromise, to avoid both the exploitation of the public by a

private monopoly, and the day-to-day political interference to which ordinary Departments of State are normally subjected. The capital might be held by the State or by former owners, including private shareholders, but there was the most complete separation between ownership and control ... The Public Corporation enjoyed general support and roused widespread interest as a new administrative device.

(Pollard 1983, pp. 106–107)

Pollard also provided support for Keynes's second assertion that a distinct historical trend toward the regulation and control of competition in the private sector through various organizational and administrative devices developed in the interwar years. After presenting evidence on the rapid growth in the scale of the typical production unit, Pollard argued as follows:

Even this does not show fully the extent of industrial concentration, for many firms, while nominally independent, were being combined frequently in their own industry, but sometimes even in different industries in complex ways inadequately described as "lateral" or "diagonal" integration. The links between the firms forming a group were sometimes economic or technical, but often they were little more than financial. Holding companies or subsidiaries were the most common means of control, but there were also inter-locking capital holdings, frequently unknown to the public, and inter-locking directorates ... In the main, however, growing concentration was associated with restrictions of competition and the creation of monopolistic markets. The logical conclusion of this development was the creation of a single large monopolistic firm dominating an industry by controlling, say, 70% or more of its capacity. Several of these survived from before 1914. Apart from the single firm, the most widespread form of monopoly to arise in the inter-war years was the trade association. At the end of the war ... John Hilton, the Secretary of the Committee [on Trusts], estimated that over 500 associations were then in existence ... Many of these trade associations collapsed in the slump of 1921–2, but in the "rationalization" movement of 1924–29, *much of it Government supported*, others were formed. By the late 1930s there were probably 1000–2000 in existence in manufacturing alone, with a similar number to be found in distribution and other spheres. Most of them were driven sooner or later to concern themselves with price fixing and control ... Some trade associations went further and approached those of the German-type cartel by controlling not only prices, but also output quotas or capacity [through control of investment].

(Pollard 1983, pp. 102–103, emphasis added)

The end result, according to Pollard, was:

> Monopolistic combination of one kind or another became much more common during the inter-war years, to the extent that *by the end of the period restrictive practices had become the normal framework of economic life*, buttressed as they were by associations, agreements and Acts of Parliament. "As a feature of industrial and commercial organization," wrote an observer in 1937, "free competition has nearly disappeared from the British scene."
>
> (Pollard 1983 pp. 103–104, emphasis added)

Pollard also documented a "striking" change in the attitude toward monopoly on the part of the British public and the British government starting in the 1920s. Initially, the change was simply an acceptance of the suppression of free competition in the name of economic rationality by private firms – a sea change for a people raised on the sanctity of "free" competition. Later, the government and the public came to support the suppression of competition through government coordination of private-sector economic activity, a task made easier by the rise of self-administered inter-firm relations.

> The drive towards "rationalization" of industry, first introduced in this country from Germany about 1924, was perhaps the first harbinger of change. It began as a movement to improve techniques, but it was soon mainly looking for savings by structural and economic, rather than technical, reorganization, "the right arrangement of the relations of the producers to each other." This often required the collaboration of firms to provide common services, or, more commonly, to provide a full load for the more up to date plant while scrapping the less efficient. Such measures were more logically applied to the whole of an industry, and thus rationalization led directly to schemes of control and monopoly.
>
> (Pollard 1983, p. 104)

By the end of the 1920s, Pollard argued, *all three political Parties supported the trend toward cooperative relations among dominant firms in markets organized as oligopolies and the use of industry planning by the state.*

> The new Labour members of the Committee on Trusts had as early as 1919 emphasized their belief that evolution towards combination and monopoly was "both inevitable and desirable, as long as it was controlled in the public interest." Conservative opinion by the early 1930s was equally strongly in favour of regulation and control. Some Conservatives were even prepared to go further, and plan industry as a whole.
>
> (Pollard 1983, p. 105)

## 114  The Economic Consequences... *to* The General Theory

Many in the Conservative Party supported this "rationalization" movement as a necessary condition for an efficiently managed qualitative increase in government planning or guidance of the economy. Pollard quoted a 1933 book on economic reconstruction written by the influential Conservative politician Harold Macmillan, who was the British Prime Minister from 1957 to 1963:

> [State economic planning] is impossible without the cooperation of industry. Production cannot be planned in relation to established demand while industries are organised on competitive lines. In present circumstances there are no channels through which any economic policy at all can be effectively administered throughout the field of productive effort. It is for this reason that I regard it as a matter of primary importance to produce an orderly structure in each of our national industries amenable to the authority of a representative directorate conducting the industries as self-governing units in accordance with the circumstances of the modern world.
>
> (Pollard 1983, p. 105)

The growing movement toward private-sector self-regulation of competition under the guidance of the state in concert with the vast amount of capital controlled by public and semi-public bodies and the support of all three political parties did indeed seem to have created the foundations needed for Keynes's policy revolution to succeed.

## Notes

1. Some readers might not be familiar with the expression "smoking gun" used here. In a murder mystery, the police may have collected a good deal of circumstantial evidence that a particular suspect is guilty, but do not have enough evidence to ensure conviction in a trial. What is needed is additional evidence that will guarantee a guilty verdict; for example, someone who saw the "smoking gun" used to kill the victim in the hands of the murderer.
2. See, for example, pages 3, 23, 274, 341, 348, and 412.
3. The Local Loans Fund was a central fund that could be used to finance investment by Local Authorities and other bodies that were permitted by law to borrow from it.
4. Over the life of the Trade Facilities Act from 1921 to 1927, guarantees were given for a total of £74 million worth of private-sector borrowing.
5. For example, an important but not fully worked-out regulation is that when private companies become very powerful within their industry, BIF proposed that they be forced to register with the Board of Trade as "Public Corporations" subject to the regulatory powers of the Board and a new government body called the Trust Tribunal.
6. This was a central assumption of Schumpeter's theory of competition as well (see Schumpeter, 1946).

7 Keynes's efforts on behalf of the Liberal Party in this election were not rewarded. Labour won the election with 288 seats in the House of Commons, while the Conservatives took 260 seats and the Liberals 59.
8 It might seem odd to use the Liberal Industrial Inquiry as corroboration for Keynes's first thesis since he himself was so heavily involved in its research and writing. But since Pollard cites the study without criticizing its methods or conclusions, the reader must assume he believed it to be a reliable source.

# 9 On the edge of the Great Depression

Keynes continues his efforts to gain political support for the radical policies in *Britain's Industrial Future*

For several years following the publication of BIF, Keynes continued to try to gather political support for his radical policy proposals using all of the means at his disposal, including speeches, newspaper and magazine articles, radio broadcasts, interaction with important government, business, and party officials, and membership on important government committees. When it turned out that these prodigious efforts in pursuit of his objective were ineffective, he turned his focus to the creation of a theoretical edifice he hoped would lead most economists and many important businessmen and politicians to move to his side of the debate. This project culminated with the publication of *The General Theory* in 1936.

In November 1929, the Chancellor of the Exchequer appointed a Committee on Finance and Industry under the chairmanship of a Scottish judge named Macmillan to propose policies to resolve Britain's economic problems. Keynes was one of a large number of committee members, as was Ernest Bevin of the Transport and General Workers Union. The Macmillan Committee met about 100 times; it issued its Report in May 1931, after the onset of the Great Slump. Though the financial market collapse in the USA was well underway at this point, it is not mentioned as a matter of importance in the record of the Committee hearings. This may be because Britain did not suffer from a financial crisis.

Donald Moggridge, the editor of Keynes's *Collected Writings*, commented that Keynes "dominated the proceedings of the Committee, both in examining witnesses and shaping [its] report" (CW 20, p. 38). The transcript of his own testimony before the committee occupies 270 pages of Volume 20 of the *Collected Writings*. We can only select a few points here to emphasize the consistency of his analysis as it appears in this record with the major themes he had been expressing for years.

In his testimony to the Committee, Keynes critically analyzed all of the main proposals – good and bad – for dealing with Britain's now almost decade-old economic malaise. He declared that his "own favorite remedy – the one to which I attach the greatest importance," was a program of public investment (CW 20, p. 126). Hazarding a guess that a permanent increase in investment would ultimately induce new imports equal to about a quarter of the spending on new investment, Keynes observed that "in order to increase the total investment by £100,000,000 you might have to increase the home investment by £125,000,000" (CW 20, p. 132). Home investment of £100,000,000 per year, "which is only 2.5 per cent of the national income, would cure nearly half of the existing unemployment" (i.e. decrease it from 12.3 percent in 1930 to perhaps 6 percent) (CW 20, p. 132). When you take account of the multiplier, he said, the program will substantially raise income and profits (and thus taxes) and will dramatically reduce spending on the "dole." With "the increase of employment you automatically get the resources for at least half of what you are doing out of the 'dole' and analogous resources" (CW 20, p. 131). Keynes believed there would be no significant long-run budget deficits generated by the rise in public investment.

His opponents, he said, contend "that it is in fact impracticable to find objects of an economic character which are, as it is sometimes expressed, sufficiently productive to justify the expense" (CW 20, p. 137). What they mean is that the projects to be undertaken will yield less than the going rate of interest. Suppose the interest rate is 5 percent and the projects are expected to yield only 4 percent. Should they be undertaken?

> [The] choice may be between investing at four per cent and not investing at all; between getting a four per cent return and getting nothing with the savings ... [R]ather than get less than five per cent on £100, [his opponents] would prefer that someone should lose the £100.
> (CW 20, p. 137)

The problem, Keynes said, comes from confusing sensible policy under the current dismal economic conditions with policy when the economy is in market-clearing equilibrium. Under the assumption of perpetual static full-employment equilibrium, net present value calculated at the current rate of interest may be an efficient criterion for the selection of investment projects – though this is not likely to be the case.[1] But under current conditions of stagnation:

> new investment yielding four per cent or in special cases three per cent would be naturally preferable to [continued high] unemployment and business losses. It is better that we should have a man employed in using plant which will produce an investment to yield four per cent in perpetuity than that the man and the plant should be unemployed. It is not a choice between investing at four per cent or five per cent; it is a choice between investing at four per cent and having 80 per cent of the [national] savings wasted and spilled on the ground.
> (CW 20, p. 138)

Keynes went on to argue that the current division of direct responsibility for large-scale investment programs among public and semi-public bodies gave the central government – the most effective level of government to coordinate public investment spending – responsibility for only about 20 per cent of public investment funds. To remedy this problem, *he suggested that the central government should be given control over all public investment funds.* It could then allocate these funds among the government bodies that do most of the public investment through loans at subsidized interest rates. That is, Britain needs:

> encouragement by the Treasury, and other Whitehall Departments, of expenditure by local authorities and public boards. I believe that this might be on a very large scale, as soon as one admits that it is legitimate to let them have money at a lower rate of interest than that which is fixed by conditions abroad ... [That is] to say to local authorities "If you will anticipate your expenditure, or produce anything that is at all reasonable we will let you have money out the Local Loan Funds below the standard rate of 5.25 per cent, or whatever it is now, going down to 4 per cent or even 3 per cent as a temporary expedient to the employed only so long as there is a serious difficulty in home investment."
>
> (CW 20, p. 144)

Keynes understood that many of the largest long-term public or semi-public capital projects under the state's influence were very interest elastic. This is one reason why he focused so strongly over the interwar period on the necessity of substantially lowering the long-term interest rate. Housing was perhaps the most important example. Each 1 percent decline in the interest rate paid on borrowed capital would significantly reduce the rent or mortgage payments needed to make the purchase of a house financially viable.

He reiterated here his argument that capital controls were needed to prevent capital flight from keeping domestic interest rates at a level far too high to sustain domestic capital accumulation at the rate consistent with full employment. Britain invested a very large percentage of its saving overseas, which forced the Bank of England to keep interest rates high enough to prevent a loss of gold. The combination of high interest rates and a low expected profit rate on new capital investment caused chronically high unemployment. Since capital controls would enable a substantial reduction in interest rates, they would be necessary to adequately reduce unemployment.[2]

Keynes also repeated here, in an especially strong form, something he said from time to time when offering policy advice to official government bodies. A large increase in public and semi-public investment to kick-start economic growth in the midst of high unemployment would eventually raise the profit rate on private capital investment. Once this program sufficiently increased economic activity and, presumably, substantially lowered excess capacity:

> then private enterprise will be revived. I believe you have first of all to do something to restore profits and then rely on private enterprise to carry the thing along ... [W]e must look to a bold Government programme to lift us out of the rut; and if this is done, if it has the result of restoring business profits, then the machine of private enterprise might enable the economic system to proceed under its own steam; and since I should look forward to that, I shall also look forward to being able gradually to diminish the amount of Government intervention.
>
> (CW 20, p. 147)

This statement is strange! Had Keynes changed his mind about the need for permanent economic planning? Keynes had stated over and over again, including in BIF, that a massive and *sustained* period of public investment under the control of a Board of National Investment would be necessary to achieve and maintain full employment. In May 1931, he called for a "comprehensive scheme of national planning" (CW 20, p. 495). In *The General Theory*, he would argue that sustained full employment would drive the profit rate to zero; sustained full employment based on private investment was therefore impossible. So, what is going on here?

I believe the solution to this puzzle lies in the fact that when Keynes was asked to advise official government bodies about the best policies to move the country out of the current slump, he would typically propose nothing stronger than the most aggressive intervention he thought the government would possibly support. This was usually a far weaker policy than he actually believed necessary to permanently solve Britain's economic problems in the interwar years. This approach to policy advice disappeared when Britain's entry into WWII seemed inevitable.

A five-person drafting committee was formed to work on the Committee Report over the winter of 1930–1931. Keynes was a very active member. By the government's design, the full Macmillan Committee could not possibly agree on appropriate government policy. The government had deliberately selected members of the Committee whose ideological positions were so diverse that they could never agree on anything of importance. This was the ideal situation from the government's perspective. A deadlocked Committee Report would leave the government free to choose whatever policies it wanted.

In the end, a fairly innocuous Report was prepared with four addendum items setting out the views of various contending members. One addendum was written by "a group centred around Keynes" (CW 20,

p. 280). The group of six included Ernest Bevin, the union leader. Keynes and Bevin agreed on most of the issues considered by the Committee.

The addendum argued that there were only three policies arguably capable of achieving a substantial reduction in unemployment: cutting wages and salaries; import tariffs and export subsidies; and state action or state subsidies to raise domestic investment. The signers believed that the first option – the one favored by the government and conservative economists – was likely to be disastrous: "the social costs of an attempt which failed would be incalculable" (CW 20, p. 308). They supported the second and third options. Keynes's support of the third option showed that he was, at least temporarily, willing to oppose free trade.

The section on "Schemes of Capital Development" began with a refutation of the government claim that public investment will cause private investment to decline – the standard "crowd-out" perspective referred to at the time as the "Treasury View." The crowding-out thesis is embedded in many macro models even today. The signers supported the counter-thesis sometimes referred to as the "crowd-in" thesis, which stated that when the economy has substantial excess capacity, a permanent stimulus to AD through government policy will *increase* private investment.

> But in general, provided the schemes are wisely chosen, we see no presumption in favour of the view that "official" investment need seriously compete or interfere with "unofficial" investment. Indeed, on the contrary, if "official" investment is successful in restoring the volume of output and of profits, this may help restore the business optimism which is a necessary condition of expansion.
>
> (CW 20 p. 302)

The signers offered some general observations about the process through which public investment should be dramatically expanded. First, there must be a central institution whose job is to design and direct the program as a whole, especially in light of the current fragmentation of authority over public investment. *They specifically supported the creation of a powerful Board of National Investment broadly similar to the one proposed by BIF.*

> It may be that we should develop an improved organisation for handling all matters of this kind. It would be outside our scope to pursue this subject in detail. But we think that efficiency and forethought might be much increased if a body were to be set up which might be designated the Board of National Investment, in the hands of which all matters relating to the deliberate guidance of schemes of long-term national investment would be concentrated. This Board might be entrusted with the duty of raising funds not only for the local authorities which now borrow through the Local Loans Fund but also for

other local authorities including municipalities, for the telephones, for the roads and for such further schemes of national development as those we have suggested above.

(CW 20, p. 307)

Second, the scope of important productive public investment projects is extremely large. For example:

> A considerable part of the larger towns and industrial centres of the country need rebuilding and replanning on a comprehensive scale ... Much of the industrial housing of the country is of an age when buildings of that character are, of necessity, only fit to be demolished. It seems an insanity to keep a large proportion of the building trade out of employment when this is the case. Some of our staple industries need to be refitted and replanned on modern lines, at the cost of a substantial capital expenditure. In several cases, there is much to be said for replanning an industry as a whole ... In cases of proved necessity, we should not be opposed to measures of compulsion, in conjunction with the provision of adequate and cheap finance.
>
> (CW 20, pp. 306–307)

Keynes was also a member of the government's Economic Advisory Council. On July 10, 1930, at Keynes's suggestion, the Prime Minister appointed a five-member subcommittee called the Committee of Economists with Keynes as chair. Though this committee, in the end, could not agree on either the cause or the solution to Britain's economic problems, Keynes's contributions are of interest. Publicly supported investment remained the key. Now having a firmer estimate of the value of the multiplier – his best guess at this time is about two (CW 20, p. 442) – Keynes was aggressive in arguing for a considerable state subsidy to investment programs not under direct government control. This is an important point to understand about Keynes's plan: the Board of National Investment was to be empowered to finance at below-market interest rates a substantial volume of non-public capital investment projects as long as they were congruent with the Board's overall objectives.

> In cases where it is clear that the projects would not be entered upon without a subsidy, it would be easy, generally speaking, to justify a subsidy amounting to fully one-third of the interest cost. Indeed, on certain assumptions as to the [value of the multiplier], a subsidy up to a half of the interest cost which would have to be paid in the open market would be justified. We think, therefore, that any projects, of which the prospective yield reaches 2.5 to 3 per cent, are worthy of assistance.
>
> (CW 20, p. 447)

Turning to projects directly under the auspices of either the central government or local governments, Keynes simply states that the case in their favor is now so widely accepted by economists that there is not much point in reviewing it.

> We should dwell in this remedy at greater length if it were not for the fact that the advantages of such schemes are now generally accepted, and that the obstacle to pushing this remedy still is to be found, not so much in theoretical views, as in the difficulty in finding suitable schemes to assist.
>
> (CW 20, pp. 447–448)

Keynes's draft report for the subcommittee was too optimistic about public investment for the conservatives on the Council and was rejected. Lionel Robbins, with the enthusiasm of the true believer in classical theory, and Hubert Henderson, Keynes's former ally in the Liberal Party who had recently shifted to the right, argued that wage cuts and balanced budgets, not a large public investment program, were the only viable approaches to resolving the crisis.[3]

In December 1930, Sir Oswald Mosley, a right-wing Member of Parliament (MP) and the founder of the British Union of Fascists, resigned from the Cabinet. He published a widely discussed "Manifesto" signed by 17 Labour MPs that called for national economic planning centered on public investment, arguing that this was the only viable solution to what he believed to be a politically explosive economic situation. He had been substantially influenced by Keynes's long-term support of a policy of this perspective.[4] Keynes reviewed the Manifesto in *The Nation and Athenaeum*. In the review, his language and his enthusiasm for a radical approach to national planning are obviously liberated from the substantive restrictions and muted tone he imposed on himself in the official government discussions and reports we have been reviewing. Keynes stated that he did not agree with every detail in the Manifesto:

> But I like the spirit which informs the document. A scheme of national economic planning to achieve a right, or at least a better, balance of our industries between the old and the new, between agriculture and manufacture, between home development and foreign investment; and wide executive powers to carry out the details of such a scheme. That is what it amounts to ... [The] manifesto offers us a starting point for thought and action.
>
> (CW 20, pp. 473–474)

The Manifesto will shock many readers of *The Nation and Athenaeum*, he said, "who have *laissez-faire* in their craniums ... But how anyone professing and calling himself a socialist can keep away from the manifesto is a more obscure matter" (CW 20, p. 475). Note the clear implication embedded in the following quotation that Keynes considers himself to be a socialist. The choice faced by Britain:

> will be ever more openly and obviously set between forcing a reduction of wages and a scheme of national planning. But, however this may be, looking further ahead I do not see what practical socialism can mean for our generation in England, unless it makes much of the manifesto its own – this peculiar British socialism, bred out of liberal humanitarianism, big-business psychology, and the tradition of public service.
>
> (CW 20, p. 475)

Finally, we consider an article Keynes published in March 1931 titled "Proposals for a Revenue Tariff." *It is Keynes's first public rejection of free trade*. Of course, in private correspondence and internal government documents he had been in support of a revenue tariff for some time. Moggridge notes that "as the recantation of an avowed free trader, it caused a sensation" (CW 9, p. 231). Its relevance for our purpose is that Keynes defended a tariff on the grounds that it would facilitate, under the restrictions of the existing gold standard, a program of vigorous domestic expansion. The stress on the budget and on "confidence" may reflect his desire to assuage the concerns of others that he did not himself share.

> I am of the opinion that a policy of expansion, though desirable, is not safe or practicable today, unless it is accompanied by other measures which would neutralise its dangers ... There is the burden on the trade balance, the burden on the budget, and the effect on [business and financial] confidence.
>
> (CW 9, p. 236)

Keynes proposed that the tariff rate be set such that it would generate between £50 and £75 million per year, enough to finance a very large program of public investment of the kind he had in mind.

In a follow-up piece, Keynes argued that the only permanent solution to Britain's economic problems would be a "comprehensive scheme of national planning."

> But if I look into the bottom of my own heart, the feeling which I find there is, rather, that a tariff is a crude departure from *laisser-faire* [sic], which we have to adopt because we have at present time no better weapon in our hands, but that it will be superseded in time, not by a return to *laisser-faire* [sic], but by some comprehensive scheme of national planning.
>
> (CW 20, p. 495)

The takeaway point from Keynes's activities in the opening years of the 1930s is that he remained committed to the radical economic policies described in detail in BIF.

## Keynes and "Liberal Socialism" (1931–1932)

In several essays written in these years, Keynes outlined his vision of liberal or democratic socialism. Though most of his energy was engaged in dealing with the global financial crisis in 1930–1932, he continued to push the radical policies called for in BIF. Here are three examples of his efforts in this regard.

In December 1931, Keynes delivered an address to the Society for Socialist Inquiry (which appeared in early 1932 in *The Political Quarterly*). Perhaps the most interesting aspect of this address is that it makes clear Keynes's sympathy for, comfort with, and allegiance to beliefs that he referred to as "Liberal Socialism." *This is clearly an address from one socialist to other socialists.*

> The real question is whether we are prepared to move out the nineteenth-century laissez-faire state into *an era of liberal socialism*, by which I mean a system where we can act as an organised community for common purposes and to promote social and economic justice, whilst respecting and protecting the individual – his freedom of choice, his faith, his mind and its expression, his enterprise and his property.
> (CW 21, p. 500, emphasis added)

The central message – an old theme for Keynes – was that the only sensible and effective way to move from the disastrous political economy of the present to an efficient and humane organization of economic life was through a thoughtful evolutionary transition toward a planned economy, one with a significant though clearly subsidiary role for markets and private enterprise in determining the dynamic path of the British economy. As always, he argued against a revolutionary path that would "stir up the embers of the class war" and destroy the economic and political foundations necessary for the construction of his ideal republic.

> For it will have to be on the basis of increased resources, not on the basis of poverty, that the grand experiment of the ideal republic will have to be made ... To be sufficiently deep-founded on the best intelligence and finest and strongest emotions of the community, to be able to keep up steam when things are going reasonably well; to thrive, not on the vapors of misery and discontent, but on the living energy of the passion for right construction and the right building up of a worthy society – that is the task.
> (CW 21, pp. 34–35)

He pointed to two important reasons to support evolutionary institutional and policy reform over a revolutionary strategy bound to be economically disastrous in the short run. The first is that, in the current era, the evolutionary reforms needed to restore prosperity in fact lead in the direction of the eventual socialist objective – a planned economy based on government control of the capital accumulation process and dedicated to social justice.

> I am convinced that those things which are urgently called for on practical grounds, such as the central control of investment and the distribution of income in such a way as to provide purchasing power for the enormous potential output of modern productive technique, will also tend to produce a better kind of society on ideal grounds.
> (CW 21, p. 36–37)

The second is that the economic payoff to society from unleashing the enormous potential productivity of today's economy, with its unused resources and its powerful technical and engineering knowledge, is simply too large to pass up. "For it may be capable of solving once for all the problem of poverty" (CW 21, p. 37). Thus, for Keynes, the evolution toward middle-way planning was also the best initial path toward the future goal of socialism as well.

In March 1932, with the general unemployment rate at 17 percent and investment in a state of collapse, Keynes delivered a radio lecture (later published) titled "The State and Industry," enthusiastically supporting government economic planning. Its main message was that state planning is a good idea whose time has come; it is the wave of the near future. Soviet Communism and Italian Fascism were merely two particular variants of the kind of change in economic organization that must take place in all countries to defeat the current forces of deflation and depression and unleash the great potential productivity available to them. The striking thing about this lecture is how comfortable Keynes is with the boldness of these experiments. He wants the British experiment in central planning to be equally ambitious, as long as it protects democracy, individual liberty, and a continued (though much more circumscribed) role for markets and the profit motive. As always, the term "Socialist" with a capital "S" refers to the Labour Party's commitment to Soviet-style quantitative planning with all productive property controlled by the state. The broadcast opened as follows:

> There is a new conception in the air today – a new conception of the possible functions of government ... It is called planning – state planning; something for which we had no accustomed English word for even five years ago. It is not [state] Socialism; it is not Communism. We can accept the desirability and even the necessity of *planning* without

being a Communist, a [state] Socialist or a Fascist. But whether it is going to prove possible to carry out *planning* in actual practice without a great change in the traditions and in the machinery of democratic government – that is the big question mark. It is perhaps *the* problem of problems which the post-war generation of young Englishmen, who will be in their prime of life over the next twenty years, have to solve.

(CW 21, p. 84, emphasis in original)

There are two forces driving state planning onto the British political agenda. The first is the example of those countries currently undertaking "magnificent experiments" with central planning.

> The Russian Five-Year Plan has assaulted and captured the imagination of the world. This dream is not yet a realized success – it is much too soon to say that – but it is not the preposterous failure, which many wise and experienced people expect it to be ...
>
> [L]et us not belittle these magnificent experiments or refuse to learn from them. For it is a remarkable and a significant thing that the two most extraordinary political movements of the modern age, approaching their task from opposite moral and emotional poles, should agree in this vital particular – *that state planning, that intelligence and deliberation at the centre must supersede the admired disorder of the 19th century.*
>
> (CW 20, pp. 85–86, emphasis added)

The second reason is that the "absolute failure in terms of their own potentialities" of the unplanned economies of England and the USA had established a *"prima facie* case for planning" (CW 21, p. 87).

The third reason is that central planning during the war was a huge success.

> For what are the economic events of the modern world which must most strike the apprehension of the dullest observer? The extraordinary capacity for the production of material wealth ... which we developed during the War; and the opposite picture today of starvation amidst plenty, our incredible inability to carry to our mouths the nourishment which we have produced with our hands. *For the War was the nearest thing we have ever had in this country to a planned regime.* The environment was unfavourable, the haste was excessive and hurried improvisations were inevitable. Yet it showed us the potentialities of modern technique to produce.
>
> (CW 21, p. 87, emphasis added)

Keynes called his listeners' attention to the crucial distinction between Soviet-style planning and the planning he envisioned. He supported central control of the "general organisation of resources" – of the level of aggregate economic activity, the allocation of resources across broad categories of competing uses, and the distribution of income – "as distinct from the *particular* problems of production and distribution which are the province of the individual business technician and engineer" (CW 21, p. 87, emphasis in original). Modern capitalism suffered from a chronic incapacity to actualize its potential capacity to produce. This failure was not just a problem of the slump; it was structural. To remedy this institutional incapacity, it would be necessary to bring in collective intelligence and central deliberation through planning. But we have to remedy this failure "without impairing the constructive energy of the individual mind, without hampering the liberty and the independence of the private person" (CW 21, p. 88).

> If the England of the coming generations can solve that problem – and my proud patriotic heart harbours a hope that our national qualities may be best of all suited to do it – we shall have contributed, I think, something more valuable to civilisation than the Bolshevist or the Fascist can; – though I do not overlook that each of these movements may be capable in its way of contributing something to the dignity of human nature which transcends the field and the scale of operation that I attributed to national planning however complete and however successful ... [S]tate planning ... differs from [state] Socialism and from Communism in that it does not seek to aggrandise the province of the state for its own sake. It does not aim at superseding the individual within the fields of operations appropriate to the individual, or of transforming the wage system, or of abolishing the profit motive. Its object is to take deliberate hold of the central controls and to govern them with deliberate foresight and thus modify and condition the environment within which the individual freely operates with and against other individuals.
>
> (CW 21, p. 88)

Keynes went on to list various examples of appropriate areas for centralized decision-making, including town planning, rural preservation, and "deliberate planning to influence the localisation of industry." The most important object of state planning is:

> the maintenance of the general level of industrial production and activity at the optimum level and ... the abolition of unemployment ... [This] will lead us to far more deliberate and more far-reaching policies of credit control, to a greater preoccupation with the appropriate

level of the interest rate, and in general to an attempt to control the rate at which new investment is encouraged and facilitated to take place ... [I]t is the failure of the unplanned industrial world ... which is predisposing many persons to consider without prejudice those far-reaching experimental projects of the most constructive minds of the post-war world which go, conveniently, by the name of planning.

(CW 21, p. 91)

Keynes ended his talk with a repetition of his standard political themes. There is no need to suffer a loss of individual liberty and initiative to enjoy the fruits of ambitious central planning. Totalitarianism could make the task of planning easier, but democratic planning will have the enthusiastic support that accompanies popular consent and will have greater and more disinterested talent available to it. As always, planning institutions should have "semi-autonomy" from democratic control, and "state planning by Public Corporations" will be the cornerstone of the planning system.

Moreover, it should be compatible with democratic and parliamentary government to introduce modern improvements and new organs of administration ... State planning, as I conceive it, would not be administered or supervised in detail by democratically elected bodies. The latter would be judges, not of the first, but of the final instance, reserve forces to effect a change when grave mistakes have been made. The day-to-day tasks of state planning would be carried out in the same sort of way and with the same kind of instruments of administration under a democratic government as they would under an autocratic government ... It may be that other countries will enjoy the rare opportunity of seeing three experiments carried on simultaneously, differing vastly on the surface yet each directed to the solution of the same essential problem, – the Five Year Plan in Russia; the Corporative State in Italy; and *state planning by Public Corporations responsible to a democracy in Great Britain.* And as lovers of our species, let us hope that they all will be successful.

(CW 21, p. 92, emphasis added)

In September 1932, Keynes published two important articles based on a talk at the Annual Conference of the Labour Party. Keep in mind that Keynes believed that his radical policy agenda could only be successfully implemented by an electoral alliance between the Liberal and Labour Parties, with Labour providing the bulk of the votes.

Keynes "warmly" applauded Labour's support for "the principle of setting up a National Investment Board," but argued it "did not go nearly far enough for me" (CW 21, p. 133). Capital controls and the huge size of capital assets held by public or semi-public bodies stressed here were, of course, persistent themes for Keynes. Note that Keynes updates his data on the size of public and semi-public investment.

> The real problems, as I see them, are concerned with the quantitative, rather than with the qualitative, control of new investment, and partly with securing that the amount of foreign lending should be appropriate to the circumstances. The resolution ... seems to overlook *the smallness of the part which purely private enterprise now plays, and is likely to play in the future*, in the direction of home investment ... Apart from the control of overseas loans, which certainly should not be left in the future to *laissez-faire*, ... the main issue is concerned with the regulation of the pace of that *predominant proportion of new investment at home which has already passed irrevocably out of the control of private enterprise and into the control of public and semi-public bodies* ... Thus £200,000,000 was invested through [local authorities and building societies] in 1930 compared with £30,000,000 in 1914. The above omits capital expenditure by the central government (including the Post Office) or by public boards such as the Central Electricity Board, the Port of London, the Metropolitan Water Board, the Agricultural Mortgage Corporation, and the component parts of what will be the London Traffic Authority, or by universities and hospitals and the like ... *Thus in the two years 1930 and 1931 the aggregate finance provided by building societies was appreciably greater than the ... aggregate of new capital for all purposes within the United Kingdom.* In short, *considered quantitatively private industrial investment is very far from being of the first importance.* What we need is a coordinated policy to determine the rate of aggregate investment by public and semi-public bodies, in which case we could safely leave industry to raise what funds it needs as and when it chooses.
>
> (CW 21, pp. 134–135, emphasis added)

That body would be the Board of National Investment. It would seek "the maintenance of equilibrium between the total flow of new investment on the one hand, and on the other hand the total resources available for investment ... and secondly a division of new lending between foreign and domestic borrowers" (CW 21, p. 136). Though the Board would have to concern itself with preventing dysfunctional price movements, and thus in times of inflation might have to lower investment, its main goal:

> would be to maintain the level of investment at a high enough rate to ensure the optimum level of employment. Without such an instrumentality we may be sure that the disastrous fluctuations will continue in the future as severely as in the past, and perhaps more severely.
>
> (CW 21, p. 137)

This warning is quite serious: the total unemployment rate in 1932 was 17 percent. The challenge for socialists like himself was quite clear. "The grappling with these central controls," he told the Convention, "is the rightly conceived socialism of the future" (CW 21, p. 137).

In May 1932, Harold Macmillan, who would later become Prime Minister in a Conservative government, circulated a policy paper advocating selective import protection, low interest rates, and an "Investment Development Board." Macmillan was considered a very liberal Conservative. Keynes sent him comments.

> My main feeling is that you are not nearly bold enough with your proposals for developing the investment functions of the state. You are trying it would seem to get your results by a sort of combination of private enterprise and subsidy ... But at the present time it would be extraordinarily difficult to bring about an adequate volume of investment even if one had the whole force of the state behind one. The greater part of investment is concerned with building, transport and public utilities, and the scope for private enterprise is in modern times somewhat limited.
> (CW 21, p. 109)

MacMillan wrote Keynes that he agreed with all his criticisms "in theory." But, he said:

> I am still trying the perhaps hopeless task of influencing the Government in the direction I want them to go, and, for this purpose, I have to conceal a certain amount and to preserve certain political tendencies! I am going to try to make some modification in the way you suggest, if I can do it without destroying the chance of anybody in my party reading and being influenced by my pamphlet.
> (CW 21, p. 111)

It is important to understand, as noted above, that this was precisely the dilemma Keynes himself confronted whenever he found himself in a situation in which the best outcome he could possibly hope for was to convince those around him to support moderate and perhaps temporary measures to increase public investment. It helps explain the occasional modesty of some of Keynes's own policy proposals to or testimony before various government commissions. He too sometimes seemed to "conceal a certain amount" in order to attempt to influence conservative politicians and civil servants to support moderate positive policy initiatives. In situations in which the best feasible outcome was moderate reform, Keynes at times supported moderate reform.

Keynes came to believe that the current government was too reactionary to be influenced by progressive argument. He stated this view in another letter to MacMillan.

The main point in my opinion is that we are now in the grip of reactionary forces, and however fair-spoken those in authority may be, they fully intend to take advantage of present circumstances to reverse a great deal of what they regard as semi-socialistic policy. They also conscientiously disbelieve in the kinds of schemes for planning, etc., which you and I favour. There is probably no practical sense in any efforts except those deliberately aimed at ousting them.

(CW 21, p. 127)

In early 1933, Keynes issued a major policy statement, both in Britain and in the USA, called "The Means to Prosperity." It provoked much discussion in both countries. Its primary purpose was to support "schemes of capital development at home as a means to restore prosperity" (CW 9, p. 339). The importance of both these articles, in my view, is that they combined the "magic" of the multiplier with Keynes's long-held belief that there was a huge number of large-scale public investment projects that it made economic sense to undertake. Keynes's use of the multiplier was always in support of reliance on public and semi-public investment to restore and sustain prosperity.[5] But in developing this analysis, Keynes was now armed with the formal multiplier theory that first appeared in Kahn's famous article in *The Economic Journal* in June 1931. It suggested that, for every new dollar of public investment, there would be an increase in output two or more times as large. The formalization of the multiplier also meant that he was closing in on the basic short-run model of income determination that would be a cornerstone of *The General Theory*.

After taking the reader through the potential "leakages" from the income stream following an injection of spending, Keynes estimated the value of the multiplier in Britain to be two (CW 9, p. 343), with the American multiplier "greater than two" (CW 9, p. 345).[6] Keynes assumed that it required "£150 of primary expenditure to put one man to work for a year," and that "Great Britain had the task of putting at least 1 million men back to work" (CW 9, p. 364). Keynes is clearly being conservative here because, in 1933, Britain had over 2.5 million people in insured unemployment alone. He thus estimated that "we should need an increased loan-expenditure *plus* an increased foreign balance amounting altogether to £150 million" (CW 9, p. 364, emphasis in original).

To calculate the effect of this level of spending on the government budget, he assumed that "the total benefit to the Exchequer of an additional loan-expenditure of £100 is at least £33 [reduced spending on the dole] plus £20 [increased taxes], or £53 altogether, i.e., a little more than a half of the loan-expenditure" (CW 9, p. 347). Since these projects will normally yield more than their cost in present-value terms and more than half the loan will be covered by reduced unemployment payments and increased taxes, they will actually lower government debt over time. Keynes believed that there was a vast reservoir of large-scale investment projects with positive net present values that could help move the economy back to full employment. Thus, there was no budgetary impediment to undertaking a major program of public investment.

> Take, for example, the proposal to spend £7 million on the new Cunarder [a large ocean liner]. I say that this will benefit the Exchequer by at least half this sum ... which vastly exceeds the minimum aid which is being asked of the exchequer. Or take the expenditure of £100 million on housing whether for rebuilding slums or under the auspices of a National Housing Board, this would benefit the budget by the vast total of some £50 million – a sum far exceeding any needful subsidy. If the mind of the reader boggles at this and he feels that it must be too good to be true, let him recur carefully to the argument which has led up to it.
> (CW 9, p. 348)

Since it is the depression itself that created the large budget deficits of the era, the argument that we should avoid large public investment programs because they will raise the deficit is tragically mistaken. "There is no possibility of balancing the budget except by increasing the national income, which is much the same thing as increasing employment" (CW 9, p. 347).

With the budget deficit problem disposed of, Keynes pressed home the urgency of large-scale public investment. His standard caveats are here. Bank credit must be "cheap and abundant." The long-term interest rate must be "low for all reasonably sound borrowers" (CW 9, p. 353). The foreign balance must be protected through capital controls from the deterioration that domestic expansion in a stagnant word economy would bring under laissez-faire. Finally, the task of domestic economic renewal would be easiest to accomplish if programs of public investment and easy money were undertaken worldwide, but since there is no chance of this taking place in the foreseeable future, Britain will have to go it alone. Thus, public investment is "the means to prosperity."

Keynes concluded the essay, as was his style, with the combination of an attractive policy solution and a dire warning to his powerful critics in and out of government. The warning is based on the fragility of financial systems loaded with debt in the face of deflation and falling incomes. Governments have tried the deadly combination of trying to protect the value of the pound through high interest rates and shrinking domestic deficit spending (or loan expenditure). If they fail now to adopt debt-financed, large-scale public investment accompanied by capital controls, the outcome will be catastrophic.

On the other hand, Great Britain has the other combination still untried – the policy of protecting the foreign balance and at the same time doing all in our power to stimulate loan-expenditure. I plead, therefore, for a trial of this untried combination in our domestic policy; and for the [upcoming] World Economic Conference an advocacy by our representatives of an expansion of international reserve money on the general lines proposed above. For we have reached a critical point ... Few of us doubt that we must, without much more delay, find an effective means to raise world prices; or *we must expect the progressive breakdown of the existing structure of contract and instruments of indebtedness*, accompanied by the utter discredit of orthodox leadership in finance and government, *with what ultimate outcome we cannot predict*.

(CW 9, p. 366, emphasis added)

Keynes went to the USA again, arriving on May 15, 1934, and leaving on June 8. He met with a large number of important American political and financial figures. On May 28, he had an hour-long meeting with President Roosevelt. Keynes apparently found the meeting "fascinating," while FDR "reported that he had 'a grand talk with Keynes and liked him immensely'" (CW 21, pp. 320–321).

Before leaving the USA, Keynes wrote an analysis of Roosevelt's policy problems and perspectives for both the *New York Times* and the *London Times*. He provided a quantitative analysis of the fiscal policy of the preceding year, one that is extremely important for our purposes. Stimulus to production and employment, he said, must depend chiefly on "the Government's [loan financed] emergency expenditure" (CW 21, p. 325). The specific programs mentioned are the Civil Works Administration and the Public Works Administration. Such spending had fluctuated between about $100 million and $400 million a month over the previous nine months. Each $100 million represented about 2.75 percent of monthly national income, according to Keynes. Thus, to raise such loan-financed spending from the lower figure to the higher represents an increase of a little over 8 percent of national income. Keynes believed that such a policy would "increase the national money income by 25 to 30 per cent" (CW 21, p. 326). By implication, he believed the applicable multiplier to be about 3.0–3.5. And he thought that fluctuations in US government spending and income over the past year have already confirmed his basic analytical framework. Keynes also insisted that it was a great mistake for the Roosevelt administration to cut back on public spending as significantly as it did.

Some five months ago I wrote that the relapse [in income] in the latter half of 1933 was the predictable consequence of the failure of the Administration to organise new loan expenditure ... on an adequate scale ... Fortunately the expenditures did increase, rising from less than $100,000,000 in the month preceding my letter to an average of $300,000,000 in the next four months. As I predicted the fruits of this have been enjoyed, and I estimate that there has been an improvement of something like 15 per cent in output, incomes and employment. This is an immense achievement in so short a time. But latterly, the expenditures have been declining and, once more as a predictable result, a recession of 3 per cent and perhaps 5 per cent is impending.

(CW 21, pp. 328–329)

In a *Redbook* piece in December 1934, Keynes is perhaps even more enthusiastic about the efficacy of public investment, raising his estimate of the American multiplier to a very – probably overly – optimistic level.

[F]or each man actually employed on the government scheme, three, or perhaps, four, additional men are employed in providing for his needs and for the needs of one another. In this way a given rate of government expenditure will give rise to four or five times as much employment as a crude calculation would suggest. Thus there would be some advantage even if the scheme itself were to yield but little revenue hereafter. If, however, it is even a moderately sound scheme capable of yielding (say) three per cent on its cost, the case for it is overwhelming.

(CW 21, p. 336)

In 1934 and especially 1935, Keynes was preoccupied with completing *The General Theory*.

## Notes

1 On the other hand, current prices are not an efficient guide to the investment decision, especially in depressed conditions. Future prices are the appropriate, though unknowable, guide.
2 "I should, however, like to say this, that I do very greatly doubt whether we shall ever be free in this country to return to unbridled laissez-faire in the matter of foreign lending" (CW 20, p. 147).
3 Henderson taught at Cambridge University, where he became an associate of Keynes. He was one of the group who set up and ran the Liberal Party Summer School starting in 1922. When a group headed by Keynes bought the influential *Nation and Athenaeum* magazine in 1923, Keynes persuaded Henderson to leave his job at Cambridge and become the editor of the magazine. Henderson was a significant contributor to BIF and coauthor with Keynes of the Liberal Party's 1929 campaign pamphlet "Can Lloyd George Do It?" However, as the global depression worsened in the early 1930s, he rejected the analysis and policy proposals of BIF, opposed Keynes's budget proposals, and shifted toward support of the conservative "Treasury View." He will reappear later in the book.

4 See also the Keynes-Mosley correspondence in CW 20 (pp. 312–315).
5 This would be the case in chapter 10 of *The General Theory*, where Keynes introduced the concept of the public investment multiplier.
6 Keynes wrote an article ("The Multiplier"; CW 21, pp. 171–178) a month later, extending this analysis.

# 10 Keynes on "insane" financial markets and the emergence of stagnation in the USA in the early 1930s

Keynes's theory of financial markets underwent a sea change after the end of the stock market boom in the USA in 1929 and the onset of the financial crisis that followed. The eventual outcome of this transformation was his theory of financial markets as unstable, "insane" "gambling casinos" presented in chapters 12, 13, 15, and 22 of *The General Theory* and in his defense of these ideas in the *Quarterly Journal of Economics* (hereafter QJE) in 1937, where he stressed their perverse influence on capital investment spending. This chapter provides an overview of his thinking about US financial markets in particular and global financial markets in general in the early 1930s. It also presents a few of Keynes's observations about the early onset of stagnation in the US economy and the deepening global depression during this period.

## America's "insane" financial markets and the global economic crisis

Keynes's two-volume *Treatise on Money* was written during the stock market boom in the USA in the late 1920s and published on December 1930 (CW 5 and 6, 1930), shortly after the US stock market entered the early stages of its collapse. The book contains interesting insights into Keynes's thinking about the character of modern financial markets at that time. In it, Keynes makes a first pass at explaining why financial asset prices are inevitably subject to bouts of volatility. As Schumpeter put it in his evaluation of Keynes's contributions to economics in 1946, there was now an "emphasis on expectations, upon the 'bearishness' in the downturn" that is not yet the theory of the "liquidity preference" to sell securities in the downturn in *The General Theory* (Schumpeter 1946, p. 508). In this sense, the *Treatise* anticipated Keynes's treatment of financial instability in *The General Theory*.

In the *Treatise*, Keynes described security-price cycles in terms of the balance between the optimistic expectations of "bulls" and the pessimistic expectations of "bears." His theory of financial market cycles emphasizes that the *endogeneity of security-price expectations* leads to the high volatility of stock and bond changes.

We typically enter a financial boom, he said, when economic conditions are improving rapidly and most investors have confident expectations that this will continue. In Keynes's words, in the upswing there is a "'bull' market with a consensus of opinion" (CW 5, p. 226). But as security prices continue to rise, some cautious investors will come to expect that the bull market has run its course, inducing them to sell some risky long-term securities and hold the receipts as "money" –savings accounts and Treasury bills. Keynes argued:

> as soon as the price of securities have risen high enough, relatively to the short-term rate of interest, to occasion a difference of opinion as to the prospects, a "bear" position will develop, and some people will begin to increase their savings deposits ... Thus, in proportion as the prevailing opinion comes to seem unreasonable to more cautious people, the "other view" will tend to develop, with the result of an increase in the "bear" position.
>
> (CW 21, p. 229)

If underlying economic conditions deteriorate, so that performance disappoints the expectations of many investors, a downturn in security prices will begin. We now have a "'bear' market with a division of opinion" (CW 21, p. 226). Finally, when pessimistic expectations spread widely, we enter a '"bear' market with a consensus of opinion" (CW 21, p. 226). Now everyone wants to sell long-term securities and hold the money they receive in the form of cash or short-term financial assets that cannot suffer a nominal loss of value. In terms used in *The General Theory*, "liquidity preference" has spiked. Security prices may fall rapidly. Thus, to a limited extent, the *Treatise* anticipated the emphasis on the potential for extreme financial instability in *The General Theory*.

However, the theory of security-price volatility in the *Treatise* had a major flaw that would be corrected in *The General Theory*. It assumed that financial cycles take place around fixed equilibrium income and output levels. This limits the potential amplitude of stock- and bond-price fluctuations. You cannot get a near-total collapse in stock prices such as occurred in the USA in the early 1930s in the fixed-equilibrium model of the *Treatise*. But you can, as we will see, in *The General Theory*, where changes in expectations will cause changes in security prices, equilibrium income, and corporate profits that lead to further changes in security expectations, and so on.

Keynes's seeming lack of serious attention to financial-market instability as a potential threat to US economic progress in the 1920s ended with the collapse of the US stock market in the fall of 1929. At the end of May 1931,

Keynes left on his first visit to America since 1917. This trip would complete a process that radically changed his opinion about the character of US financial markets and about the prospects for a revival of US economic growth.

Keynes returned from the USA on July 18, 1931, with the American economy on a downhill slide, US security prices in an uneven process of collapse, the banking system in a state of crisis, and the unemployment rate skyrocketing – it rose from 4 percent in 1929 to 15 percent in 1931 on its way to a 1933 peak of 25 percent. Meanwhile, the rate of unemployment among all workers in Britain doubled between 1929 and 1931, rising from 8.0 to 16.4 percent. It peaked at 17.0 percent in 1932 (Garside 1990, p. 5).[1]

By the end of his trip, Keynes had come to believe that America was in a catastrophic condition. All of his previous hopes for a US-led global recovery had evaporated. His belief that British prosperity could only be restored by a revolutionary change in her economic system such as the one described in BIF was strongly reinforced, as was his belief that Britain needed much greater independence from the global economy – what he would refer to in 1933 as greater "national self-sufficiency."

Rather than looking at Keynes's comments in the early 1930s in chronological order, we will first present excerpts from his statements about the destructive character of the process of price deflation that was currently greatly exacerbating the ongoing global economic crisis. We will then examine the stark transformation that took place in Keynes's understanding of the nature and condition of US financial markets. After explaining why Keynes came to believe, for the first time, that the US had now entered a period of secular stagnation, we end with a few of his observations concerning the dire situation in the global economy.

Keynes's views in the early 1930s might be summarized as follows: the UK and now perhaps the USA and much of the world economy had entered an era of long-term or secular economic stagnation. He argued that the rate of profit on capital investment experienced a significant decline in the vigorous capital spending boom in the USA and elsewhere by the end of the late 1920s that was now exacerbated by the sharp rise in excess capacity associated with the onset of depression. In *The General Theory*, he described the situation as follows:

> New investment during the previous five years [1924–1929] had been, indeed, on so enormous a scale in the aggregate that the prospective yield on further additions was, coolly considered, falling rapidly. Correct foresight would have brought down the marginal efficiency of capital [or expected profit rate on new capital goods] to an unprecedentedly low figure; so that the "boom" could not have continued on a sound basis except with a very low long-term rate of interest.
>
> (CW 7, p. 323)

This fall in the incentive to invest was reinforced by the outbreak of financial crises in America and elsewhere – though not in Britain. The financial crisis was the result of a number of factors. The main problem was massive overborrowing that led to weakening balance sheets in both financial and nonfinancial corporations. In the USA, there was excessive borrowing in agriculture, in real estate, in residential and business construction, and for stock and bond market speculation. A large volume of foreign funds had flooded into New York City to get in on the great financial market boom there, which ratcheted up the likelihood that a financial crisis originating in the USA would quickly spread around the globe. This left the US economy in a state of extreme financially fragility. Governments in Europe were also heavily overindebted. Britain's staggering war debt was mostly domestically held, but there were massive cross-border loans resulting from war finance and the reparations imposed on the losers of the war by the winners in the Treaty of Versailles. The entire global financial system had become incredibly fragile.

By the early 1930s, balance sheets in real-sector and financial firms in the USA and elsewhere showed that the value of assets was either not much higher than the value of liabilities or, in many cases, even lower than the value of liabilities, so that anything that caused interest rates to rise (and bond prices to fall) or the value of the real or financial assets used as collateral for loans to fall could trigger a financial crisis capable of spreading across countries through highly integrated national financial markets. The "Great Crash" in US securities markets that began in late 1929 provided the trigger. It created falling financial security prices, rising interest rates – especially real or deflation-adjusted interest rates – and a collapse in the supply of credit in the face of a wave of margin calls, defaults, and bankruptcies. As output and income began to decline, deflation spread to the real sector – profit rates and investment spending plummeted and unemployment exploded. The real-sector collapse exacerbated the financial crisis and vice versa in a kind of economic dance of death. Interconnected international financial and real-sector markets spread the devastation almost everywhere. A massive deflation of goods and financial market prices spread rapidly around the world, threatening to destroy national economies.

The global economy had thus entered a disastrous downward disequilibrium process that demonstrated that Keynes's fear of the impact of deflation in a fragile "regime of money contract" was well-founded. But even Keynes was shocked to see how quickly the destructive self-reinforcing dynamics of the global crisis were proceeding.

Keynes gave two lectures at the New School for Social Research in New York in June, where he stressed the urgent need to first stop the current deflationary spiral, then reflate the global economy. He argued, as he had before, that deflation was an economically, politically, and socially dangerous process, one that violated basic norms of social justice.

Deflation was dangerous in part because, in the UK at least, "the social resistance to a drastic downward readjustment of salaries and wages [will] be an ugly and dangerous thing." Keynes referred to the conventional belief that wage deflation would "present comparatively little difficulty in a country such as the United States where economic rigidity has not yet set in." He disagreed with this proposition: "I find it difficult to believe this" (CW 20, p. 545).[2] His remark here is prescient in that social and economic conflict did become widespread in the USA in the mid-1930s. The emergence of a militant industrial union movement was but one dimension of the struggle. The rise of communist, fascist, socialist, and various other forms of political rebellions accompanied the insurgent union movement.

Keynes had long argued that deflation is particularly dangerous in a fragile "regime of money contract" because, as prices fall, "we increase proportionately the burden of monetary indebtedness" (CW 20, p. 545). He focused on the condition of balance sheets in a globally integrated financial system as a crucial indicator of the potential dangers caused by a period of serious deflation. In a general deflation, the value of the collateral relied on by lenders evaporates, threatening both lender and borrower with default. Keynes said that if this deflationary disequilibrium process proceeds far enough in a heavily indebted environment, it can become a threat to the entire financial system and indeed the entire economic and social order.

> For the burden of monetary indebtedness in the world is already so heavy that any material addition would render it intolerable. The burden takes different forms in different countries. In my own country it is the national debt for the purposes of War which bulks largest. In Germany it is the weight of reparation payments fixed in terms of money. For creditor and debtor countries there is the risk … of general default. In the United States the main problem would be, I suppose, the mortgages of farmers and loans on real estate generally.
>
> (CW 20, p. 546)

> The truth is that the financial structure of the United States is no more able than the rest of the world to support so terrific a change in the value of money. The vast growth of bank deposits and bonded indebtedness in that country interposes a money contract between the real asset on the one hand and the ultimate owner of wealth on the other. A depreciation of the money value of the real asset, sufficient to cause [bank safety] margins to run off, necessarily tends to burst up the whole structure of money contract, particularly those short-term contracts represented by bank deposits.
>
> (CW 20, p. 571)

In a letter written from the USA to his friend Hubert Henderson in June 1931, Keynes expressed shock at the extreme vulnerability of the US banking system. The crash in stock and bond prices after late 1929 exposed securities markets as speculative gambling casinos whose instability contributed to the collapse of capital investment. But Keynes had not fully appreciated before his trip to America the degree of rot that existed in the heart of America's financial markets – its banks. "I had most underestimated before I came ... the position of many banks in the country" (CW 20, p. 556). It was not just securities markets, but the entire financial system that was on the verge of destruction.[3] The threat of a financial collapse in the USA was a threat to the global financial system. It is not surprising, therefore, that Keynes went on to argue in *The General Theory* that financial markets were the Achilles' heel of modern capitalism.

US banks had lent heavily to farmers, to land speculators, for residential and commercial real estate and construction, to financial market speculators – and to each other. They had significant investments in bonds that had collapsed in value and had borrowed heavily from their depositors, including those who lived outside the USA. The ongoing deflation in so many real and financial markets had left the balance sheets of many banks in near-disastrous condition.

A large number of banks had recently failed and thousands of others were in a perilously fragile condition. Keynes observed:

> there is great unrest amongst depositors. There is a possibility at any moment of bank runs breaking out in different parts of the country, similar to what was lately experienced in Chicago. The consequence is that depositors not infrequently take their money out in cash and keep it in a safe deposit box ... This means that the banks in their turn are extraordinarily nervous, even those that are perfectly solvent, since they never know when they may have to support a run from their depositors. Accordingly *they have an absolute mania for liquidity*. They put pressure on their customers to repay loans, since loans and advances are non-liquid in an emergency. Generally speaking, they turn all the assets they can into a fairly liquid form and in some cases keep an abnormally large amount of till money. As long as this mentality exists on the part of depositors and banks, and it is obvious that in the circumstances it is entirely intelligible, since many banks are in fact not safe, whilst the members of the general public cannot tell which the dangerous ones are, it overshadows the whole situation[4] ... It is the weakness of the banking system all over the country which primarily stands in the way of the usual remedy, cheap and abundant credit, failing to take effect. It will be difficult to make much progress until there is a challenge to this mentality.
>
> (CW 20, pp. 556–557, emphasis added)

Note Keynes's emphasis on the "absolute mania for liquidity" – the intense pressure to trade every kind of marketable asset, real or financial, to get the cash needed to pay debts and to avoid additional capital loss. This mania found its reflection in the intense focus on "liquidity preference" as a behavior toward risk in the relevant chapters on financial markets in *The General Theory*.

Keynes focused on the fact that the condition of balance sheets was a major cause of the economic chaos of the era. For Keynes, *balance sheets matter*! I emphasize this because, for reasons that are not clear to me, Keynes discussed but did not adequately stress the centrality of balance sheet conditions in his analysis of the crisis tendencies of modern capitalism in *The General Theory*, though he does refer to the importance of balance sheets in his analysis of disequilibrium dynamics in chapters 19 and 22. This lack of adequate emphasis may have led most modern "Keynesian" economists to assume that Minsky added this dimension to Keynes's analysis of the destructive dynamics of capitalist economies. Nothing could be further from the truth.

Another serious problem was that long-term interest rates in the USA were very high just when the actual and the expected rates of profit on capital investment had been dramatically reduced. "In the light of past experience, the rate of interest in the U.S. is, it seems to me, absurdly, incredibly high – sufficient by itself to explain the slump in which we are labouring" (CW 20, p. 552). Keynes then addressed the question of what the effect on output and employment might be if the interest rate were to be substantially reduced. His answer was that low interest rates alone could not increase industrial capital investment in such depressed conditions. But this was not a devastating problem because, as Keynes said over and over again, manufacturing investment is not large relative to other kinds of investment such as in infrastructure, real estate, and public utilities: "Manufacturing enterprise [alone] is never capable of absorbing any large proportion of current saving" (CW 20, p. 553). But low interest rates would help stimulate investment in buildings, transport, and public utilities, the kind of investments that he believed should be controlled by public and semi-public entities.

Keynes returned to these themes in a lecture on July 1, 1931. He addressed the question of why long-term interest rates did not fall even though the Fed had substantially cut short-term rates. Adjusted for deflation and for increased risk as reflected in bond ratings, long-term interest rates had risen dramatically – *the opposite of what classical theory (and Modern Keynesian theory) predicted would happen when unemployment was high*. Keynes tells us that the "morbid psychology" of financial institutions is a big part of the problem. They are caught in a situation in which the deflationary process has caused their net worth to evaporate to the point where they are forced to sell all risky assets. This pushes interest rates up and bond prices down, which makes the situation even more dangerous.

There is a certain point where almost everybody in charge of funds reaches the stage of what I call "abnormal psychology." In an ordinary way, any kind of financial institution has a certain cushion of some kind, reserves and margins, and is prepared to run reasonable risks, prepared to be sensible on the evidence, but when these margins run down to a certain point they get into a state of mind where they are not prepared to run ... any risk at all, because they have got to the end of their margins. If they would run any risk at all, and it was to go wrong, they would be in a horrid situation, and ... they get into *a state of mind* where they won't run [even] a sound risk. That *morbid psychology*, though quite intelligible and natural, is a tremendous obstacle to a right development of affairs when it exists. There is an element of that morbid psychology present today; there are financial institutions and individuals who want to safeguard against any possible future loss, and are therefore unwilling to run sound risks.

(CW 20, p. 537, emphasis added)

Keynes also learned a great deal about the "abnormal psychology" of financial market investors while in America. He mentioned that he discussed the state of the stock market with

all sorts of people, but found no-one who even thought their opinion [about the future path of stock prices] was worth two-pence. When the elements of bluff and skilled market-manipulation and mass psychology and pure chance are added to the intrinsic difficulties of forecasting the courses of the credit cycle itself, the case is hopeless.

(CW 20, p. 586)

This discovery had a profound effect on Keynes's evolving theory of "insane" financial markets. In the language of chapter 12 of *The General Theory*, this "hopeless" feeling will be described as a complete loss of "*confidence*" by investors in their ability to generate useful forecasts of future stock-price movements to guide their behavior in the market. In chapter 12, Keynes will argue that such a loss of "confidence" by investors will lead to extreme volatility in security prices, a condition he refers to as "abnormal times."

A conventional valuation [of security prices] which is established as the outcome of the mass psychology of a large number of [unavoidably] ignorant individuals is likely to change violently as the result of a sudden fluctuation of opinion ... since there will be no strong roots of conviction to hold it steady.

(CW 7, p. 154)

Many investors were not willing to buy or hold long-term securities under these conditions and others bought or sold securities as their optimism about future prices rose and fell in cycles.

Keynes began a lecture in Germany in January 1932 with an acknowledgment that the most immediate threat to the global economy was now a financial crisis, not the industrial slump he had pointed to only a year earlier.

> The immediate problem for which the world needs a solution today is essentially different from the problem a year ago. Then it was a question of how we could lift ourselves out of the acute slump into which we had fallen and raise the volume of production and employment back towards a normal level. But today the primary problem is how to avoid a far-reaching financial crisis ... *Can we prevent an almost complete collapse of the financial structure of modern capitalism?* ... [N]o one is likely to dispute that the avoidance of financial collapse, rather than the stimulation of industrial activity is not the front-rank problem.
> (CW 21, p. 39, emphasis added)

The world was now witnessing one of the greatest deflations in the price of real and financial assets in the modern era. As early as May 1930, Keynes had written: "Apart from the [immediate post-WWI] slump of 1921, one can go back seventy years without finding anything equal to it" (CW 20, p. 346). The average annual rate of deflation in the US consumer price index from December 1929 to June 1933 was 8.3 percent. In the quotation immediately below (from January 1932), note again that Keynes believed that Britain was probably the only major nation not involved in the financial panic because it did not have a casino financial system.

> [T]he immediate causes of the financial panic [are found in] a catastrophic fall in the money value not only of commodities but of practically every kind of asset – a fall which has proceeded to a point at which the assets, held against money debts of every kind including bank deposits, no longer have a realizable value in money equal to the amount of the debt. The "margins" as we call them, upon which confidence in the maintenance of which the debt and credit structure of the modern world depends, have "run off." The assets of banks in very many countries – *perhaps in all countries with the probable exception of Great Britain* – are no longer equal, conservatively valued, to their liabilities to their depositors. Debtors of all kinds no longer have assets equal in value to the fixed money charges for which they have made themselves liable. Few governments still have revenues equal to the fixed money charges for which they have made themselves liable.
> (CW 21, p. 39, emphasis added)

Keynes went on to explain yet again how the outbreak of crisis in a financially fragile system with precarious balance sheets can trigger destructive disequilibrium dynamics. Note his stress on the "competitive panic" to get liquid. In *The General Theory*, Keynes observed that in the USA in 1932 "there was a financial crisis or crises of liquidation, when scarcely anyone could be induced to part with holdings of money on any reasonable terms" (CW 7, pp. 207–208).

> Moreover, a collapse of this kind feeds on itself. We are now in the phase where the risk of carrying assets with borrowed money is so great that there is a competitive panic to get liquid. And each individual who succeeds in getting more liquid forces down the price of assets in the process of getting liquid, with the result that the margins of other individuals are impaired and their courage undermined. And so the process continues. It is, perhaps, in the US that it has proceeded to the most incredible lengths. But that country only offers an example, extreme owing to the psychology of its people, of a state of affairs which exists in some degree almost everywhere.
>
> (CW 21, p. 40)

The destructive disequilibrium dynamics also involved national governments; it induced them to adopt beggar-thy-neighbor trade policies. The gold standard made the situation worse. Keynes, of course, supported managed trade and capital controls to minimize these problems.

> The competitive struggle for liquidity has now extended beyond individuals and institutions to nations and to governments, each of which tries to make its international balance sheet more liquid by restricting imports and stimulating exports by every possible means, the success of each one in this direction meaning the defeat of someone else. Moreover every country tries to stop capital development within its own borders for fear of the effect on its international balance. Yet it will be successful in its object only in so far as its progress towards negation is greater than that of its neighbours.
>
> (CW 21, p. 40)

In an article published in *The Economic Journal* in September 1932, Keynes unleased a ferocious attack in the strongest possible language on the structure and performance of US financial markets. He argued they were short-term-oriented, speculative, "insane gambling" casinos subject to extreme instability, and that they were causing economic devastation around the world. This is the Schumpeterian "pre-analytic vision" that inspired Keynes's analysis of US financial markets in *The General Theory*. He argued that US financial markets were:

dominated by *insane gambling* to get in at the bottom, just as they were dominated in the boom by insane gambling to get out at the top. If one is offered $20 for the price of $10, it may be foolish to refuse; but it may not seem so, if the $20 is on offer for $8 a week later. Yet positions of this kind – games of musical chairs in which all the players but one will fail to get a seat – which are not based, and do not even pretend to be based, on intrinsic values and long views, change suddenly ... I do not so much refer to the fact, though it is truly remarkable, that the paper value of all the railways and public utilities, *after having fallen to one tenth of what it had been two years previously*, has then proceeded to double itself within five weeks. For this is no more than a vivid illustration of *the disadvantages of running a country's development and enterprise as a bye-product of a casino*.

(CW 21, pp. 120–21, emphasis added)

This language used here – about games of "musical chairs" and the "disadvantages of running a country's development and enterprise as a bye-product of a casino" – reappeared in chapter 12's analysis of the instability of stock market prices and the destructive effects of this instability on capital investment. In chapter 12, Keynes concluded:

Speculators may do no harm as bubbles on a steady stream of enterprise. But the position is serious when enterprise becomes the bubble on a whirlwind of speculation. When the capital development of a country becomes a by-product of the activities of a casino, the job is likely to be ill-done.

(CW 7, p. 159)

## Stagnation seeps into the US economy

Keynes's overall assessment of economic conditions and prospects in the early 1930s was bleak. "[I]t would not surprise me to see a closing of stock exchanges in almost all countries and an almost universal moratorium in the repayment of existing debts" (CW 21, p. 40). The only piece of really good news was that on September 21, 1931, Britain abandoned the gold standard.

Prior to the "Great Crash" in US financial markets, Keynes believed that the US economy was not infected by the secular stagnation that had set in in Britain. By the early 1930s, he had become disabused of this belief. In February 1931, in a lecture to the Royal Institution, Keynes reminded his audience that innovations had played a large role in creating the boom of the late 1920s in the USA, but that this source of the demand for capital investment had, at least temporarily, dried up.

Until recently, new inventions such as the motor car and the motor lorry and the new roads which they require, new cinema developments, and wireless instruments, have played a big part in maintaining prosperity, but there seems at the moment a lull in new inventions,
(CW 20, p. 480)

On the way home from his visit to the USA, Keynes prepared a memorandum for the British government on economic conditions in the USA in mid-1931. For our purposes, the most interesting conclusion of the report was his belief that the USA had apparently entered a state of economic stagnation. He offered numerous reasons, in addition to the disasters in the financial system, as to why the US economy was now "stuck in a rut" just like the British economy.

The "population is no longer increasing rapidly" (CW 20, p. 573). The USA had joined Britain in the list of countries with rapidly slowing rates of population growth; for Keynes, this was one of the key conditioning factors for long-term stagnation.

Just as was the case in Britain, there appeared to be no system-transforming innovations on the horizon in the USA. There "is a marked absence of new invention, and it may be necessary, again, for a very great fall in the rate of interest before enough new techniques based on existing knowledge will be brought within the payable zone" (CW 20, p. 574).

Excess capacity in industry is so high it constitutes a powerful impediment to increased capital investment. "In the leading manufacturing industries, such as steel, motors and many others, it is certain that no new plant will be required for a long time to come" (CW 20, p. 573).

"There is a good deal of renewal and reconstruction which the railways might do. But the great falling off in their revenues, more severe than in Great Britain, has broken their spirit and destroyed their credit" (CW 20, p. 573).

There is a great need to construct adequate housing for "the common man." Unfortunately, "with his present reduced earning power he cannot pay a higher rent" (CW 20, p. 574).

The "slump is primarily a slump in construction ... It is difficult to see how there can be a real recovery without renewed construction enterprise on a large scale" (CW 20, p. 572). But "the opportunities to buy existing properties at bargain prices must stand in the way of new building" (CW 20, pp. 572–573). The large excess supply of buildings on the market played a role similar to that of excess capacity in manufacturing, stifling new investment.

An index of building activity was about 40 percent higher in 1928 than it had been in 1923–1925, but it experienced a severe collapse after 1928, falling to a level more than 20 percent below 1923–1925 by the end of 1930.

In a comment that prefigured his theory of business cycles in *The General Theory*, Keynes observed that builders who continued to borrow in the 1927–1929 boom were ready "to neglect the rate of interest and to agree to pay [interest] rates which, cautious calculation should have shown, could not be earned by the enterprise" because housing was overbuilt, the population was no longer growing rapidly, and "the cream had been taken by now off most of the new construction business." He said that the "rate of interest may have to fall a tremendous way before it will pay on a cool calculation to repeat the enterprise of 1927–29" (CW 20, p. 573). However, "just when it is so important to bring about a really drastic reduction in the long-term rate of interest, the extreme nervousness of lenders and their recent unhappy experiences conspire to bring the rate up" (CW 20, pp. 573–574).

"There are severe limitations on the possibilities of new construction expenditures by public authorities, though very large expenditures on roads are still proceeding" (CW 20, p. 574). Keynes said that the Roosevelt administration was committed to large expenditures on new construction in principle, but "the President told me that he had just gone over the figures again, that they had already shot their bolt, and there was not above $150m worth of projects still to be done" (CW 20, p. 575). Keynes concluded that "an adequate recovery is really out of the question pending the elapse of time and a great fall in the long-term rate of interest" (CW 20, p. 575).

Keynes also observed that US labor markets had lost some of the flexibility he had previously attributed to them. US nominal wages in industry were not falling rapidly in the face of shockingly high unemployment as assumed in classical theory, but rather had become relatively stable. In "large-scale industry ... my conclusion is that [nominal] hourly wage rates have not been affected very much more than in [rigid] England," falling from 1929 to mid-1931 by some 3–4 percent (CW 20, p. 576). (Wages in farming and small business had declined much further.) Keynes believed that this was a good thing because high wages help sustain AD in the face of rising unemployment, but they blocked a major disequilibrium process – falling real wages – portrayed in the orthodoxy of the time as a cure for high unemployment. What he failed to note here, but would emphasize in *The General Theory*, was that since prices were falling by as much as or more than nominal wages, real industrial wages in the USA were not falling at all. He used this "fact" in chapters 2 and 19 of *The General Theory* to attack the classical argument that when unemployment was temporarily high, falling nominal wages would automatically lead to falling real wages, which in turn would restore full employment. If prices fall by as much as or more than nominal wages, the classical theory of the labor market falls apart, but Keynes's theory of wage determination is supported.

He also argued, against his previous assumption, that high unemployment would indeed cause social unrest in the USA, just as in Britain. The difference was that in the USA "it is not so much a question of strikes and lockouts as of direct social disorder, looting and other forms of lawlessness in that lawless country," a reaction strengthened by the fact that "there is no organized relief to the unemployed" (CW 20, p. 579).

## The future looks dismal

Keynes acknowledged that his trip to the USA had left him much more pessimistic about the future than he had been when he left Britain. His long-held belief that only radical change in the political economy of Britain could prevent economic disaster was strongly reinforced by this trip.

> Before I went to the United States I was disposed to hold with some confidence that the first impetus to recovery would have to come from America. I held this view so firmly that it was some time before I even questioned it. But eventually it was put to me point-blank in discussion that perhaps the opposite was true. And in the end I began to wonder whether this might be the more probable opinion.
> (CW 20, p. 586)

Meanwhile, government economic policy in Britain had become even more deflationary. Ramsay MacDonald, a Labour Party member who served as Labour Prime Minister in 1924 and in 1929–1931, became Prime Minister of a National Unity Government from 1931–1935. He was committed to a priority of savage budget-cutting to reduce the government deficit and to a defense of the exchange rate of the pound. As a result, MacDonald was expelled from the Labour Party. Keynes wrote to his mother in August 1931: "One's hopes were always precarious and now they have disappeared. The country has been stampeded into an attempt to make this deflation effective, and heaven knows how it will all end" (CW 20, p. 596).

Keynes's mood was equally somber when he addressed a group of MPs in September 1932. He attacked the draconian budget proposed by the MacDonald government, arguing both that it was deflationary and that it violated tenets of social justice.

Keynes said that the MacDonald "budget will increase the number of unemployed by more than 10 per cent by Christmas" (CW 20, p. 609). He proposed instead a large increase in debt-financed public investment projects that were economically and socially desirable – "things which have some utility such as education, public health and public works" (CW 20, p. 608). The following quotations are taken from the notes Keynes made for this speech.

The budget fails on every test. In my opinion the Govt's programme is one of the most wrong and foolish which Parliament has deliberately perpetrated in my lifetime. I should like to say a word first of all on social justice. Can barely trust myself to speak. The attacks on the school-teachers seem to be a most foul iniquity. The well-to-do suffer 3 or 4 per cent, the schoolteachers 15 ... Cutting schoolteachers' salaries will not help us capture lost markets.

(CW 20, pp. 608–609)

He was extremely pessimistic about the future.

I speak from a full heart. The course of policy pursued so far has reduced us to a point of humiliation one could not have conceived. During the last 12 years I have had very little influence, if any, on policy. But in the role of a Cassandra, I have had considerable success as a prophet. I declare to you, and I will stake my reputation on it, that we have been making in the last few weeks as dreadful errors of policy as deluded statesmen have ever been guilty of.

(CW 20, p. 611)

One effect of this qualitative decline in economic prospects was that Keynes was now more confident than ever that even after the demise of the gold standard in Britain, cheap and abundant credit by itself could not restore prosperity. In early 1932, Keynes wrote: "I am not confident, however, that on this occasion the cheap money phase will be sufficient by itself to bring about an adequate recovery of new investment" (CW 21, p. 60). For this reason, "there will be no means of escape from prolonged and perhaps interminable depression except by direct state intervention to promote and subsidise new investment" in the context of greater autonomy from the avalanche of destructive forces now crushing the global economy (CW 21, p. 60).

## Notes

1 There were two different ways that the unemployment rate was calculated in this era. One dealt with "insured" workers covered by Britain's unemployment insurance program. The other used "total unemployed." The rate of unemployment among insured workers was always higher than the rate of total unemployment, as the hardest-hit industries were those most involved in the highly unionized export sectors. For example, the insured unemployment rate was 10.4 percent in 1929 and 21.3 percent in 1931.
2 In the 1920s, Keynes had argued that while Britain's economy *was* rigid and inflexible, America's economy did not suffer from this problem.
3 Of course, the two systems were intertwined since banks had lent enormous sums of money for financial market speculation in the late 1920s on margin.

Any serious price decline would trigger margin calls that would lead to more selling – and so on.
4 This situation, in which no one knows which banks are safe and which are not, and therefore investors, including other banks, pull all liquid funds out of the banking system, is reminiscent of the financial collapse in 2008–2009. Since no bank knew the value of the complex mortgage-based derivatives held by other banks during the crisis, the interbank loan market collapsed.

# 11 National self-sufficiency: 1933

In April 1933, Keynes delivered a lecture entitled "National Self-Sufficiency" to a packed hall at University College Dublin. The lecture was published a few months later both in England and in the USA. It was thus a widely noted and important address. Though rarely read by mainstream economists, this essay may be the best-known of Keynes's "radical" writings among progressive economists. Roy Harrod, Keynes's "official" biographer, tried to explain away the radical character of the essay by arguing that it was written while Keynes was in a fleeting mood of deep depression triggered by his profound disappointment at the collapse of the World Economic Conference in July 1933. "It may have been partly by revulsion from the futility of the Conference," Harrod argued, that Keynes wrote and published this article (which he does not mention by name). "He was depressed by the gathered wisdom of the nations." The article "lacked his usual precision of thought," and was "a little rambling" in Harrod's view (Harrod 1951, p. 446). Unfortunately for Harrod's thesis, Keynes delivered the lecture two months before the conference even began. In any case, Keynes is on the record as being rather pessimistic about any progress being made at the Conference. Prior to its opening, he said that "it will be extraordinarily difficult to avoid a fiasco" (CW 21, p. 251).

The essential thing to understand about this article is that it contained not one belief or opinion that Keynes had not held for many years and had not publicly expressed many times before.[1] And it contained no important belief or opinion that Keynes did not continue to hold and to publicly propagate for the rest of his life. Far from being an aberrant and temporary response to his disappointment over the inability of the major powers to agree on international cooperation as Roy Harrod claimed, "National Self-Sufficiency" is Keynes's carefully considered views as they had evolved over the previous decade. *It is, simply put, the mature Keynes!*

The article is devoted in the main to an exploration of Keynes's positions on international economics. It takes his long-held and well-known support for state planning built around an extensive program of public capital accumulation more or less for granted. It also assumed that the listener and reader were aware that there were ambitious experiments in national economic planning and in national control of international economic activity ongoing in many countries, including in Ireland, where the lecture was delivered. (Mussolini came to power in 1922 and Hitler in March 1933.) It opened with a moving description of Keynes's early and almost religious belief in "free trade" and open capital markets.

> I was brought up, like most Englishmen, to respect free trade not only as an economic doctrine which a rational and instructed person could not doubt but almost as part of the moral law. I regarded departures from it as being at the same time an imbecility and an outrage. I thought England's unshakable free-trade convictions, maintained for nearly a hundred years, to be both the explanation before man and the justification before heaven of her economic supremacy.
> 
> (CW 21, p. 234)

It went on to explain that nineteenth-century free-traders believed their position to be consistent with economic efficiency (through comparative advantage), individual liberty, and international peace; he did not argue that they were wrong in that specific historical context.

But time and circumstance have changed; Britain was, as Keynes had been insisting since 1919, in a qualitatively new era. Under modern conditions, he argued, the ancient verities no longer held. The first concern he expressed was about the relation of free trade and, especially, international capital mobility to world peace. Note the strong support for capital controls.

> [I]t does not now seem obvious that a great concentration of national effort on the capture of foreign trade, that the penetration of a country's economic structure by the resources and the influence of foreign capitalists, that a close dependence of our own economic life on the fluctuating economic policies of foreign countries, are safeguards and assurances of international peace. It is easier, in the light of experience and foresight, to argue quite the contrary. The protection of a country's existing foreign interests, the capture of new markets, the progress of economic imperialism – these are a scarcely avoidable part of a scheme of things which aims at the maximum of international specialisation and at the maximum geographical diffusion of capital wherever its seat of ownership. *Advisable domestic policies might be easier to compass, if, for example, the phenomena known as "the flight of capital" could be ruled out.* The divorce between ownership and the real responsibility of management ... when ... applied internationally ... is, in times of stress, intolerable – I am irresponsible towards what I own and those who operate what I own are irresponsible towards me ... [E]experience is accumulating that remoteness between ownership

and operation is an evil in the relations between men, likely or certain in the long run to set up strains and enmities which will bring to nought [all] financial calculation.

(CW 21, p. 236, emphasis added)

These ideas led Keynes to the following conclusions:

I sympathize, therefore, with those who would minimise, rather than with those who would maximise, economic entanglement between nations. Ideas, knowledge, art, hospitality, travel – these are the things which should of their nature be international. But let goods be homespun whenever it is reasonably and conveniently possible; and, *above all, let finance be primarily national* ... For these strong reasons, therefore, I am inclined to the belief that ... a greater measure of national self-sufficiency than existed in 1914 may tend to serve the cause of peace, rather than otherwise.

(CW 21, pp. 236–237, emphasis added)

No one who had followed Keynes's public discourse over the decade would be at all surprised by these conclusions. He had been leery of the implications for world peace of international financial entanglements since the negotiations over the Treaty of Versailles. In 1921, he wrote that "the practice of foreign investment, as we know it now, is a very modern contrivance, a very unstable one, and only suited to peculiar circumstances" (CW 9, p. 39). The *Treatise on Money* argued that the case for British free trade had been weakened by

the gradual disappearance, in a world of mass-production and of the universal adoption of modern techniques, of the special advantages in manufacturing which used to be ours, and to the high real wages (including in this the value of social services) to which our workers are accustomed as compared with our European competitors.

(CW 6, p. 169)

And in mid-1930, Keynes had written in an internal government memorandum:

*I am no longer a free trader* ... in the old sense of the term to the extent of believing in a very high degree of national specialisation and in abandoning any industry which is unable for the time being to hold its own.

(CW 20, p. 379, emphasis added)

Of course, while Keynes's positions on these questions had not changed, the recent world trend toward higher protectionist tariffs and toward increased economic autonomy in many nations had hardened or solidified or reinforced his views. *It is important to understand that Keynes was not arguing in favor of autarky.*

> I must not be understood to carry my argument beyond a certain point. A considerable degree of international specialisation is necessary in a rational world in all cases where it is dictated by wide differences in climate, natural resources, native aptitudes, level of culture and density of population. But over an increasingly wide range of industrial products, and perhaps of agricultural products also, I become doubtful whether the cost of national self-sufficiency is great enough to outweigh the other advantages of gradually bringing the producer and the consumer within the ambit of the same national, economic and financial organisation.
> 
> (CW 20, p. 238)

This gets us to the crux of the paper. Decreased international specialization may cost less than it used to, but it still costs something. Is there some national purpose with sufficient prospective benefits that required greater national autonomy or at least greater national control over international trade and investment to achieve? In Keynes's words: "National self-sufficiency, in short, though it costs something, may be becoming a luxury which we can afford if we happen to want it. Are there sufficient good reasons why we happen to want it?" (CW 20, p. 238). Keynes's answer is yes – *to make national economic planning possible!* The most urgent task facing Britain is to find the right path leading to a "transition towards greater national self-sufficiency and a planned domestic economy" (CW 20, p. 245).

Keynes stressed the fact that while many countries were currently experimenting with national economic planning of one sort or another, there was no satisfactory model of democratic and efficient national planning in existence for the British to copy. Thus, the transition toward a planned economy had to be accomplished through bold but thoughtful experimentation, taking care at every point to ensure that no irreparable damage was done in the process to democracy, individual liberty, or economic efficiency. His discussion of the need to experiment opens with a statement that very few economists today would recognize as Keynes's. Here, he condemns modern capitalism in the harshest terms – not just the capitalism of the Great Depression, but the capitalism of the 1920s as well.

> The decadent international but individualistic capitalism, in the hands of which we found ourselves after the War, is not a success. It is not intelligent, it is not beautiful, it is not just, it is not virtuous – and it doesn't deliver the goods. In short, we dislike it and *we are beginning to despise it*. But when we wonder what to put in its place, we

> are extremely perplexed. Each year it becomes more obvious that the world is embarking on a variety of politico-economic experiments ... Russia is still alone in her particular experiment, but no longer alone in her abandonment of the old presuppositions. Italy, Ireland, Germany have cast their eyes, or are casting them, towards new modes of political economy. Many more countries after them will be seeking, one by one, after new economic gods. Even countries such as Great Britain and the United States, though conforming in the main to the old model, are striving, under the surface, after a new economic plan. We do not know what will be the outcome. We are – all of us, I expect, about to make many mistakes. No one can tell which of the new systems will prove itself best.
>
> (CW 20, p. 239, emphasis added)

His main point is that these experiments in national planning will not succeed if each country remains tightly tied into an orthodox international financial and trading system. Keynes believed that very low long-term interest rates were a necessary condition for the large-scale public investment program he supported. Yet under the traditional open system of international finance, they would be impossible to maintain because higher interest rates in other countries would trigger the flight of capital from Britain. And in the absence of managed trade, a substantial increase in economic growth in Britain while the rest of the world continued to deflate would cause unsustainable British trade deficits.

The whole point of national self-sufficiency was to untie the economy from its existing restraints; to free it up for experimentation with an economically more powerful state. Keynes was simply making the argument – which he never recanted – that the government would have to manage trade and capital flows as part of an overall state planning process, and that England should continue to produce domestically whatever goods or services were thought to be essential to the quality of Britain's economic or social life, even if such commodities could be purchased elsewhere somewhat more cheaply.

> We wish – for the time being at least and so long as the present transitional, experimental phase endures – to be our own masters, and to be as free as we can make ourselves from the interferences of the outside world. Thus, ... the policy of an increased national self-sufficiency is to be considered not as an ideal in itself but as directed to the creation of an environment in which other ideals can be safely and conveniently pursued ...
>
> I have become convinced that the retention of the structure of private enterprise is incompatible with the degree of material well-being to which our technical advancement entitles us, unless the rate of interest falls to a much lower figure than is likely to come about by

natural forces operating on the old lines. Indeed, the transformation of society, which I preferably envisage, may require a reduction in the rate of interest towards the vanishing point within the next thirty years.[2] But under a system by which the rate of interest finds ... a uniform level throughout the world, after allowing for risk and the like, this is most unlikely to occur. Thus, ... economic internationalism embracing the free movement of capital and loanable funds as well as of traded goods may condemn this country for a generation to come to a much lower degree of material prosperity than could be attained under a different system. But this is merely an illustration. The point is that there is no prospect for the next generation of a uniformity of economic systems throughout the world, such as existed, broadly speaking, during the nineteenth century; that we all need to be as free as possible of interference from economic changes elsewhere, in order to make our own favorite experiments towards the ideal social republic of the future; and that a deliberate movement towards greater national self-sufficiency and economic isolation will make our task easier, in so far as it can be accomplished without excessive cost.

(CW 21, pp. 240–241)

Keynes ended this essay with a warning. Looking to the experience of Russia and Germany with national autonomy and central planning, he saw much waste and inefficiency as well as many things that were politically and socially frightening. "I must not be supposed to be endorsing all those things which are being done in the political world today in the name of economic nationalism" (CW 21, p. 244). He listed three particular dangers. "The first is Silliness – the silliness of the doctrinaire." Here, he stressed the importance of economic efficiency and the tendency of social movements to let ideology dominate good sense. "An experimental society has need to be far more efficient than an old-established one if it is to survive safely" (CW 21, p. 244).

The second danger was "Haste." This was a theme he had stressed over and over again – careful evolutionary change offers much greater prospects of eventual success than hasty revolutionary change.

We have a fearful example in Russia today of the evils of insane and unnecessary haste. The sacrifices and losses will be vastly greater if the pace is forced. This is above all true of a transition towards greater national self-sufficiency and a planned domestic economy.

(CW 21, p. 245)

The third danger is "Intolerance." Referring to Russia again, Keynes warned against the practice of forcing one's views on society through violence rather than persuasion. It may be a natural tendency, he suggested, for revolutionary movements to continue to practice the same methods in power that they were forced to use in the struggle to acquire power. But only a deeply rooted commitment to foster criticism can create the atmosphere of tolerance of criticism that is essential for successful experimentation. Keynes made it clear that he would personally prefer laissez-faire – with all its inefficiency, waste, injustice, and propensity for war – to a Stalinist mode of economic development.

> Yet the new economic modes, towards which we are blundering, are, in the essence of their nature, experiments. We have no clear idea laid up in our minds beforehand of exactly what we want. We shall discover it as we move along, and have to mould our material in accordance with our experience. Now for this process bold, free and remorseless criticism is a *sine qua non* of ultimate success. We need the collaboration of all the bright spirits of the age. Stalin has eliminated every independent, critical mind, even when it is sympathetic in general outlook ... Let Stalin be a terrifying example to all who seek to make experiments. If not, I, at any rate, will soon be back again in my old nineteenth-century ideals.
> 
> (CW 21, p. 246)

The central themes of this essay, especially the necessity for managed trade and capital controls to facilitate domestic planning, were to find explicit embodiment in the 1940s. In the war years, Keynes's proposals for a new international financial system included the obligation of all member nations to institute tight capital controls.[3] And he continued his campaign for domestic full-employment policy based on state control of investment.

## Notes

1. His rejection of free trade was of recent vintage. As noted, he had rejected this doctrine at least three years before in the Addendum to the Macmillan Committee Report, and two years earlier in his public writings.
2. Keynes had for some time been gravitating toward the view that if state planning could sustain full employment for, say, one generation or so, the rate of profit on capital would fall toward zero. To maintain capital investment at a full-employment level would therefore require that the risk-adjusted long-term interest rate fall toward zero as well. Keynes will present and defend this argument in *The General Theory*, where he looks forward to "the euthanasia of the rentier" (CW 7, p. 376).
3. Crotty (1983) provides a defense of the claim that Keynes was determined to incorporate tight capital controls on the post-WWII international financial order.

# Part II
## *The General Theory*
The ultimate defense in theory of Keynes's radical policy agenda

# 12 Methodology and ideology
Keynes versus the classicists

## Introduction

*The General Theory* was designed to accomplish three main objectives. First, it contains a devastating attack on classical theory, the purpose of which was to convince economists and members of Britain's intellectual, business, and political elites that the theory that informed their economic worldview and provided essential support for the disastrous conservative economic policies of the era was fundamentally flawed. Second, it presented a radically new theory of modern capitalism informed by a different methodology than the one used in classical theory. Third, Keynes used his new theory to argue in *The General Theory* that unless Liberal Socialism replaced capitalism in Britain and elsewhere, the world was likely to remain mired in economic stagnation amid rising political distress.

## Keynes's attack on classical theory

In the chapters that follow, I will show that *The General Theory* focused on three fundamental errors in classical theory that Keynes had been attacking since WWI: (1) its conclusion that a capitalist economy has a unique equilibrium point at full employment; (2) its conclusion that high unemployment created by exogenous shocks would be quickly eliminated by stabilizing market disequilibrium processes; and (3) its conclusion that there are no endogenous sources of destabilizing disequilibrium dynamics in capitalism. As Schumpeter put it, classical theory was not an evolutionary theory.

His attack on the first conclusion is well known. Everyone who studied economics in college is familiar with the "Keynesian Cross" and perhaps the IS/LM model that demonstrate the potential multiplicity of underemployment equilibriums.

His attack on the second classical conclusion is not at all well known. In mainstream interpretations of *The General Theory*, it is explicitly or implicitly assumed that all equilibriums are stable, an assumption sometimes bolstered by phase diagrams unsupported by historical or empirical studies. This assumption, shared with classical theory, is a necessary condition for the ubiquitous use of comparative statics in "Keynesian" models – including, at times, by Keynes himself in several places in *The General Theory*, a point to which we will return. But the fact is that the book devoted substantial space to the analysis of precisely those destabilizing out-of-equilibrium dynamic processes of wage and price deflation and rising real interest rates that had been the focus of his attacks on conservative laissez-faire policy for over a decade. These destabilizing dynamic processes are ruled out by assumption in standard comparative static analysis. *Yet seven chapters totaling almost 140 pages of The General Theory – over a third of the book* – plus many scattered comments in other chapters are devoted to his war against the thesis that high unemployment would self-correct if only the government left the economy alone and unions did not interfere with downward money wage flexibility.

In February 1930, in testimony before the Macmillan Committee, Keynes addressed the issue of disequilibrium processes, an issue to which, he said, "I attach enormous importance."

> Economists spend most of their time describing and discussing what happens in a position of equilibrium, and they usually affirm that a position of disequilibrium is merely transitory. I want to study what happens during the process of disequilibrium.
> 
> (CW 20, pp. 72–73)

Keynes's attack on the third classical conclusion that there are no endogenous sources of the disruption of equilibrium is rarely acknowledged in mainstream macro theory, though it is often stressed in Post Keynesian theory. *The General Theory* puts heavy emphasis on endogenous disruption of equilibrium positions that create instability that is at times seriously dysfunctional, occasionally leading the economy into unsustainable economic booms and financial bubbles followed by self-reinforcing processes of economic collapse. Endogenously generated instability in financial markets is especially likely to be destructive. Destabilizing endogenous disequilibrium processes are an integral part of *The General Theory*, yet they are missing in both classical and Modern Keynesian theory. Chapter 19 of this book discusses the incompatibility of Keynes's theory and Modern Keynesian theory in this regard.

## Methodology and ideology

*Does the realism and completeness of the assumption set matter to the validity of derived hypotheses?*

We preface our analysis of *The General Theory* with comments on the roles played by methodology and ideology in Keynes's clash with classical theory and laissez-faire policy in *The General Theory*. In the one-page opening chapter, Keynes sought to differentiate his general theory of capitalism from what he saw as the special case embedded in classical theory. The assumption set of classical theory, he said, is "applicable to a special case only and not to the general case, the situation which it assumes being a limiting point of the possible positions of equilibrium" (CW 7, p. 3). In the last chapter of the book, Keynes made a fundamental attack on classical methodology.

> Our criticism of the accepted classical theory of economics has consisted not so much in finding logical flaws in its analysis as in pointing out that its tacit assumptions are seldom or never satisfied, with the result that it cannot solve the problems of the actual world.
> (CW 7, p. 378)

In other words, Keynes insists, you cannot build a realistic theory of capitalism based on crudely unrealistic assumptions. The realism and completeness of the assumption set matters. Keynes's views on this issue are in sharp conflict with classical theory and with Milton Friedman's argument that, in his favored methodology of positivism, the truth content of derived hypotheses is unrelated to the realism or completeness of the assumption set.[1] Friedman's positivism is the quasi-official methodology of both neoclassical and Modern Keynesian economic theory.

Classical theory has only one equilibrium state, one in which all markets clear. This equilibrium state is stable by assumption. If temporarily moved from equilibrium by some exogenous shock, market forces ensure a speedy return to a general equilibrium bliss point. Keynes argued that classical theorists did not build their theory of market-clearing equilibrium with stabilizing disequilibrium dynamics on concrete empirical or historical analysis. Rather, they searched for an assumption set that could generate their predetermined economic and policy conclusions. Not surprisingly, this assumption set is stunningly unrealistic because only an unrealistic and incomplete assumption set could possibly support the laissez-faire policy conclusions of classical theory.

Classical theory had both historical and ideological roots. The historical underpinning was the fact that the British economy grew rapidly and became economically and financially dominant in the global economy from the mid-eighteenth century through most of the nineteenth century, a period that Keynes often referred to as the "glorious nineteenth century." This understanding of capitalism hid from view the fact that Britain's high trend growth was caused by an inherently transitory set of conditions. These unique and transitory factors were thus not understood to be unique and transitory in the classical model used to explain Britain's impressive nineteenth-century long-term growth rate. They were implicitly considered to be permanent conditions of modern laissez-faire capitalism, at least in Britain.

This brings us to the ideological function of classical theory. It needed an assumption set capable of supporting in theory the ideological belief that unregulated capitalism was an ideal system – the Schumpeterian "pre-analytic vision" that lay behind the theory. The classical thesis that any significant attempt by the state to interfere with free markets, no matter how well intended, could not help but lead to inferior results was thus not based on careful observation of British economic and political history and an understanding of the transitory nature of its nineteenth-century growth path – it was an ideological presupposition built into its construction.

Keynes argued to the contrary that, in order to be useful, a theory must begin with a set of assumptions that realistically describes the historically specific institutions and behaviors that constitute actually existing capitalism in any particular place and time. For Keynes, for example, nineteenth-century British capitalism and interwar British capitalism had different inherent tendencies that cannot be understood unless the assumption sets used to derive the theories adequately reflect the actual "facts" of the era. He argued that the assumptions used to create the "special case" of general equilibrium represented by the classical theory "happen not to be those of the economic society in which we actually live, with the result that its teaching is misleading and disastrous if we attempt to apply it to the facts of experience" (CW 7, p. 3).

Keynes stressed the ideological roots of classical theory and policy. At the end of chapter 3, he posed the question as to how it came to be that classical theory could dominate economics in Britain in the interwar era even though it had no convincing way to explain the sustained high unemployment of the era that was consistent with the facts and supported policies bound to reproduce this problem. In the quotation below, Ricardo represents the classical tradition.

> Ricardo conquered England as completely as the Holy Inquisition conquered Spain ...
>
> The completeness of the Ricardian victory is something of a curiosity and a mystery. It must have been due to a complex of suitabilities in the doctrine to the environment into which it was projected. That it reached conclusions quite different from what the ordinary uninstructed person would expect, added, I suppose, to its intellectual prestige. That its teaching, translated into practice, was austere and unpalatable, lent it virtue. That it was adapted to carry a vast and consistent logical superstructure, gave it beauty. That it could explain much social injustice and apparent cruelty as an inevitable incident in the scheme of progress, and the attempt to change such things as likely on the whole to do more harm than good, commended it to authority. *That it afforded a measure of justification to the free activities of the individual capitalist, attracted to it the support of the dominant social forces behind authority.*
>
> (CW 7, pp. 32–33, emphasis added)

So, classical economists loved classical theory in part because of its aesthetic qualities: "its vast and consistent logical superstructure gave it beauty." This elaborate superstructure also made it possible to pretend that economics was a real science, like physics or chemistry, rather than a soft social science, and it eventually gave to those best equipped mathematically to do advanced theory great prestige within the profession. Most importantly, it enabled conservative economists, who, in main, opposed progressive economic and social change, to claim that economic science supported their policies. And it gave the capitalist class, which, along with rentiers, controlled government economic policy or was "the dominant social force behind [political] authority," a pseudoscientific defense of their belief that the political process should reflect their worldview and ensure that nothing stood in the way of their untrammeled pursuit of wealth. Classical theory, he said, teaches that under laissez-faire capitalism, "all is for the best in the best of all possible worlds" (CW 7, p. 33).

## *What is general about* The General Theory?

There are two important ways in which *The General Theory* is general. The first is that the book presents a very simple abstract model of the determination of income and employment and then uses that model to create five more specific or applied models of different aspects or dimensions of economic activity in a capitalist economy. Mainstream Keynesians typically assert that there is only one model in *The General Theory* – a short-term stable equilibrium model such as Hicks's IS/LM model – but this is not true. In Chapter 19 of this book, we show that there are five different applied models of Keynes's "general theory" in *The General Theory*. They are: (1) a long-term model of sustained high unemployment sometimes referred to as secular stagnation (see Chapters 13 and 14 in this book); (2) a short-term model of high-unemployment equilibrium embodied in the simple Keynesian Cross and IS/LM models (see Chapter 19); (3) a dynamic intermediate-run model of the business cycle that focuses on endogenously generated instability in real and financial markets, a model in which instability in either sector can be transmitted to the other (see Chapter 18); (4) a model of destructive disequilibrium processes focused on wage and price deflation and endogenously generated instability in financial asset prices (see Chapters 15–17 and 19);[2] and (5) a very-short-run quasi-model or mini-model of periods or points of extreme instability or crises, especially in financial markets (see Chapters 16 and 17).

The second way in which Keynes works from the abstract or general theoretical level to the concrete or applied level is through the specification of the behavioral relations or functions that constitute the applied models of the economy. In Keynes's methodology, the equations in the applied models must adequately reflect the concrete institutional, behavioral, and empirical "facts" of the historically specific form of capitalism under investigation. These change over time. If these differences are significant enough, they change the variables in and parameters of the behavioral equations of the applied models of the economy. This alters the static and/or dynamic properties of the model. The applied models therefore must faithfully reflect these differences in order to adequately represent the behavior of the specific national capitalisms under investigation. This makes it possible for the theorist to deduce effective policy regimes for these particular economies. The insistence that applied theory must be built on a realistic assumption set that reflects the important "facts" of the historically specific economy under investigation is a core component of Keynes's anti-positivist methodology.

We consider first the issue of moving from the abstract level to the applied level. Everyone who has taken a basic course in "Keynesian" macro theory knows that Keynes created a short-run model that demonstrated that equilibrium income and employment are strongly influenced by the strength of AD or aggregate spending (AS) and that high-unemployment equilibrium is a potential state of modern capitalist economies because AD can remain below the level of income consistent with full employment.[3]

The value of equilibrium output and income depend, in all of these applications of his general model, on the relationship between AD (or total spending) and AS (or the value of output and income). In the simplest abstract model, AD is the sum of capital investment and household consumption spending. In *The General Theory*, capital spending depends on the *expected* profit rate on investment, referred to as the "marginal efficiency of capital" (or mec), and the long-term interest rate (r). These variables are functions of *expectations* of future profit flows and future bond prices, respectively. (Endogenously generated expectations play a crucial role in all of Keynes's models.) If the expected profit rate exceeds the interest rate, investment projects should be undertaken, and vice versa. Household consumption spending is assumed to be a positive function of income. The "marginal propensity to consume" out of income (or mpc) measures the sensitivity of consumption spending to changes in income.[4]

Model 1 provides an example of both the concrete application of the "general" theory to Keynes's applied model of secular stagnation and of his insistence that the assumption set must incorporate the "facts" of specific time and place. Chapters 13 and 14 of this book discuss Keynes's analysis of long-run stagnation in both *The General Theory* and in an important lecture on long-term stagnation in the year following its publication. Model 1 is based on the same abstract-level variables used in his general model, but in *The General Theory*, he analyses and explains their behavior over the entire interwar period based on his understanding of the concrete historical facts of the period. We presented his explanation of why he predicted post-WWI stagnation in his 1919 book *The Economic Consequences of the Peace* in Chapter 2 of this book, an explanation he augmented and updated in *The General Theory*.

Based on the institutional and behavioral "facts" of the interwar period through the mid-1930s, Keynes argued that both capital investment spending and household consumption spending were likely to continue to remain too low to sustain full employment over the foreseeable future. Investment would continue to be constrained by a declining actual and expected rate profit rate (mec) and by a long-term interest rate that could not fall by enough to stimulate investment in the face of a declining mec. In his projection of the character of the post-WWI economy in *The Economic Consequences of the Peace* and in his explanation of secular stagnation between WWI and *The General Theory*, Keynes explained why the rate of profit on capital goods in Britain was higher in the "glorious" nineteenth century than it was in the 1920s and 1930s. The high profit rate and growth rate of the British economy in the nineteenth century were caused by unique historical conditions that could not possibly be sustained forever, but classical theory was based on the implicit assumption that they were permanent conditions of modern capitalism.

His explanation of the decline of the rate of profit between the two periods stressed key changes in the historical "facts" from one era to the next. Key factors that helped drive nineteenth-century growth but were missing in the interwar period included: system-transforming technical change (such as the building of the national railroad system); the brutal creation, exploitation, and impoverishment of Britain's working class, especially prior to the mid-nineteenth century; imperialism with Britain at the center of the world's trading and financial systems; successful wars; rapid population growth; and a globally dominant British cotton industry dependent on slave labor and military force.[5] As noted in Chapter 2, the British historian Eric Hobsbawm summed up this situation as follows:

> There was a moment in the world's history when Britain can be described, if we are not too pedantic, as its only workshop, its only massive importer and exporter, its only carrier, its only imperialist, almost its only foreign investor; and for that reason its only naval power and the only one that had a genuine world policy.
> (Hobsbawm 1969, p. 13)

By the interwar period, all of these conditions had vanished.

Keynes also argued that the long-term rate of interest could not decline by as much as the mec in the interwar years for institutional and behavioral reasons that he discussed in various places in *The General Theory*.[6] It is important to understand that, for Keynes, the interest rate at the abstract level of the model represents the conditions of financial markets at the concrete institutional level. International and many national financial markets changed substantially between the two eras, a fact to which we shortly return. Consumption spending would continue to be held down in Britain and the USA in the current era, he said, by a high degree of income and wealth inequality that caused the share of income spent by households on consumption goods (or mpc) to be low. Keynes thus argued that both the level of investment and the value of the investment "multiplier" were too low to generate a long-run rate of growth of AD sufficient to eliminate high unemployment.

He concluded that the facts of the interwar years made it necessary to replace the laissez-faire capitalism of nineteenth-century Britain with Liberal Socialism in order to achieve sustained full employment in Britain.

Consider a second example. As explained in chapter 22 of *The General Theory* and Chapter 18 of this book, Keynes explained why business cycles of this era in the USA were unusually volatile. Model 3 incorporates the endogenously created dynamic interaction of the real sector and financial markets in driving booms far beyond sustainability while creating financial commitments that cannot be fulfilled when the booming economy eventually hits a "crisis." Minsky called this a condition of "financial fragility" in which the shift from boom to bust in the context of overstressed balance sheets in both real and financial sectors sharply exacerbates the rate and depth of the collapse.

Keynes's theory of financial investors and financial markets in model 3 (and in model 5) is fundamentally different from the theories of agents and agent choice of classical theory and Mainstream Keynesian theory because they are based on a realistic set of assumptions about institutions and agent behavior that lead to different specifications of the equations in the applied models. Keynes built his theory of agent choice on the core assumption that future states of the economy, including future financial asset prices, are unknowable or fundamentally uncertain in the present moment. This means that Keynes's financial market investors cannot be the fully informed, optimizing mathematicians of classical and Modern Keynesian theory. His agents have to construct predictions of future financial asset prices through behavioral and psychological conventions or heuristics and determine how much "confidence" they have in the truth content of their forecasts before they can decide on an investment strategy. Since Keynes argued that because both asset-price expectations and confidence in those expectations are endogenous and pro-cyclical, financial asset prices are inherently subject to bouts of instability. But he also insisted that the degree of instability in any institutionally specific financial market depended heavily on the "facts" that characterized that market. In times of light market regulation, heavily debt-financed asset purchases, fragile balance sheets, and exceptionally "liquid" markets (in which transactions can be made quickly and cheaply), financial markets can create and reproduce spectacular speculative booms and busts – as in the late 1920s and early 1930s in the USA. Keynes observed that "When the [real] capital development of a country becomes a by-product of activities of a casino, the job is likely to be ill-done" (CW 7, p. 159).

Keynes stressed that the kind of "insane" financial gambling in the USA in this period was not an inherent characteristic of all national capitalisms in all eras. He stated that one of the reasons why the London stock market did not suffer from the financial instability or mania observed in the USA in this period was because "compared to Wall Street" it was "inaccessible and very expensive" to buy and sell securities. It was, in other words, much more illiquid (CW 7, p. 159).[7] "The jobber's 'turn' [or market-makers fee], the high brokerage charges, and transfer [or turnover] tax ... sufficiently diminish the liquidity of the market ... to rule out a large proportion of the transactions characteristic of Wall Street" (CW 7, pp. 159–160). The different institutional and behavioral characteristics of British and US financial markets in the interwar period led Keynes to use different specifications of applied models of stock and bond market performance in Britain and the USA in this period. The differences between the two financial markets help explain why Britain did not experience a tsunami of bank failures as in the USA. Indeed, it never experienced a financial crisis in the 1930s.

Neither the classical theory nor the Mainstream Keynesian theory of financial markets follows Keynes's methodology in this regard. Both offer general or very abstract theories in which financial markets are always well behaved. They offer a theory of the bond market in which agents know the probability distributions of the future interest rates; in which interest rates always fall when AD receives a negative shock; in which "insane" financial market gambling casinos cannot exist and therefore financial instability and financial crises cannot exist; and in which there is one model of interest rate determination that applies to all economies that are sufficiently capitalist. That is why classical theory was incapable of predicting or explaining the US financial market chaos of the late 1920s and early 1930s and why modern mainstream financial market theory did not predict and cannot explain *ex post* the global financial crisis that began in 2007. Keynes's applied theory of financial markets was designed to explain their behavior in both relatively stable times and in periods of great market instability.

In his writings on Britain's economic problems in the interwar period, Keynes reported the results of his extensive research on the concrete historical, institutional, and empirical analyses – including at the firm and industry levels – needed to understand *why* the economy performed so badly in the interwar years. Mainstream macroeconomists rarely do this because it does not fit their deductive positivist methodology. Their goal is to demonstrate either that capitalism has a unique and stable equilibrium at full employment (true of monetarism, New Classical theory, real business cycle theory, and dynamic stochastic general equilibrium theory)[8] or that a capitalist economy always has the basic institutions, practices, and incentives to achieve and sustain full employment as long as "Keynesian" countercyclical macro policy keeps the economy on its efficient long-term growth path (Mainstream Keynesian theory). To accomplish their objectives, mainstream economists do not need to delve too deeply into the specifics of the sub-macro levels of the economy.[9]

## Keynes's support of Liberal Socialism in *The General Theory*

Though Keynes insisted, correctly, that *The General Theory* was primarily about theory, he laid out in clear and certain terms the radical policy implications of his new theory in that book. Yet the radical policy regime presented and defended in the book disappeared in postwar Mainstream Keynesianism. As we saw in the Introduction, the full policy list includes: government control over most large-scale capital investment to be used as the primary economic policy tool to achieve sustained full employment; permanently low interest rates; strict capital controls; substantial progressive redistribution of income and wealth; the end of rentier-controlled and Bank of England-supported finance capitalism (the "euthanasia of the rentier") under the guidance of a nationalized Central Bank; managed trade; policies to regulate competition; and many kinds of industrial policies. During WWII, Keynes expressed strong support for a robust social welfare system. *The General Theory* discusses the first five of these policies. You cannot miss his radical policy position if you read the entire book carefully without the preconceived belief that Keynes's ideas have been accurately reflected in the interpretations of post-WWII "Keynesians." The radical policies he argues for in *The General Theory* are reviewed in Chapter 20 of this book.

## Notes

1 See chapter 1 in Crotty (2017) for a detailed discussion of this important issue.
2 Chapter 19 argues that Keynes insisted that a capitalist economy is always subject to endogenous dynamic motion and that, therefore, in Keynes's theory, comparative static models can only constitute the initial step in a full analysis of the phenomenon under investigation.
3 Keynes discussed the influence of AS in chapter 21 of *The General Theory*, titled "The Influence of Prices."
4 As Keynes explained in chapters 7 and 8 of *The General Theory*, the mpc is a complex and institutionally contingent variable.
5 This story of the centrality of cotton to nineteenth-century growth in Britain is well told in Beckert (2015).
6 As we have seen, the rate of interest had a high lower bound from 1925 to 1931 because Britain was back on the gold standard at an overvalued pound.
7 Keynes explained why market liquidity and price volatility are positively related in chapter 12 of *The General Theory*.
8 In a 2014 article titled "Reflections on the new 'Secular Stagnation hypothesis'," Larry Summers said, "Just seven years ago all seemed well in the field of macroeconomics. The phrase 'great moderation' captured the reality that

business cycle volatility seemed way down from levels of the first part of the post-war period. A broad methodological consensus supported the use of DSGE (dynamic stochastic general equilibrium) models to understand macroeconomic fluctuation and to evaluate macroeconomic policies." DSGE models are deliberately constructed to generate a stable general-equilibrium position and they limit their financial sector to the determination of the interest rate – no casinos allowed – even as one of the greatest financial booms ever was about to bust. Yet they commanded a broad consensus among economists until the global crisis actually broke out. (See "Economic crisis has led to a crisis in the field of macroeconomics." Available at: https://voxeu.org/article/larry-summers-secular-stagnation, October 30, 2014.)

9 The recent spike in interest in the theory of secular stagnation has been accompanied, in some cases, by attempts to understand the structural forces inhibiting growth.

# 13 The priority of high-unemployment long-run equilibrium or "secular stagnation" in *The General Theory*

## *The General Theory* and concrete historical facts: secular stagnation[1]

Our survey of Keynes's ideas about the concrete historical and institutional reasons as to why Britain was "stuck in a rut" in the 1920s and why the USA, the UK, and much of the world were mired in depression in the 1930s is a useful example of his methodology as it was interpreted in the previous chapter. Here, I simply list some of the long-term institutional or structural problems that Keynes believed caused Britain and/or the USA to suffer from high unemployment through some or all of the interwar years: a secularly low rate of profit on capital in the UK and by the late 1920s in the USA exacerbated by massive excess capacity in the USA in the 1930s; the development of unstable "casino" financial markets in the USA that accelerated the real-sector and financial-market booms of the late 1920s and created the preconditions for the great crash to follow; the buildup of excessive leverage in financial institutions and in many sectors of the real economy in the USA and elsewhere that created extreme financial fragility in a "regime of money contract" by the end of the 1920s; the destructive impact of severe deflation on over-leveraged financial institutions in the USA and elsewhere in the 1930s, which occurred because most of their loans were based on collateral whose value was being destroyed by the rapidly falling prices that in classical theory were assumed to restore full employment; large unpayable inter-nation loans in the aftermath of WWI and a large domestic debt in the UK as a result of the war; the excessive globalization of capital markets, which created a dangerous degree of systemic risk as serious financial problems in important national financial markets were transmitted around the globe; destructive competition in Britain's traditional export industries (such as textiles and coal) that were dominated by small firms, in large industries with substantial economies of scale, and in all industries with chronically large excess capacity in this era; Britain's "first-mover" disadvantage – the existence of industrial structures and forms of business organization that grew up in the nineteenth century reduced incentives in Britain to build newer, more efficient, and larger-scale enterprises as was being done in the USA and Germany; the collapse of Britain's traditional export markets after WWI, in part because rising competitors such as the USA and Germany were now much more efficient in the production of tradable commodities – the decline in the size of Britain's traditional trade surplus in cotton textiles, coal, and shipbuilding are examples; destructive competition among nations to cut imports and expand imports in the 1930s – "beggar-thy-neighbor" trade policies; Britain's chronic export of financial capital to the world, which contributed to high domestic interest rates and helped finance modernization in competitor economies; the absence of job-creating, system-transforming innovation in the era[2]; the inability of unemployed workers and capital to move rapidly from deeply depressed regions to regions of higher growth because the economy was stagnant; the decision in Britain to return to gold at the prewar par that created a constant upward pressure on interest rates both before and after the return; a dramatic decline in the rate of Britain's population growth; the slowdown in the incorporation of new areas of the world to exploit; a high propensity to save in the advanced countries due to a high level of inequality; and so on.

Keynes's macro theory provides the broad abstract concepts – mec, mpc, and interest rate – used to organize all of these "facts" and the logic of causality between them and income and employment. Though these "facts" were crucial for explaining the present – the interwar years – and for making informed projections about the future, they were not adequately incorporated into classical theory, just as today's concrete facts are not adequately incorporated into neoclassical theory or "Modern Keynesian" theory.

Keynes did not expect these constraints on output and employment in the interwar years to disappear in the foreseeable future. He believed that long-term expectations of both the profit rate on capital investment and future security prices would remain both pessimistic and deeply rooted in the 1930s, a situation that did not end until the buildup to the prosecution of WWII. Confidently held expectations of endless depression themselves became a powerful "psychological" impediment to the restoration of prosperity precisely because they were based on strong institutional and empirical foundations.

Recall that Keynes repeatedly said of the nineteenth century that "prosperity is cumulative" – that decades of high growth generated a firm belief that prosperity was permanent. This belief helped minimize the decline in investment spending even in cyclical downturns. But a long, deep depression is also "cumulative" because it creates a strongly held expectation that the depression will continue for the foreseeable future. Deeply pessimistic expectations can become self-fulfilling.

Keynes concluded from his concrete study of the period that the serious impediments to full employment in the interwar era were so strong and deeply rooted that it would require a socialist transformation of the UK and, hopefully, the rest of the "West" to restore long-term prosperity. As I will demonstrate in Chapter 20, Keynes repeatedly said in *The General Theory* that only what he elsewhere called "Liberal Socialism" could defeat secular stagnation, eliminate "insane" financial markets, and restore long-term prosperity.

## The priority of secular stagnation in *The General Theory*

For Keynes, stagnation was not a chronic or universal condition of capitalist economies, but rather a chronic *tendency* of *mature* capitalist economies. There are periods in which the underlying forces pulling a mature capitalist economy into sluggish growth can be overwhelmed by what Marx called "counter-tendencies" in his own version of secular stagnation theory, usually referred to as the theory of "the falling rate of profit." Marx did not title the section of volume III of *Capital* on the propensity of mature capitalist economies to stagnate "The Law of the Falling Rate of Profit," but rather "The Law of the Tendency of the Rate of Profit to Fall." In chapter 14 ("Counter-Acting Factors"), he discussed a list of potential developments that could, for an extended period of time, prevent the profit rate from falling.

> [T]hen the difficulty which has hitherto troubled the economist, namely to explain the falling rate of profit, [has been superseded by] its opposite, namely to explain why this fall is not greater and more rapid. There must be some counteracting influences as work, which cross and annul the effect of the general law, and which give it merely the characteristic of a tendency, for which reason we have referred to the fall of the general rate of profit as a tendency to fall.
> (Marx 1967, p. 232)

For example, Marx argued that when labor markets are tight, workers' bargaining power is at its peak, which enables labor to claim an increasing share of firm revenues, causing the profit rate to fall and the rate of capital accumulation to decline. Capitalists typically respond to the rising power of labor through the use of labor-saving technical change embedded in new machinery (as well as by "the widespread introduction of female and child labour"; Marx 1967, p. 232). This leads to an increase in what Marx called the "reserve army" of unemployed workers. A large reserve army of unemployed workers will compete with employed workers for scarce jobs. This weakens the bargaining power of labor and enables capitalists to raise the profit share of income and the profit rate on capital investment by increasing the intensity of labor and the length of the workday. This is an example of a Marxian counter-tendency to the tendency of the rate of profit to fall over time.

*High-unemployment long-run equilibrium* 175

However, these developments create their own problems for profitability in the long run. The falling wage share and resulting rising inequality can lead to inadequate consumption demand and thus inadequate AD – what Marx called problems in the "realization" of "surplus value" (profit plus interest plus rent). Under Marx's theory of value, a rising capital–labor ratio, or rising "organic composition of capital," will lower the rate of profit on capital over time.[3] The "law of the tendency" embodies Marx's belief that, in unregulated capitalism and in the long run, the forces pushing the profit rate down would ultimately prevail over the counter-tendencies that raise the profit rate from time to time. Keynes held a generally similar view.

This book has listed a large number of factors Keynes believed contributed to the secular stagnation of the period. In *The General Theory*, he mentioned an important subset of these factors. The larger the number of factors that constitute impediments to long-term growth that are present in any particular historical era and the stronger their negative impact on output and employment, the more likely the existence of stagnation – and vice versa.

The basic structure of the argument in support of secular stagnation in *The General Theory* rests on three main propositions. First, in the absence of powerful countervailing tendencies, the larger the capital stock, *ceteris paribus*, the lower the actual profit rate on capital investment and therefore the lower the expected profit rate or mec. The lower the mec, *ceteris paribus*, the lower the level of investment. Second, the higher the level of per capita income and wealth in a country, the greater its degree of inequality is likely to be, which reduces the mpc and therefore lowers the investment multiplier. Third, the first two propositions imply that, in order to sustain full employment as the economy matures, the long-term interest rate would have to decline dramatically over time. However, Keynes argued, there were several reasons why this was not possible – even after the UK and then the USA went off the gold standard in 1931 and 1933, respectively. We discuss chapter 17 of *The General Theory*, in which Keynes supports this hypothesis, in Appendix 2 below.

Some of the "facts" Keynes mentions in the book in support of his stagnation thesis are: that high income and wealth inequality in mature capitalist economies such as in interwar Britain and the USA did cause the mpc to be low; that "institutional and psychological factors" in mature economies placed a high lower bound on the value of the long-term interest rate; and that while the mec was kept at an exceptionally high level in the nineteenth century by "the growth of population," the "growth of invention" (or the existence of system-transforming, capital-augmenting technical change), the "opening up of new lands," the "state of confidence," and "the frequency of war." All of these factors had weakened qualitatively in the interwar period. In the absence of these counter-tendencies, Keynes argued, the inherent tendency of the mec to fall in a mature economy as the capital stock rises over time will prevail. Moreover, the creation of "insane" casino financial markets in the era facilitated rising financial fragility in real-sector and financial firms, building a potential crisis trigger mechanism. The generation of extreme financial instability in the late 1920s and early 1930s in turn increased the perceived riskiness of capital investment, which lowered what we might call the risk-adjusted mec. A falling mpc, a falling mec, and a high interest rate (along with casino financial markets and financial fragility) had created and sustained stagnation.

The first mention of stagnation in *The General Theory* occurs in chapter 3, where Keynes explained his "principle of effective demand" – the idea that it is the expected sales of a company's products when they eventually got to market that primarily determines its decision about how much to produce and how many people to employ today. Here, he laid out for the first time in the book the outline of his basic argument in support of the secular stagnation hypothesis.

He presented the stagnation thesis in this chapter in an attempt to explain the "paradox of poverty in the midst of plenty," in which mass unemployment and poverty haunted the richest countries in the world. His explanation contains the assertions that the mpc falls as the economy matures due to rising inequality and that the mec has a tendency to decline as the stock of capital increases. Together, these assertions imply a tendency toward stagnation unless the interest rate falls rapidly.

> [T]he richer the community, the wider will tend to be the gap between its actual and its potential production; and therefore the more obvious and outrageous the defects of the economic system. For a poor community will be prone to consume by far the greater part of its output, so that a very modest measure of investment will be sufficient to provide full employment; whereas a wealthy community will have to discover much ampler opportunities for investment if the savings propensities of its wealthier members are to be compatible with the employment of its weaker members. If in a potentially wealthy community the inducement to invest is weak, then in spite of its potential wealth, the working of the principle of effective demand will compel it to reduce its actual output, until, in spite of its potential wealth, it has to become so poor that its surplus over consumption is sufficiently diminished to correspond to the weakness of the inducement to invest.
>
> But worse still. Not only is the propensity to consume weaker in a wealthy community, but, owing to its accumulation of capital being already larger, the opportunities for further investment are less attractive unless the interest rate falls at a sufficiently rapid rate.
>
> (CW 7, p. 31)

Keynes also said here that he would explain later why the interest rate "does not automatically fall to the appropriate level" at which investment is large enough (given the value of the multiplier) to sustain full employment.

Chapter 8 of *The General Theory* discusses the determinants of the mpc and marginal propensity to save (mps). One important point stressed in this chapter is that saving by business and government is a very large share of total national saving and that this form of saving had grown by enough to become a major drag on AD growth in the UK and the USA in the interwar years. Excessive depreciation reserves by business and large government reserves to pay back the huge debt accumulated during WWI – which Keynes refers to here as "sinking funds" – had substantially raised the proportion of national income saved. This lowered the expected profit rate on additional investment because the mec is a positive function of expected consumption spending. These sinking funds "diminish the current effective demand" (CW 7, p. 100).

> [I]n Great Britain at the present time (1935) the substantial amount of house-building and of other new investments since the war has led to an amount of sinking funds being set up much in excess of present requirements for expenditures on repairs and renewals, a tendency which has been accentuated, where the investment has been made by local authorities and public boards, by the principle of "sound" finance which often requires sinking funds sufficient to write off the initial cost some time before the replacement will actually fall due; with the result that even if private individuals were ready to spend the whole of their net incomes it would be a severe task to restore full employment in the face of this heavy volume of statutory provision by public and semi-public authorities, entirely disassociated from any corresponding new investment. The sinking funds of local authorities now stand, I think, at an annual figure of more than half the amount which these authorities are expending on the whole of their new developments.
>
> (CW 7, p. 101)

The same problem existed in the USA.

> In the United States, for example, by 1929 the rapid capital expansion of the previous five years had led cumulatively to the setting up of sinking funds and depreciation allowances, in respect of plant which did not need replacement, on so huge a scale that an enormous volume of entirely new investment was required merely to absorb these financial provisions; and it became hopeless to find still more new investments on a sufficient scale to provide for such new saving

as a wealthy community in full employment would be disposed to set aside. This factor alone was probably enough to cause a slump.

(CW 7, p. 100)

The result was that financial accounting practices exacerbated the existing problem of savings at full employment being far in excess of investment levels that were already shrunken by a collapsing expected profit rate. This was an institutional problem that Keynes believed placed a severe constraint on AD.

> We cannot, as a community, provide for future consumption by financial expedients but only by current physical provision for the future [in the form of capital investment]. In so far as our social and business organization separates financial provision for the future from physical provision for the future so that efforts to secure the former do not carry the latter with them, financial prudence will be liable to diminish aggregate demand [by increasing savings] and thus impair well-being, as there are many examples to testify. The greater, moreover, the consumption for which we have provided in advance [through capital investment], the more difficult it is to find something further to provide for in advance, and the greater our dependence on current consumption as a source of demand. Yet the larger our incomes, the greater, unfortunately, is the margin between our incomes and consumption ... [T]here is no answer to this riddle, except that there must be sufficient unemployment to keep us so poor that our consumption falls short of our income by no more than the [current capital goods] which it pays to produce today.
>
> (CW 7, pp. 104–105)

He summed up this argument as follows: since the demand for capital goods is ultimately derived from the expected demand for consumption goods in the future, a falling propensity to spend either income or wealth on consumption goods is one reason why the profit rate on new investment would fall as the capital stock grew.

> Thus the problem of providing that new capital-investment shall always outrun capital disinvestment [i.e. the current level of depreciation provision] sufficiently to fill the gap between net investment and consumption, presents a problem which is increasingly difficult as capital increases ... Each time we secure to-day's equilibrium by increased investment we are aggravating the difficulty of securing [full-employment] equilibrium tomorrow.
>
> (CW 7, p. 105)

## High-unemployment long-run equilibrium 179

Keynes finished the chapter by pointing out that while the belief that the economically productive opportunities for public investment are quite limited was the conventional wisdom, the opportunities for profitable private-sector investment were widely considered to be virtually unlimited. He found this belief to be "curious." Note his assertion that the UK had entered an era with a stationary population: this was a core assumption of his theory of secular stagnation. In fact, population data in England show that the rate of population growth in the interwar period was dramatically lower than it had been in the nineteenth century.

> It is a curious thing, worthy of mention that the popular mind seems only to be aware of this ultimate perplexity where public investment is concerned, as in the case of road-building and house-building and the like ... "What will you do," it is asked, "when you have built all the houses and roads and town halls and electric grids and water supplies and so forth, which the stationary population of the future can be expected to require?" But it is not so easily understood that the same difficulty applies to private investment and to industrial expansion; particularly to the latter, since it is much easier to see an early satiation of the demand for new factories and plant which absorb individually but little money, than of the demand for dwelling-houses.
>
> The obstacle to a clear understanding is ... an adequate appreciation of the fact that capital is not a self-subsistent entity existing apart from consumption. On the contrary, every weakening in the propensity to consume regarded as a permanent habit must weaken the demand for capital as well as the demand for consumption.
>
> (CW 7, p. 106)

This quote provides a simple statement of the general problem: "what will you do" with respect to private investment demand if you can imagine the private sector building all the investment projects that it makes sense to build on the assumption of a falling interest rate? What Keynes envisages here is a massive increase in the stock of public and private capital over one or two generations, during which he expects no system-transforming or substantially capital-augmenting technical change, little if any population growth after a century of rapid population growth, no wars, and no large export surplus. Under such assumed conditions, it is perfectly sensible to assume that the rate of profit on capital and the mec will fall substantially. Indeed, with physical capital growing exponentially and the labor force hardly growing at all, the resultant rise in capital per worker would lower the marginal product of capital in a classical/neoclassical model.

The proposition that there is a tendency of the rate of profit on investment to fall is addressed most directly in chapter 16, titled "Sundry Observations on the Nature of Capital." Here, Keynes argues that profit on capital is *a form of rent* paid to the owner of capital goods because capital goods are scarce; the scarcer they are, the higher the rent, and vice versa. If the capital stock was to grow very rapidly for a long period of time under state control as Keynes intended, its scarcity value and the profit rate would decline, eventually approaching zero. If the zero profit rate was achieved, the economy would, temporarily at least, be in a stationary state. Keynes argued that it is the inability of the interest rate to fall along with the rate of profit in a regime of free capital movements across borders and adherence to a gold standard that preserved the scarcity value of capital and thereby prevented the level of investment from being high enough to sustain full employment.

> It is much preferable to speak of capital as having a yield over its lifetime in excess of its original cost, than as being *productive*. For the only reason why an asset offers a prospect of yielding during its life services having an aggregate value greater than its initial supply price is because it is *scarce*; and it is kept scarce because of the competition of the rate of interest on money. If capital becomes less scarce, the excess yield will diminish, without its having become less productive – at least in the physical sense.
>
> I sympathise, therefore, with the pre-classical doctrine that everything is *produced* by *labour*, aided by what used to be called art and is now called technique, by natural resources which are free or cost a rent according to their scarcity or abundance, and by the results of past labour, embodied in assets, which also command a price according to their scarcity or abundance.
>
> (CW 7, p. 213, emphasis in original)

Keynes went on to say that capital goods could conceivably become so abundant that the profit rate could even be negative – the present value of its expected future cash flows could be less than its cost. "A correct theory, therefore, must be reversible so as to be able to cover the cases of the marginal efficiency of capital corresponding either to a positive or negative rate of interest" (CW 7, pp. 214–215).

In wealthy economies with large stocks of capital goods, a sustained high rate of investment will, in the absence of substantial change in long-term "facts" that condition the profit rate, cause the mec to fall below the prevailing interest rate at output levels associated with high unemployment. This process, which leads to stagnation, he said, currently existed in Britain and the USA.

> The post-war experiences of Great Britain and the United States are, indeed, actual examples of how an accumulation of wealth [capital goods], so large that its marginal efficiency has fallen more rapidly than the rate of interest can fall in the face of the prevailing institutional and psychological factors, can interfere, in conditions mainly

of laissez-faire, with a reasonable level of employment and with the standard of life which the technical conditions of production are capable of furnishing.

(CW 7, p. 219)

Keynes reinforced his argument with a hypothetical example that compared two nations with the same level of technology but different-sized capital stocks.

It follows that of two equal communities, having the same technique but different stocks of capital, the community with the smaller stocks of capital may be able for the time being to enjoy a higher standard of life than the community with the larger stock; though when the poor community has caught up with the rich – as, presumably, it will – then both alike will suffer the fate of Midas.

(CW 7, p. 219)

This example was chosen to reflect Britain's economic history. Britain was the global "first mover" in creating the innovations and capital investments that constituted the first industrial revolution, and it became the world's largest exporter of many of the goods that dominated world trade at the time. It thus became the "rich" community in the quote above that was now suffering the "fate of Midas." Other European countries and the USA were the initially "poor" communities; they were the second movers in the first industrial revolution who could copy and even improve on the technologies first created and/or implemented in Britain and could create and/or efficiently implement some of the technologies of the second industrial revolution. Thus, these other countries industrialized quickly and grew rapidly, while Britain's industrial advantages evaporated. But now that they have caught up with and even surpassed Britain and have large capital stocks that embody the technologies of both the first and second industrial revolutions, in the absence of an unexpected third industrial revolution, they must face the same fate as Britain.

At this point in the chapter, Keynes returned to a point he made in chapter 10 about public investment and the multiplier. If the mec is low and the long-term interest rate is relatively high, so that capital investment is far too small to generate full employment, and if the state will not or cannot undertake enough productive economic investments to qualitatively alter this situation, it would be a second-best policy if the state and the private sector invested even in projects with little direct economic return, because such projects "will increase economic well-being" through their multiplied impact on jobs and income. And since these are not productive investments themselves, they will postpone the date on which a zero profit rate on productive investment is reached. If the relation of the mec to the long-term interest rate is such that the economy cannot generate full employment and the government refuses to undertake the required level of economically efficient public investments:

> then even a diversion of the desire to hold wealth towards assets, which in fact yield no economic fruits whatever, will increase economic well-being. In so far as millionaires find their satisfaction in building mighty mansions to contain their bodies when alive and pyramids to shelter them after death, or, repenting of their sins, erect cathedrals and endow monasteries or foreign missions, *the day when capital abundance will interfere with abundance of output may be postponed.* "To dig holes in the ground," paid out of savings, will increase, not only employment, but the real national dividend of useful goods and services [via the multiplier].
> 
> (CW 7, pp. 219–220, emphasis added)

He had made the same point in chapter 10:

> Pyramid-building, earthquakes, even wars may serve to increase wealth, if the education of our statesmen on the principles of the classical economics stands in the way of anything better ... Ancient Egypt was doubly fortunate, and doubtlessly owed to this its fabled wealth, in that it possessed two activities, namely, pyramid-building as well as the search for precious metals, the fruits of which, since they could not serve the needs of man by being consumed, did not stale with abundance. The Middle Ages built cathedrals and sang dirges. Two pyramids, two masses for the dead, are twice as good as one; but not so two railways from London to York. Thus, we are so sensible, have schooled ourselves to so close a resemblance to prudent financiers, taking careful thought before we add to the "financial" burdens of posterity by building them houses to live in, that we have no such easy escape from the sufferings of unemployment.
> 
> (CW 7, pp. 129, 131)

Keynes then returned to an exposition of his preferred economic policy centered on public investment.

> Let us assume that steps are taken to ensure that the rate of interest is consistent with the rate of investment which corresponds to full employment. Let us assume, further, that *State action* enters in as a balancing factor to provide that the growth of capital equipment shall be such as to approach saturation-point [the point at which the average rate of profit on capital is zero] ... On such assumptions I should guess that a properly run community equipped with modern technical resources, of which the population is not increasing rapidly, *ought to be able to bring down the marginal efficiency of capital to zero within a*

*single generation*, so that we should attain the conditions of a quasi-stationary community where change and progress would result only from changes in technique, taste, population and institutions, with the products of capital selling at a price proportional to the labour, etc., embodied in them on just the same principles as govern the prices of consumption-goods into which capital-charges enter in an insignificant degree.

(CW 7, pp. 220–221, emphasis added)

Here, again, Keynes suggests that the profit rate will decline as the stock of capital increases *only* if there are no powerful "counter-tendencies": if the population "is not increasing rapidly," there are no systemically powerful and employment-creating "changes in technique," no large changes in consumer "tastes," and no important changes in the "institutions" on which the economy is based.

It is clear from his discussion of stagnation that Keynes had great confidence in the empirical validity or historical truth content of the tendency of the rate of profit on capital to fall in this era and in the assumption that no system-shaking innovations had taken place in Britain for some time and that none were visible on the horizon. Of course, he could not yet (in 1935) clearly foresee the profound effects that WWII and its political and economic aftermath would have on his conditioning assumptions.

Thus, in the absence of the implementation of Keynes's preferred radical policy regime, he assumes that: the mec will remain low in mature and wealthy communities such as Britain and the USA, in which much of the income and wealth of the country are in the hands of a small percentage of the population; this will cause the investment multiplier to be low; and the interest rate will remain high relative to the rate of profit on capital. With both capital investment and household spending low, secular stagnation is likely to continue to plague mature capitalist countries.

In the controversial chapter 17, titled "Properties of Interest and Money," Keynes defended the secular stagnation thesis by attempting to show that there is a high lower bound to the interest rate over the long run that prevents trend investment spending from being large enough to achieve full employment in the context of a falling mec. He makes several effective arguments in support of this hypothesis in the chapter. Unfortunately, their impact on the reader is blurred by the fact that he utilizes a long-run stock-equilibrium model to build his case, yet he relies on a number of supporting short-run arguments whose relation to the long-term static equilibrium model is unclear, at least to me. I review chapter 17 in some detail in Appendix 2.

Why did Keynes take on the daunting task of trying to fit potentially volatile short-run expectations into a long-term asset equilibrium model in chapter 17? I suspect it was because he believed that there *was* a very long-term dimension to the problem of constrained investment demand associated with a long-term version of a variant of liquidity preference for stores of wealth other than the capital stock. He argued that, throughout much of history, capital investment was restrained by the propensity of wealth-holders to hold alternative assets whose exchange value was believed to be more secure or less risky than capital goods over very long periods of time. Moreover, a propensity to hold wealth in the form of land over many generations created a cultural imperative in which landowning became a "way of life" for the hereditary land-owning class, as it did in Britain.

The exit argument in the chapter reflects this historical perspective. It points out that land ownership used to play the role that money ownership now plays as an insurance policy against possible future capital loss. "The high rates of interest on mortgages on land, often exceeding the net yield from cultivating the land, have been a feature of many agricultural economies," which inhibited "current investment in produced capital assets."

> And rightly so. For in earlier social organization where long-term bonds in the modern sense were non-existent, the competition of a high interest-rate on mortgages may well have had the same effect in retarding the growth of wealth from current investment in produced capital assets, as high interest rates on long-term debts have had in more recent times.
>
> (CW 7, p. 241)

He summed up his perspective on the powerful long-term negative influence of liquidity preference on economic development as follows:

> That the world after several millennia of steady individual saving, is so poor as it is in accumulated capital-assets, is to be explained, in my opinion, neither by the improvident propensities of mankind, not even by the destruction of war, but by the high liquidity-premiums formerly attaching to the ownership of land and now attaching to money.
>
> (CW 7, p. 242)

Keynes repeated this claim later in the book: liquidity preference, he said, was *the* major cause of inadequate capital investment over millennia. "The destruction of the inducement to invest by an excessive liquidity preference was the outstanding evil, the prime impediment to the growth of wealth, in the ancient and medieval world" (CW 7, p. 351). This is the long-run perspective that he tried to embed in the long-run stock-equilibrium model of the chapter with at best partial success.

Chapter 19 contains an important theoretical–historical discussion of the topic of secular stagnation. Near the chapter's end, Keynes said that the unique economic conditions prevailing from the late eighteenth century through the nineteenth century led to exceptional long-term growth in income and employment. This list of conditions incorporates many of the elements of his own explanation of why this century was so prosperous and why the interwar years brought stagnation followed by global depression. The list therefore constitutes a guide to his theoretical perspective on secular stagnation theory.

> During the nineteenth century, the growth of population and of invention, the opening up of new lands, the state of confidence and the frequency of war over the average of (say) each decade seem to have been sufficient, taken in conjunction with the propensity to consume, to establish a level of the marginal efficiency of capital which allowed a reasonably satisfactory average level of employment to be compatible with a rate of interest high enough to be psychologically acceptable to wealth owners. There is evidence that for a period of almost one hundred and fifty years the long run typical rate of interest in the leading financial centres was about 5 per cent, and the guilt-edged rate [on government bonds] between 3 and 3.5 per cent; and that these rates of interest were modest enough to encourage a rate of investment consistent with an average rate of employment which was not intolerably low.
>
> (CW 7, pp. 307–308)

So, the nineteenth century was exceptionally buoyant because of: the population growing rapidly (creating rising demand for consumer goods, especially housing); system-transforming innovations and technical progress (such as the creation of the railroad system and the key inventions and innovations of the first and early second industrial revolutions); the opening up of new lands around the globe (which created profitable trading opportunities for Britain, who dominated trade in cotton textiles, the most important commodity in world trade, and controlled global commerce and finance); frequent wars (which stimulated AD); and a high state of business "confidence" in an attractive profit rate on investment that became so deeply embedded in the British business and financial elites that it could not be shaken by short-term economic difficulties – "prosperity is cumulative." These factors led to an average value of the mec that was high enough that it sustained rapid capital investment and employment for over a century, even though the propensity to save was also high (and the investment multiplier therefore low) because of the extreme inequality of wealth and income in the era. The high rate of savings kept the long-term interest rate low enough to sustain rapid capital accumulation and yet high enough to be "psychologically acceptable to wealth holders." This line of reasoning is reminiscent of his arguments in *The Economic Consequences of the Peace*, discussed in Chapter 2 of this book.

However, Keynes said, the special circumstances that generated high growth and acceptable employment levels had now evaporated and showed no signs of returning. Thus, Britain faced long-term stagnation unless it radically changed the structure of its political economy. "To-day and presumably for the future the schedule of the marginal efficiency of capital is, for a variety of reasons, much lower than it was in the nineteenth century" (CW 7, p. 308).

This is a clear statement of Keynes's belief in the truth content of the stagnation thesis. Given the current low secular trend of the mec and the low value of the mpc and the multiplier, the only hope for substantially stimulating the rate of private investment spending would be a large and permanent reduction of the long-term interest rate. Thus, sustained full employment could not be achieved until the central bank was nationalized and committed to a falling rate of interest – a point he made a number of times.

> The acuteness and the peculiarity of our contemporary problem arises, therefore, out of the possibility that the average rate of interest which will allow a reasonable average level of employment is one so unacceptable to wealth-owners that it cannot be readily established merely by manipulating the quantity of money ... But the most stable, and the least easily shifted, element in our contemporary economy has been hitherto, and may prove to be in the future, the minimum rate of interest acceptable to the generality of wealth-owners. If a tolerable level of employment requires a rate of interest much below the average rates which ruled in the nineteenth century, it is most doubtful whether it can be achieved merely by manipulating the quantity of money.
>
> (CW 7, pp. 308–309)[4]

Keynes noted in this chapter that there are several deductions to be made from the nominal long-term interest rate to arrive at the actual return to the bond holder: "the cost of bringing the borrower and lender together"; "income and surtaxes"; and "the allowance which the lender requires to cover his risk and uncertainty." It is this net yield that must "tempt the wealth-owner to sacrifice his liquidity" in spite of the potential for the capital loss and possible default inevitably associated with long-term bonds (CW 7, p. 309). Liquidity or capital-safety preference may remain strong enough to keep the long-term interest rate too high to permit acceptable rates of unemployment in the face of a weak expected rate of profit. "If, in conditions of tolerable average employment, this net yield turns out to be infinitesimal, time-honored methods [of sustaining high employment] may prove unavailing," and therefore radical economic intervention by the state will be required to achieve sustained full employment (CW 7, p. 309). Keynes even quoted the nineteenth-century financial-market savant Bagehot on this issue: "John Bull can stand many things, but he cannot stand [a long-term interest rate of] 2 per cent" (CW 7, p. 309).

In chapter 22 on the business cycle, Keynes argued that the latter part of the vigorous capital investment boom in the late 1920s in the USA eventually drove the *actual* profit rate but not yet the *expected* profit rate or mec down to a level that was below the long-term interest rate by the forces associated with his secular stagnation reasoning. This led to the end of the US boom in 1929 as the mec eventually reflected the decline in the actual rate of profit. However, even at the peak of the boom (with the measured unemployment rate near 4 percent), the profit rate remained well above zero, according to Keynes. It would take rapid investment for "twenty-five years or less" to drive the profit rate to zero.

> It is, indeed, very possible that the prolongation of approximately full employment over a period of years would be associated in countries so wealthy as Great Britain or the United States with a volume of new investment, assuming the existing propensity to consume, so great that it would eventually lead to a state of full investment in the sense that an aggregate gross yield in excess of replacement cost could no longer be expected on a reasonable calculation from a further increment of durable goods of any type whatever. Moreover, this situation might be achieved comparatively soon – say within twenty-five years or less. I must not be taken to deny this, because I assert that a state of full investment in the strict sense has never yet occurred, not even momentarily.
>
> (CW 7, pp. 323–324)

Chapter 23, aptly titled "Notes on Mercantilism, Etc.," is a smorgasbord of observations by Keynes about both the errors and the important insights associated with mercantilism, an economic doctrine that dominated British thinking for 200 years prior to the nineteenth century, when it became displaced by the classical school. Mercantilists supported: managed trade; industrial policy designed to create conditions supportive of the growth of British industry through the pursuit of what is sometimes referred to as dynamic comparative advantage; and government-guided low interest rates. Keynes applauded the mercantilists for rejecting what became classical dogma: that free trade and the free movement of capital across borders would automatically set the interest rate at a level consistent with domestic full employment. Keynes vigorously opposed the free movement of money capital flows across Britain's borders because this increased domestic interest rates and lowered domestic employment.

> Great Britain in the pre-war years of the twentieth century provides an example of a country in which the excessive facilities for foreign lending and the purchase of properties abroad frequently stood in the

way of the decline in the domestic rate of interest which was required to ensure full employment at home.

(CW 7, p. 337)

The mercantilists turned out to be more insightful about this problem than the classicists that succeeded them, Keynes said, and for this reason they supported state intervention to keep the interest rate low.

> Mercantilists' thought never supposed that there was a self-adjusting tendency by which the rate of interest would be established at the level consistent with sustained full employment. On the contrary, they were emphatic that an unduly high interest rate was the main obstacle to the growth of wealth.
>
> (CW 7, p. 341)

They also rejected the core classical belief that disequilibrium processes could be trusted to quickly restore full employment when the economy suffered from underemployment. In the middle of the eighteenth century, David Hume helped solidify the shift of focus from potentially unstable disequilibrium processes to stable equilibriums.

> [He] began the practice amongst economists of stressing the equilibrium position as compared with the ever-shifting movement towards it, though he was still enough of a mercantilist not to overlook the fact that *it is in the transition that we actually have our being*.
>
> (CW 7, p. 343, emphasis added)

Keynes emphasized that the crucial insight embedded in mercantilist thought was that the core problem of laissez-faire capitalism is the combination of a tendency of the profit rate to fall over time and of the rate of interest to remain high. Indeed, he argued that this has been the core economic problem throughout history. What he said here is a good short statement of his strong belief in the long-run stagnation thesis.

> It is impossible to study the notions to which the mercantilists were led by their actual experiences, without perceiving that there has been *a chronic tendency* throughout human history for the propensity to save to be stronger than the inducement to invest. *The weakness of the inducement to invest has been at all times the key to the economic problem. To-day the explanation of the weakness of this inducement may chiefly lie in the extent of existing accumulations*; whereas, formerly, risks and hazards of all kinds may have played a larger part. But the result is the same. The desire of the individual to augment his personal wealth by abstaining from consumption has usually been stronger than the inducement of

the entrepreneur to augment the national wealth by labor on the construction of durable assets.

(CW 7, pp. 347–348, emphasis added)

Keynes then commented again on how the classical school was able to rule out of serious discussion self-evident truths that had been established across "several millenniums" – including the belief that, left only to private financial markets, interest rates will usually be too high to achieve full employment.

> There remains an allied, but distinct, matter where for centuries, indeed for several millenniums, enlightened public opinion held for certain and obvious a doctrine which the classical school has repudiated as childish, but which deserves rehabilitation and honour, I mean the doctrine that the rate of interest is not self-adjusting at a level best suited to the social advantage but constantly tends to rise too high, so that a wise government is concerned to curb it by statute and custom and even by evoking the sanctions of moral law ... The destruction of the inducement to invest by an excessive liquidity preference was the outstanding evil, the prime impediment to the growth of wealth, in the ancient and medieval world.
>
> (CW 7, p. 351)

How, then, did classical theory become the conventional wisdom in spite of the fact that it was inconsistent with most of world history? Keynes notes here "the analogy between the sway of the classical school of economic theory and certain religions" (CW 7, p. 351). His main answer to this question was consistent throughout the interwar years: the era from the mid-eighteenth century through the end of the nineteenth century in Britain was in fact a relatively unique period in the history of capitalism, but it was pictured in classical theory as if it were the perpetual state of laissez-faire capitalism in all eras and all places. The growth of capital investment in Britain remained high throughout this era because Britain was the main beneficiary of: the rise of capitalism; the construction of a globally integrated economy; the creation of Britain's empire; the domination of the world's cotton industry, the most important global industry during this era; Britain's role at the center of global commerce and finance; and the industrial revolutions that took place in this period. These events created enormous opportunities for highly profitable investment projects. "For nothing short of the exuberance of the greatest age of the inducement to invest could have made it possible to lose sight of the theoretical possibility of its insufficiency" (CW 7, p. 353).

Keynes acknowledged that during the long nineteenth century, the policy positions derived from classical theory worked reasonably well, even though classical theory was a deficient general theory of long-run capitalist dynamics. But when the unique conditions that led to rapid growth in the long nineteenth century ended, the laissez-faire policies supported by classical theory proved to be disastrous for Britain and the global economy because the assumptions of classical theory conflicted sharply with actual conditions in mature capitalism.

## Conclusion

It is clear that, by the 1930s, Keynes believed that the major economic problem that had confronted Britain throughout the interwar years now afflicted the USA and other mature capitalist countries. The problem was deeply rooted long-term or secular stagnation. In this chapter, I have tried to demonstrate that convincing the reader that secular stagnation was real and deeply rooted was Keynes's major *theoretical* objective in the sections of *The General Theory* that dealt with underemployment equilibriums. One might argue as Schumpeter did that it was *the* major theoretical objective of the book.

In Chapter 20, I will show that Keynes's major *policy* objective in *The General Theory* was to convince the reader that the only adequate solution for this long-term stagnation problem was a revolution in Britain's political economy that would replace the current malfunctioning and archaic capitalist system with a form of democratic socialism. In the new economy, the state would directly control or guide the lion's share of large-scale capital investment and use this power, aided by capital controls, progressive tax policy, industrial policies, and sustained expansionary monetary policy to generate and sustain full employment and to sharply reduce income and wealth inequality.

## Appendix 1: Did history demonstrate that Keynes's theory of secular stagnation was wrong?

Did the high growth and rapidly rising real incomes of the postwar Golden Age prove that Keynes's projection of secular stagnation was a mistake? Obviously, the world has not remained in depression since the 1930s, but in my view, the appropriate formulation of the question is this: were there good reasons for Keynes to expect secular stagnation in the absence of an improbable dramatic increase in the role of the state in the economy, in the absence of unforeseeable system-transforming technical change, in the absence of rapid population growth, and in the absence of war? Keynes thought there were, and he proposed a radical change in the economic role of the state precisely because this was the best way to end economic stagnation in Britain.

What actually ended stagnation was not stabilizing disequilibrium market processes as in classical theory, but rather the radical transformation of both the US and UK economies, starting in the 1930s (with the

New Deal and the tight regulation of financial markets in the USA), accelerating in WWII with both governments in control of all crucial economic decision-making in the planned economies of the period, and culminating with the era of big government and the welfare/warfare state after the war.

However, even this radical transformation, along with the spread of the second industrial revolution across much of the developing world, did not permanently end the specter of secular stagnation. Rather, it led to the "Golden Age" of capitalism in the 1950s through the late 1970s, a period of about a single generation. Following economic turmoil in the 1970s, the institutions and processes of the Golden Age were replaced by those of the emerging global neoliberal order, which in its turn eventually brought about a "Leaden Age" of rising unemployment, rising inequality and slower growth in the West, and rising inequality within the faster-growing developing economies.

In recent decades, the "insane" financial markets of the 1920s and 1930s were reincarnated as the new superheated global financial casino of this era. This contributed to the onset of the global economic crisis in the mid-2000s that caused much of the global economy, including the developed economies in the West, to fall into deep recessions with rapidly rising public debt, widespread economic policies of austerity, and, again, increasing income and wealth inequality. Several influential mainstream economists (including Paul Krugman, Robert Gordon, and Larry Summers) have recently expressed support for a theory of secular stagnation.

These developments again raise the fundamental question at the heart of Keynes's focus on secular stagnation theory: is prosperity that is occasionally interrupted by bouts of stagnation the normal state of modern or mature capitalism – or is it the other way around?[5] Keynes believed it was the other way around, and for this reason argued for a change of economic systems from capitalism to liberal socialism.

In *The General Theory*, Keynes presented and defended his understanding of the long-term crisis of the American and British economies in the midst of the Great Depression. If these countries were to continue to operate under the relatively unregulated capitalist systems they had in the 1920s, he argued, they would continue to experience slow growth and perpetually high unemployment. These problems could neither be eliminated by market disequilibrium processes nor by moderate policy change within existing political–economic regimes. If the government response to the turmoil of the 1930s remained constrained by classical maxims, Keynes expected to see continuing social, economic, and political unrest, with an ongoing increase in popularity of political movements of the extreme left and extreme right. Such movements had already taken power in Italy, Germany, and the Soviet Union. Keynes understood that the forces that created secular stagnation were strong enough to create the potential for political chaos, even in the USA – a threat so powerful that it had already induced major experimentation in many countries, with such dramatically increased government intervention in the operation of the economy as to be unprecedented outside of wartime. As one recent commentator on the political turbulence in Europe in this era put it:

> By 1939, most of the continent's functioning democratic systems were in extreme ruins. Weimar Germany, the most modern constitutional polity of its day, gave way to the Third Reich. Across eastern and southern Europe, the interwar transition to democracy was thrown into reverse as no fewer than 16 countries shifted right.
> (*Financial Times*, January 31/February 1, 2015, p. 7)[6]

To sum up: textbook Keynesian theory concludes that it is logically possible for a capitalist economy to be stuck in a high-employment equilibrium. Since the theory implicitly assumes that market economies are efficient long-term allocation mechanisms, most Keynesians, at least until very recently, argued that when the economy is in recession, all that is required is a temporary "kick-start" to AD through monetary and/or fiscal policy that will cause the economy to return to its *natural* low-unemployment long-term growth path. This conclusion is an act of faith in the efficiency of modern capitalism rather than a deduction from a careful, open-minded historical and institutional analysis. Keynes, who conducted just such an analysis, did not share this faith.

So, it is not true, as many have argued, that *The General Theory* is solely about the short and intermediate runs with no theory of the long run. Indeed, in the 1930s, Keynes and Alvin Hansen, a Harvard economist strongly influenced by Keynes's work, were the non-Marxist economists most associated in the eyes of the economic profession with secular stagnation theory.

## Appendix 2: The perplexing chapter 17 of *The General Theory*[7]

Minsky argued that Keynes "dug deeper – but not clearly" into the crises tendencies of modern capitalism in chapter 17 and that the chapter's secular stagnation arguments were "obscure" because the general equilibrium model presented there brought the reader "back into the world of the classical economy" and away from the endogenous instability stressed in chapters 2, 3, 5, 12–15, 19, and 22 of *The General Theory* and in Keynes's defense of *The General Theory* in the QJE in 1937 (Minsky 1975, p. 79).[8] But endogenous instability arguments, including the theory of "liquidity preference" to hold money as an asset presented in chapter 15 to explain the volatility of the long-term interest rate, *are* in fact used effectively in chapter 17. It is the relation of such phenomena to his long-run model that is unclear. Keep in mind that Keynes presented a number of arguments in *The General Theory* elsewhere than in chapter 17 about why the interest rate has a lower bound that is too high to allow for sustained full employment, so he did not have to rely solely on the validity of the arguments in this chapter to defend this assertion.

The chapter opens with this question:

> It seems, then, that the *rate of interest on money* plays a peculiar part in setting a limit to the level of employment, since it sets a standard to which the marginal efficiency of a capital-asset must attain if it is to be newly produced ... It is natural to enquire wherein the peculiarity of money lies as distinct from other assets ... Until we answer [this] question, the full significance of our theory will not be clear. The money-rate of interest – we remind the reader – is nothing more than the percentage excess of a sum of money contracted for forward delivery, e.g. a year hence.
>
> (CW 7, p. 222, emphasis in original)

Keynes identifies three types of assets that can be used to store wealth: capital investment goods, durable "consumption goods" such as housing, and "money." He focused on three attributes of assets that determine their annual yields in terms of their own values, or their "own-rates of interest," or their marginal efficiencies: (1) their "yield or output q measured in terms of themselves"; (2) the wastage or carrying cost of holding assets "irrespective of their being used to produce a yield," called c; and (3) "the power of disposal over an asset during a period," denoted l, which is called its "liquidity premium" (CW 7, pp. 225–226).

The key to Keynes's argument in the chapter is that while real assets have a higher net yield (q-c) than money, money earns a substantial "liquidity premium" while the real assets do not. The liquidity premium is defined as:

> the power of disposal over an asset during a period [which] may offer a potential convenience or security, which are not equal for assets of different kinds ... There is, so to speak, nothing to show for this at the end of the period in the shape of output; yet it is something for which people are willing to pay something. The amount (measured in terms of itself) which they are willing to pay for the potential convenience or security given by this power of disposal (exclusive of the yield [q] or carrying cost [c] attaching to the asset), we shall call its liquidity premium l.
>
> (CW 7, p. 226)

Liquidity, or the "power of disposal" of an asset, is, surprisingly, not defined here, but it is typically understood to be the ability to sell an asset quickly with a low transaction cost and without a significant capital loss. In the absence of inflation, money is the ultimate liquid asset because it cannot suffer a nominal capital loss. The real assets considered here are potentially quite illiquid. If the owners of these assets are forced to sell them into a weak market, they will experience a substantial capital loss. The liquidity premium is thus a kind of insurance payment against the risk of being forced to sell an asset at a steep loss. However, it is not clear to me that it belongs in a long-run stock-equilibrium model.

Minsky argued that the last sentence in the quote immediately above should begin: "The amount [in foregone cash flows] ..." Risky assets have higher cash flows over the long run than safe assets. Their "ease of disposal" and the "certainty of [their] sale price" can be quite volatile over the business cycle, but they should not be volatile in a long-term equilibrium state.

> If an asset is liquid the cash flow in the form of interest and profits per dollar [q] of market value will be smaller than if the asset is illiquid. The visible rate of return on an asset will vary inversely with the quality of the market for the asset or with the time to maturity, or with other measures of the ease of disposal and the certainty of its sale price.
>
> (Minsky 1975, pp. 81–82)

The "liquidity premium" used here appears to be closely related to the concept of "liquidity preference" that is the centerpiece of the theory of the determination of the long-term interest rate discussed in chapter 15 of *The General Theory*. The conclusion of that chapter is that fluctuations in expected capital gains or losses in the bond market, along with investor ignorance in a world of Keynesian uncertainty about the likelihood of unforeseeable future needs to raise cash quickly, cause investors to switch their preferences from holding mostly "money" to mostly long-term bonds and back as the pessimism of financial market downturns is replaced by the optimism of booms.[9] The theory of liquidity preference of chapter 15 does not transfer smoothly into a static long-term equilibrium model precisely because interest rate instability is powered by the volatility of expectations of future asset prices and the confidence with which investors hold these expectations. But if the economy is in a state of long-term equilibrium, then long-term expectations are stable by assumption and *liquidity preference should be zero by assumption*. As Minsky put it: "At a crucial juncture in the argument, stagnation and the exhaustion-of-investment-opportunity ideas take over from a cyclical perspective in which investment, asset holding, and liability structures are guided by speculative considerations" (Minsky 1975, pp. 79–80).

Keynes does discuss the influence of short- to intermediate-term expectations in chapter 17. "To determine the relationships between the *expected* returns on different types of assets which are consistent with equilibrium, we must also know what the changes in relative values during the year *are expected* to be" (CW 7, p. 227, emphasis added). Keynes does not tell us here whether these are the psychologically complex "Keynesian" expectations stressed in the rest of the book. If they are not – if the expected yields are the truth about the future – then no one needs to hold money as an asset as an insurance policy against unpredictable outcomes. If the future is assumed to be representable by pre-given and stationary probability distributions, as in the classical theory and modern "rational expectations" models, all risk can presumably be hedged. On the other hand, if the future is unknowable and expectations are conventionally and behaviorally constructed as in the rest of the book, there *will be* a liquidity preference for money that keeps the interest rate high, especially at times of economic and financial instability.

The kernel of Keynes's thesis in chapter 17 is that "money ... has special characteristics which lead to its own-rate of interest ... being more reluctant to fall as the stock of assets in general increases than the own-rates of interest of other assets" in the long run (CW 7, p. 229). He calls attention to two main "peculiarities" in the money rate of interest that limit its long-term decline.

The first characteristic is that, under existing institutional and political conditions, the money supply is relatively inflexible or the elasticity of supply is low with respect to changes in demand for money. There are two reasons for this. One is that the central bank is committed to maintaining that level of supply needed to keep the exchange rate relatively stable; another is that Britain cannot mine gold domestically whenever there is a rising demand for gold. Keynes could have added the fact that the policy of the Bank of England reflected the interests of the rentier class and the big banks, and thus would be likely to keep a tight rein on the money supply to sustain high interest rates even when Britain was not on the gold standard.

Therefore, as the demand to hold money *as an asset* grows over time, unless the supply of money is deliberately increased by the central bank, the excess demand can only be eliminated by a rising interest rate. By way of contrast, as the supplies of real assets grow over time, Keynes believed, there will be a decline in their marginal efficiencies or own-rates of interest. These facts led Keynes to the conclusion that the interest rate is unlikely to fall as fast as the value of (q-c) for capital goods and consumer durables such as housing over the long run, causing the gap between current investment and saving at full-capacity output to grow over time.

> The first characteristic which tends toward the above conclusion is the fact that money has, both in the long and in the short period, a zero, or at any rate a very small, elasticity of production, so far as the power of private enterprise is concerned, *as distinct from the monetary authority* ... Now, in the case of assets having an elasticity of production, the reason why we assumed their own-rate of interest to decline was because we assumed the stock of them to increase as the result of

> a higher rate of output. In the case of money, however – postponing for the moment, our consideration of the effect of [deflation] *or of a deliberate increase by the monetary authority* – the supply is fixed.
>
> (CW 7, p. 230, emphasis added)

Keynes makes clear that this particular cause of an excessively high interest rate in the short and the long run could be eliminated by a central bank committed to the goal of sustained full employment. The prime objective of such a central bank would be to increase the money supply by enough to allow the interest rate to fall to zero as the mec on real assets falls to zero under the relentless growth of public and semi-public investment. Capital controls would obviously be needed to accomplish this goal.

> Unemployment develops, that is to say, because people want the moon; – men cannot be employed when the object of their desire (i.e. money) is something which cannot be produced and the demand for which cannot be readily chocked off. There is no remedy but to persuade the public that green cheese is practically the same thing and to have a green cheese factory (i.e. a central bank) under public control.
>
> (CW 7, p. 235)[10]

In other words, elimination of this problem required that the central bank be nationalized and its main objective changed from defense of rentier income to the pursuit of sustained full employment. The Bank of England had been owned by its private shareholders and was strongly influenced by their interests from its founding in 1694. It was finally nationalized by the Labour Party in 1946.

Keynes commented that land rent shares with the interest rate the property that rising demand elicits no increase in supply. To distinguish between the two, Keynes introduced a "second condition" that differentiated between them.

> The second *differentia* of money is that it has an elasticity of substitution equal, or nearly equal, to zero, which means that as the exchange value of money rises there is no tendency to substitute some other factor for it ... This follows from the peculiarity of money that its utility is solely derived from its exchange-value, so that the two rise and fall pari passu, with the result that as the exchange value rises there is no motive or tendency, as in the case of rent-factors, to substitute some other factor for it.
>
> (CW 7, p. 231, emphasis in original)

If the price or exchange value of housing or of capital goods rises, *ceteris paribus*, the demand for these assets will fall. But if a drop in the price level causes the exchange value of money to rise, the demand to hold money as an asset will not fall, so there is no reason to exchange money for real assets. Indeed, in an era of deflation – an ongoing process of price decline expected to continue into the future rather than a once-and-for-all change in the price level – there will be a strong incentive to sell real assets and hold more money. Deflation causes "capital gains" in the purchasing power of money.[11] Recall that Britain experienced a serious process of deflation from the early 1920s through much of the 1930s,

On other hand, deflation will reduce the demand for money to make transactions, and this will increase the stock of money available to buy bonds, which will reduce the interest rate.

Since there are forces operating on the interest rate in both directions:

> It is not possible to dispute on purely theoretical grounds that this reaction might be capable of allowing an adequate decline in the money-rate of interest. There are, however, several reasons, which taken in combination are of a compelling force, why in an economy of the type to which we are accustomed it is very probable that the money-rate of interest will often prove reluctant to decline adequately.
> (CW 7, p. 232)

Keynes offered four reasons why the interest rate was likely to rise in a deflation. First, anticipating an argument made in chapter 19, Keynes states that "If the effect [of falling prices] is to produce an expectation of a further fall, the [negative] reaction on the marginal efficiency of capital may offset the decline in the rate of interest" caused by lower transactions balances (CW 7, p. 232). If businesses and households expect an ongoing process of deflation to continue, they will postpone purchases today in anticipation of lower prices next period, which will reduce AD and employment today and fuel further deflation. This argument is quite reasonable but is specifically about *disequilibrium processes* and thus does not seem suitable for inclusion in a long-term equilibrium model.

Second, wages are downwardly "sticky in terms of money" (CW 7, p. 232). If they were not, "this might often tend to create an expectation of a further fall in wages with unfavourable reactions on the marginal efficiency of capital," as explained in the previous paragraph (CW 7, p. 232). This helps protect the economy from the potential for high unemployment to trigger a destructive deflationary spiral. Keynes devotes considerable space in *The General Theory*, especially in chapters 2 and 19, to a defense of his belief that downward wage rigidity created by strong labor unions is a necessary condition for avoiding disastrous deflation under conditions of sustained high unemployment – the inverse of the classical position.

The third reason as to why the interest rate cannot fall as far as the own-rates on real assets, Keynes said, "is the most fundamental consideration in this context, namely, the characteristics of money which satisfy liquidity-preference" (CW 7, p. 233).

> For, in certain circumstances *such as will often occur*, [liquidity preference] will cause the rate of interest to be insensitive, particularly below a certain figure, even to a substantial increase in the quantity of money in proportion to other forms of wealth. In other words, beyond a certain point money's yield from liquidity does not fall in response to an increase in its quantity to anything approaching the extent to which the yield from other types of assets fall when their quantity is comparably increased.
>
> (CW 7, p. 233, emphasis added)

This argument is presumably intended as a longer-term variant of the famous "liquidity trap" discussed in chapter 15 on "Incentives to Liquidity." The liquidity trap is a condition in which increases in the money supply elicit no decline in the interest rate because it is already so low that the reward for holding risky bonds relative to riskless money in the form of the interest rate is negligible, and expectations of a future capital loss on bond-holding become almost universal.

> There is the possibility ... that, after the rate of interest has fallen to a certain level, liquidity-preference may become virtually absolute in the sense that almost everyone prefers cash to holding a debt which yields so low a rate of interest. In this event the monetary authority would have lost effective control over the rate of interest. But whilst this limiting case might become practically important in future, I know of no example of it hitherto.
>
> (CW 7, p. 207)

Keynes used US financial markets in the early 1930s as an example of this kind of phenomenon: "In the United States at certain dates there was ... a financial crisis or crisis of liquidation, when scarcely anyone could be induced to part with holdings of money on any reasonable terms" (CW 7, pp. 207–208).

Keynes also pointed out there would be an important upside to a liquidity trap in the Liberal Socialist economy he desired. It would allow a Board of National Investment to borrow extensive funds to finance public investment at an exceptionally low rate of interest. "Moreover, if such a situation were to arise, it would mean that the public authority itself could borrow [to finance public investment] through the banking system on an unlimited scale at a nominal rate of interest" (CW 7, p. 207).

In his 1937 defense of *The General Theory* in the QJE (Keynes 1937), Keynes famously asked of the classical theory, which assumed a static equilibrium in which the (stochastic) future would look like the present until an exogenous shock to the system took place: what possible motive could people have for holding money as a store of value in long-term equilibrium? His answer was that the existence of a demand for money as an asset requires radical or Keynesian uncertainty about future states of the economy. Since expectations and the confidence with which they are held are endogenously restless, the "equilibrium" Keynes refers to in the last sentence can, logically, only be a temporary or moving equilibrium and not a long-term static equilibrium. In chapter 15, Keynes said:

> In a static society or in a society in which for any other reason no one feels any uncertainty about the future rates of interest, the liquidity function [or demand to hold money as an asset function], or the propensity to hoard function (as we might term it), will always be zero in equilibrium.
>
> (CW 7, pp. 208–209)

Liquidity preference to hold money as an asset is a positive function of our sense of the unpredictability of future non-money asset prices. Even if we were to think of the future as identical to the present in the sense that outcomes would be random draws from a stationary probability function, the sense of uncertainty would be at its nadir in static equilibrium and all risk could be hedged.

Fourth, Keynes argued that "the fact that contracts are fixed, and [money] wages [and therefore prices] are usually somewhat stable, in terms of money unquestionably plays a large part in attracting to money so high a liquidity-premium" (CW 7, p. 236). Both factors – that contracts are written in terms of money (rather than real assets such as, say, wheat) and that money wages are *usually* stable so that prices are *usually* stable – certainly help to make money an attractive store of wealth, even though its yield is small. In Britain, there had been substantial price stability over most of the nineteenth century and deflation over most of the interwar years, which made money an even more attractive store of wealth. This presumably put upward pressure on the long-term interest rate.

*Summary*

In my opinion, chapter 17 does contain a number of interesting arguments in support of the main proposition of the chapter that interest rates are unlikely to fall fast enough or far enough to keep investment spending at a level consistent with full employment as the mec and the mpc fall over time. In this important sense, the chapter is a success. However, I also believe that a substantial part of the liquidity premium on money is attributable to *ever-changing* short-term and long-term expectations that, upon occasion, can become wildly unstable – see chapters 12 and 15. This phenomenon simply cannot be integrated comfortably into a long-term asset *equilibrium* model.

## Notes

1. To the best of my knowledge, Keynes never used the term "secular stagnation."
2. I do not mean that there were no important innovations in the interwar period in the USA and Britain. In fact, there were a number of important new industries created or further developed during this period. However, their impact on output and employment was too small to overcome the long list of impediments to growth mentioned here. They were not sufficiently system transforming, at least in this era.
3. The neoclassical theory of the firm has a similar property. A rising capital-to-labor ratio will reduce the marginal product of capital, which, *ceteris paribus*, will lower the rate of profit on capital.
4. Even with a nationalized central bank, a persistently low interest rate could not be achieved without the use of capital controls.
5. Thomas Piketty's widely read book, *Capital in the Twenty First Century* (Piketty 2014), has again raised the question of whether rising inequality is the natural or normal state of capitalism.
6. "From dawn to dusk – European democracy enters dangerous times."
7. Readers without an interest in this topic can skip Appendix 2.
8. We should bear in mind that Minsky and other Golden Age "Keynesian" economists were uncomfortable about being associated with Keynes's commitment to the theory of secular stagnation in an era of seemingly endless prosperity. In this period, it was almost universally believed that, with big government, activist monetary and fiscal policy, financial market regulation designed to end casino capitalism in America, huge defense budgets, and large social welfare spending, secular stagnation could not happen again.
9. The reader should keep in mind that Keynes defines "money" as cash plus short, safe financial assets such as savings accounts and Treasury bills that pay interest, but normally at a much lower rate than is paid on long-term bonds.
10. Adherence to the belief that the "moon is made of green cheese" is a sign of credulity or dim-wittedness.
11. In periods of high inflation, of course, money is a terrible store of value, normally far inferior to gold or land or works of art, and so on. Keynes was certainly aware of this fact. But inflation was not on the horizon when Keynes wrote *The General Theory*. Britain experienced serious deflation in every year from 1921 through 1933 and relative price stability in the three years that followed. Moderate price inflation did not return until after 1936 when Britain began its military buildup in anticipation of its likely participation in war in Europe.

# 14 Upon further reflection
## Keynes on secular stagnation in 1937

Keynes received a letter three months after *The General Theory* was published in which the writer said that he could not find a fully adequate defense of the secular stagnation thesis in the book. He said that Keynes's defense of the stagnation thesis was:

> inadequate in not formulating the difference between diminishing m.e. [mec] in one line (when investment in other lines is kept constant) and diminishing m.e. in all lines when investment in all lines is extending. I see no reason to suppose that in the latter case m.e. (long period) will decline all that steeply.
>
> (CW 29, p. 212)

The writer believed that an endless creation of "technological progress" and "conscious entrepreneur planning" created unlimited profitable investment opportunities that made it possible to have "almost indefinite growth" (CW 29, p. 212).

Keynes could have defended himself by repeating and perhaps providing additional support for his argument that endless system-transforming technical change was nowhere to be seen in the mid-1930s UK, nor had it made an appearance in the decade-plus that preceded it. He could have repeated his standard list of all the structural, behavioral, and institutional impediments to a return to rapid growth.[1] But, surprisingly, he did neither of these things. Instead, he acknowledged that his defense of secular stagnation in the book was not fully adequate. In fact, he appears to bend over backwards to accept the writer's critique. Keynes suggests that his arguments in support of secular stagnation were half-hearted – a mere "obiter dictum," rather than an adequate defense.

> I agree that I must develop more realistically the point I threw out that we might without excessive difficulty reach saturation point in the supply of capital. As expressed in the book it is not much better than

an obiter dictum. I may very well be wrong, but I should like to make an attempt to justify more adequately the way in which I feel about the matter.

(CW 29, p. 213)

We know that Keynes's efforts to support the stagnation thesis were anything but just "thrown out." As we have seen, he devoted a substantial part of the book to its defense. While the reader of *The General Theory* may or may not have been converted to the stagnation thesis, he or she was left with no doubt as to the seriousness of Keynes's attachment to it. And he had expressed his commitment to his version of the tendency of the rate of profit to fall over and over again since WWI. Of course, because Keynes received and answered a veritable mountain of mail on a regular basis, he may have pleaded guilty to the charge to avoid a lengthy correspondence about it.

Nevertheless, it is probably true that Keynes understood that the arguments about stagnation in the book left many readers unconvinced of its validity and that he could – and should – improve upon them. This led him to undertake a different kind of defense of the stagnation thesis in an important lecture he gave to the Eugenics Society in February 1937 titled "Some Economic Consequences of a Declining Population." It is referred to in the literature as the Galton Lecture. Keynes was a Director of the Society, which included a wide swath of Britain's intellectual and political elite among its members, from 1937 to 1944.

In his lecture, Keynes presented a macroeconomic-empirical argument in defense of the existence of secular stagnation in the current era, something he had not to my knowledge done before. He opened his essay with a warning – reminiscent of arguments he made in chapter 12 – that though the future is unknowable, people have an inherent psychological need to fool themselves into thinking that they can forecast the future with some degree of accuracy.

> The future never resembles the present – as we all know … We do not know what the future holds. Nevertheless, as living and moving beings, we are forced to act. Peace and comfort of mind require that we should hide from ourselves how little we foresee. Yet we must be guided by some hypothesis. We tend, therefore, to substitute for the knowledge which is unattainable certain conventions, the chief of which is to assume, contrary to all likelihood, that the future will resemble the past. This is how we act in practice.

(CW 14, p. 124)

Keynes ridiculed the classical school as an extreme example of this tendency to assume people have true knowledge of the future.[2] It asserted that agents can estimate the probability distributions of all possible future outcomes associated with every possible alternative current choice. Note that this implies that the future is already determined and therefore unaffected by agent choice in the present – no "micro-foundations" of macroeconomic outcomes here.

> In this way a mythical system of probable knowledge was employed to reduce the future to the same calculable status as the present. No [real person] has ever acted on this theory. But even today I believe our thought is sometimes influenced by such pseudo-rationalistic principles.
>
> (CW 14, p. 124)

However, he said, "the most outstanding example of a case where we in fact have a considerable power of seeing into the future is the prospective trend of population" because of the existence of detailed population statistics. He argued that there is near-certain knowledge that the rate of population growth has declined sharply and will continue to be low for a long time.

> We know much more securely than we know almost any other social or economic factor relating to the future that, in the place of a steady and indeed steeply rising level of population which we have experienced for a great number of decades, we shall be faced in a very short time with a stationary or a declining level ... [I]t is virtually certain that the change-over, compared with what we have been used to, will be substantial ... because of the long but definite time lag in the effects of vital statistics.
>
> (CW 14, p. 125)

Keynes then introduced a macro demand-for-capital-goods relation or function. "The demand for capital depends, of course, on three factors: on population, on the standard of life, and on capital technique" (CW 14, p. 126).

Keynes did not formalize this function in his lecture, but it can be represented, I believe, without significant distortion to the logic of his argument as the identity $K^D = f(N, Y/N, K/Y)$,[3] where K is capital stock, N is population, Y is national income, Y/N represents the "standard of life," and K/Y is an index of the "capital technique" Keynes referred to as the "period of production."

Keynes, as always, stressed the crucial impact of population growth on the demand for capital goods. "In assessing the causes of the enormous increase in capital during the nineteenth century and since, too little emphasis, I think, has been given to the influence of an increasing population as distinct from other influences" (CW 14, p. 126). (The data show that the population of Britain did grow very rapidly in this period.) He warned that "a changeover from an increasing to a declining population may be very dangerous."[4]

Keynes stated that the demand for capital goods will, *ceteris paribus*, "increase more or less in proportion to population [N], and the progress of invention may be relied on to raise the standard of life [Y/N]" (CW 14, p. 125). But the effect of invention on "the period of production [K/Y] depends on the type of invention which is characteristic of the age" (CW 14, p. 126). He defined the period of production as "the amount of capital employed to produce a unit of output" (CW 14, p. 127). The longer the "period of production" represented by K/Y, the greater the demand for capital stimulated by any increase in AD.

He then observed that technical change in the nineteenth century was capital-augmenting – it increased K/Y – and thereby increased the demand for capital goods. But it had become either neutral or, more likely, capital-reducing in the interwar period.

> It may have been true of the nineteenth century that improvements in transport, standards of housing and public services [such as public utilities] ... did tend to increase [K/Y] ... But it is not equally clear that the same thing is true today. Many modern inventions are directed toward finding ways of reducing the amount of capital necessary to produce a given result [and thus are capital-saving].
> (CW 14, p. 127)

Moreover, "as the result of our experience as to the rapidity of change in tastes and technique, our preference is decidedly toward those types of capital goods which are not too durable." Finally, "as we get richer, our consumption tends to be directed toward those articles of consumption, particularly the services of other people," which are also not durable (CW 14, p. 127). He concludes that, if anything, K/Y is likely to fall in the current era: "apart from changes in the interest rate, [K/Y] may be tending to diminish."

> Now, if the number of consumers is falling off and we cannot rely on any significant technical lengthening of the period of production, the demand for a net increase of capital good is thrown back into being wholly dependent on an improvement in the average level of consumption or on a fall in the rate of interest.
> (CW 14, p. 127)

Recall that Keynes did not expect the mpc and multiplier to increase and believed that the long-term interest rate was unlikely to fall much further under current policy institutions and practices.

At this point in the lecture, Keynes used long-term time series data to support his hypothesis that the rate of capital investment is likely, under current institutional arrangements, to continue to be far too low to move the British economy to sustained full employment. He presents data on the change in the four variables in the demand for capital equation – K, N, Y/N, and K/Y – over the period 1860–1913, warning the reader that, with the exception of the estimate of population growth, the available data are "very rough," so that any conclusions drawn from the data should "be regarded only as broad pointers to what is going on" (CW 14, p. 128).

Keynes estimated that the capital stock rose by 170 percent over the period; population grew by 50 percent; the standard of life (Y/N) increased by 60 percent; and the capital-intensity of production (K/Y) increased by just 10 percent (CW 14, p. 128). He drew a number of important conclusions from these data. The first is that the high rate of capital accumulation that drove the tremendous growth in per capita income and productivity in that era was caused to a substantial degree by a rapid rise in population at home and abroad.

> It follows that a stationary population with the same improvement in the standard of life and the same lengthening of the period of production would have required an increase in the stock of capital of only a little more than half of the increase which actually occurred. Moreover, whilst nearly half of the home investment was required by the increase in population, probably a substantially higher proportion of the foreign investment of that period was attributable to that cause.
> (CW 14, p. 128)

What, then, Keynes asked, are the implications for macroeconomic performance in the current era of a seismic demographic shift toward a stationary or slowly growing population?

He starts his answer with the guess that changes in family size, average incomes, taxation rates, and institutional and social change "may have raised the proportion of the national income which tends to be saved in conditions of full employment" (CW 14, p. 129). Saving at full employment must be equaled by capital investment at full employment or else full employment is unattainable and unsustainable. Taking account of the lack of precision in estimates of future economic conditions on the propensity to save, Keynes estimates that national savings at full employment will "lie somewhere between 8 per cent and 15 per cent of income each year" (CW 14, p. 129). Given his calculation of the current size of the capital stock, he estimates that "new investment at a rate of somewhere between 8 per cent and 15 per cent of a year's income means a cumulative increment in the stock of capital of somewhere between 2 per cent and 4 percent per annum" (CW 14, p. 129).

If we assume no large change in the rate of interest and no change in existing institutions and policies, then in order to ensure full employment "we shall have to discover a demand for *net [of depreciation] additions* to our stock of capital amounting to somewhere between 2 per cent and 4 percent annually. And this will have to continue year after year indefinitely" (CW 14, pp. 129–130, emphasis added). Selecting the lower bound of 2 percent to make his argument as persuasive as possible – if his secular stagnation thesis is supported at 2 percent, it will be overwhelmingly supported at 4 percent – Keynes showed that, in the absence of qualitative institutional change of the kind he supported, the likely rate of growth of the capital stock will be much too low to be compatible with sustained full employment.

Keynes reminds his audience that his data from 1850–1913 show that the demand for new capital in that era of high growth came primarily from two sources, each of about equal strength: the rapid growth of the population and the effect of innovations that increase labor and capital productivity and thus permit a higher standard of life (Y/N). Looking forward, Keynes assumes no growth in population in the foreseeable future, as well as no growth in K/Y. He projects that the average rate of growth of Y/N over the past 100 years will continue into the future at "somewhat less than 1 per cent per annum cumulatively" (CW 14, p. 130).[5] Given that savings at full employment are expected be at least 2 percent of the capital stock annually and as much as 4 percent, and that investment will be at most 1 percent of the capital stock annually, *the large to massive gap between savings and investment at full employment will ensure the continuance of sustained high unemployment and secular stagnation.*

The validity of Keynes's empirical support for his stagnation thesis was, of course, contingent on the assumption that there would be no unforeseen qualitative future changes in Britain's economic institutions and structures in the next few decades and that no future system-transforming innovations were on the horizon. The facts of the economic transformation caused by the planned economies of WWII and of the creation of a massive increase in the economic role of governments in the social democratic welfare/warfare states that were created in the USA and UK afterwards therefore do not undermine the validity of Keynes's conditional prediction. Absent the buildup to and prosecution of the war and all of the unforeseeable economic and political changes that followed, no one knows what the trajectory of European and North American economies would have been or what the ultimate results of the then-ongoing dangerous process of social and political unrest would be.

Keynes concluded his talk by drawing conclusions about necessary changes in Britain's economic system similar to those he drew in the exit to chapter 24 in *The General Theory* discussed in Chapter 20 of this book. Bear in mind that his audience was quite familiar with the policy debate triggered by the recent publication of *The General Theory*; they knew that Keynes was a liberal socialist because he had said this in public on many occasions, and they knew that his preferred policies centered around public control of most large-scale capital investment.

The first conclusion deals with the need for immediate reforms within the current political economy of Britain. He argues that if those who dominate economic policy in Britain, especially the powerful rentier class, refuse to take effective reforms to sharply raise the propensity to consume and sharply lower interest rates, investment will remain in the doldrums and the investment multiplier will remain low. This will condemn Britain to perpetually high unemployment. Chronic joblessness and meager living standards for the majority will eventually create a political revolt that will end "civil peace" and eventually destroy the current "form of society."

> With a stationary population we shall, I argue, be absolutely dependent for the maintenance of prosperity and *civil peace* on policies of increasing consumption [and the multiplier] by a more equal distribution of income and of forcing down the rate of interest so as to make profitable a substantial change in the period of production [K/Y] ... *Yet there will be many social and political forces to oppose the necessary change.* We must foresee what is before us and move to meet it half-way. If capitalist society rejects a more equal distribution of incomes and the forces of banking and finance succeed in maintaining the rate of interest somewhere near the figure which ruled on average during the nineteenth century (which was, by the way a little lower than the rate of interest which rules today), then a chronic tendency towards the underemployment of resources must in the end sap and *destroy that form of society*.
> (CW 14, p. 132, emphasis added)

The second conclusion supports the peaceful revolution to achieve Liberal Socialism that Keynes had been calling for throughout the interwar years, based on state control or guidance of the lion's share of large-scale capital investment and the perpetually low interest rates made possible by the "euthanasia" of the rentier class discussed in chapter 24 of *The General Theory*. This is the "evolution in our attitude toward [capital] accumulation" referred to by Keynes. The position taken here is fully consistent with the policy views in *The General Theory*.

> But if, on the other hand, persuaded and guided by the spirit of the age and such enlightenment as there is, it permits – as I believe it may – a gradual evolution of our attitude toward [capital] accumulation, so that it shall be appropriate in the circumstances of a stationary or declining population, we shall be able, perhaps, to get the best of both worlds – to maintain the liberties and independence of our present system, whilst its more signal faults [such as rentier influence on policy] gradually suffer euthanasia as the diminishing importance of capital accumulation and the rewards to it fall into their proper position in the social scheme.
> (CW 7, pp. 132–133)

Keynes ended his lecture with an upbeat message. If the country would take the steps necessary to see that capital investment equaled full-employment saving in an economy with a stable population, people could achieve a rising standard of living along with full employment.

> But a stationary or slowly declining population may, if we exercise the necessary strength and wisdom, enable us to raise the standard of life to what it should be, whilst retaining those parts of our traditional scheme of life which we value the more now that we see what happens to those who lose them.
>
> (CW 14, p. 133)

## Notes

1 Given the almost universally held belief that trend population growth rate had dropped substantially in Britain, Keynes could have argued that if the capital stock grew rapidly over the long run, the labor-to-capital ratio would decline substantially over time, causing the marginal product of capital, and thus the return to physical capital, to fall. This is an argument he makes, at least by implication, in chapter 11.
2 His distain would apply equally to the assumption of "rational expectations" in today's macroeconomic orthodoxy.
3 This relation is an identity that, when its variables are confronted with historical data, is subject to substantial measurement error, especially over long historical periods.
4 One reason for this was that it would increase the cost of eliminating excess capacity due to overproduction based on the extrapolation of past trends in industries such as residential housing, business construction and the building of infrastructure. "This creates a pessimistic atmosphere" (CW 14, p. 126).
5 Keep in mind that $Y/N$ is not labor productivity – output per labor hour or per worker – but rather output per person in the entire population, including those too young, too old, or too infirm to be in the labor force. Average growth in output per worker in these data would be higher than 1 percent per year.

# 15 Keynes versus the classicists on the effects of wage and price deflation

Keynes spent most of the 1920s arguing that Britain's economy was "stuck in a rut" with persistently high unemployment, but the situation worsened considerably in the 1930s. The rate of total unemployment (as opposed to the higher rate of insured unemployment) fluctuated between 12 and 17 percent in the six years preceding the publication of *The General Theory*. These "facts" made it patently obvious to almost everyone but die-hard classical economists that is was possible for the economy to exist in a high-unemployment equilibrium state or in a series of such states for prolonged time periods. In Part I of this book, we saw that Keynes argued over and over again in the period from WWI through the publication of *The General Theory* that the main out-of-equilibrium processes that ensure stability of equilibrium in classical theory – wage and price deflation and adjustments in financial markets – were not only ineffective in this era, they were terribly destructive as well, worsening the economic problems that initiated them.

To most economists who call themselves Keynesian, the claim that destructive disequilibrium processes are a crucial part of Keynes's economics would seem highly questionable, if not bizarre. This is not just because many never carefully read *The General Theory* from start to finish, but also because the book is almost universally understood to concern itself exclusively with short-term, stable equilibriums and to rely heavily on comparative static exercises that assume stability of equilibrium to derive economic policies.

This is partly Keynes's fault. His main policy goal was to convince economists and other influential people that a permanent increase in public investment would inevitably lead to a much larger (or multi-plied) increase in production and a substantial permanent decline in unemployment. The most effective way to do this was in a determinist short-run stable-equilibrium model. This is what he did in chapter 10 of *The General Theory*, where he provided examples of how a permanent rise in public investment would, over an extended period of time, lead to a rise in production equal to the increase in public investment times the multiplier, *ceteris paribus*. This is a much more compelling defense of the effectiveness of public investment than the more accurate statement that a rise in public investment will kick off a complex dynamic and path-dependent expansionary process in an uncertain environment of unknowable magnitude. On the other hand, the careful reader of the whole book will clearly see the importance of destructive disequilibrium processes in Keynes's thinking.

Recall that there are two essential processes in classical theory that quickly restore general equilibrium if the economy suffers a negative exogenous shock to AD while in general equilibrium. The first is that an excess labor supply will cause wage and price deflation that *inevitably* lead to real-wage deflation and thus to an assured rise in employment and output. Real-wage deflation will continue until the excess supply of labor is eliminated. The second disequilibrium process that restores general equilibrium is found in financial markets where any negative shock to AD is met by a quick and sharp drop in interest rates that restores AD to full-capacity level. We will examine Keynes's critique of the classical theory of efficient financial markets when we treat chapters 12, 13, 15 and 22 below.

The classical vision of an ideal capitalist economy requires that money-wage deflation always takes place without restriction in the face of high unemployment, that prices fall by less than wages, and that real-wage deflation always causes employment to increase until full employment is restored. In *The General Theory*, Keynes argued that none of these assertions are true – classical theory had the essential facts of disequilibrium dynamics wrong.

We have already seen that Keynes persistently argued that serious deflation had catastrophic effects. He railed against repeated attempts by the government to deliberately create wage deflation in traditional export industries by increasing unemployment, calling the policy an economic disaster and a violation of basic principles of social justice. The fact that Keynes used the first substantive chapter of *The General Theory* to attack the classical theory of deflation indicates how important it was to him to destroy the idea that Britain could deflate its way to prosperity. Keynes also argued that the USA and global financial systems had become so fragile and over-leveraged that the serious deflation of the early 1930s had triggered a financial market collapse and global depression. Deflation under conditions of financial fragility is especially disastrous. This was a major theme of his 1923 *Tract on Monetary Reform* (CW 4) with its emphasis on a "regime of money contract."

In chapter 2, Keynes focused on the classical theory of the labor market, the market that directly determines the state of employment. He accepted what he referred to as the first postulate of classical theory – that the real wage is always equal to the marginal product of labor (MPL) or the increase in output caused by the addition of one more worker. In other words, we are always on the classical labor demand curve. Just as in the neoclassical short-run theory of the labor market, classical theory assumed – in obvious conflict with reality – that the whole capital stock (K) is utilized no matter how many workers (L) are employed. Capital is a "jelly" that can be spread thick (if L is low) or thin (if L is high).[1] In the classical (and neoclassical) short run, it is assumed that the MPL always declines as output and employment rise and always falls when unemployment rises. *This means that the real wage always falls as unemployment rises.*[2]

There were a number of important "facts" that Keynes believed the classicists got wrong about the labor demand curve. First, classical theory asserts as a fact that when unemployment rises, nominal wages fall. Prices are also likely to fall, but always by less than the decline in money wages. Real wages therefore must fall, leading to an increase in the demand to hire workers. But in fact, he said, while nominal wages may fall (as in the USA from 1929 to 1933) or may stay the same in recessions or depressions (as in manufacturing in the UK in the early 1930s), Keynes argued that real wages tend to remain relatively steady and may even rise when unemployment is high.

The fact is that in the USA, with weak unions, nominal wages in manufacturing fell by 21 percent from 1929 to 1933, but real wages rose by 4 percent as unemployment increased from 4 to 25 percent.[3] Prices fell by slightly more than wages as the result of massive excess capacity and more intense competition, forces not considered in classical disequilibrium theory.[4] In the UK, where unions were strong, nominal wages stayed relatively constant in manufacturing from 1929 to 1936, while the real wage rose by at least 10 percent because prices fell.[5]

Keynes concluded: "The change in real wages associated with a change in money wages ... is almost always in the opposite direction" (CW 7, p. 10). This "fact" implies that the crucial classical assumption that wage deflation is a mechanism that automatically eliminates involuntary unemployment in a capitalist economy was not true. He observed that classical economists had never even attempted to empirically verify the central classical assumption that a fall in the money wage automatically leads to a fall in the real wage: "it is strange that so little attempt should have been made to prove or to refute it" (CW 7, p. 12).

Keynes offered two reasons as to why this assumption should have been suspect even to classical economists. The first reason has to do with the nature of competition, assumed by classical theory to always be fierce or "perfect."

> For it is far from being consistent with the general tenor of the classical theory, which has taught us to believe that prices are governed by marginal prime cost in terms of money and that money wages govern marginal prime cost. Thus if money-wages change, one would have expected the classical school to argue that prices would change

> in almost the same proportion, leaving the real wage and the level of employment practically the same as before.
>
> (CW 7, p. 12)

In the real world of the 1930s, fierce competition in an environment of high unemployment and crushing excess capacity should have been expected to drive prices down as fast or faster than marginal cost was falling – which is what actually happened. The core problem is that in the world of classical theory, there was no attempt to build an empirically and institutionally realistic theory of out-of-equilibrium processes, one that acknowledges the effects of excess capacity and destructive competition.[6] Unrealistic stabilizing out-of-equilibrium processes are assumed to exist in classical theory because they are necessary to defend laissez-faire policy. Recall that in "Am I a Liberal?" Keynes argued that classical "perfect competition" is a theory of a blissful *state*; it does not contain any theory of potentially destructive disequilibrium processes in real time. We have already seen Keynes's analysis of the destructive character of intense competition in the British cotton and coal industries in the 1920s, as well as his argument that "perfect competition," which assumes that price equals marginal cost, would destroy the growing number of important industries with large economies of scale and, therefore, large fixed costs per unit. In his view, the classical theory of competition as a process was utterly bankrupt.

The second reason to reject the classical argument that real and money wages move in the same direction is that its assumptions are inconsistent. High unemployment may well force workers to accept lower money wages if they are not well-organized as in the USA in the 1920s and early 1930s. However, when employment falls, the classical demand for labor or the MPL function shows that the real wage rises because output per worker rises – which contradicts the central claim of the theory of efficient disequilibrium processes. Note the similarity between Keynes's assertion that labor is "readier to accept wage-cuts when employment is falling off" and Marx's theory of the "reserve army" of the unemployed.

> [W]hen money-wages are rising … it will be found that real wages are falling, and when money-wages are falling, real wages are rising. This is because, in the short period, falling money-wages and rising real wages are each, for independent reasons, likely to accompany decreasing employment; labour being readier to accept wage-cuts when employment is falling off, yet real wages inevitably rising in the same circumstances on account of the increasing marginal return to a given capital equipment when output is diminished.
>
> (CW 7, p. 10)[7]

Second, involuntary unemployment is a "fact" that should not be theorized away for political or ideological convenience. In the depression, there were millions of unemployed workers in the USA and Britain who wanted to work at the going wage but could not get jobs. Several statements in the chapter make Keynes's view on this clear: "Who would deny it?" he asked. (Well, Robert Lucas, Edward Prescott, and Thomas Sargent, among others.)

Third, unless workers have full cost-of-living adjustments in their wage contracts or wages are set by national bargaining among labor, capital, and the state, workers have no way to negotiate a bargain with employers for a real as opposed to a money wage. Labor as a whole cannot make a bargain with employers in which they trade lower real wages for more jobs, as the narrative associated with classical theory suggests.[8] Classical theory assumes that if all workers would accept lower nominal wages, the real wage would fall, leading to lower unemployment. The "most fundamental objection … flows from our disputing the assumption that the general level of real wages [and thus employment] is directly determined by the character of the wage bargain" (CW 7, p. 13). "There may exist no expedient by which labour as a whole can reduce its *real* wage to a given figure by making revised *money* wage bargains with the entrepreneurs" (CW 7, p. 13, emphasis in original).

Given the money wage, which is set through wage bargaining, the real wage will be determined by the aggregate price level.[9] But the price level is directly determined in the goods market, not the labor market. This means that the real wage cannot be established until conditions in the output market are taken into account. AD – not the money wage – is the *main* determinant of the demand for labor. Keynes insisted that *the MPL curve is not a demand curve for labor*. Rather, given the demand for labor, which is primarily determined in the goods market, the MPL curve translates the level of labor demanded into an appropriate real wage.[10] To simplify just a bit, Keynes said that AD determines labor demand through the production function, and then the amount of labor demanded determines real wage along the MPL curve – and not the other way around.

Finally, Keynes built his innovative, non-classical labor-supply function in chapter 2 based on the institutional fact that where organized labor is strong, workers will, if they can, resist money-wage cuts, causing the money wage to become downwardly rigid or at least downwardly sluggish. They will try to fight money-wage cuts for two main reasons.

First, in a depressed economy, the elasticity of employment with respect to a fall in the money wage will be very low. If steel workers take a pay cut in a depression, this will not lead to a significant expansion of jobs in the steel industry because the rate of growth of steel industry employment depends on the growth of production in steel-using industries such as capital goods, autos, and consumer durables. Their growth of production in turn depends on the rate of growth of economy-wide AD, which steelworkers cannot significantly influence. Keynes said that workers instinctively know this: "workers, though unconsciously, are instinctively more reasonable economists than the classical school" (CW 7, p. 14).

Second, workers also know that "reductions of money wages are seldom or never of an all-around character." Workers in stronger unions will be better able to strike or work to rule or otherwise obstruct production in order to resist wage cuts than workers in weak unions or non-unionized workers. Workers with less or no bargaining power therefore will be unable to resist wage cuts and will drop down the *relative wage and status ladder*, an outcome that is socially unjust and that workers know is unjust. All workers will thus try to resist money-wage cuts.

> Since there is an imperfect mobility of labour, and wages do not tend to an exact equality of net advantage in different occupations, any individual or group of individuals, who consent to a reduction of money-wages relative to others, will suffer a *relative* reduction in real wages, which is a sufficient reason to resist it ... In other words, the struggle about money-wages primarily affects the *distribution* of wages between the different labour groups.
> 
> (CW 7, p. 14, emphasis in original)

> Except in a socialized community where wage-setting is settled by decree, there is no means of securing uniform wage reductions for every class of labour. The result can only be brought about by a series of gradual, irregular changes, justifiable on no criterion of social justice or economic expedience, and probably completed only after wasteful and disastrous struggles where those in the weakest bargaining positions will suffer relative to the rest.
> 
> (CW 7, p. 267)

In interwar Britain, workers did indeed strike in the face of money-wage cuts, even when unemployment was high. The militant General Strike of 1926 was only the most prominent example of this.

Keynes made similar comments in other writings. In 1930: "A reduction of wages [in Britain] can only be [achieved] as a result of a sort of civil war or guerrilla war carried on, industry by industry, all over the country, which would be a hideous and disastrous prospect" (CW 20, p. 419). In 1931: "In my country a really large cut in money wages ... is simply an impossibility. To attempt it would be to shake the social order to its foundation" (CW 20, p. 546).

Keynes believed that though workers will struggle against and strike to prevent money-wage cuts if they can, they are likely to accept modest real-wage declines that arise from moderate price increases because this will not change their place in the relative wage distribution.

Every trade union will put up some resistance to a cut in money wages, however small. But since no trade union would dream of striking on every occasion of a rise in the cost of living, they do not raise the obstacle to any increase in aggregate employment which is attributed to them by the classical school.

(CW 7, p. 15)

Note that, contrary to textbook treatments of Keynes, downward money wage rigidity is not caused by "money illusion" – workers' inability to distinguish between nominal wages and the purchasing power of their wage. There is no mention of money illusion in *The General Theory*.

The derivation of Keynes's labor supply function is clearly based on an anti-classical methodology and reflects a methodological innovation. It is not derived by deduction from optimization processes over standard pre-given agent preferences given complete and correct information about the future, but rather *inductively* by a study of the facts. It is a historically, behaviorally, and conventionally determined function. Workers resist changes in relative wages as much for "moral" as economic reasons. Wage cuts that lower their position in the vector of wages across jobs and industries are considered unfair.[11]

Of course, the real wage must also be in the labor supply function because workers are not irrational: they care about the purchasing power of their wage. For Keynes, labor supply is a function of both the current money wage and the current real wage. This means that every time the money wage changes in a disequilibrium process, the classical and neoclassical labor supply function shifts. The classical presumption that wage and price deflation will automatically cure unemployment cannot be derived from such a labor supply function.

The attack on the alleged employment-creating benefits of deflation as the main path to full employment was so important to Keynes that he returned to it in chapter 19, after the basic macro model in the book had been constructed. To discuss the arguments in chapter 19, we first have to briefly review the basic structure of the simple Keynesian AD/AS model.

To simplify somewhat for present purposes, we might say that in Keynes's theory, employment and income are primarily determined by AD – Say's Law does not hold. In his simple model with no government, AD is the sum of capital investment spending, consumption spending, and net exports. As we will discuss in detail below, Keynes assumed that future economic states are unknowable in the present. This means that corporations and households have to form expectations of the future based on mere guesswork or behavioral conventions to make decisions about how much to invest and how much of their current income to spend on consumption goods. The value of AD in any period thus partly depends on the state of expectations in that period.

As we shall see in our discussion of chapter 12, Keynes argued that expectations of the future are normally formed through extrapolation or projection from the relevant past. The longer this expectation formation process generates forecasts that are accurate enough to seem serviceable, the more "confidence" people will place in them. When people have confidence in optimistic expectations, they will be willing to spend more of their income on consumption goods and services and businesses will spend more on capital investment. When they have pessimistic expectations or have lost confidence in their ability to forecast with reasonable accuracy, they will spend less. Therefore, expectations *must* be incorporated into an exploration of the likely effects of falling money wages on employment in Keynes's model.

Chapter 19 reflects Keynes's insistence that analyses of out-of-equilibrium dynamics can only be adequately addressed if they allow key variables normally held constant in comparative-static exercises to become endogenous. This is especially important with respect to expectations and confidence. Classical theory asked a comparative-static question: would a once-and-for-all fall in the money wage raise employment holding AS and, implicitly, expectations and confidence constant? Keynes argued that the appropriate question is: would a *process* of falling money wages over time with nothing arbitrarily held constant eliminate unemployment? How will a time-consuming process of falling wages affect the determinants of AD – the mec, the mpc, the rate of interest, and the trade balance? Keynes acknowledged that deflation would help the trade balance, but argued that its overall effect would be to lower AD and employment.

I want to focus on three issues discussed in chapter 19: the effects of deflation on expectations of future wages and prices, on the interest rate, and on financial fragility. Comparative statics are useless here because they incorporate the assumption that expectations never change in the disequilibrium process. Keynes argued that the most likely situation in a depressed economy is – in the absence of strong unions – a process of *falling* money wages over time caused by an excess supply of labor. He said: "The most unfavorable contingency is that in which money wages are sagging downwards and each reduction in wages serves to diminish confidence in the prospective maintenance of wages [in the near future]" (CW 7, p. 265). But this is the most likely outcome in periods of sustained high unemployment in the absence of strong unions.

Keynes said that in a depressed economy expectations of future prices are elastic with respect to falling current prices. He argued that when prices are expected to continue falling, the purchase of capital goods and consumer durables will be postponed in anticipation of lower prices in the future. This means that AD and employment will continue to fall, maintaining downward pressure on money wages. The takeaway here is that downwardly flexible wages in a period of high unemployment can result in a deflationary wage and price spiral such as the one that took place in the USA in the early 1930s.

Keynes also examined what is often called the "Keynes effect," in which falling prices combined with a constant money supply lead to a rising real money supply and a consequent reduction of the interest rate, *ceteris paribus*.[12] Keynes made two arguments against this proposition in chapter 19. First, the money supply is endogenous. As nominal income falls, the transactions demand for money falls. But both the demand for and supply of credit fall as well, which will lead to a decline in the money supply. Second, a steep drop in the nominal wage associated with high unemployment is likely to be accompanied by economic and political turbulence, as it was in Britain in the 1920s and in the USA in the 1930s. This causes investors to shun risk and seek capital safety. They will sell long-term securities that can suffer large capital losses and shift to liquid short-term assets that cannot suffer a serious capital loss. Stock prices will fall and interest rates, especially risk- and inflation-adjusted interest rates, will rise – as they did in the deflation of the 1930s. "If, moreover, the reduction in wages disturbs political confidence by causing popular discontent, the increase in liquidity preference due to this cause may more than offset the release of cash from active circulation" (CW 7, pp. 263–264). In an IS/LM model, a rise in liquidity preference (or the desire to hold less of your wealth in the form of bonds) would be represented by an upward shift in the LM curve.

Moreover, when prices, incomes, and the value of collateral assets collapse in a financially fragile "regime of money contract," the nominal value of debts remains constant, but the real value of debts rises dramatically – as in the 1930s. Nominal incomes decline, but nominal debt values do not. This can lead to a wave of defaults and bankruptcies, the evaporation of new loans, and an unwillingness to roll over existing loans.

> The depressing influence on entrepreneurs of their greater [real] burden of debt may partly offset any cheerful reactions from the reduction of wages. Indeed, if the fall of ... prices goes far, the embarrassment of those entrepreneurs who are heavily indebted may soon reach the point of insolvency, with severely adverse effects on investment.
> (CW 7, p. 264)

We have seen that Keynes believed the combination of treacherously fragile balance sheets and rapidly collapsing asset values in the deflation of the early 1930s was a major cause of the depression.

Keynes went on to attack the widely held thesis that capitalism would be capable of generating sustained full employment if only there were no strong unions to limit or prevent money-wage deflation. The conventional wisdom of the time in Britain was that the main cause of sustained high unemployment in the era was not inherently ineffective disequilibrium dynamics in free-market capitalism, but rather the existence of strong unions that prevented adequate money-wage deflation. This was the firm belief of classical economists and the presumption relied on in policy formulation. Support for the lockout in the coal industry in 1926 and for the brutal repression of the General Strike that followed was motivated not only by fear of revolution, but also by the semireligious belief in the necessity of driving down miners' wages to restore British trade dominance in coal as part of a general strategy of forcing large nominal wage cuts in all major export industries. Lower export costs would also facilitate the return to gold at prewar par. And, of course, price deflation was also attractive because it would enrich the politically powerful rentier class who owned long-term bonds and received interest payments denominated in nominal values.

*Keynes insisted that free-market capitalism – not unions – was the cause of high unemployment.* Where is that mentioned in your macro textbook? He attacked the claim that union-supported money-wage rigidity was the chief impediment to full employment in the strongest possible terms, arguing to the contrary that if a process of substantial wage deflation set in, it could completely destabilize the economy. British unions were performing a service to Britain by preventing a catastrophe, he argued.

> It follows therefore that if labour were to respond to conditions of gradually [rising unemployment] by offering its services at a gradually diminishing money wage, this would not, as a rule, have the effect of reducing real wages and might even have the effect of increasing them, through its adverse influence on the volume of output.[13] *The chief result of this policy would be to cause a great instability of prices, so violent perhaps as to make business calculations futile in an economic society functioning after the manner of that in which we live.* To suppose that a flexible wage policy is a right and proper adjunct of a system which on the whole is one of laissez-faire, is the opposite of the truth. It is only in a highly authoritarian society, where sudden, substantial, all-around changes could be decreed that a flexible wage-policy could function with success.
>
> (CW 7, p. 269, emphasis added)

This is not the only place in *The General Theory* where Keynes argued that the unrestricted downward flexibility of wages – a cornerstone of classical stability analysis – would be disastrous. "For if competition between unemployed workers always led to a very great reduction in money wages, there would be violent instability in the price level" (CW 7, p. 253). As Keynes argued in the *Tract on Monetary Reform*, violent instability of prices would create intolerable uncertainty and could easily trigger both a collapse of capital investment and a financial crisis in a state of systemic financial fragility. I have never seen this view – that a substantial degree of downward wage and price rigidity is a condition of existence of a capitalist free-market economy – attributed to Keynes.

## Notes

1 This assumption makes excess capacity zero at all levels of production.
2 There was no compelling economic reason for Keynes to accept the classical MPL function. Indeed, he published an article in 1937 (Keynes 1937) that rejected it. The article cited empirical work by Dunlop and by Kalecki that showed that over a wide range of output, the MPL is constant. This implies that the real wage is constant – deflation cannot lower the real wage. My guess is that Keynes accepted the classical first postulate to sooth the feelings of economists who were open-minded but not yet converted to his views, the people who were his main target audience. It seems that in *The General Theory* Keynes was willing to accept as much of received doctrine as he could while still being able to develop a theory that supported his radical interventionist policies.
3 Data from Carlstrom and Fuerst (2001). See also United States Bureau of the Census (1975).
4 The classical theory of the labor market assumed perfect competition or competition of maximum intensity; variations in the degree of competition and excess capacity were assumed away.
5 Total labor income fell because of increased unemployment and fewer hours worked per week.
6 The theory of destructive competition, associated both with Schumpeter, who explored the process of "creative destruction," and with Marx is explored in Crotty (2017, chapters 10 and 11). Schumpeter assumed the forces of creation were always stronger than those of destruction because he assumed Say's Law always holds.
7 The last fragment of the quote is puzzling because when L falls, K/L rises and L/K falls, which should lower the marginal product of capital. What Keynes presumably means here is that since it is assumed in the "short run" that capital is fully employed no matter how many workers there are, the K/L ratio rises as employment declines, causing the MPL to rise. Since real wages are positively related to the MPL, they will rise as well.
8 This is not an explicit assumption: classical theory understands that the wage bargain is only over a money wage. But since it assumes that money-wage cuts automatically translate into real-wage cuts, it is *as if* the bargain is over a real wage. "The traditional theory maintains, in short, *that the wage bargains between the entrepreneurs and the workers determine the real wage*; so that, assuming free competition amongst workers, the latter can, if they wish, bring their real wages into conformity with the marginal disutility of the amount of employment offered by the employers at that wage" (CW 7, p. 11, emphasis in original). In reality, workers can agree to take a money-wage cut, but they have no control over the determination of the price level.
9 In the absence of unions and/or tight labor markets, the wage "bargain" is simply a take-it-or-leave-it dictate of the employer.
10 I use the word "primarily" because the real wage has a feedback effect on AD.

11 The mec (defined in chapter 11 of *The General Theory*) and the impact of liquidity preference on the interest rate are two other examples of conventionally or behaviorally determined variables.
12 As the amount of money needed to facilitate transactions declines due to deflation, it creates an excess supply of money that will be used to buy bonds, driving bond prices up and interest rates down.
13 Recall that as output falls, the MPL rises. If we assume that the economy is always on the MPL curve, unemployment and real wages move in the same direction.

# 16 Keynes versus the classicists on disequilibrium processes in the bond market

In *The General Theory*, Keynes presented his theory of financial markets in two parts. He first analyzed the stock market in chapter 12, where he argued that because the future is unknowable in the present, expectations of future stock price movements can only be formed through the use of inherently unstable social, behavioral, and psychological conventions. This was a key reason why the US stock market in the 1920s and early 1930s turned into an "insane gambling casino." He also argued in this chapter that capital investment spending is strongly affected by the movement of stock prices, making investment itself an inherently unstable variable. Keynes concluded that in the event of a significant and rapid fall in income, employment, and the rate of profit, stock prices were likely to fall rapidly, exacerbating rather than helping reverse the downturn. The stock market has potentially destructive disequilibrium dynamics.

Having established this result, he moved on to analysis of the bond market and the behavior of the long-term interest rate in chapters 13–15. Since these chapters come after chapter 12, they assume the reader already understands Keynes's ideas about uncertainty and the properties of conventional expectations formation. He used these ideas to show that interest rates are likely to rise in the face of a sharp economic decline, as they did in the early 1930s – a result in direct conflict with classical theory and with IS/LM models as well.

I have reversed Keynes's order of presentation and turn first to his analysis of the bond market because he had spent the 1920s attacking the claim made by classical theorists that falling interest rates will always restore full-employment equilibrium in response to a substantial negative shock to demand. He did not spend substantial time trying to tie stock prices into his emerging macro theory until the early 1930s.

We begin with chapter 14, which presents and attacks the classical theory of the determination of the interest rate. Classical theory has a flow equilibrium model in which the interest rate balances the flow of saving and investment at full-capacity income and output, a theory that assumes markets always clear in equilibrium. It also at least implicitly assumes that the stochastic future is knowable in the present.

Classical theory:

> has regarded the rate of interest as the factor which brings the demand for capital investment goods and the willingness to save into equilibrium with one another ... [T]he rate of interest necessarily comes to rest under the play of market forces at the point where the amount of investment at that interest rate is equal to the amount of saving at that rate.
>
> (CW 7, p. 175)

But, Keynes insisted, this could only be true "if the level of income is assumed to be given" or unchanged by shifts in the investment and savings functions (CW 7, p. 178). Full-employment equilibrium is the only possible equilibrium in classical theory. If, for example, there is a negative exogenous shock to the investment function at full employment, its effect on the interest rate as captured in classical theory is a reasonable approximation to reality if and only if the full-employment "level of income is assumed to be given" or constant throughout the disequilibrium process. In other word, this disequilibrium process proceeds *almost timelessly while AS and income remain at their full-employment levels.*

> For the classical theory ... assumes that it can proceed to consider the effect on the rate of interest of (e.g.) a shift in the demand curve for capital, without abating or modifying its assumption as to the amount of the given income out of which savings are to be made. The independent variables of the classical theory of the rate of interest are the demand curve for capital and the influence of the rate of interest on the amount saved out of a given income.
>
> (CW 7, p. 179)

The key point here is that the classical conclusion that a negative shock to investment demand will cause interest to fall by the amount needed to restore the economy back to full employment turns out to be a tautology; full-employment production (AS) can be shown to be stable in the event of negative demand shock (AD) only by assuming its level never changes in response to that demand shock.

Let us examine the classical argument about the determination of the interest rate in some detail. We have just seen that in classical theory a negative shock to AD at full-employment equilibrium creates an excess AS of goods and services. This immediately leads to falling wages and prices and then to falling real wages. Falling real wages are assumed to keep AS perpetually at or near its full-employment level. However, if AD was to remain below AS for a long time when unemployment fell, unwanted inventories would pile up and workers would be laid off again. Thus, classical theory must provide an explanation of the forces that cause AD to quickly rebound back to its pre-shock level where it equaled full-capacity AS.

What are the out-of-equilibrium forces in the classical theory of financial markets that ensure that this AD rebound takes place? The answer is that an efficient bond market responds quickly to a negative AD shock by lowering the long-term rate of interest. This causes both investment spending and consumption spending to increase until their sum, which is AD in the simple model, is again equal to full-capacity supply.[1] The classical theory of efficient bond markets thus plays a crucial role in the out-of-equilibrium dynamics that ensure a return to full employment after a negative shock to demand. Efficient bond markets are an essential foundation of Say's Law.

The classical theory of how changes in the interest rate keep AD approximately equal to full-employment output is, according to Keynes, roughly as follows. Income, Y, is identically equal to the value of output, AS. It is assumed that flexible wages perpetually hold AS near $AS^F$ (full-capacity supply). But what causes AD to move back to equal $AS^F$ in the face of a negative shock to investment spending? The classical answer lies in the bond market.

The classical Quantity Theory of Money says that because bonds pay interest and money does not, people hold the minimum amount of money needed to finance transactions. This means that all household saving (above the minimum needed to augment money holdings for transactions purposes) *automatically* flows into the bond market as an assured source of funds to finance business investment. Saving is therefore the demand for corporate bonds ($B^D$). Classical theory assumed a time-preference theory of saving and consumption, with $S = S(r, Y)$ and $C = C(r, Y)$.[2] The higher r, the more of our income we save and the less we consume. So $B^D = S(r, Y)$. If we assume with the classicists that all investment is funded by bond issues, the bond supply will be determined by the needs of business to finance investment: $B^S = I(r, Y)$.

Since classical theory assumed that factor prices change quickly enough to hold AS approximately equal to $Y^F$ (full-employment income) even in the face of negative shocks to demand, for purposes of analyzing financial market out-of-equilibrium processes, Y is treated in classical theory as an exogenous constant equal to full-employment Y or $Y^F$. Thus, even in the face of a negative shock to AD, we can write $S = S(r: Y^F)$ and $I = I(r: Y^F)$, where $Y^F$ is an exogenous constant.[3] The interest rate is thus the variable that regulates the balance between S and I or between $B^S$ and $B^D$ given that Y remains constant at $Y^F$ in the process.

Assume that the expected profit rate deteriorates. This is an exogenous negative shock to the investment demand function. Holding Y constant at $Y^F$, investment spending will decline at every level of the interest rate. At the original interest rate, S (the demand for bonds) will be greater than I (the supply of bonds). This will cause the price of bonds to rise and the interest rate to fall. A declining interest rate will increase consumption spending and cause investment spending to rise relative to its value at the original interest rate. The interest rate must continue to fall until S declines and C and I increase by enough to restore equality between AD and $Y^F$ again.

Since Y never changes by assumption (that is: $\Delta Y = \Delta C + \Delta S = \Delta C + \Delta I = 0$), the interest rate will fall with almost infinite speed to cause $\Delta S$ to equal $\Delta I$, and $\Delta C$ to equal $-\Delta I$. The rise in consumption spending equals the fall in investment spending so that AD again equals AS at $Y^F$.[4]

It is thus the superefficiency of both labor markets and financial markets that gives classical theory its marvelous out-of-equilibrium stability-restoring processes. Full employment is not only stable, *it is almost instantaneously stable*. AS did not decline in response to the drop in AD (caused by the decline in investment) because wages and prices moved quickly to make the appropriate adjustments to AS. Then, given this rigidity in AS, the bond market moved at lightning speed to lower r, forcing I and C to rise and AD to move quickly back to equal $Y^F$. This comes very close to the auctioneered Walrasian general equilibrium model in which prices move the system back to general equilibrium in the aftermath of a shock before any actual or calendar time passes.

## Keynes's theory of potentially destabilizing bond markets, part I: AS falls when AD falls

Keynes presented a two-pronged attack on the classical theory of the role played by the bond market in the restoration of full employment. The first prong was his insistence that AS depends on and quickly reacts to changes in AD. As all students of economics know, this is a cornerstone of his theory. If AD or sales decline substantially, Y and employment will fall in response. Seeing sales fall, firms will lower production by laying off workers in order to prevent an excessive inventory buildup. If Y falls because AD falls, Say's Law is a fairy-tale and there are multiple potential equilibrium positions. "The traditional analysis has been aware that saving depends on income, but it has overlooked the fact that income depends on investment" (CW 7, p. 184). Keynes argued repeatedly that the classical theory had to assume its conclusion that competitive markets keep AS close to $Y^F$ even in the face of shocks and shifts in AD in order to prove it. But once AS (or Y) is allowed to become endogenous and a function of AD, the whole classical financial market story losses credibility and coherence.

Consider once again our classical story of how bond markets stabilize the equilibrium value of income via the example used above in which there is a negative exogenous shock to the investment function. This will cause AD and Y to fall. The initial fall in Y caused by the shift in the parameters of the investment function $I(r, Y)$ – the exogenous shock – will induce a further decline in I as well as drop in C(r, Y), causing AD and Y to fall even farther. "If the investment demand-schedule shifts ... income will, in general, shift also." But the classical theory can "not tell us what its new value will be" because it assumes income is constant (CW 7, p. 181). With both the demand for bonds (S) and the supply of bonds (I) falling due to the fall in Y, there is no guarantee that r will even decline, never mind fall to the point that its impact on AD would be as large as the negative impact of the fall in Y on the level of I. Indeed, if the decline in I is large and unexpected, panic in financial markets might cause interest rates to spike, accelerating the decline. This is what happened in the early 1930s.

Keynes argued in chapter 8 that the interest elasticity of consumption with respect to a decline in the interest rate was likely to be small and possibly even zero. The influence of a decline in the interest rate:

> on the rate of spending out of a given income is open to a good deal of doubt. For the classical theory of the rate of interest, which was based on the idea that the rate of interest was the factor which brought the supply and demand for savings into equilibrium, it was convenient to suppose ... that any rise in the rate of interest would appreciably diminish consumption. It has long been recognized, however, that the total effect of changes in the interest rate on the readiness to spend on present consumption is complex and uncertain, being dependent on conflicting tendencies, since some of the subjective motives towards saving will be more easily satisfied if the rate of interest rises, whilst others will be weakened ... Over a long period substantial changes in the rate of interest probably tend to modify social habits considerably, thus affecting the subjective propensity to spend – though in which direction in would be hard to say ... The usual type of short-period fluctuation in the rate of interest is not likely, however, to exercise much direct influence on spending either way ... [T]he main conclusion, suggested by experience is, I think, that the short-period influence of the rate of interest on individual spending out of a given income is secondary and relatively unimportant, except, perhaps, where unusually large changes are in question.
> (CW 7, pp. 93–94)

We know that the elasticity of consumption with respect to a fall in income is large. We also know that consumption is much larger than investment. Therefore, even if the interest declined significantly – which is highly unlikely – any positive impact of a fall of the interest rate on AD through an increase in investment would be swamped by the negative impact on both consumption and investment caused by the fall in Y. The key point is that by allowing Y to become an endogenous function of AD, Keynes made the classical demonstration of the efficient, stability-enhancing character of financial markets irrelevant. It simply does not apply to the real world in which a substantial fall in investment will typically lead to a multiplied fall in AD and therefore in output, income, and employment, and the response of the bond market could make the collapse even greater.

## Keynes's theory of potentially destabilizing bond markets, part II: uncertainty and interest rate instability

Keynes's main goal in writing chapters 13 and 15 was to create a theory founded on the assumption of fundamental uncertainty about future economic states that, unlike classical theory, could explain why long-term interest rates in the USA declined in the late 1920s but then leapt up in the early 1930s, exacerbating the economic and financial crises of the period. The real or inflation-adjusted (Baa) long-term interest rate hit 20 percent in 1932.[5] While Keynes's theory of the interest rate is compatible with periods of relative bond market stability, his main goal in these chapters was to show why, in a world of uncertainty, bond prices are inherently prone to occasional periods of high volatility and can exhibit destructive pro-cyclical disequilibrium dynamics.

To accomplish this goal, he focused on the choice investors have to make between holding their financial wealth in the form of risky long-term bonds that normally have a substantial interest rate but are vulnerable to capital loss when interest rates rise or holding it instead in the safe "liquid" form of "money" that has zero-interest yield but whose value cannot suffer a capital loss.[6,7] When investors begin to fear that interest rates will rise and bond prices will fall, they may sell bonds and hold on to the money they get from the sale. This will cause interest rates to rise, reinforcing the pessimistic expectations that induced the bond sales. If pessimism about future bond prices becomes strong enough in a period in which financial markets have become financially fragile, a panic may ensue.

In *The General Theory*, Keynes observed that in the USA in 1932, "there was a financial crisis or crises of liquidation, when scarcely anyone could be induced to part with holdings of money on any reasonable terms" (CW 7, pp. 207–208). In 1931, he wrote: "There is an element of that morbid psychology present today; there are financial institutions and individuals who want to safeguard against any possible future loss, and are therefore unwilling to run [even] sound risks" (CW 20, p. 537). That same year, he wrote that US banks "have an absolute mania for liquidity ... [T]hey turn all the assets they can into a fairly liquid form and in some cases keep an abnormally large amount of till money" (CW 20, pp. 556–557). In 1932, he marveled at the "insane gambling" that took place in US bond markets. "It is truly remarkable," he said, "that the paper value of all the railways and public utilities, after having fallen to one tenth of what it had been two years previously, had then proceeded to double itself within five weeks" (CW 21, pp. 120–121). These were the financial market dynamics that Keynes tried to explain in chapters 13 and 15 through his innovative theory of liquidity preference as a behavior toward uncertainty in bond markets.

Keynes began the second prong of his attack on the classical theory of interest rate determination and his presentation of his own theory of the bond market with an attack on the Quantity Theory of the demand to hold "money" because it does not incorporate what has become known in economics as the "speculative" motive for so doing – to hold money rather than bonds in order to avoid an expected future capital loss on bonds and to be in a position to make capital gains by buying bonds whenever expectations of rising bond prices return. Once expectations of future bond prices are incorporated into the demand for bonds function and, with Keynes, we assume that the future is unknowable in the present, out-of-equilibrium processes in the bond market can become destructive or destabilizing. In particular, a negative "shock" to AD may cause interest rates to rise, accelerating the rate of decline of income and employment. This destructive dynamic cannot exist in classical theory, but it was an important part of the disasters of the early 1930s in the US economy that Keynes wanted to explain.

Keynes argued that households and businesses will not automatically restrict themselves to holding the minimum amount of money required for transactions and invest the rest of their savings in long-term bonds as classical theory assumes. After the decision about what percentage of income to save has been made by a wealth holder:

> there is a further decision which awaits him, namely in what form will he hold the command over future consumption which he has reserved, whether out of his current income or *from previous savings* [or wealth]. Does he want to hold it in the form of immediate, liquid command (i.e. in money or its equivalent)? Or is he prepared to part with immediate command for a specified or indefinite period, leaving it to [unknowable] future market conditions to determine on what terms he can, if necessary, convert deferred command over specific goods into immediate command over goods in general? In other words, what is his *liquidity-preference*? ... [The] definition of the rate of interest is the reward for parting with liquidity ["money"] for a specified period. For the rate of interest is, in itself, nothing more than the inverse proportion between a sum of money and what can be obtained for parting with control over the money in exchange for a debt for a stated period of time.
> 
> (CW 7, pp. 166–167, emphasis in original)

Once we acknowledge with Keynes that the future is uncertain or unknowable and therefore that there is, at times, a serious possibility of substantial capital loss in the holding of long-term securities like bonds, the classical theory of the determination of the long-term interest rate becomes fatally flawed. Saving is no longer identically equal to the demand for bonds. There is a separate decision about how much saving should be used to purchase bonds and how much to hold in the liquid form of "money." Much more importantly, the agent has to ask: what percentage of his or her accumulated wealth or "previous savings" does he or she want to hold in the risky long-term asset bonds rather than in the financial asset "money" that is immune from nominal capital loss? What is his or her "liquidity preference?"

Keynes's theory of the determination of the interest rate is a stock-equilibrium theory.[8] He refers to "the amounts of his resources" that an investor "will wish to retain in the form of money" (CW 7, p. 166). The rate of interest, he said, "is the 'price' which equilibrates the desire to hold wealth in the form of cash with the available quantity of cash" (CW 7, p. 167). "[I]t is in respect of his stock of accumulated savings, rather than of his income, that the individual can offer his choice between liquidity [money] and illiquidity [bonds]" (CW 7, p. 194). This makes the interest rate potentially quite volatile because accumulated financial wealth can be 20 times larger than annual savings. If investors decide to sell a substantial part of their accumulated bond holdings in order to avoid a large expected capital loss and to hold on to the money generated by these sales, the long-term interest rate would move sharply higher.

The classical theory of interest rate determination assumes that investors know the correct value of the future interest rate and bond price as a point estimate or as a known and stationary probability distribution. There is no Keynesian uncertainty. But if the future interest rate and bond price are known with certainty, the demand to hold bonds would equal total financial wealth minus the amount of money needed for transactions and precautionary purposes. The demand to hold money as an investment asset would be zero in equilibrium at every positive rate of interest, no matter how low, because the possibility of capital loss has been ruled out by assumption.[9] The demand to hold money would thus be a function of Y alone, with zero elasticity with respect to changes in the rate of interest. Keynes's argument here applies as well to the LM model; if there is no uncertainty about future interest rates, the LM curve would be a vertical line and all money would be held for transactions purposes.[10]

> In a static society or in a society in which for any reason no one feels any uncertainty about the future rates of interest, the liquidity [or demand to hold money] function L, or the propensity to hoard [money] (as we might term it), *will always be zero in equilibrium.*
> (CW 7, pp. 208–209, emphasis added)

It is impossible to overstate the importance of the assumption of fundamental uncertainty to Keynes's attack on classical bond market theory and to the construction of his own theory of potentially unstable bond markets centered on the concept of liquidity preference. Keynes put this point as follows in his 1937 QJE article:

> Partly on reasonable and partly on instinctive grounds, our desire to hold money as a store of wealth is a barometer of the degree of our distrust [or lack of confidence] of our own calculations [expectations] and conventions concerning the future. Even though this feeling about money is itself conventional or instinctive, it operates, so to speak, at a deeper level of our motivations. It takes charge at the moments when the higher, more precarious conventions have weakened. The possession of actual money [rather than expectations of money generated by interest payments or bond sales in the future] lulls our disquietude; and the premium which we require to make us part with money [the long-term interest rate] is the measure or our disquietude.
> (Keynes 1937, p. 116)

Or, as he put it in 1945 in a statement that assumes that investors can choose between risky long-term bonds and relatively safe short-term debt to include in their wealth holdings:

> What determines the reward the individual requires to surrender his liquidity for a long or short period? In practice, of course, what some stockbroker who knows nothing about it advises him, or convention based on old dead ideas of past irrelevant experience. But assuming enlightened self-interest (which probably influences convention) it is your expectation of or a lack of expectation and temporary uncertainty about future changes in the r. of i. [rate of interest].
> (CW 27, p. 391)

Keynes said that "the existence of *uncertainty* as to the future of the rate of interest" is "a necessary condition [for] the existence of a liquidity preference for money as a means of holding wealth" (p. 168, emphasis in original). "[U]*ncertainty* as to the future course of the rate of interest is the sole intelligible explanation of … liquidity preference" (CW 7, p. 201, emphasis in original). Again, if the future is knowable, the demand to hold money as an asset is zero in equilibrium at all interest rate levels.

Keynes argued that, in a world of uncertainty, the bond–money choice will depend on two things. One is the investor's expectations of the movement of bond prices in the near to intermediate future. If bond prices are expected to either increase, remain the same, or at least fall by less than the interest payment on the bond, bonds will, on this criterion alone, be a better investment than zero-interest money. If they are expected to experience a significant decline or a capital loss larger than interest payment, investors will sell bonds.

But there is a second crucial determinant of the desired bond–money split: the "confidence" investors place in the validity or truth content of their expectation-formation process – "on how likely we rate the likelihood of our best forecast turning out quite wrong" (CW 7, p. 148). Even if an investor's best guess is that bonds are not likely to suffer a significant future capital loss, they may want to sell some of their bonds and hold on to the money they receive if they have little confidence in the validity or accuracy of their forecast. Keynes said, as quoted above, that when we "distrust our own calculations [or expectations] and conventions concerning the future" and when "our precarious conventions have weakened," we shift from bonds to money. What he means is that when investors lose "confidence" in their ability to form reliable expectations of future interest rates, they will sell some bonds and hold on to the money they receive. This will cause bond prices to fall and interest rates to rise. This process, if strong enough, can trigger a financial panic. Keynes's crucial theory of "conventional" expectation and confidence formation is discussed in chapter 12 of *The General Theory* and in Chapter 17 of this book.

Because expectation and confidence formation are discussed in chapter 12, Keynes assumed that the reader of chapters 13–15 would be familiar with the material in that chapter. In chapter 12, he argued that in forming expectations, "our usual practice [is] to take the existing situation and to project it into the future, modified only to the extent that we have more or less definite reasons for expecting a change" (CW 7, p. 148). In other words, in normal times, agents formulate expectations by extrapolating the recent trajectory of the economy into the intermediate future, and they presumably have more or less confidence in the reliability of expectations thus formed depending on how accurate such forecasts have been in the recent past. Because both expectations and confidence are endogenously determined, the economy does not need to be exogenously shocked to move – it moves on its own, endogenously.

*Any change in expectations or in confidence will cause a shift in the liquidity preference (or demand to hold money rather than bonds as an asset) function as it is typically specified in Modern Keynesian textbooks and by Keynes on page 199 of* The General Theory: $L = L_1(Y) + L_2(r)$. $L_1$ is the transaction demand plus the precautionary demand to hold money, while $L_2$ represents the crucial "speculative" demand to hold financial wealth in the form of money rather than bonds. "$L_1$ mainly depends on the level of income, whilst $L_2$ *mainly depends on the relation between the current interest rate and the state of expectation*" (CW 7, p. 199, emphasis added).[11] Keynes's liquidity preference function should therefore have been written as $L_2(r_t, r^e_t)$ or perhaps $L_2(r_t - r^e_t)$, where $r_t$ is the current interest rate and $r^e_t$ is the expected future interest rate in period t.[12]

Since the expected future value of the interest rate is included in Keynes's $L_2$ function in *The General Theory* as an exogenous shift parameter, changes in the degree of liquidity preference "are primarily due to changes in the expectation affecting the liquidity preference function itself" (CW 7, p. 197). In other words, every time expectations change – and they change much of the time – *the $L_2$ function shifts*. Keynes explained that in order to generate the standard classical result that a fall in r will cause an increase in the demand to hold money, the $L_2$ function must assume a constant or "given rate of expectation" (CW 7, p. 202). Given that Keynes assumed in chapter 12 that expectations are typically formed by extrapolation from the recent past, every time the interest rate changes in an unexpected way the expected interest rate also changes, causing the $L_2(r)$ function to shift and the actual interest rate to change again in an ongoing endogenous process.

Chapter 12 also points to the importance of confidence in the reliability of expectation formation to agent choice under uncertainty. The complete specification of Keynes's liquidity preference function therefore should have been written as $L_2(r_t, r^e_t, C_t)$, where $C_t$ is an index of confidence in the reliability of expectations. If the interest rate moves through time as expected, confidence in the reliability of expectations will increase, causing a shift in the standard $L_2 = L(r)$ function that will cause the interest rate to change. Since both expectations and confidence change endogenously, the *standard $L_2$ function is always shifting, constantly changing the temporary "equilibrium" value of the interest rate.*[13] The interest rate is thus what Shackle called "an inherently restless variable" (Shackle 1972, pp. 163–164). Minsky argued that the longer the price of a financial asset remained stable, the more confident investors would become that the asset is not very risky, which would lead them to buy more of that asset, raising its price. In his words: "stability is destabilizing."

Keynes pointed out that shifts in the $L^2$ function could, at times, be sharp or "discontinuous," creating or exacerbating interest rate volatility. "Changes in the liquidity function itself, due to a change in the news which causes revision of expectations, will often be discontinuous, and will, therefore, give rise to a corresponding discontinuity of change in the rate of interest" (CW 7, p. 198). This discontinuity will be especially pronounced if a large majority of investors come to believe with conviction or confidence that bond prices are likely to suffer a significant fall. To state the case in extreme form: "If the change in the news affects the judgment and requirements of everyone in precisely the same way, the rate of interest ... will be adjusted forthwith to the new situation without any transactions" (CW 7, p. 198). This is obviously not a vision of a bond market that always has deeply rooted equilibriums.

Keynes also argued that the forces that made stock prices so volatile in the "insane" US gambling casino also operated in the US bond market in this era. In chapter 12, he wrote:

> A conventional valuation [of stock prices] which is established as the outcome of the mass psychology of a large number of ignorant individuals is liable to change violently as the result of sudden fluctuations of opinion due to factors that do not really matter much to the prospective yield; since there will be no strong roots to hold it steady.
>
> (CW 7, p. 154)

In chapter 13, he wrote:

> Just as we found the [price of a stock] is fixed, not by the "best" opinion, but by the market valuation as determined by mass psychology, so also expectations as to the future of the rate of interest as fixed by mass psychology have their reactions on liquidity preference.
>
> (CW 7, p. 170)

There is a paradox of sorts in the role played by money, the safe asset, in Keynes's theory of bond market instability. Where markets themselves are liquid, so that securities can be traded quickly for money at low transaction costs, the ability to rapidly shift from risky long-term securities to money in the event of market trouble will calm the nerves of investors. This will induce them to take what are objectively (though not subjectively) greater risks in a financial boom because they believe they can quickly shift to money and out of risky securities if trouble develops.[14] If markets were not liquid and there was no safe asset, investors would have to be much more cautious about holding risky securities, which would, *ceteris paribus*, raise interest rates and lower income and employment. But at the same time, the existence of an asset without risk of nominal capital loss can worsen the degree of panic in *all* long-term financial markets because, by providing a safe haven for frightened investors, it enables them to flee all long-term risky assets, potentially creating or exacerbating a financial panic. Keynes said that the high degree of liquidity in modern markets:

> presents us with a dilemma. For, in the absence of an organised market, liquidity-preference due to the precautionary motive would be greatly increased [raising interest rates]; whereas the existence of an organised market gives an opportunity for wide fluctuations in liquidity-preference due to the speculative motive.
>
> (CW 7, pp. 170–171)

The highly liquid bond market is therefore subject to points of "wide fluctuations" in the value of the long-term interest rate – a constant theme in these chapters.

## Keynes's theory of liquidity preference and the behavior of US interest rates in the late 1920s and early 1930s

How does Keynes's theory of the bond market help contribute to an explanation of booms and busts such as the one that took place in the USA in the late 1920s and early 1930s? Since both Keynes's theory of the business cycle in chapter 22 and a sketch of a Keynes–Minsky cycle will be presented later, we limit our discussion here to a few points.

It is easy to tell a simple abstract story about how Keynes's theory of the interest rate operates in a boom. Rising bond prices in a general environment of investor optimism lead to the expectation held with increasing confidence by an increasing proportion of investors that bond prices will continue to rise or at least not fall significantly over the foreseeable future. Investors therefore are likely to shift portions of their financial wealth from money to bonds over time. This causes interest rates to keep falling and bond prices to keep rising. Falling interest rates help stimulate rapid growth in AD, creating or accelerating a boom in the real sector by making it more attractive for firms and households to engage in debt-financed spending. This will increase the financial fragility of firms, households, and banks. At some point, unexpected problems in the real and/or financial sectors create pessimistic expectations and possibly a collapse in confidence, kicking the expansion into reverse.

It is more difficult to tell a simple yet adequate story about the actual behavior of interest rate determinants in the bubble of the late 1920s by focusing exclusively on the bond market through the lens of chapters 13–15. This is due in part to a complex relation between interest rates and stock prices in the boom that is not discussed in these chapters. Though it is assumed in the chapters that investors have to choose between money and bonds, in fact they can buy either stocks or bonds or both. Long-term bond prices did rise by almost 20 percent in the boom of 1926 through early 1929. But stock prices rose by about 125 percent between 1926 and late 1929, generating increasingly optimistic expectations of capital gains on stocks held with increasing confidence. This induced many investors to sell bonds and buy stocks, which kept long-term interest rates higher (and bond prices lower) in 1927–1929 than they otherwise would have been. Meanwhile, there was an enormous increase in speculators' demand for short-term broker loans to buy stocks near the peak of the bubble.[15] This caused a jump in short-term interest rates on broker loans – from 4 percent in early 1928 to 14 percent in mid-1929. The spread between long and short interest rates fell precipitously from 1928 through 1929, inverting the yield curve.[16] Speculation-driven short rates actually moved above long rates in 1928 and most of 1929 (Federal Reserve Bank of Cleveland 1998, p. 199).[17]

Now consider what might happen once a strong bond market bubble bursts, bond prices start to fall, and interest rates begin to rise. Expectations would shift rather quickly from optimism to pessimism about the future path of bond prices, triggering an increase in the rate of bond sales that would accelerate the pace of interest rate increases. This would generate even more pessimistic expectations. Because expectations of rising bond prices just prior to the start of the crash turned out to be profoundly mistaken, confidence in the expectation-formation process would be likely to collapse. This alone would cause an additional sharp upward pressure on the interest rate. Rapidly rising interest rates would accelerate the decline in AD caused by falling capital investment and deteriorating consumption spending, which would reinforce the ongoing rise in liquidity preference. Should a process of this kind take place at a time when firms, households, and financial institutions have developed fragile balance sheets, the financial system itself might face collapse, as it did in the USA in the early 1930s.

## What happened to interest rates in the early 1930s?

Relevant data from the USA in the first half of the 1930s are consistent with Keynes's theory, but starkly inconsistent with classical theory. This is hardly a surprise because Keynes had US financial markets in this period in mind when he wrote the "insane casino" chapters of *The General Theory*. For example, in 1930, just as the crisis hit, AAA-rated corporate bonds (the safest class of corporate bonds) had an interest rate of 4.6 percent, while riskier Baa bonds paid 5.9 percent. In May 1932, in the midst of the collapse, the AAA rate rose to 5.4 percent. However, many bonds initially in the AAA category in the boom of the late 1920s had been downgraded to Baa by 1932. The Baa interest rate rose to 11.6 percent (Board of Governors of the Federal Reserve System 1943, p. 468). Long-term bond prices were in a state of collapse.

Keep in mind that there was a severe deflation in this period starting in early 1930 that saw a 25 percent price decline in the USA between 1929 and 1932, so real long-term rates increased by much more than nominal rates. *The real Baa interest rate was more than 20 percent in 1932 –* with a nominal interest rate of 11.6 percent added to a 10.3 percent rate of deflation that blew up the real value of nominal interest payments.[18] The real AAA interest rate was 15.7 percent. This huge leap in real long-term rates, along with the severe stock price collapse that accompanied it, obviously made the real-sector crisis qualitatively worse. Rather than reducing instability in the real sector as asserted by classical theory, the bond market greatly magnified it. This was an immensely destructive disequilibrium process.

Keynes pointed out that there was little the Fed could do to stop this onslaught.

> Where, however, (as in the United States, 1933–34) open-market operations have been limited to the purchase of very short-dated

securities, the effect may ... be mainly confined to the very short-term rate of interest and have but little reaction on the much more important long-term rate of interest.

(CW 7, p. 197)[19]

In the context of a panic in the long-term bond market, open market operations merely widened the long–short interest rate spread.

Of course, at the same time and through the same process, the short-term interest rate on "money" fell as investors fled the risk of capital loss in stocks and bonds and used the cash generated by these sales to buy the capital safety provided by short, safe financial assets. This caused the Treasury bill rate, which was 4.4 percent in 1929, to decline to 2.2 percent in 1930 and 1.2 percent in 1933 and led to an explosion of the long–short interest differential. But the fall in the short rate could do nothing to stop the collapse of capital investment spending.

By 1936, in the midst of the depression, the nominal Baa rate had declined to 5 percent, but by this time the actual and the expected gross profit rates on capital investment were so low and excess capacity so high that even a sharp drop in the long-term interest rate could not possibly get capital investment out of the doldrums. Net investment (gross investment minus depreciation) in the USA was actually negative in 1933. And the banks were more concerned with their solvency than with providing ample credit to businesses and households.

## Conclusion

Having demonstrated that wage-price deflation in the context of high unemployment is a destructive process in chapters 2 and 19 and that interest rates are likely to rise when the economy is failing in chapters 13–15, Keynes completed his attack on the classical theory of stabilizing disequilibrium processes. But these chapters did not complete his analysis of the "insane" financial markets of this era. This required a theory of the stock market and its effect on capital investment, which he provided in chapter 12.

## Appendix[20]

There has been some confusion in the literature on Keynes's theory of interest rate determination in *The General Theory* created by his definition of the term "money."

> [W]e can draw the line between "money" and "debts" [or "bonds"] at whatever point is most convenient for handling a particular problem. For example, we can treat as *money* any command over purchasing power which the owner has not parted with for a period in excess of three months, and as *debt* what cannot be recovered for a longer

> period than this; or we can substitute for "three months" one month or three days or three hours or any other period; or we can exclude from *money* whatever is not legal tender on the spot. It is often convenient in practice to include in money time-deposits with banks and, occasionally, even such bills as (e.g.) treasury bills.
>
> (CW 7, p. 167, emphasis in original)

These short-term interest-bearing assets should dominate zero-interest cash as a safe haven when bond prices are expected to decline.

Moreover:

> In general discussion, as distinct from specific problems where the period of the debt is expressly specified, it is convenient to mean by the rate of interest the complex of the various rates of interest current for different periods of time, i.e. for debts of different maturities.
>
> (CW 7, p. 167)

In this case, the theory of liquidity preference would be about the determination of the *term structure of interest rates* rather than the long-term bond rate alone, or, in a simpler two-maturity debt model, about the *spread* between the interest rate on risky long-term bonds and the normally much lower rate of interest on very-short-term debts that are almost invulnerable to nominal capital loss. If investors began to expect that bond prices are likely to decline, they would sell some bonds and hold the cash they received in the sale in the form of savings accounts or short-term Treasury bills. These transactions would raise the long rate and lower the short rate, increasing the spread.

This is a bit awkward for the interpreter of Keynes's theory of liquidity preference: is it a theory of the long-term interest rate or a theory of the term structure of interest rates – the "spread" between a long-term and short-term interest rate? Indeed, if only the spread is determined in the model, the level of the long-term interest rate is missing an "anchor" and its equilibrium value is undetermined.[21]

Fortunately, this "anchor" issue is not of primary importance for the main purpose of this chapter. We are concerned here primarily with the dynamic response of the long-term interest rate to a substantial decline in AD, especially, as in the early 1930s, in a situation of financial fragility and with the endogenously induced dynamics associated with financial market cycles and not with some hypothetical static-equilibrium value of the long-term interest rate in the depth of the Great Depression. We have shown that in the financial meltdown of the early 1930s investors sought capital protection by dramatically shifting from long-term bonds to the short-term interest-bearing assets included in Keynes's broad definition of "money," a process that caused the long–short spread to skyrocket as long rates rose dramatically while short rates fell.

# Notes

1. Keynes abstracted from both government expenditures and taxes as well as net exports that deal with this issue in chapters 13–15.
2. This discussion assumes that corporate profits are zero or that all saving is done in the household sector.
3. See the diagram on page 180 of *The General Theory*.
4. Note that this exercise is an example of how classical financial markets are also efficient mechanisms that alter production priorities to reflect changes in time preference, risk preference, and technology. When the real sector signaled that investment was no longer as productive as before, financial markets efficiently raised the C/Y ratio and lowered the I/Y ratio. So financial markets not only kept the economy at its full-capacity equilibrium in the face of an exogenous shock, they also accomplished the appropriate transfer of resources between investment and consumption. Financial markets are our friends.
5. Keep in mind that the price of a bond and the interest rate on the bond are inversely related.
6. In *The General Theory*, Keynes separated the analysis of bond and stock markets. The stock market is treated in chapter 12 and the bond market in chapters 13–15. This was a change from the strategy he used in the *Treatise on Money* published in 1930, where he discussed the behavior of stocks and bonds together, referring to them collectively as security prices. "This treatment, however, involved a confusion between results due to a change in the rate of interest and those due to a change in the schedule of the marginal efficiency of capital, which I hope I have here avoided" (CW, pp. 173–174). This strategy creates a serious problem. It pictures investors as faced in chapters 13–15 with a choice of holding either "money" or long-term bonds. In fact, their choices are more complex and include the choice between stocks and bonds, which are potential substitutes in investors' portfolios. We point out below that in the late 1920s stocks became more attractive than bonds because of the incredible stock market bubble in this period.
7. Keynes defined "money" broadly to include not only zero-interest "cash," but also such short-term interest-bearing assets as savings accounts and Treasury bills that are relatively resistant to nominal capital loss. This raises the question as to whether he offered a theory of the long-term interest rate or of the long–short interest rate "spread." This issue is discussed in the Appendix.
8. Ideally, the model should take into account that the amount of financial wealth in the economy is changed by the flow of savings at every moment of model time.
9. If the stationary probability distributions that correctly described future states were knowable, all risk could be hedged.
10. This point was emphasized by Hicks, as we note in Chapter 19.
11. Y is included in the function as a proxy for the transactions and precautionary motives to hold money.
12. As explained above, his theory of liquidity preference requires the assumption that agents are uncertain about the value of $r^e_t$. If, for example, all investors knew with certainty that $r^e_t$ was lower than $r_t$ or that the future bond price was higher than the current bond price, no one would be willing to hold money and $r_t$ would be forced to rise until it equaled $r^e_t$, at which point $L_2$ would equal zero in equilibrium.

13 The same thing is also true about the LM curve. Endogenously generated changes in expectations and/or confidence in expectations keep the LM curve in perpetual motion.
14 While each individual investor might find comfort in the belief that he or she can quickly exit the stock or bond market when prices begin to fall, this cannot be true for all investors. When fear hits a market and everyone begins to sell, most investors will suffer large capital losses.
15 Brokers' loans more than doubled from the third quarter of 1927 through the third quarter of 1929. They then fell by more than 90 percent from the third quarter of 1929 to the fourth quarter of 1931 (*Banking and Monetary Statistics: 1914–1941*, Board of Governors of the Federal Reserve System, p. 494. Accessed at: http://fraser.stlouisfed.org/).
16 The relevance of the long–short "spread" is explained in the Appendix.
17 Data from "Interest Rates in the 1920s," Federal Reserve Bank of Cleveland, Economic Trends, No. 98-02, p. 7, 02.01, 1998.
18 Moody's (2018) and United States Bureau of Labor Statistics (2018).
19 Keynes argued that significant changes in monetary policy in response to problems in the real sector can actually aggravate the situation because they will increase uncertainty with respect to future central bank intervention: they "may also give rise to changed expectations concerning the future policy of the central bank" (CW 7, p. 198).
20 Non-specialist readers can skip this Appendix.
21 One resolution of the problem is to assume that the central bank can set or "anchor" the shortest-term interest rate, but in a model with Keynesian uncertainty, this creates an additional problem. In periods of instability, the central bank would be forced to keep changing its money supply target in an attempt to maintain a constant short-term interest rate, and this itself would add to the uncertainty confronting investors.

# 17 Chapter 12 of *The General Theory*
## The "insane" stock market, capital investment, and instability

### Introduction

The section of *The General Theory* in which chapter 12 is located is titled "The Inducement to Invest" and chapter 12 is titled "Long-Term Expectation." The objective of the chapter is to explain the nature or character of long-term expectation formation with respect to the profitability of new capital investment goods, and in so doing to explore the effects of long-term expectations on the behavior of capital investment. The chapter thus deals with a crucial area of the interpretation of Keynes's theory about which there is considerable debate. It is an important debate because the determination of the stability or instability of equilibrium and the character of out-of-equilibrium processes in Keynes's theory depend critically on the character of long-term expectation formation, as does the existence of endogenous sources of instability. Does *The General Theory* argue that long-term expectations are exogenous or endogenous? If they are exogenous, where do they come from? If they are endogenous, are long-term expectations strongly or weakly sensitive to or even affected by recent outcomes? The more sensitive that long-term expectations are to recent economic outcomes, the more potentially unstable the economic system will be. Conversely, if long-term expectations do not respond to events in the recent past, it is more likely that equilibriums will be relatively stable and business cycles will have moderate amplitude.[1]

For Keynes, as we have seen, answers to questions about the "laws of motion" of a capitalist economy require the specification of the historical and institutional characteristics of the economy under investigation in the time period under investigation. In other words, answers must be derived from the analysis of concrete capitalisms and not some abstract capitalism-in-general model. This is of special importance in chapter 12 because Keynes believed that the character of the long-term expectations that co-determines the level of capital investment had dramatically altered between the nineteenth century and the interwar years, especially in the USA. Two institutional changes were particularly important in this regard. First, Keynes argued that, in the interwar era, the site of decision-making about capital investment in effect shifted from the investing corporation itself to the stock market. He argued that this change dramatically increased the elasticity of long-term expectations with respect to recent realizations, making the economy much more volatile. Second, he said that the stock market had become an "insane" "gambling casino" in the postwar period dominated by short-term speculators. The result of these two changes, Keynes concluded, was less investment and more volatile investment. "When the capital development of a country becomes a by-product of the activities of a casino," he said, "the job is likely to be ill-done" (CW 7, p. 159).

In order to achieve his objectives in this chapter, Keynes had to create a theory of the dynamics of the era's casino stock markets. Chapters 12, 13, 15, and 22 together constitute a theory of the inherent instability of lightly regulated financial markets that is the foundation of Keynes–Minsky models of financial volatility and financial fragility, the best models available to analyze today's global "casino" financial markets.

In this important chapter, Keynes analyzed the effect of fundamental or radical uncertainty on the capital investment decision of the firm. Fundamental uncertainty means that the probability distributions that describe future states of the economy are not knowable in the present because these states have yet to be determined in the present and will be influenced by decisions taken today and tomorrow by agents ignorant of the future. This assumption is a crucial underpinning of Keynes's revolutionary transformation of macro theory. It also led him to create a largely unrecognized transformation in micro theory or the theory of agent choice, a transformation discussed in Appendix 1.

We saw in the previous chapter how the assumption of fundamental uncertainty led to a theory of potentially unstable interest rates that were likely to rise in the face of any serious downturn in the real sector, worsening the problem. Chapter 12 applies Keynes's theory of agent choice under uncertainty to the determination of the mec or expected profit rate on investment, and thus to the determination of capital investment spending. The mec is defined in chapter 11 of *The General Theory*. It has to be a function of the *expected* future cash flows associated with a capital investment project because, under fundamental uncertainty, no one has certain knowledge of what these future cash flows will be at the time the investment decision is made.

> I define the marginal efficiency of capital as being equal to that rate of discount which would make the present value of the series of annuities given by the returns expected from the capital-asset during its life just equal to its supply price [or cost] ... The reader should note that the marginal efficiency of capital is here defined in terms of the *expectation* of yield.
> 
> (CW 7, pp. 135–136, emphasis in original)

Keynes tells us that investment projects should only be undertaken if their marginal efficiency or mec exceeds the long-term interest rate.

## Long-term expectation formation under radical uncertainty

Keynes argues that the assumption that the future is inherently unknowable in the present is both obviously true and theoretically transformational.

> The outstanding fact is the extreme precariousness of the basis of knowledge on which our estimates of prospective yield have to be made. Our knowledge of the factors which will govern the yield of an investment some years hence is usually very slight and often negligible. If we speak frankly, we have to admit that our basis of knowledge for estimating the yield ten years hence of a railway, a copper mine, a textile factory, the goodwill of a patent medicine, an Atlantic liner, a building in the city of London amounts to little and sometimes to nothing; or even five years hence. In fact, those who seriously attempt to make any such estimate are often so much in the minority that their behaviour does not govern the market.
> 
> (CW 7, p. 150)

Keynes repeated this "outstanding fact" about the theory of agent choice under uncertainty in the 1937 QJE article that stressed the differences between his theory and classical theory.

> [In classical theory,] at any given time facts and expectations were assumed to be given in a definite and calculable form; and risks, of which, tho admitted, not much notice was taken, were supposed to be capable of an exact actuarial computation. *The calculus of probability, tho mention of it was kept in the background, was supposed to be capable of reducing uncertainty to the same calculable status as that of certainty itself* ...
> 
> Actually, however, we have, as a rule, only the vaguest idea of any but the most direct consequences of our acts. Sometimes we are not much concerned with their remoter consequences, even tho time and chance may make much of them. But sometimes we are intensely concerned with them, more so, occasionally, than with the immediate consequences. Now of all human activities which are affected by this remoter preoccupation, it happens that one of the most important is economic in character, namely, Wealth. The whole object of the accumulation of Wealth is to produce results ... at a comparatively distant, and sometimes at an indefinitely distant, date. Thus the fact that our knowledge of the future is *fluctuating, vague and uncertain*, renders Wealth a peculiarly unsuitable subject for the methods of the classical economic theory ...

## 242 The General Theory

> By "uncertain" knowledge, let me explain, I do not mean merely to distinguish what is known for certain from what is only probable. The game of roulette is not subject, in this sense, to uncertainty: nor is the prospect of a victory bond being drawn ... Even the weather is only moderately uncertain. The sense in which I am using the term is that in which the prospect of a European war is uncertain, or the price of copper and the rate of interest twenty years hence, or the obsolescence of a new invention, or the position of private wealth-owners in the social system in 1970. About these matters there is no scientific basis on which to form any calculable probability whatever. *We simply do not know.*
> 
> (Keynes 1937, pp. 212–214, emphasis added)

Keynes then argued that in the absence of true knowledge of the future consequences of our current decisions we are forced to form expectations of the future through the use of socially sanctioned behavioral or psychological *conventions*. In the QJE article and in other writings, Keynes presented a complex view of conventional expectation formation. As we have seen, in his 1937 Galton Lecture, Keynes said that people have a profound psychological need to reassure themselves that they can foresee the future with at least some degree of accuracy when they make choices that will significantly affect their future happiness or prosperity, even though they know at some psychologically deeper level that this is not possible.

> The future never resembles the present – as we all know ... We do not know what the future holds. Nevertheless, as living and moving beings, we are forced to act. Peace and comfort of mind require that *we should hide from ourselves how little we foresee*. Yet we must be guided by some hypothesis. We tend, therefore, to substitute for the knowledge which is unattainable certain conventions, the chief of which is to assume, *contrary to all likelihood*, that the future will resemble the past. This is how we act in practice.
> 
> (CW 14, p. 124, emphasis added)

Keynes thus argues that even though "we simply do not know" the information that we must have to make safe decisions, we have a human need "to behave in a manner which saves our faces as rational, economic men" (Keynes 1937, p. 214), a manner that allows us the comfort of the illusion of safety and rationality. He tells us that we have a psychological need to calm our anxieties, to remove the constant stress created by forced decision-making under inadequate information, a need that is neither irrational nor socially or economically dysfunctional. We have good reason, in other words, to try to "overlook this awkward fact" that the reproduction of our economic and social status requires a knowledge of things that, in fact, "we simply do not know." In Keynes's words above: "Peace and comfort of mind require that we should hide from ourselves how little we foresee" (CW 14, p. 124).

To help us accomplish this calming of our nerves, Keynes argues, we collectively develop a "conventional" process of expectation formation. Keynes's concept of conventional decision-making is a sine qua non of his macro theory. It is also one of Keynes's most important theoretical innovations. The dictionary definition of conventional as "arising from custom and tradition" captures Keynes's meaning to some degree. In place of the complete probabilistic information appropriate to the world of classical, New Classical, and neoclassical agent choice, Keynes substitutes an expectation-formation and decision-making process based on custom, habit, tradition, instinct, and other socially constituted practices that make sense only in a model of human agency in an environment of genuine uncertainty.[2]

In his 1937 QJE article, Keynes tells us that we save our faces as rational economic men and calm our nerves in the following ways, none of which are available to the mainstream fully informed "rational" actor.

(1) We assume that the present is a much more serviceable guide to the future than a candid examination of past experience would show it to have been hitherto. In other words we largely ignore the prospect of future changes about the actual character of which we know nothing.
(2) We assume that the *existing* state of opinion as expressed in prices and the character of existing output is based on a *correct* summing up of future prospects, so that we can accept it as such unless and until something new and relevant comes into the picture.
(3) Knowing that our own individual judgment is worthless, we endeavor to fall back on the judgment of the rest of the world which is perhaps better informed. That is, we endeavor to conform with the behavior of the majority or the average. The psychology of a society of individuals each of whom is endeavoring to copy the others leads to what we may strictly term a *conventional* judgment.

(Keynes 1937, p. 214, emphasis in original)

All three of these conventional methods of expectation formation would be irrational in a world of agents who were, or at least believed they were, fully informed about future economic states. However, it is not surprising that they are a reasonable explanation of how psychologically complex agents make choices in the context of fundamental uncertainty.

Keynes immediately warns the reader that an economy based on these principles of expectation formation will inevitably be subject to bouts of extreme instability, especially in periods such as the late 1920s through the mid-1930s in which financial security markets were globally integrated and lightly regulated.

> Now a practical theory of the future based on these three principles has certain marked characteristics. In particular, being based on so flimsy a foundation, it is subject to sudden and violent changes. The practice of calmness and immobility, of certainty and security, suddenly breaks down. New fears and hopes will, without warning, take charge of human conduct. The forces of disillusion may suddenly impose a new conventional basis of valuation. All these pretty, polite techniques, made for a well-paneled Board Room and a nicely regulated market, are liable to collapse. At all times the vague panic fears and equally vague and unreasoned hopes are not really lulled, and lie but a little way below the surface.
> (Keynes 1937, p. 215)

Keynes then criticizes classical theory because it turns a blind eye to this severe flaw in the economic system by assuming away fundamental uncertainty, a criticism equally applicable to neoclassical and New Classical theory.

> Tho this is how we behave in the market place, the theory we devise in the study of how we behave in the market place should not itself submit to marketplace idols. I accuse the classical economic theory of being itself one of these pretty, polite techniques which tries to deal with the present by abstracting from the fact that we know very little about the future.
> (Keynes 1937, p. 215)

In chapter 12, Keynes simplified his theory of long-term expectation formation in response to institutional changes we discuss below. He argued that the long-term expectations that determine the mec were now set in the stock market and therefore had shallow roots. They were formed by extrapolation from the recent past, unless there were concrete reasons to believe the trajectory of the economy had changed or would change in the near future. Our usual practice, he said, is "to take the existing situation and to project it into the future, modified only to the extent that we have more or less definitive reasons for expecting a change" (CW 7, p. 148).

This theory is compatible with periods of relative stability or continuity. Expectations that the economic trajectory of the economy in the recent past will continue in the foreseeable future can lead to decisions that cause it to continue. If agents expect a period of prosperity to continue, they may make decisions that cause it to continue, and vice versa. Convention-based extrapolative forecasts can thus help make possible those periods of continuity that Keynes called "normal times" and that Joan Robinson referred to as periods of "tranquility."

However, Keynes immediately warns the reader of chapter 12 that while the convention that the future will look like the recent past extrapolated is compatible with periods of tranquility, economic history demonstrates that expectations thus formed are also inherently vulnerable to serious error. Conventional forecasts have at times been substantially, even disastrously, mistaken. The convention itself is therefore quite psychologically fragile.

> This does not mean that we really believe that the existing state of affairs will continue indefinitely. We know from extensive experience that this is most unlikely. The actual results of an investment over a long term of years very seldom agree with the initial expectation … [P]hilosophically speaking, [the expectation] cannot be uniquely correct, since our existing knowledge does not provide a sufficient basis for a calculated mathematical expectation.
> 
> (CW 7, p. 152)

Keynes cautions the reader – as he would do again in his QJE article – that the precarious nature of an expectation-formation process built on such a fragile foundation cannot sustain persistently high investment, especially in an era in which casino stock and bond markets have a dominant role in the capital investment decision.

> [I]t is not surprising that a convention, in an absolute view of things so arbitrary, should have its weak points. It is its precariousness which creates no small part of our contemporary problem of securing sufficient investment.
> 
> (CW 7, p. 153)

## The role of "confidence" in the truth content of expectations in Keynes's theory

There is a second crucial aspect or dimension of the formation of expectations in chapter 12 that has virtually vanished from Modern Keynesian theory. As mentioned in the previous chapter, because Keynes's agents are aware that they do not know the future, it is difficult for them to have complete psychological *confidence* that their expectations will turn out to be correct. The decision to invest is therefore not determined solely by the best expectations the firm can have of the future profit or cash flows from a potential investment project. The mec is also strongly influenced by the degree of confidence the agents who make the capital investment decision have in the truth content or correctness of their expectations. The degree of confidence in expectations plays a key role in Keynes's theory of investment instability.

The state of long term expectation, upon which our decisions are based, does not solely depend on the most probable forecast we can make. It also depends on the *confidence* with which we make this forecast – *on how likely we rate the likelihood of our best forecast turning out quite wrong. If we expect large changes but are very uncertain as to what precise form these changes will take, then our confidence will be weak.* The state of confidence, as they term it, is a matter to which practical men always pay the closest and most anxious attention. But economists have not analysed it carefully and have been content, as a rule, to discuss it in general terms. In particular it has not been made clear that its relevance to economics comes in through its important influence on the marginal efficiency of capital. *There are not two separate factors affecting the rate of investment, namely, the schedule of the marginal efficiency of capital and the state of confidence. The state of confidence is relevant because it is one of the major factors determining the former, which is the investment demand schedule.*

(CW 7, p. 148–149, emphasis added)

Social and behavioral conventions calm our nerves and "save our faces" as rational economic agents because they create confidence that expectations thus formed have a degree of meaningfulness or validity or truth content sufficient to sustain an investment decision of great moment for the agent. An optimistic forecast of the mec will not induce a firm to undertake a risky long-term investment if the firm has little confidence that their forecast is the truth about the future.

The creation of confidence in the meaningfulness of forecasts or in the "scientific" character of the "conventional wisdom" is absolutely essential to both the growth potential and the conditional stability of the Keynesian model.[3] A key reason why agents can sensibly attribute a quasi-objective or quasi-scientific character to conventionally formed expectations is that conventions are socially constituted and socially and externally sanctioned. They are not mere idiosyncratic figments of the isolated individual's imagination. This assumption is reflected in Keynes's assertion, just cited: "Knowing that our own individual judgment is worthless, we endeavor to fall back on the judgment of the rest of the world which is perhaps better informed" (Keynes 1937, p. 214).

Consider the following example of this assumption. When the collective wisdom of "Wall Street" (as reflected in the views of the business and financial press, investor newsletters, television's market analysts, and so forth) is near unanimous in predicting that a buoyant stock market will continue into the foreseeable future, it is not unreasonable for an individual investor to conclude that this expectation has a solid foundation. After all, the institutions and individuals who constitute "Wall Street" are professionals and insiders, knowledgeable students of the market whose expertise in these matters is richly rewarded by society. Moreover, when

Wall Street is selling the belief that markets are in a long upturn, financial economists and government officials are likely be in agreement with this forecast. To assume that this collection of experts is as ignorant of the future as the isolated individual investor is to question the very rationality of our economic and social institutions. In normal times, people do not do that.

Conventions that inform confidence formation prevent agents from being perpetually confused and perhaps even psychologically immobilized by their comprehension of the extreme precariousness of their economic status. In the end, it is the propensity of agents to believe in the solidity and validity of the conventional forecast and not just "animal spirits" – some innate or genetically transmitted "spontaneous urge to action rather than inaction" – that defeats the forces of ignorance and prevents perpetual stagnation or perpetual chaos in a Keynesian world (CW 7, p. 161). But, as Keynes warned, it "is not surprising that a convention, in an absolute view of things so arbitrary, should have its weak points" (CW 7, p. 153). In what Keynes referred to as "abnormal" times, when forecasts of stock market or real-sector booms turn out to be disastrously wrong, confidence in expectations can quickly evaporate, causing security prices and capital investment to plummet. "The practice of calmness and immobility, of certainty and security, suddenly breaks down" (Keynes 1937, p. 215).

For our purposes in this chapter, we will rely on the simple assumptions that the degree of confidence agents have in their expectations is a positive function of the accuracy of their forecasts in the recent past in normal times, and that confidence can collapse or evaporate in Keynes's "abnormal" times of panic and crisis.

## From the boardroom to the financial gambling casino: how the long-term expectations that determine capital investment became unstable and confidence in expectations evaporated in the 1930s

In chapter 11, Keynes created a theory in which, given the interest rate, investment in capital goods depended on the long-term profit expectations of business firms as reflected in the mec. However, in chapter 12, he shifted the site of effective determination of the mec from the managers of the firm to speculators in the stock market. We might say that the site of investment decision-making shifted from the longer-term perspective of the corporate boardroom to the very short-term speculator's perspective of the era's stock and bond market "gambling casinos." According to Keynes, this sea change in the institutional structures that determine capital investment spending caused investment to become much more unstable than it had been in the nineteenth century.

Keynes explained how this structural change came to pass.

> In former times, when enterprises were mainly owned by those who undertook them or by their friends and associates, investment depended upon a sufficient supply of individuals of sanguine temperament and constructive impulses who embarked on business as a way of life, not relying on a precise calculation of prospective profit.
> (CW 7, p. 150)

In the nineteenth century, most firms were owned by founders and their families and friends, but by the interwar period, many large firms had gone public as the founding families cashed out their illiquid stock of real capital by selling ownership of the firm on the stock market. The assumed replacement of the management of the firm by investors in the stock market as the site of the determination of the mec required a rethinking by Keynes of the theory of capital investment.

Family-owned and -operated firms were committed to the long-term growth of the firm primarily because this made possible the long-term reproduction of the economic and social status of the family. This required such firms to invest in order to grow and stay competitive over the longest of runs. They therefore had long-run capital investment planning horizons. The rise of publicly owned corporations whose stock is traded on the market as the dominant form of enterprise ownership in the interwar years created a stark difference between the liquidity properties of capital goods owned by family firms and the liquid stock certificates owned by public shareholders.

Keynes stressed the importance of this change in liquidity in his explanation of the instability of the period.[4] An asset is liquid if it can be sold quickly with a small transaction cost without the sale causing a significant drop in the price of the asset. Physical capital can be highly illiquid. Once put in a specific place, with a specific technology, and integrated into an existing production system, the resale of the asset may take a substantial period of time and can result in a substantial capital loss. If the firm is forced to sell plant or equipment when business in the industry is bad and the demand for capital goods has collapsed, the sale will result in a large capital loss for the firm.

Family-owned firms did not consider selling their factories in economic downturns or buying factories for the purpose of reselling them a short time later for capital gains. They were not short-term speculators. "Decisions to invest in private business of the old-fashioned type were, however, decisions that were irrevocable, not only for the community as a whole, but also for the individual" (CW 7, p. 150). This limited the volatility of capital investment over time.

On the other hand, a shareholder owns a piece of paper he or she can buy or sell at a moment's notice at a small transaction cost. In the unstable stock markets of the late 1920s and 1930s, speculators operated – often with borrowed money – on very short-term horizons, seeking quick capital gains when prices were rising, while quickly selling to avoid short-term capital losses when prices were falling. This helped make stock prices extraordinarily unstable.

Why was Keynes so focused on the properties of the stock market in a chapter devoted to long-term expectations as they affect the mec and the level of investment spending? It is because in this chapter Keynes argues that *a rise in a firm's stock price is tantamount to an increase in its mec,* and it therefore creates an increase in the demand for capital goods. If, then, the stock market is an insane gambling casino, investment spending will be exceptionally volatile and thus exceptionally risky: over the long run there will be too little investment, and what investment there is will not be efficiently allocated.

> With the separation between ownership and management that prevails today and with the development of organised investment [i.e. stock] markets, a new factor of great importance has entered in, which sometimes facilitates investment but *sometimes adds greatly to the instability of the system.* In the absence of security markets there is no object in frequently attempting to revalue a [capital] investment to which we are committed. But the Stock Exchange revalues many investments every day and the revaluations give a frequent opportunity to the individual (though not to the community as a whole) to revive his commitments. It is as though a farmer, having tapped his barometer after breakfast, could decide to remove his capital from the farming business between 10 and 11 in the morning and reconsider whether he should return to it later in the week.
>
> (CW 7, p. 150–151, emphasis added)

> [T]he daily revaluations of the Stock Exchange, though they are primarily transfers of old investments between one individual and another, *inevitably exert a decisive influence on the rate of current investment.* For there is no sense in building up a new enterprise at a cost greater than that at which a similar existing enterprise can be purchased; whilst there is an inducement to spend on a new project what may seem an extravagant sum, if it can be floated off on the stock exchange at an immediate profit.[5]
>
> (CW 7, p. 151, emphasis added)

He repeated this assertion in chapter 22.

> I have shown above (Chapter 12) that, although the private [stock market] investor is seldom himself responsible for new [capital] investment, nevertheless, the entrepreneurs, who are directly responsible, will find it financially advantageous, and often unavoidable, to fall in with the ideas of the market, even though they themselves are better instructed.
>
> (CW 7, p. 316)

Some distinguished Modern Keynesians followed Keynes's lead in this. James Tobin wrote that his famous "q" theory of investment, in which investment is determined by the ratio of the financial market value of the firm to its reproduction cost, was inspired by chapter 12.[6] Hyman Minsky also flirted with theory q, but he was not consistent about this (Minsky 1975).

This thesis is consistent with Keynes's methodological tenet that the dynamics of capitalist economies are informed by their historically specific institutional and behavioral foundations. In this case, the tenet suggests that the impact of changes in stock prices on capital investment depends on historically and institutionally specific conditions. Keynes himself said that the proposition that the mec was set in the stock market rather than the boardroom was not true in the pre-WWI era. I argued (Crotty 1990) that Keynes's assertion that stock price behavior, not managerial discretion, determined investment spending was not correct in the period of the dominance of the "managerial firm" in the USA and elsewhere. This historical dynamic is described in detail by the business historian Alfred Chandler (Chandler 1990). On the other hand, as explained in Crotty (2005), the relation between stock prices and capital investment was altered by the emergence of the hostile takeover movement of the 1980s and the "shareholder-value" movement in the 1990s. In the first case, hostile takeovers forced management to pursue the objectives of their attackers even though they did not share them and in fact resisted most takeovers – which is why they were called hostile. By the 1990s, the compensation of top managers had become heavily weighted with stocks and stock options and thus was closely tied to the short-term performance of their company's stock. This led to massive buybacks of company stock financed by heavy borrowing in order to prevent stock prices from falling as managers sold their stocks and to a short-term horizon for the firm's investment decisions. Both the heavy indebtedness of the firms and their short-term planning horizons constrained long-term investment. Keynes's assumption that managers are forced or induced to obey stock market signals when making capital investment decisions was therefore not consistent with the facts in the era of the "managerial firm," while it was broadly consistent with manager–shareholder relations after the 1970s.

Keynes then asked a question whose answer has a major impact on the determination of the mec: what is the character of the expectations that move stock prices and – at least in this historical period and especially in the USA – alter capital investment spending?

Early in the chapter, he offered one psychologically based convention that led to the conclusion that long-term expectations would be formed by extrapolation from fairly recent trends, which would make them pro-cyclical and therefore potentially destabilizing. This convention centers on the assumption that people have more confidence in short-term than long-term expectations, or alternatively, that long-term expectations are based mostly or only on the behavior of the recent past.

> It would be foolish, in forming our expectations, to attach great weight to matters which are very uncertain.[7] It is reasonable, therefore, to be guided to a considerable degree by the facts about which we feel somewhat confident, even though they may be less decisively relevant to the issue than other facts about which our knowledge is vague and scanty. For this reason the facts of the existing situation enter, in a sense disproportionately, into the formation of our long term expectations; our usual practice being to take the existing situation and to project it into the future, modified only to the extent that we have more or less definite reasons for expecting a change.
> (CW 7, p. 148)

Taken by itself, this statement suggests that the mec of a factory with an expected life of two decades will be primarily determined by forecasts of the state of the economy, say, two or three years in the future, with the years beyond that being behaviorally irrelevant. Though the profit yielded by this factory in the last 17–18 years of its expected life are more important to the determination of the mec than that generated in the first 2–3 years, the firm, Keynes suggested, has little confidence in its ability to forecast beyond the first few years – "our knowledge is vague and scanty" – and therefore does not put much weight on the out years. But it does believe it can forecast the coming few years with reasonable confidence by extrapolating economic trends over the last couple of years. Therefore, the mec calculation will be disproportionately influenced by performance in the past few years rather than by long-term trends.

Keynes returned to this question immediately after he argued that the mec was set in the volatile stock market and not in corporate boardrooms. In the first paragraph that followed this argument, he asked: "How then are these highly significant daily, even hourly, revaluations of existing [capital] investments carried out in practice?" (CW 7, p. 151). He answered his own question as follows:

> In practice we have tacitly agreed, as a rule, to fall back on what is, in truth, a *convention*. The essence of this convention – though of course it does not work out quite so simply – lies in assuming that the existing state of affairs will continue indefinitely, except in so far as we have specific reason to expect a change. This does not mean that we really believe that the existing state of affairs will continue indefinitely. We know from extensive experience this is most unlikely.
> (CW 7, p. 152, emphasis in original)

Keynes seems to be saying that if you want to forecast stock prices in a period like the 1930s, in which they were enormously volatile, the best you can do is to extrapolate price movements from the very recent past: long-term trends cannot help with this task. Keynes said that the speculators that determined stock prices in the era only needed to forecast prices "three months or a year hence" to ply their trade (CW 7, p. 155). This can lead to alternating waves of buying and selling.

Moreover, when stock price movements are volatile and thus difficult to predict with any accuracy, agents will lose confidence in their ability to forecast accurately. The US economy was in a disastrous situation in the first half of the 1930s because expected long-term profit rates on capital investment as seen from the boardroom were dismal *and* financial markets were incredibly unstable, a situation that created an extreme lack of confidence in the ability of investors to predict future security prices. This caused a huge decline in the mec in Keynes's model. We repeat here a comment Keynes made about the utter loss of investors' confidence in their ability to predict stock price movements in the USA in 1930. He said he discussed the state of the stock market with:

> all sorts of people [in America], but found no-one who even thought his opinion was worth two-pence. When the elements of bluff and skilled market-manipulation and mass psychology and pure chance are added to the intrinsic difficulties of forecasting the course of the credit cycle itself, the case is hopeless.
>
> (CW 20, p. 586)

Keynes paid particular attention to the almost unlimited instability of conventionally generated expectations in what he called "abnormal times."

> A conventional valuation which is established as the outcome of the mass psychology of a large number of ignorant individuals is liable to change violently as the result of sudden fluctuations of opinion due to factors that do not really matter much to the prospective yield; since there will be no strong roots to hold it steady.[8] In abnormal times in particular, when the hypothesis of an indefinite continuance of the existing state of affairs is less plausible than usual even though there are no express grounds to anticipate a definite change, the market will be subject to waves of optimistic and pessimistic sentiment, which are unreasoning and yet in a sense legitimate where no solid basis exists for a reasonable calculation.
>
> (CW 7, p. 154)

Financial markets are thus potentially very unstable because the future is unknowable, which makes investors *inevitably* "ignorant" of the future and dependent upon psychological mechanisms to guide their decisions. Volatile expectations are "unreasoning" yet "legitimate" because the information needed to make assuredly optimal decisions does not exist. There are no knowable future fundamentals to guide investor choice. "It is not surprising that a convention, in an absolute view of things so arbitrary, should have its weak points. It is its precariousness which creates no small part of our contemporary problem of securing sufficient investment" (CW 7, p. 153).

Keynes is here asserting that *secular stagnation and casino financial markets are related* in that the propensity of financial markets to create excessive capital investment instability is part of the explanation of secular stagnation. Investment is insufficient to sustain full employment in part because it is so potentially unstable that it makes the future states of the economy more unpredictable than they otherwise would be. This makes the investment decision riskier than it otherwise would be. We might say that financial market instability lowers the risk-adjusted mec, or, more accurately, it lowers confidence in the truth content of the mec.

Keynes went on to list a series of factors "which accentuate this precariousness" of the mec that is largely determined in the stock market. They include the following:

> As a result of the gradual increase in the proportion of equity in the community's aggregate investment which is owned by persons who do not manage and have no special knowledge of the circumstances, either actual or perspective, of the business in question, the element of real knowledge in the valuation of investments by those who own them or are contemplating purchasing them has seriously declined ... Day-to-day fluctuations in the profits of existing investments, which are obviously of an ephemeral and non-significant character, tend to have an altogether excessive, and even an absurd, influence on the market.
>
> (CW 7, pp. 153–154)

Keynes explained why the stock market is a short-term speculative gambling casino in which professional investors cannot form long-term expectations of corporate profits, which, in turn, determine market prices.

> It happens, however, that the energies and the skill of the professional investor and speculators are mainly occupied otherwise. For most of these persons are, in fact, largely concerned, not with making superior long-term forecasts of the probable yield of an investment over its whole life, but in forecasting the conventional basis of valuation a short time ahead of the general public. They are concerned, not with what an investment is really worth to a man who buys if "for keeps," but with what the market will value it at, under the influence of mass

> psychology, three months or a year hence. Moreover, this behavior is ... an inevitable outcome of an investment market organized along the lines described. For it is not sensible to pay 25 for an investment of which you believe the prospective yield to justify 30, if you also believe that the market will value it at 20 three months or a year hence.
>
> Thus the professional investor is forced to concern himself with the anticipation of impending changes, in the news or in the atmosphere, of the kind by which experience shows that the mass psychology of the market is most influenced. This is the inevitable result of investment markets organized with a view to so-called "liquidity" ...
>
> The battle of wits to anticipate the basis of conventional valuation a few months hence, rather than the prospective yield of investment over a long term of years ... can be played by professionals amongst themselves. Nor is it necessary that anyone should keep his simple faith in the conventional basis of valuation having any genuine long-term validity. For it is, so to speak, a game of Snap, of Old Maid, of Musical Chairs – a pastime in which he is the victor who says Snap neither too soon nor too late, who passed the Old Maid to his neighbor before the game is over, who secures a chair for himself when the music stops ...
>
> Or, to change the metaphor slightly, professional investment may be likened to those newspaper competitions in which the competitors have to pick out the six prettiest faces from a hundred photographs, the prize being awarded to the competitor whose choice most nearly corresponds to the average preferences of the competitors as a whole; so each competitor has to pick, not the faces who he himself finds prettiest, but those who he thinks likeliest to catch the fancy of the other competitors, all of whom are looking at the problem from the same point of view ... We have reached the [point] where we devote our intelligence to anticipating what average opinion expects the average opinion to be.
>
> (CW 7, pp. 154–156)

Keynes then replies to a hypothetical reader who argues that "there must surely be large profits to be gained from the other players in the long run by a skilled individual who, unperturbed by the prevailing pastime, continues to purchase [financial] investments on the best long-term expectations he can frame" (CW 7, p. 156). He says that there are some investors of this type, but several factors limit their influence on security pricing.

> Investment based on genuine long-term expectations is so difficult today as to be scarcely practicable. He who attempts it must surely lead much more laborious days and run greater risks that he who tries to

guess better than the crowd how the crowd will behave; and, given equal intelligence, he may make more disastrous mistakes ... It needs more intelligence to defeat the forces of time and our ignorance of the future than to beat the gun. Moreover, life is not long enough; human nature desires quick results, there is a peculiar zest in making money quickly.

(CW 7, p. 157)

Keynes then lists two reasons why the buy-and-hold long-term investor may bear a heavier risk than the short-term speculator. First, there is the balance sheet or financial fragility problem resulting from the fact that the long-term investor must be able to bear substantial capital losses in a market collapse whereas the speculator can cut his or her losses by selling early in the downturn. An "investor who proposes to ignore near-term [downward] market fluctuations needs greater resources for safety and must not operate on so large a scale, if at all, with borrowed money" (CW 7, p. 157).

Second, Keynes tells us that a manager of investment funds has an asymmetric incentive structure that induces him to join the crowd in the midst of a market bubble of some duration even if he knows the bubble will eventually collapse. If he fails to shift his clients' funds into hot stocks, he will soon lose his clients to his competitors, but if he follows the crowd in its herd behavior, his clients will not blame him when the boom turns into a bust because everyone will have suffered the same losses. If "in the short run [in the boom] he is unsuccessful, which is very likely, he will not receive much mercy. Worldly wisdom teaches that it is better to fail with the crowd than to succeed unconventionally" (CW 7, pp. 157–158).

Keynes was well aware that much of the frantic speculation of the period in the USA was heavily funded by short-term margin loans from banks and from brokers who borrowed from banks. Therefore, he said, a theory of stock price determination must incorporate a theory of margin lending by financial institutions. If either the demand to hold stocks falters or the market providing margin credit seizes up, a collapse in stock prices and capital investment spending will follow. Once this collapse takes place, even a sharp drop in interest rates on margin loans will not be able to revive the stock market and capital investment.

> So far we have had chiefly in mind the state of confidence of the speculator or speculative investor himself and may have seemed to be tacitly assuming that, if he himself is satisfied with the prospects, he has unlimited command over money at the market rate of interest. This is, of course, not the case. Thus we must also take account of the other facet of the state of confidence, namely, the confidence of the lending institutions towards those who seek to borrow from them,

> sometimes described as the state of credit. A collapse in the price of equities, which has disastrous reactions on the marginal efficiency of capital, may have been due to the weakening either of speculative confidence or the state of credit. But whereas the weakening of either is enough to cause a collapse, recovery requires the revival of *both*. For whilst the weakening of credit is sufficient to bring about its collapse, its strengthening, though a necessary condition of recovery, is not a sufficient condition.
>
> (CW 7, p. 158, emphasis in original)

So, capital investment depends on the mec, which depends on the stock market and on the long-term interest rate. Stock prices (and therefore the mec) depend in part on short-term interest rates on margin borrowing by speculators. And, of course, stock prices depend on capital investment because the level of investment affects current and expected future profit rates. Long-term interest rates also depend to some extent on capital investment, which is partially funded by new bond issues. Finally, the response of AD to problems originating in the real or financial sectors depends on the degree of financial fragility in both sectors. Economic performance in this period thus depended crucially on the behavior of stock markets, bond markets, and the market providing margin loans to stock and bond speculators, markets that Keynes characterized as insane gambling casinos. And all of this was taking place in the context of extreme financial fragility.

Thus, extreme stock market, capital investment, and employment volatility are the:

> inevitable result of investment markets organized with a view to so-called "liquidity." Of the maxims of orthodox finance none, surely, is more anti-social than the fetish of liquidity, the doctrine that it is a positive virtue on the part of investment institutions to concentrate their resources upon the holding of "liquid" securities. It forgets that there is no such thing as liquidity of investment for the community as a whole.
>
> (CW 7, p. 155)

Keynes defined speculation as "the activity of forecasting the [short-term] psychology of the market" and enterprise as "the activity of forecasting the prospective yield of [real] assets over their whole life" (CW 7, p. 158). For markets to be economically functional, he said, the capital investment decision must be guided by enterprise, not speculation. But as market liquidity increases, "the risk of the predominance of speculation [also] increases" (CW 7, p. 159). The higher the market liquidity, the greater the proportion of short-term speculators in the market and the greater the potential volatility of capital investment spending.

Speculators may do no harm as bubbles on a steady stream of enterprise. But the position is serious when enterprise becomes the bubble on a whirlpool of speculation. When the capital development of a country becomes a by-product of the activities of a casino, the job is likely to be ill-done. The measure of success attained by Wall Street, regarded as an institution of which the proper social purpose is to direct new investment into the most profitable channels in terms of future yield, cannot be claimed as one of the outstanding triumphs of laissez-faire capitalism – which is not surprising, if I am right in thinking that the best brains of Wall Street have been in fact otherwise engaged.
(CW 7, p. 159)

Keynes concluded that the disastrous consequences of speculation on investment and employment "are a scarcely avoidable outcome of our having successfully organized 'liquid' [financial] investment markets" (CW 7, p. 159).

Keynes's most important policy proposal to resolve the dilemma created by highly liquid financial markets, offered in the exit paragraph of chapter 12, will not come as a surprise to readers of this book. *The state will have to directly control and/or guide the majority of large-scale capital investment in the country to achieve the goal of sustained full employment.*

> I expect to see the State, which is in a position to calculate the marginal efficiency of capital goods on long views and on the basis of the general social advantage, taking an ever greater responsibility for *directly organizing investment*; since it seems likely that the fluctuations in the market estimation of the marginal efficiency of different types of capital, calculated on the principles I have described above, will be too great to be offset by any practicable changes in the rate of interest.
> (CW 7, p. 164, emphasis added)

Keynes's analysis in chapter 12 of the destabilizing effects of volatile and speculative financial markets on the mec, and therefore on capital investment, complement his analysis of the destabilizing effects of bond markets in chapters 13–15. Both help accelerate economic expansions, pushing them to unsustainable levels, and as Keynes described in chapter 22 on business cycles, if conditions are right, both can also turn real-sector downturns into deep recessions and financial market downturns into devastating crashes. He believed that the disequilibrium properties of financial markets that always help restore full-employment equilibrium in the face of negative AD shocks as embodied in classical theory were ideology disguised as theory. In the real world, the "insane" financial markets of his time (and of any time in which largely unregulated financial markets play a dominant role in the economy) can propagate and strengthen negative aggravate demand shocks and initiate economic instability endogenously.

## Appendix 1: Fundamental uncertainty and the bankruptcy of classical and neoclassical theories of rational agent choice

In building his theory of agent choice on the assumption that the future is fundamentally uncertain and therefore unknowable in the present, Keynes raised basic questions about the very meaning of "rationality" in New Classical and neoclassical theories of "rational" agent choice, and in so doing created a little-noticed transformation of the theory of agent choice.

In New Classical theory, agents are assumed to have probabilistic knowledge of future states of the economy that, by some unexplained miracle, is actually complete and correct. In the illogical language of the theory, agents have "rational expectations," though only an irrational person could hold such views. Future economic states are assumed not just to be known in the present, but also to be stationary; they will not change in response to current and future agent decisions or exogenous shocks to these probability distributions. We might think of such models as macro-founded because, since the future must be determined before agents make current decisions, the task of the agents individually and collectively is not to influence or create future economic states, but rather to adjust their own decisions so as to make them consistent with pre-given future economic states – no micro-foundations here. If we remove the absurd assumption that agents have complete and correct knowledge of the stationary future in New Classical theory, it is unclear how rational agents would select among alternative courses of action. Indeed, there would be no definition of what a rational choice is.

In the subjective probability models of agent choice used in traditional neoclassical micro theory, it is assumed that agents believe they know the true probability distributions that represent future states of the economy even though it is acknowledged by those who created the theory that it is impossible for anyone to have true knowledge of the future. "For the subjectivist, in fact, probabilistic knowledge does not necessarily correspond to anything in objective reality" (Lawson 1988, p. 41). The problem here is that it is impossible for a rational agent to assume he or she has perfect knowledge of the future if in fact the basis for perfect knowledge is formally assumed to be unavailable to him or her. The neoclassical theory of rational agent choice thus implicitly assumes that agents are irrational because they believe they have infallible knowledge of the future when the theory explicitly assumes they cannot possess such knowledge. This problem would, of course, be solved by introducing Keynes's concept of the degree of confidence agents have in the truth content of their fallible expectations, but this would destroy the foundation of the theory of rational and optimal choice. It is remarkable that neoclassical theorists seem unaware of this striking logical contradiction at the heart of their models.

In both theories, agents are assumed to have a known objective function (at least implicitly assumed not to change during the time that elapses from when a choice is made until the outcome is determined) and perfect stochastic knowledge about the relation between current choice and the future results of that choice. An agent is thus considered to be rational if he or she performs the optimization math correctly and irrational if he or she does not. If we replace the obviously unrealistic perfect-future-knowledge assumption used is these theories with Keynes's obviously correct assumption of fundamental uncertainty, mainstream theories have absolutely nothing to say about how sensible agents make choices.

Robert Lucas believes that, "in cases of uncertainty, economic reasoning will be of no value" (Lucas 1981, p. 224). But in the case of Keynes's radical uncertainty, this is simply not true. Keynes offers an alternative behavioral theory of what might be called "sensible" agent choice under radical uncertainty in chapter 12 based on his development of "conventional" expectation and confidence formation. This micro theory, which is a central part of his analysis of financial markets and the capital investment decision, is a crucial building block of his macro-theoretical apparatus. This theory of sensible agent choice under fundamental uncertainty should have created a revolution in mainstream micro theory, but alas, it did not.

One might think that modern behavioral economic theory, which has been used to resolve anomalies in the standard theory of efficient markets, has incorporated most of the core insights of Keynes's theory of agent choice under fundamental uncertainty, but one would be wrong to do so. These theories are not intended to be substitutes for the vision incorporated in neoclassical theory. Rather, they are meant to be amendments to it that do not challenge its dominant position in the profession. "The behavioral finance literature ... simply adopts the neoclassical view with biases added (e.g., overshooting, undershooting, framing, etc." (Findlay and Williams 2008, p. 224). Camerer and Lowenstein insist that behavioral finance does not seek "a wholesale rejection of the neoclassical approach to economics based on utility maximization, equilibrium *and efficiency*" (Camerer and Lowenstein 2004, p. 1, emphasis added). Matthew Rabin, a star in the behaviorist camp, argues that their research program is "not only built on the premise that mainstream economic *methods* are great, but also that most mainstream economic *assumptions* are great" (Rabin 2002, p. 658, emphasis in original).

In my opinion, the core problem in mainstream theories of rational agent choice is not the standard assumption that all agents are rational, though we know people may act irrationally at times. Rather, it is that agents' unavoidable ignorance of future economic conditions makes assuredly optimal choice – the foundation of mainstream micro theory – impossible. That is, the damage done to neoclassical micro theory by the assumption of fundamental uncertainty is far greater than that caused by agent irrationality.[9]

## Appendix 2: The "dilemma" created by a liquid stock market

Keynes raised an important question in this chapter: why are financial investors willing to buy and hold risky equity securities whose price behavior at times is volatile and unpredictable? There are two parts to Keynes's answer. The first is implicit in his theory of conventional expectations and confidence formation, a behavioral theory that implies that agents' perceptions of market risk will be low in periods of stable security prices and even lower during market booms when confidently held expectations of rising prices become widespread. In ebullient markets, agents come to believe that stocks are not really risky investments. This is a core building block of Minsky's theory of the endogenous creation of financial fragility.

The second answer is that investors will only agree to buy and hold risky long-term stocks because the high liquidity of the stock market allows them to convince themselves that in the event that stock prices unexpectedly begin to decline, they can exit the market before prices fall very far. This makes potentially high-risk investment in stocks appear to be relatively safe, which stimulates stock purchases. It therefore contributes to the propensity to generate market bubbles, and the longer and stronger the bubble, the more likely it is to be followed by a serious crash. Keynes concluded that the liquidity properties of lightly regulated modern stock markets helped create the insane gambling casinos of the era.

Keynes suggested that conventionally constituted expectations are held with substantial confidence during periods of relatively stable trends in security prices. Yet there are many examples in the historical record when such expectations have been disastrously misleading to investors. Investors are never sure that a market crash will not occur over the intermediate to long run. Because they cannot totally erase their fear that another market crash could happen, investors are hesitant to commit their money to risky long-term securities unless financial markets are extremely liquid so that these securities can be sold at a moment's notice when problems first develop.

In my view, Keynes should have made this property of investor psychology historically specific. For example, it seems reasonable for the 1930s, but not for the stock market boom in the USA in the late 1920s. Historically, substantial stock market booms over long periods have been accompanied by a widely accepted belief that "this time is different." When financial asset prices rise fast enough for long enough, market analysts, financial economists, financial firms, politicians, and others will always find or create reasons to believe that today's financial markets are not subject to the imperfections that led previous booms to self-destruct. Many of those insisting that "this time is different" will believe in the dream they are propagating. In the stock market boom in the USA from 1984 through 2000, it was the short-term behavior of stock prices that was thought to be unpredictable: "don't sell on the dips" became the conventional wisdom. It became widely believed that as long as investors held on to their stocks during the short periods of downward price movement that inevitably occur during any long-term boom, they were bound to receive large capital gains on their stock holdings. Optimism about longer-term market prospects facilitated the longevity of that boom.

If investors can count on the fact that stocks can be sold quickly and with a low transaction cost in liquid markets, and if most investors rely on conventional expectations and confidence formation at least over the short run, they will normally be happy to buy and hold stocks until a serious downturn actually begins to develop.

> An investor can legitimately encourage himself with the idea that the only risk he runs is that of a genuine change in the news *over the near future*, as to the likelihood of which he can attempt to form his own judgment, and which is unlikely to be very large. For assuming the convention holds, it is only these changes which can affect the value of his investment, and he need not lose any sleep merely because he has not any notion what his investment will be worth ten years hence.
> (CW 7, pp. 152–153, emphasis in original)

That is, investors believe that outcomes beyond a short- to intermediate-run future are not relevant to their portfolio investment decisions as long as markets remain highly liquid. If, as Keynes claimed, the likelihood that significant unexpected negative events that will substantially affect stock prices over the course of a few weeks is legitimately considered to be "unlikely to be very large" and investors can sell their stock in an instant at little cost, they may come to believe that aggressive investment strategies that would be extremely risky if the securities had to be held over a longer period are in fact relatively safe.

> Investment becomes reasonably "safe" for the individual over short periods, and hence over a succession of short periods however many, if he can fairly rely on there being no breakdown of the convention and on his therefore having an opportunity to revise his judgment and change his investment position before there has been time for much to happen.
> (CW 7, p. 153)

Of course, if all investors actually do try to exit the market simultaneously when prices drop, all but the quickest to act will suffer large capital losses. What is sensible for the individual investor can be disastrous for the investing class. Keynes made the implicit assumption here that agents are not fully conscious of the collective illogic of their position, though he rejected that assumption elsewhere in the book.

Without the assumed "insurance" against large losses provided by high liquidity, investors would be far less willing to hold a large part of their wealth in the form of stocks and average stock prices would be much lower, as would the mec – and Tobin's q. Moreover, the demand to hold long-term bonds would also decline, driving up interest rates. As a result, capital investment itself would be much lower, *ceteris paribus*.

If capital investment is strongly influenced by stock prices, as Keynes says it is in chapters 12 and 22, then a highly liquid stock market is a necessary (though certainly not sufficient) condition for there to be extended periods of high stock prices and high investment. And, as Keynes stressed in chapter 13 and 15, as long as investors have the option to hold their wealth in the form of risk-free "money," they cannot be induced to hold risky bonds unless they believe that they can sell them at a moment's notice at a negligible transaction cost. This results in what Keynes twice refers to as a "dilemma" in the chapter. Under existing institutional arrangements, highly liquid markets for stocks and bonds are required to provide adequate funds at moderate cost to finance high levels of capital investment. Yet the liquidity of these securities contributed to the great instability of stock and bond markets in the era, leading investors to buy in the booms, often on credit, and to dump their holdings in the downturn. This leads to unstable capital investment spending that creates unstable employment and income. High liquidity also leads to inadequate average investment spending, which creates high secular unemployment, because it reduces the level of the capital stock below what it would have been otherwise, thereby reducing employment opportunities.

## Notes

1 The ideas in this chapter are discussed at length in Crotty (1994).
2 This assertion is defended in Appendix 1.
3 I am not sure why the central role in the determination of the mec played by agents' confidence in their expectations disappeared from Modern Keynesian investment theory. One likely reason for this is that the concept that agents have variable subjective confidence in the truth content of their expectations is incompatible with the use of both objective and subjective probability distributions as representations of agent expectations in New Classical and neoclassical theories of rational agent choice, respectively.

However, Keynes may have contributed to this development himself with his formal definition of the mec in chapter 11. The mec is defined there as that value of m for which the following equation holds: $\Sigma Q_t^E/(1 + m)^t = P_1^S$, where t is a time index from 1 to T, T is the *expected* life of the investment good, $Q_t^E$ is the net cash flow *expected* to be generated by this investment in future period t, and $P_1^S$ is the cost of the investment good in period t. The mec is clearly a profit rate of sorts – an internal rate of return – since it will be higher the larger the expected profit flows, the more the total expected profit flows are front-loaded, and the lower the cost of the investment good. Keynes also said, "I define the marginal efficiency of capital as being equal to that rate of discount which would make the present value of the *series of annuities* given by the returns expected from the capital-asset during its life just equal to its supply price" (CW 7, p. 135, emphasis added).

This definition creates a serious problem in Keynes's theory because annuities are payments due the owner whose value is specified in a contract; there is no uncertainty about their nominal value. Thus, contrary to Keynes's claim in chapter 12 that the mec is a function of both expected profit flows and confidence in those expectations, *the mec formula does not incorporate the effect of confidence on the capital investment decision at all*. Under this definition of the mec, fundamental uncertainty has no influence on the level or the volatility of capital investment spending. Minsky commented that "the introduction of uncertainty … was never formalized to the same extent as the other functional relations" (Minsky 1975, p. 60). To remain consistent with everything in *The General Theory* but the formal definition of the mec in chapter 11, we will assume that the degree of confidence that agents have in the truth content of their expectations of the future is a crucial determinant of their decisions.

4  The problems caused by excessive liquidity are explored in Appendix 2.
5  In a footnote, Keynes tells us that "when a company's shares are quoted very high so that it can raise more capital by issuing more shares on favourable terms, this has the same effect as if it could borrow at a low rate of interest. I should now describe this by saying that a high quotation for existing equities involves an increase in the marginal efficiency of the corresponding type of capital and therefore has the same effect (since investment depends on a comparison between the marginal efficiency of capital and the rate of interest) as a fall in the rate of interest" (CW 7, p. 151). This seems to me to be an unhelpful and confusing conflation of two quite different variables.
6  There is a large and contentious literature about the empirical validity of Tobin's q theory of investment.
7  Keynes put a footnote here that stressed that by "'very uncertain' I do not mean the same thing as 'very improbable'" (CW 7, p. 148). He is theorizing radical uncertainty, not probabilistic risk.
8  The words "no strong roots to hold it steady" mean that confidence in the truth content of expectations has evaporated.
9  The argument in the last few paragraphs is presented in greater detail in Crotty (1994).

# 18 The theory of the business cycle in chapter 22

Integrating the profit rate and the bond and stock markets in a theory of financial and economic instability

In chapter 22, Keynes brought the analytical apparatus developed earlier in the book to an analysis of the business cycle. In Keynes's cycle theory, developed in the midst of the Great Depression, financial markets not surprisingly play a crucial role in creating cyclical instability. His theory of the cycle incorporates key real and financial sources of disequilibrium. Chapter 22 is of special importance because the dynamic model developed in the chapter is supposed to explain in outline form the causes of the late 1920s boom in the USA and its collapse into depression in the 1930s.

He starts his description of the cycle when the economy begins to expand following a recession. The actual rate of profit starts to rise, which causes the expected rate of profit or mec to follow suit. The actual profit rate will continue to increase until it peaks at some point in mid-expansion; it then declines as the expansion continues due to the rapid rise in and decreasing scarcity of the capital stock.[1] He said that this is what actually happened at the end of the late-1920s US boom. The mec or expected profit rate will continue to increase for some time after the actual profit rate peaks because most investors will initially see this leveling off as a temporary deviation from its upward trend. Keynes used a numerical example in which the actual rate of profit hits 6 percent in mid-boom and falls thereafter. If the expansion reached full employment, he assumed the profit rate would reach an expansion low of 2 percent.

The continuation of the economy past its profit-rate maximum by itself might not cause a crisis and economic downturn; it could simply lead to a slowdown in the rate of growth. What creates the crisis is that extrapolative expectation and confidence formation cause the mec to continue to rise for some time after the actual profit rate has peaked. This leads to an overvaluation of long-term securities.[2]

At this point in the analysis, Keynes repeated his chapter 12 claim that the mec is effectively set in the stock market and that financial investors are more susceptible to boom euphoria than the managers of nonfinancial firms. He believed that those directly responsible for making the capital investment decision "will find it advantageous, and often unavoidable, to fall in with the ideas of the market, even though they themselves are better instructed" (CW 7, p. 316). The problem is that financial investors are likely to be overly optimistic after mid-boom, extrapolating the recent rise of the actual profit rate to levels at or beyond its 6 percent mid-expansion peak. They will thus continue to push stock higher even as the actual profit rate begins to decline.

> This situation, which I am indicating as typical, is not one in which capital is so abundant that the community as a whole has no reasonable use for any more capital, but where investment is being made under conditions which are unstable and cannot endure, because it is prompted by expectations which are destined to disappointment.
> (CW 7, p. 321)

It "is an essential characteristic of the boom that investments which will in fact yield, say, 2 per cent in conditions of full employment are made in the expectation of a yield of, say, 6 per cent, and are valued accordingly" (CW 7, p. 321).

The "valued accordingly" assumption is the key to the market collapse for Keynes. It means that stock prices are based on the assumption of a 6 percent return, so that when the actual return declines toward 2 percent, it will reveal that the market is badly overpriced and capital losses are unavoidable. If the upward phase of the cycle was sluggish, the overvaluation of security prices might be modest and the exit from the market orderly. But if the upward phase was long and strong, the revelation that prices are substantially overvalued can trigger a rush to exit the market.

Moreover, it seems reasonable to assume that if firms confidently expected a 6 percent return on capital investment, they would have been willing to borrow at, say, 4 percent, which could cause heavy losses for borrowing firms when the rate of profit fell to 2 percent. It could also lead to capital losses for banks and bond-holders. This would lead to rising interest rates. Though Keynes did not adequately stress the role of increasing leverage used by real-sector and financial-sector firms to sustain capital investment spending in the boom in this chapter, the kernel of the idea is planted here and in chapter 19, as well as in his reports to British government while on his visits to the USA in early 1930s.

If the actual profit rate does fall well below the rate embedded in security prices, Keynes argued, investors' optimism and confidence will be shaken, causing a shift from a bull to a bear market. This will cause investment spending to decline, which will reduce AD. "The latter stages of the boom are characterised by optimistic expectations as to the future yield of capital-goods sufficiently strong to offset their growing abundance and their rising costs of production and, probably, a rise in the rate of interest" (CW 7, p. 315). But a time must come when the forces that lower the rate of profit and raise the interest rate as the boom matures adversely affect expectations and confidence in financial markets. "The disillusion comes because doubts suddenly arise concerning the reliability of the prospective [or expected] yield, perhaps because the current yield shows signs of falling off, as the stock of newly produced durable goods steadily increases" (CW 7, p. 317). The boom may end with a financial and economic crisis rather than a smooth slowdown largely because of the dysfunctional character of financial markets.

> It is in the nature of organized investment markets, under the influence of purchasers largely [and unavoidably] ignorant of what they are buying and of speculators who are more concerned with forecasting the next shift of market sentiment than with a reasonable estimate of the future yield of capital-assets, that, when disillusion falls over an optimistic and over-bought market, *it should fall with sudden and even catastrophic force.*
>
> (CW 7, pp. 315–316, emphasis added)

> When the disillusion comes, this expectation [that investment will yield 6 per cent] is replaced by a contrary "error of pessimism," with the result that the investments, which would in fact yield 2 per cent in conditions of full employment, are expected to yield less than nothing; and the resulting collapse of new investment then leads to a state of unemployment in which the investments, which would have yielded 2 per cent in conditions of full employment, in fact yield less than nothing.
>
> (CW 7, pp. 321–322)

The outbreak of pessimism and the loss of confidence in the conventions that underlie expectation formation will also cast a pall over the bond market, a point Keynes also stressed in his 1937 defense of *The General Theory* in the QJE.

> The dismay and uncertainty as to the future which accompanies a collapse in the marginal efficiency of capital naturally precipitates a sharp rise in liquidity preference and hence a rise in the interest rate. Thus the fact that a collapse in the marginal efficiency of capital tends to be associated with a subsequent rise in the interest rate may seriously aggravate the decline in investment.
>
> (CW 7, p. 316)

This is an endogenously generated shift in the LM curve caused by a preceding shift in the IS curve caused by the fall in the mec.[3] Once a substantial collapse in the mec and therefore in capital investment has occurred,

Keynes argued, it may be extremely difficult to restore prosperity. "It is not so easy to revive the marginal efficiency of capital, determined, as it is, by the uncontrollable and disobedient psychology of the business world" (CW 7, p. 317). If the financial system is over-leveraged and fragile before the mec falls, the reaction in financial markets may be severe.

Keynes went on to argue that the excesses of the late-1920s boom in the USA could not have been avoided by tightening monetary policy early in the boom, a policy supported by many economists at the time, except by killing the economic expansion altogether.

> [The] remedy for the boom is not a higher rate of interest but a lower rate of interest. For that may enable the boom to last. The right remedy for the trade cycle is not to be found in abolishing booms and thus keeping us permanently in a semi-slump; but in abolishing slumps and thus keeping us permanently in a quasi-boom.
>
> (CW 7, p. 322)

But herein lies a problem for monetary theory and policy: an interest rate low enough to have generated the low unemployment rates of the late 1920s also fueled an unsustainable financial-market boom whose eventual crash brought the whole system down with it. You cannot perpetually sustain a capital investment boom via low interest rates without simultaneously fueling a financial market bubble. This circle could not be squared within the confines of the then-current policy regime. It is public investment supported by low interest rates and capital controls, not monetary policy alone, which can facilitate a sustained high growth rate.

Keynes stated this position as follows:

> The boom which is destined to end in a slump is caused, therefore, by the combination of a rate of interest, which in a correct state of expectation would be too high for full employment, with a misguided state of expectation which, so long as it lasts, prevents this rate of interest from being in fact a deterrent. A boom is a situation in which over-optimism triumphs over a rate of interest which, in a cooler light, would be seen to be excessive.
>
> (CW 7, p. 322)

In other words, he argued, modern stock and bond markets are an impediment to the achievement and maintenance of full employment, and the Central Bank alone cannot resolve the problem. The solution, of course, is planned public investment in pursuit of sustained full employment supported by a secularly low interest rate, capital controls, and managed trade.

## Notes

1. Keynes argued in chapter 11 that the mec will fall as investment increases in the short run due to a declining marginal product of capital and rising unit costs in the industries that produce capital goods. In chapter 22, he said that the profit rate would hit its expansion low if and when the economy reached full employment.
2. This argument bears a resemblance to one that Marx made: the crisis comes not because the rate of profit falls, but because profit flows no longer adequately cover fixed costs such as rent and interest payments. "The rate of profit falls … The fixed charges – interest, rent, – which were based on the anticipation [expectation] of a *constant* rate of profit and exploitation of labour, remain the same and in part *cannot be paid*. Hence *crisis*. Crisis of labour and crisis of capital. This is therefore a disturbance in the reproduction process" (Crotty 2017, p. 101, emphasis in original).
3. We will return to the subject if endogenous shifts in the IS and LM curves in the next chapter.

# 19 Are the "models" Keynes created in *The General Theory* compatible with the IS/LM interpretation of the book?

A digression

Careful readers of *The General Theory* may have noticed that there is more than one concrete or applied economic model that can be culled from the abstract theory presented in the book. I list here five overlapping models: (1) a long-term model of sustained high unemployment or secular stagnation; (2) a short-term model of high-unemployment equilibrium embodied in the simple Keynesian Cross and the IS/LM model; (3) a dynamic intermediate-run model of the business cycle that focuses on endogenously generated instability in real and financial markets; (4) a model of destructive disequilibrium processes focused on wage and price deflation and instability in financial asset prices; and (5) a short-run quasi-model or mini-model of periods or points of extreme instability, especially in financial markets. The main question addressed in this chapter is: what are the consequences of the fact that Mainstream Keynesian theory teaches that only model 2, the short-run IS/LM model, adequately reflects Keynes's important theoretical contributions in *The General Theory*, despite the fact that it cannot accommodate models 1, 3, 4, and 5?

The primary contribution of the IS/LM model is that it helps explain why, in the short run, it is possible to have a high-unemployment equilibrium. The central problem is that, as a short-run static-equilibrium model, the IS/LM model does not incorporate four of the most important building blocks of Keynes's economic theory – secular stagnation; endogenous expectations in an environment of fundamental uncertainty; endogenous "confidence" in expectations; and endogenous balance sheets. The first three are constantly stressed in *The General Theory*. The fourth is discussed in chapters 2, 19, and 22, but not emphasized throughout the book. However, it was of central importance to Keynes's 1930s writings about the causes of the financial collapse and Great Depression.

The IS/LM model therefore cannot adequately represent the full set of dysfunctions in a capitalist economy that Keynes stressed, nor the sources of endogenous dynamics identified by Keynes in the book. This makes the IS/LM model incapable of explaining the extreme volatility of financial markets and investment spending or the collapse of the financial system in the USA in the late 1920s and 1930s. Ironically, the IS/LM model demonstrates that financial markets always help stabilize the economy by lowering interest rates when AD is falling and unemployment is high, and, when embedded in a standard AS/AD model in which the price level is an endogenous variable, it demonstrates that deflation helps restore full employment when AD is depressed. We have shown that Keynes believed both of these propositions were the opposite of the truth, a fact that is rarely if ever mentioned when the IS/LM model is described in undergraduate text books or even in standard advanced treatments of Keynes's economic theory.

The first model in order of presentation in this book was Keynes's model of secular or long-term stagnation. Based on his evaluation of the institutional and behavioral characteristics of the interwar period, Keynes argued that there was a historically contingent tendency of the rate of profit to fall as the capital stock increased, of the mps to be high and therefore the multiplier to be low (due to the high income and wealth inequality of the period), and of the interest rate to remain too high to stimulate a level of investment adequate to sustain full employment. The defense of this theory is centered in chapters 16 and 17 of *The General Theory*, but also appears throughout the book. Keynes's most formal defense of the secular stagnation thesis was presented in his Galton Lecture in 1937, discussed in Chapter 14 of this book.

The simple short-run IS/LM model *can* be used to organize a narrative of sorts that explains the long-term stagnation trends in the era based on the assumption that the mec has a tendency to fall over time – model 1. Indeed, arguments by influential economists such as Paul Krugman and Larry Summers in support of the proposition that we have again entered a period of secular stagnation are often embedded in an IS/LM framework.

The IS/LM framework is most aptly suited to reflect Keynes's model 2, which explains the existence of short-run, static, high-unemployment equilibriums. This is the great strength of the IS/LM translation of *The General Theory*: it demonstrates quite clearly, using core ideas from the book, why a high-unemployment equilibrium can exist in the short to intermediate run in a capitalist economy.

Keynes presented the third model, the model of endogenously generated instability, in chapter 22 on the business cycle. For chapter 22 to be consistent with Keynes's model 3, the static IS/LM model would have to be made dynamic, incorporating the endogenous sources of movement in the actual rate of profit on capital, in the expected rate of profit (which is influenced by stock prices), and in the interest rate. This would require the IS/LM model: to reflect Keynes's insistence that both expectations and confidence are endogenously determined variables generated through extrapolation from recent trends in the economy; to emphasize that the cyclical pattern of divergence between expectations and realizations is a driving force of cyclical dynamics; and to embed these patterns in a model of endogenous balance sheets to be compatible with Keynes's insistence in chapter 22 that, in the "crisis" phase of the cycle, "when disillusion falls over an optimistic and over-bought market, it should fall with sudden and even catastrophic force" (CW 7, pp. 315–316). A simple dynamization of the IS/LM model is discussed below.

Model 4 focuses on the destructive disequilibrium processes of wage and price deflation, which we treated in chapter 15, and interest rate dynamics, which are analyzed in chapter 16. Here, I will just remind the reader that chapter 15 stresses endogenous expectations and confidence formation and concludes that wage and price deflation are likely to aggravate rather than eliminate the deficiencies in AD that cause high unemployment, especially if the AD deficiency is large and balance sheets are fragile. This cannot happen in an IS/LM world.

The fifth model used by Keynes, if "model" is even an appropriate term, is the very-short-term analysis of moments or points of crises of extreme volatility, in which the expectation-formation process becomes unhinged and unstable and confidence in expectations evaporates, especially but not exclusively in casino financial markets. It is thus a crucial component of his model of extreme business cycles. Since Keynes devoted much of chapters 12, 13, 15, and 22 of *The General Theory* and much of the defense of that book in the QJE article in 1937 to explaining the outbreak and persistence of instability in the period, it seems reasonable to consider it separately here.

I already discussed (in Chapter 17) Keynes's emphasis on those points he called "abnormal times," when financial investors lose all confidence in the expectation-formation process. This causes financial asset prices to move in erratic patterns. Recall that in 1930 he said he discussed the outbreak of instability and unpredictability in US financial asset prices with "all sorts of people [in America]." He observed a complete and total collapse in investors' confidence in expectation formation. He said he:

> found no-one who even thought his opinion was worth two-pence. When the elements of bluff and skilled market-manipulation and mass psychology and pure chance are added to the intrinsic difficulties of forecasting the courses of the credit cycle itself, the case is hopeless.
> (CW 20, p. 586)

In chapter 12, Keynes described these points of extreme instability and unpredictability as follows:

> A conventional valuation [of security prices] which is established as the outcome of the mass psychology of a large number of ignorant individuals is liable to *change violently* as the result of sudden fluctuations of opinion due to factors that do not really matter much to the prospective yield; since there will no strong roots to hold it steady. In abnormal times in particular, when the hypothesis of an

indefinite continuance of the existing state of affairs is less plausible than usual even though there are no express grounds to anticipate a definite change, the market will be subject to waves of optimistic and pessimistic sentiment, which are unreasoning and *yet in a sense legitimate* where no solid basis exists for a reasonable calculation.

(CW 7, p. 154, emphasis added)

The potential for a breakdown in the continuity and stability of financial markets at the end of a long expansion is a crucial part of the model Keynes used to explain key economic developments of the era, and it should be one possible outcome of any model that claims to adequately represent *The General Theory*. This model or model component plays no role in any of the standard Mainstream Keynesian models with which I am familiar.[1]

## Comparing Keynes's five models and Modern Keynesian IS/LM and AD/AS analyses

Even economists who recognize the importance of long-term stagnation theory to Keynes, both in *The General Theory* and in his theoretical and political interventions throughout the interwar period, agree that the "model" in the book can only be formally represented as a very-short-term model.

Schumpeter stressed that the secular stagnation model is formalized as a short-run, stable static-equilibrium model. "It is true that he [Keynes] had an aversion to 'periods' and that he concentrated attention upon considerations of static equilibrium." Schumpeter said that most economists do not realize "how very strictly short-run his model is and how important this fact is for the whole structure and all the results of *The General Theory*" (Schumpeter 1946, p. 511). This "limits applicability of this analysis to a few years at most … All the [long-run] phenomena incident to the creations and change in this apparatus, that is to say, the phenomena that dominate the capitalist process, are thus excluded from consideration" (Schumpeter 1946, p. 512).

Thus, in Schumpeter's opinion, even the secular stagnation argument in *The General Theory* has to be embodied in a short-run static-equilibrium model because variables that affect the long-term trajectory of the economy, such as technical change and population growth, are assumed to be exogenous constants.

> Though it remains true that he tried to implement an essentially long-run vision by a short-run model, he secured, to some extent, the freedom for doing so by reasoning (almost) exclusively *about a stationary process* or, at all events, a process that stays at, or oscillates about, levels of which a stationary full-employment equilibrium is the ceiling.
>
> (Schumpeter 1946, p. 512, emphasis added)

Note the clear inference here that *The General Theory* has only one model. How did Schumpeter think this model could explain both the stagnation of the interwar years and the chaos of the late 1920s and early 1930s? The endogenous dynamic processes that occupy so much of *The General Theory* appear to have been hidden from Schumpeter's "vision." What happened to Keynes's "insane" gambling casino financial markets or his attack on the use of deflation to restore full employment? This seems to me to be an inadequate summary of *The General Theory*.

The IS/LM model was created by John Hicks in a 1937 paper (Hicks 1937). In a reconsideration of that paper over four decades later, Hicks wrote: "The IS/LM diagram ... is widely, but not universally, accepted as a convenient synopsis of Keynesian theory" (Hicks 1980, p. 139). Note that his IS/LM model is assumed to be a "synopsis" of the entire book, rather than one aspect among many of Keynes's complete theory.

Hicks is correct in the sense that IS/LM models, typically integrated in intermediate-run AS/AD models in which the price level is endogenous, do dominate textbook interpretations of Keynes's theory. I note again that the AS/AD model is perversely un-Keynesian. Wage and price levels are assumed to be exogenous constants in the IS/LM model. When inserted into the AD/AS model, as is typically the case in intermediate macro theory textbooks, the price level becomes endogenous. Under conditions of high unemployment, in which AS is greater than AD, the price level falls, which raises real money supply (money supply/price level; $M^s/P$). This shifts the LM curve to the right, which lowers the interest rate and thus increases investment and consumption spending, raising AD, income, and employment. In other words, deflation *always* increases employment, a proposition Keynes consistently and aggressively attacked in the interwar period.

Hicks stressed three related characteristics of *the* model: (1) it could only apply to "periods" of very short length; (2) expectations had to be strictly exogenous within the period; and (3) both goods and money markets were always in equilibrium. The third characteristic requires that realizations are always identical to expectations, chapter 22 of *The General Theory* notwithstanding.

The first characteristic is required to sustain the second. Unless the "period" is very short indeed, things that influence expectations or confidence or any other aspect of the behavioral equations are likely to change. The longer the period, then the less realistic the explicit assumption that expectations are strictly exogenous, the more likely that long-run factors such as technology will change, the more likely balance sheets will be transformed, and thus the less adequate the IS/LM model is to its task. The third characteristic is also required to sustain the second one. If expectations turn out to be wrong, a rational agent would presumably alter expectations in a manner designed to lower expected forecast errors. This would cause shifts in the IS and/or LM curves because expectations of future profits affect the investment function and expectations of future bond prices affect the demand for money function. Hicks's IS/LM model is thus stable by assumption.

Finally, and this is extremely important, note that Keynes's crucial variable "confidence" has no role to play – indeed, does not exist – in IS/LM models. I have never seen it referred to in intermediate macro textbooks and cannot remember it being mentioned in any macro literature with the exception of occasional use by Post Keynesians. This silence eliminates a major source of endogenous dynamics in *The General Theory*.

The time period in Keynes's model, Hicks said, was "a short-period ... we shall not go far wrong if we think of it as a year." "Mine [in the IS/LM model] was an "ultra-short-period; I called it a week" (Hicks 1980, p. 141). Hicks wanted to "exclude the things that might happen and might disturb the [model of the] markets" during the period because they would cause the model's behavioral equations to shift (Hicks 1980, p. 141).[2]

Hicks wrote that Keynes's model was a single-period static model in which "expectations were strictly exogenous" and always equal to realizations, which puts the model in direct conflict with much of *The General Theory* (Hicks 1980, p. 140). This allowed him to stress that the IS/LM model "must be assumed to be, in an appropriate sense, in equilibrium" at all times; "the model in some sense, must be in equilibrium" (Hicks 1980, p. 149).

Hicks argued that the IS/LM model itself offers no procedure for analyzing out-of-equilibrium processes. Outside general equilibrium, "we cannot say much about" what would happen, presumably because "saying much" would require a theory of endogenous expectation formation outside equilibrium (Hicks 1980, p. 149). If the economy was off the curves, agents' expectations would be "disturbed."

The core IS/LM model thus does not specify out-of-equilibrium dynamics; it only specifies equilibrium positions. This creates two problems. First, specifications of disequilibrium processes in IS/LM models are theoretically *ad hoc* in the sense that they are not derived from the basic theoretical propositions in the model about the investment and consumption functions or the liquidity-preference function. The theorist can add on any assumption about what happens out of equilibrium he or she pleases, be it stabilizing or destabilizing, without being in conflict with the core equilibrium model itself. Second, the disequilibrium process added to the IS/LM model is in direct conflict with the theory of disequilibrium processes used by Keynes in the book.

> We have, then, facts before us; we know or can find out what ... did actually happen in some past year (say, the year 1975) ... And since the theory is to tell us what would have happened, the variables must be determined. And that would seem to mean that the model, in some sense, must be in equilibrium. Applying these notions to the IS–LM

construction, *it is only that point of intersection of the curves which makes any claim to represent what actually happened* (in our "1975"). Other points on either of the curves ... surely do not represent, make no claim to represent, what actually happened ... *If we cannot take them to be equilibrium positions, we cannot say much about them.*

(Hicks 1980, p. 149, emphasis added)

Hicks went on to say that the assumption of equilibrium in the IS/LM model will not egregiously distort reality as long as the economy is moving in a smooth and stable manner and the length of the period in the model is not too long. "But [this assumption] is dangerous. Though there may well some periods of history, some 'years', for which it is quite acceptable, it is just at the turning points, at the most interesting 'years', where it is hardest to accept it" (Hicks 1980, p. 150). I take him to mean that the IS/LM static-equilibrium model is only useful in helping us make sense of economically stable periods that are relatively short. It is not able to explain business cycle movements (model 3) and it certainly does not apply (without substantial modification) to turbulent, out-of-equilibrium periods such as the mid-1920s to mid-1930s (models 4 and 5), the period *The General Theory* was written to explain.

Having argued that the IS/LM model must remain in equilibrium with expectations equal to realizations at all times, in his early 1980s article, Hicks acknowledged that *this cannot possibly be true for the LM curve.* His argument, which is convincing, is as follows: the LM curve is the locus of (Y, r) points at which the real money supply (M/P) is equal to the demand to hold real (or price-adjusted) money as an asset. The demand to hold money, L (for liquidity preference), is assumed to be a positive function of current income (the "transactions" demand) and a negative function of the current interest rate (the "speculative" demand). The money supply, $M^S$, is traditionally assumed to be set by the Central Bank.[3] We can write the traditional LM curve as $(M^S/P)_t = L(kY_t, r_t)$, where P is the price level, k is a constant, and $kY_t$ represents the transactions demand to hold money in period t. The values of all variables are assumed to be known with certainty. The equilibrium condition that identifies the (Y, r) points on the LM curve is that $M^S$ = money demand ($M^D$).

Keynes's speculative demand to hold money, which links money demand to the current rate of interest in the LM model, logically requires not only that investors consider the expected future bond price when deciding between holding money and bonds as a store of financial wealth, but also that they are uncertain about or have less than complete confidence in their expectations. He made this crystal clear, as was demonstrated in chapter 16. If investors knew the future value of interest rates (and bond prices) with certainty, they would hold all of their financial wealth above the minimum amount of money needed to finance transactions in the form of bonds, *no matter how low the expected interest rate was.* As Hicks put it: "there is no sense in [a desire for] liquidity, unless expectations are uncertain," and uncertainty must therefore be reflected in the equations of the model (Hicks 1980, p. 152). In the absence of uncertainty about expected future bond prices, there is no risk of capital loss on bond-holding and therefore no reason at all to hold money as an investment asset.

Thus, if investors are not uncertain about the expected future bond price, there is zero speculative demand for money and $M^D = kY$. In equilibrium, the demand for bonds must equal the total financial wealth available to invest in either money or bonds (W) minus kY, where W is a constant. Since in equilibrium $kY = W - M^S$, the LM curve would be a vertical line at $Y = (W - M^S)/k$, and the equilibrium values of Y and r would be set at the point of intersection of the IS curve and the vertical LM curve.

A vertical LM curve means that shifts in the IS curve have no effect on the equilibrium value of Y. How un-Keynesian! Thus, the multiplier on new public investment spending will be 1. To explain the process that leads to this result, we have to perform a comparative static analysis that assumes equilibriums are stable. Sustained new public investment will shift the IS curve to the right. With the rightward shift in the IS curve caused by increased investment, Y will be higher than it was at the old equilibrium interest rate. This will increase the transactions demand for money, causing $M^D$ to exceed $M^S$. Investors will sell bonds to get money, which will drive the interest up until the curves intersect at the vertical LM curve once again, leaving the equilibrium value of Y unchanged. New public investment will have "crowded out" an equal amount of private investment and consumption via rising interest rates.[4] How classical! This is one of several reasons why any model not based on genuine uncertainty about future economic states cannot legitimately claim to be a model of *The General Theory*.

## Stability properties and the legitimacy of comparative static macro-policy analysis in *The General Theory* and IS/LM models

Keynes argued that Britain needed to shift from classical laissez-faire economic policy to Liberal Socialism not only because the economy was mired in long-term stagnation, but also because of destructive disequilibrium processes based on endogenous expectation- and confidence-formation processes in an environment of fundamental uncertainty and, at times, of fragile endogenous balance sheets. These processes can both initiate instability in particular markets and aggravate instability initiated elsewhere.

One implication of Keynes's theory of disequilibrium dynamics is that comparative-static analysis, which must assume stabilizing out-of-equilibrium dynamics, is an illegitimate analytical procedure in a fully Keynesian model. Yet, as mentioned before, Keynes himself used comparative statics in chapter 10 of *The General Theory* to provide a concrete answer to the question of how much increased income and employment would result from a given amount of permanent additional public investment. This appears to make him vulnerable to the charge of inconsistency on this important question. However, I will show that Keynes warned the reader of *The General Theory* against relying solely on comparative statics to address stability questions. He insisted in the strongest terms on the need to incorporate endogenous dynamics into his model.

We turn first to an analysis of the IS curve. The IS curve is the locus of income and interest rate (Y, r) points for which $AD_t = C(Y_t) + I(Y_t, r_t) = Y_t = AS_t$, where C is consumption spending and I is investment spending. Keynes's criterion for undertaking an investment project is that the mec must exceed the long-term interest rate. The mec is a positive function of the expected annual profit flows over the entire expected life of the project, which may vary from a few years to a few decades. In the IS model, however, expected future profit flows are replaced by current income, a quantity known to the firm with certainty. This puts the IS model in serious conflict with Keynes's theory of the determinants of capital investment spending.

There are two possible ways to justify this anti-Keynesian assumption, neither of which is satisfactory. The first is to assume that agents believe that the short-term equilibrium value of $Y_t$ is *always* equal to the expected long-term equilibrium value of Y, denoted here as $Y_{LR}^{EX}{}_t$. This assumption incorporates long-term expectations into the investment equation as required, but it also implies that firms always believe that the short-term equilibrium value of $Y_t$ and $Y_{LR}^{EX}{}_t$ are equal. However, $Y_t$ will typically change between each adjacent short-period equilibrium, and these changes will be substantial in "interesting times." It would therefore be irrational for firms to believe that future values of Y will always be identical to the present value of Y in the face of persistent evidence that this is not true. The assumption that firms are irrational is not acceptable as a foundation for Keynes's theory. Given fundamental uncertainty, agents do not have the complete and correct information about future states of the economy required to be able make assuredly optimal decisions. However, they should not be modelled as making assuredly incorrect choices either.

In the second case, the value of $Y_{LR}^{EX}{}_t$ is assumed to be an exogenous constant unaffected by changes in $Y_t$ in the short and intermediate run, no matter how many short or intermediate periods there are or what the path over time of $Y_t$ looks like. This leads to two problems in the theory behind the IS curve. The first problem is caused by the fact that long-term capital investment in the short-run IS model is a positive function of $Y_t$. But, in general, $Y_t$ will be different from $Y_{LR}^{EX}{}_t$ – at times substantially different. This suggests that firms are irrational because they knowingly base their long-term investment decisions on the wrong variable – current Y – which differs in value from the correct variable – the long-term expectation of future Y.

The second problem is that this model provides no hint of how agents form their guesses about the value of $Y_{LR}{}^{EX}{}_t$, never mind their process for deciding on the degree of confidence they should place in their calculation of $Y_{LR}{}^{EX}{}_t$. Keynes insisted that long-term expectations are endogenous – see chapter 12 of *The General Theory* and his 1937 QJE article. They are formed by extrapolating the trajectory of the economy over the relevant past except if there are specific reasons to expect a change in this trajectory. Keynes specifically assumes that the elasticity of the mec with respect to recent values of the actual profit rate or of stock prices is not small. But if, contrary to Keynes, we assume that long-term expectations are unaffected by the movement of the economy over time, we have to ask: where else can they possibly come from? To paraphrase Mao Tse-tung's comment on the origin of "correct ideas": long-term expectations "do not fall from the sky." It is irrational to build an economic theory on the foundation of this *deus ex machina*, and it is decidedly un-Keynesian as well.

There are two situations in which the fully exogenous long-term expectation assumption is less objectionable, though it is still objectionable. If the economy were to sink into a deep and long depression that squeezed almost all optimism out of the economy, as in the mid-1930s, one might expect long-term expectations to become relatively – though not absolutely – unresponsive to short-term movements in the economy. It might take quite a while – perhaps as long as a few years – for an upturn to create significantly more optimistic expectations or to reduce confidence in the pessimism of the era. This would also be true to some extent of a long economic or financial upturn such as the stock market boom in the USA that lasted from the mid-1980s through 2000.[5] Toward the end of that boom, investors had come to believe that the boom was permanent. Nevertheless, in both cases, the firmly held long-term expectations of the era were endogenously created.

If we add to these problems the fact that the IS model does not incorporate the confidence variable at all, it seems clear that the specification of the IS curve is incapable of adequately representing Keynes's theory.

Is an IS equilibrium stable? Suppose the economy should find itself at a point in (Y, r) space (with Y on the horizontal axis) that is below and to the left of the IS curve. Will endogenous forces cause Y to return to a point on the IS curve or not? The answer given by textbook Keynesian theory is a definitive yes. The answer given in *The General Theory* is that sometimes it will and sometimes it will not. It all depends on the behavior of expectations and confidence.

In the IS model, it is *implicitly* assumed that the current deterioration in the economy reflected in the point below the IS curve does not alter the expected short-run or long-run value of equilibrium Y or the confidence with which expectations are held. I say implicitly because unless the current value of Y and the long-term expected value of Y, $Y_{LR}^{EX}$, are assumed to be identical, $Y_{LR}^{EX}{}_t$ must be an implicit exogenous shift parameter hidden in the specification of the investment equation. Because the expected long-term equilibrium value of Y is assumed to be unaffected by movements in $Y_t$, the IS equation will not shift as the $Y_t$ point moves off the curve. If the decline in investment plus consumption (i.e. in AD) caused by the decline in Y is less than the decline in Y (or AS) itself, inventories will fall at Y values to the left of the IS curve. This provides a signal to firms to produce more output and generate more income until the economy is back to a point on the IS curve. This condition will be met if the sum of the propensities to consume and invest out of current income is less than 1.0.[6] Since the IS model makes this assumption, it is stable with respect to values of Y that lie off the curve.

Keynes answered the stability question differently. We know from chapters 12, 19, and 22 of *The General Theory* that, in Keynes's theory, long-term expectations of future variables usually respond fairly quickly to significant movements in their actual values, and confidence in expectations is sensitive to changes in the accuracy of recent forecasts. If Y is used as a proxy for the mec, then expected future income $Y_{LR}^{EX}{}_t$ will be a function of lagged values of Y ($Y_t$, $Y_{t-1}$, $Y_{t-2}$, and so forth). Therefore, if current $Y_t$ drops significantly and unexpectedly below the point on the IS curve associated with the current short-run equilibrium value of Y, investment will decline at all (Y, r) points because $Y_{LR}^{EX}{}_t$, a shift parameter in the IS equation, will decline. The IS curve will shift left, generating a new – possibly temporary – equilibrium Y at the point of intersection of both curves. What happens next would depend on the specific character of endogenous expectation and confidence formation.

We already showed in our discussion of the Hicks critique that points on the LM curve are assumed to be stable under the assumptions that investors know future bond prices with certainty and that expected values of r and Y are unaffected by changes in the current values of these variables. An analysis of the stability of the LM curve consistent with *The General Theory* might proceed as follows: suppose the interest rate fell to a point significantly below the LM curve. This means that the price of bonds increased significantly, creating capital gains for bond-holders. Given the endogeneity of expectations, it would be reasonable for investors to increase their expectation of future bond prices – an implicit parameter embedded in the L function. This would shift the LM curve to the right, lowering the interest rate and increasing the equilibrium level of Y. The same qualitative effect would take place if investors' confidence in the forecast of future capital gains increased. What would happen after that shift would all depend on the behavior of endogenous expectations and confidence.

What might a dynamic investment function more consistent with *The General Theory* look like? It might be written as $I_t = I(r_t, Y_t, Y_{LR}^{EX}{}_t, CF_t)$, where $Y_{LR}^{EX}{}_t$ and $CF_t$ (agent confidence in the expectation-formation process at time t) are endogenous variables determined by extrapolating the recent trajectory of the economy.[7]

Keynes's theory of liquidity preference requires the inclusion of expected future bond prices and the degree of confidence agents have in these expectations to determine what share of their financial wealth investors wish to hold in the form of bonds versus money. Since bond prices and interest rates move in opposite directions, we might write a Keynes-inspired demand for money function as $M^D_t = M(Y_t, r_t, r^{EX}_t, CF_t)$, where the expected interest rate $r^{EX}_t$ (formed through extrapolation from the relevant past) and $CF_t$ are endogenous variables.

We might think of $Y_{LR}^{EX}{}_t$ and $r^{EX}_t$ as constructed by extrapolation from a distributed lag function of past rates of growth of $Y_t$ and $r_t$ with coefficients that decline as we move back in time from $t-1$. The cutoff date for the series might be the point when the current "era" began, perhaps after the most recent crisis, though the value of the coefficients on distant past observations would be relatively small. The function should be consistent with the endogenous boom–bust business cycle discussed in chapter 22. $CF_t$ might also be constructed through a distributed lag function built by extrapolating the percentage error in forecast values relative to actual values in the relevant past. Model 5 requires that these formulations be subject to disruption at crisis points when agents lose all confidence in their ability to foresee the future – as in chapter 12's "abnormal times."

The complete economic model would be composed of the structural equations of the expanded IS/LM model combined with equations that explain how expectations and confidence are formed. The logic of this dynamic process is as follows: the values for expectations and confidence are influenced by recent trends of relevant economic variables. Expectations and confidence in turn affect agent decisions that determine current economic outcomes given the structure of the economic model. Current outcomes then influence the next period's values of expectations and confidence – and so on. Steve Fazzari argued that a dynamic process such as this cannot be stationary.

> Since agents learn and realized outcomes depend on expectations, the uncertain process being forecast cannot possible be stationary. Learning leads to changing expectations and changes in expectations cause changes in the underlying process ... This kind of learning may never reach a self-sustaining state at all.
> (Fazzari 1985, p. 73)

A complete formal analysis of this system would require a full specification of a dynamic mathematical version of this model.[8] However, for our purposes, in the next section we will look at Keynes's model as a system of augmented IS/LM curves that shift over time in response to exogenous shocks and their own endogenous dynamic forces.

## Exogenous shocks, stability, and comparative statics in *The General Theory* and in IS/LM models

Let us first compare and contrast the effects of a substantial unexpected negative exogenous shock to investment spending on equilibrium income in the textbook IS/LM model and in *The General Theory*. In the IS/LM case, investment spending will decline at every (Y, r) point along the IS curve. This will cause the IS curve to experience a parallel leftward shift equal to the size of the investment shock times the multiplier. The LM curve will be unaffected by this shift because expectations of future levels of income and the interest rate are implicitly held constant even as current Y and r change, and the existence of the key variable "confidence" is omitted from the analysis. Since the position of the LM curve does not change, the equilibrium values of both r and Y will decline by a calculable amount.

The direction of the initial impact on the equilibrium value of Y is consistent with the argument in *The General Theory*. However, Keynes's insistence in chapters 13, 15, and 22 of *The General Theory* that a sharp unexpected decline in income and employment is likely to be met by a sharp rise in r that exacerbates the downturn has been theorized out of existence in the IS/LM model because it assumes there is no change in expectations and confidence. In this very important sense, the IS/LM model is an anti-Keynes model. It eliminates the possibility of dysfunctional or "insane" gambling casino financial markets such as those of the late 1920s and 1930s whose importance was stressed by Keynes.

This decline in r will minimize the size of the fall in equilibrium income caused by the exogenous decline in investment in a manner similar to the reaction of r to a negative exogenous shock in the classical model. This is the result of a decline in the transactions demand for money, which increases the demand for bonds and thus lowers the current interest rate (while leaving the expected interest rate unchanged). As in classical theory, financial markets are our friends.

Of course, in the IS/LM model, the ultimate result of the shock is a lower level of equilibrium income, which clearly differentiates it from classical theory. It is worth repeating that the IS/LM analysis may not be unreasonable if we are evaluating the very-short-term effects of modest changes in the determinants of AD.

Now compare this IS analysis with the outcome of the effects of a negative shock to investment spending within the framework of *The General Theory*. Given that expectations and confidence are endogenous, any substantial shock to any section of the economy, if it is substantial, is likely to set off a dynamic and potentially unpredictable reaction that may or may not have a final resting place. The exact dynamics of the process cannot be determined unless the theorist is willing to fully specify the mathematical properties of the functions that generate expectations and confidence, but Keynes sketched out the logic of the process. Two aspects of Keynes's analysis are especially relevant.

First, in Keynes's theory, the *permanent* fall in I and Y created by the negative investment shock should cause $Y_{LR}^{EX}{}_t$ and the expected rate of profit or mec to decline. If the shock was unexpected, as is presumed, $CF_t$ would decline as well. This would create an induced second leftward shift in the IS function as traditionally specified. The induced shift might itself cause further changes to expectations and confidence that would lead to yet a third leftward shift in the IS function – and so on.

Second, a significant and unexpected deterioration in conditions in the real sector is likely to cause financial investors to lower their expectations of future corporate profits and future bond and stock prices. They are also likely to become less confident in their ability to forecast financial asset prices accurately. Moreover, if the downturn is substantial and the financial system fragile, it could trigger debt defaults. The result of all this would be an *endogenous rise in liquidity preference* as investors dump both stocks and bonds to avoid potential capital loss and hold the proceeds in the form of "money."[9] In a serious unexpected downturn, an LM curve with endogenous expectations and confidence will shift left in response to the downward shift in the IS curve. This will cause the interest rate to rise sharply – as it did in the USA in the early 1930s.[10]

The increase in the interest rate caused by the induced LM shift will cause AD and Y to fall further, accelerating the downturn. This may cause expectations of future income and profits to decline yet again and/or confidence in the ability to forecast the future to fall, both of which will cause yet another leftward shift in the IS curve. In contrast to Mainstream Keynesian and classical theory, when serious trouble develops in the real sector, Keynes warned us that financial markets are more likely to worsen the effects than they are to help eliminate them. We know that Keynes had the catastrophic dynamic interaction between real and financial sectors in the USA in the late 1920s and early 1930s in mind when he was writing *The General Theory*. Yet this destructive dynamic is ruled out by assumption in the standard IS/LM model that, again, is supposedly the sole interesting model contained in *The General Theory*.

In the very unlikely and un-Keynesian event that both firms and financial investors had foreseen the full *effects* of an unexpected initial "shock" to either sector and adjusted their expectations to it, it might seem that the ultimate impact of the shock will be new short-run equilibrium positions for Y and r as in the comparative-static exercises in mainstream macro textbooks. Yet even then, since the original shock itself was not *anticipated* in either market, there would be a decline in the confidence with which expectations are held in both markets, which itself would lead to an induced downward shift in both IS and LM curves. This in turn might cause another change in expectations and/or confidence and thus a third shift in the curves.

The reader should understand that I am not conjuring up this intersectoral dynamic interaction based only on arcane hints offered in *The General Theory*. In chapter 22, Keynes clearly stated the problem, which can be explained in IS/LM terms. The sharp decline in the mpc will cause a fall in the IS curve, and this will trigger "a sharp rise in liquidity preference" that will cause an equally sharp upward shift in the LM curve.

> The dismay and uncertainty as to the future which accompanies a collapse in the marginal efficiency of capital naturally precipitates a sharp rise in liquidity preference and hence a rise in the interest rate. Thus the fact that a collapse in the marginal efficiency of capital tends to be associated with a subsequent rise in the interest rate may seriously aggravate the decline in investment.
>
> (CW 7, p. 316)

Keynes strongly emphasized the interconnectedness of disequilibrium processes in the real and financial sectors in his 1937 defense of *The General Theory*. He argued that the spread of pessimism or optimism from financial actors to business firms and from the latter back to the former was quite likely to occur. This makes sense: corporate leaders and the top executives of large financial institutions move in the same business and social circles, interact with and influence one another, have access to similar formal and informal sources of information about economic developments, and tend to hold similar views of the state of the economy. Thus, movement in either the IS or the LM curve, if it is significant and unexpected, will cause shifts in the other curve. Keynes said there is:

> [no] reason to suppose that the fluctuations in one of these factors [investors' or lenders' expectations and confidence] will tend to offset the fluctuations in the other [entrepreneurs' expectations and confidence]. When a more pessimistic view is taken about future yields [that lowers the mec], that is no reason why there should be a diminished propensity to hoard [or a fall in liquidity preference]. *Indeed, the conditions which aggravate the one factor tend, as a rule, to aggravate the other. For the same circumstances which lead to pessimistic views about future yields are apt to increase the propensity to hoard.*
>
> (Keynes 1937, p. 118, emphasis added)

He concluded:

> It is not surprising that the volume of investment, thus determined, should fluctuate wildly from time to time. For it depends on two sets of judgments about the future, neither of which rests on an adequate

or secure foundation – on the propensity to hoard [or liquidity preference] and on opinions of the future yield of [real] capital assets.

(Keynes 1937, p. 118)

Neither the standard IS/LM model nor more sophisticated Mainstream Keynesian theory incorporates Keynes's vision of the potential for substantial and even extreme financial and economic instability that was a major focus of *The General Theory* and of his 1937 defense of that book.

## Keynes warned about relying solely on comparative statics to analyze the effects of exogenous shocks in *The General Theory*

What Keynes is asking us to envision here is not the comparative static analysis relied on in both mainstream textbooks and, indeed, in his own analysis of the "multiplier" process associated with a permanent increase in public investment in chapter 10 of *The General Theory*. Rather, Keynes is describing a potentially endless dance of shifting curves across time whose final resting place, if any, is unknowable – a process ruled out, and thus hidden from the reader's view, by the failure to move beyond comparative statics in IS/LM theory. I repeat here a relevant comment from Keynes mentioned above:

> I should, I think, be prepared to argue that, in a world ruled by uncertainty, with an uncertain future linked to an actual present, a final position of equilibrium, such as the one we deal with in static economics, does not properly exist.
>
> (CW 29, p. 229)

Though Keynes did use a comparative-static analysis of a permanent change in the level of public and semi-public capital investment in *The General Theory*, he also warned us in that book that comparative statics should only be the first step in the full analysis required to understand the dynamic impact of economic "shocks" or unexpected policy changes on economic outcomes, not the only step. This is so important and so at odds with Modern Keynesian methodology that I quote him at length here. He began by saying that the use of comparative statics "must not lead us into supposing that [the curves or functions] are, strictly speaking, independent" as required in comparative statics (CW 7, p. 297).

> The object of our analysis is, not to provide a machine, or method of blind manipulation, which will furnish an infallible answer, but to provide us with an organized and orderly method of thinking out particular problems; and, after we have reached a provisional conclusion by isolating the complicating factors one by one, *we then have to go back on ourselves and allow, as well as we can, for the possible interactions of*

*the factors amongst themselves.* This is the nature of economic thinking. Any other way of applying our formal principles of thought (without which, however, we shall be lost in the wood) will lead us into error. *It is a great fault of symbolic pseudo-mathematical methods of formalizing a system of economic analysis ... that they expressly assume strict independence between the factors involved and lose all their cogency and authority if this hypothesis is disallowed*; whereas, in ordinary discourse, where we are not blindly manipulating but know all the time what we are doing and what the words mean, we can keep "at the back of our heads" the necessary reserves and qualifications and the adjustments which we shall have to make later on, in a way in which we cannot keep complicated partial differential equations [representing out-of-equilibrium processes] "at the back" of several pages of algebra *which they assume will all vanish.* Too large a proportion of recent "mathematical" economics are merely concoctions, as imprecise as the initial assumptions they rest on, *which allow the author to lose sight of the complexities and interdependencies of the real world in a maze of pretentions and unhelpful signals.*

(CW 7, pp. 297–298, emphasis added)

He made a similar point in chapter 18. He said that economic models divide "determinants of our economic system" into two groups: endogenous and exogenous variables. This division is "of course, quite arbitrary from any absolute standpoint. The division must be made entirely on the basis of experience" (CW 7, p. 247). If we want to ask what the initial effect of a fall in investment spending on income and employment will be when holding expectations, confidence, and the balance sheets of firms, financial investors, and households constant, a comparative-static exercise may be adequate to the task. But if we want to know what changes will result from the decline in investment in the trajectory of the economy over a longer period, we must allow those variables initially and arbitrarily held constant to react to the first-stage or comparative-static changes. If these changes affect expectations and/or confidence and/or balance sheets (or indeed any other determinant of the AD or AS functions), this will cause additional, endogenously generated movements whose end point is unpredictable. The induced effects on variables initially held constant will be of especially great significance in turbulent times such as the 1930s and the post-2007 global economic and financial crisis.

## Endogenously generated movement: "stability is destabilizing"

In Keynes's theory, the economy does not need to be exogenously "shocked" to move. Capitalism is an evolutionary system that is always in the process of generating endogenous change, sometimes slowly and sometimes rapidly. Minsky is well known for his defense of the Keynes's commitment to the thesis that "stability is destabilizing." I have already discussed this phenomenon in the sections of this book focused on *The General Theory*'s treatment of: the "liquidity preference" theory of the interest rate in chapters 13 and 15; the theory of the determination of stock prices in chapter 12; the effects of deflation in chapter 19; and the business cycle in chapter 22. Since the main ideas relevant to endogenous instability have already been covered, I only offer here a brief example of the kinds of arguments made in support of this thesis.

We could begin our narrative either with a relatively stable or a rising rate of profit on capital investment or with a relatively stable and attractive level or rate of growth of security prices over an extended period of time. Following Minsky, we begin with financial markets.

Consider a situation in which financial markets have been relatively stable for some time. If this situation persists long enough, investors will begin to expect that stocks and bonds are not especially risky in the current era and therefore will increase their purchases of these securities. This will increase stock prices and lower interest rates. Investors, relying on Keynes's conventional expectation-formation process, will begin to incorporate the recent rise in capital gains into their expectations of future security prices. The longer this process continues, the more optimistic investors will become and, equally importantly, the more confident they will become in their optimism. Because they are confidently optimistic, investors will feel comfortable taking on increasing leverage to buy stocks and bonds, and their brokers will be comfortable lending them the money to do so. If the financial market boom lasts long enough, financial analysts and economics professors will begin to assure investors that we have entered a "new era" in which the boom can go on forever – "this time is different."

Capital investment would be expected to increase because, throughout much of the boom, the expected profit rate is rising, confidence in expectations is rising, and the interest rate is falling. Rising investment spending will cause income and employment to increase. Corporations will be willing to increase borrowing to finance investment because they believe they can safely take advantage of the positive effect of leverage on the rate of return on owner-capital. Consumption spending would be buoyed by rising wages and increased job security, by household access to credit on easy terms, and by the wealth effect of capital gains on consumption spending. The stimulation of real-sector growth by the financial boom will have a positive-feedback effect on the financial sector, just as Keynes described in his discussion of interacting real and financial sectors in the QJE article of 1937.

But if this boom is long and strong, it may leave in its wake both financially fragile balance sheets and confidently optimistic expectations destined to be eventually disappointed. Economic booms always eventually end. In Keynes's view, the rapid accumulation of capital over an extended period will eventually drive down the actual rate of profit on capital. In that sense at least, it never really is a "new era." If the inevitable downturn begins in an over-leveraged environment, it may trigger a financial crisis accompanied by a collapse of both optimism and confidence that leaves investors in a psychological panic. The outcome of this process can be ugly, as it was in the USA in the 1930s or in much of the world after 2007. The claim that Keynes insisted that unregulated or lightly regulated capitalist economies inevitably generate bouts of instability and crisis from time to time is fully explored and defended in chapter 2 of Crotty (2017), but is ruled out by assumption in IS/LM models.

Minsky was right to insist that Keynes's macro theory was based on ceaseless change in positions of temporary stasis brought about by powerful endogenous forces.

> In the Marshallian long-run equilibrium there are no endogenous economic forces making for further change ... [T]he Marshallian vision is that of a system tending toward rest ... Every reference by Keynes to an equilibrium is best interpreted as a reference to a transitory set of system variables toward which the economy is tending; but, in contrast to Marshall, as the economy moves toward such a set of system variables, endogenously determined changes occur which affect the set of system variables toward which the economy tends. The analogy is that of a moving target, which is never achieved but for a fleeting instant, if at all. Each state, whether it be boom, crisis, debt-deflation, stagnation, or expansion, *is transitory*. During each short-period equilibrium, in Keynes's view, processes are at work which will "disequilibrate" the system. Not only is stability and unattainable goal; *whenever something approaching stability is achieved, destabilizing processes are set off*.
> 
> (Minsky 1975, p. 61, emphasis added)

For reasons already elaborated, I believe that Minsky's assertion that Keynes thought stagnation in the interwar period would soon be eliminated by endogenous forces and was thus "transitory" is profoundly mistaken.

## Conclusions

The main contributions of the IS/LM model to our understanding of Keynes's economic theory is that: (1) it provides a clear and logical explanation of why a capitalist economy can exist in a stable high-unemployment equilibrium state, even if only in the short run; and (2) it provides the framework for a narrative, as opposed to a formal model, of the causes of secular stagnation. Used for the second purpose, the fact that IS/LM equilibriums are always stable is a virtue. For all other purposes and for the other four models in *The General Theory*, the always-stable IS/LM model embodies a serious misunderstanding of Keynes's theory. Its widespread acceptance among economists as the one and only model in *The General Theory* led the economics profession to completely miss the destructive dynamic processes that occupy almost half of its pages. The IS/LM model shows that financial markets always help counteract negative shocks to AD by lowering interest rates and can never exacerbate them, and that financial markets can never initiate financial instability. Indeed, the late 1920s and 1930s financial boom and subsequent collapse in the USA is inexplicable within the confines of the model designated as Keynes's legacy. The fact that the post-WWII economics profession came to accept this idyllic view of the nature of lightly regulated financial markets, later embodied in "efficient financial markets" theory, helped financial corporations in their successful efforts to disassemble the strict regulation of financial markets imposed in the midst of the 1930s depression. This radical financial market deregulation was a major cause of the global financial crisis that erupted in 2007–2008. Moreover, when embedded in the standard AS/AD model, the IS/LM model demonstrates that deflation always raises AD and lowers unemployment, a proposition Keynes aggressively attacked in chapters 2 and 19 of *The General Theory*.

In *The General Theory*, Keynes constructed a theory that could be used to explain the historical record of real-world capitalism. This record contains periods of relatively stable economic evolution in "normal times," long periods of mostly rapid growth as in the "glorious" nineteenth century, normal business cycles, bouts of extreme instability in "interesting times" that are endogenously created, endogenous financial bubbles and crashes, and secular stagnation or prolonged depressions that can threaten social and political stability. These were explained by Keynes in the five models he developed in *The General Theory* to support his belief that capitalism had to be replaced by Liberal Socialism.

The main problem with the IS/LM model, then, is not just that it can be legitimately claimed to reflect or embody only a subset of the important criticisms of modern capitalism Keynes presented in *The General Theory*. The problem, rather, is the widespread belief among economists that the IS/LM model is all that Keynes bequeathed to the profession in his magnum opus, and therefore it is the sole argument he made against classical theory. This means that his support for Liberal Socialism has an inadequate logical foundation.

Prior to the Great Depression, the overwhelming majority of US economists taught that a stable high-unemployment equilibrium was impossible in a free-market economy. Even in the depths of the depression, when it was obvious to almost everyone that market forces alone could not restore prosperity to the country, the economics profession still relied on a variant of classical theory (Colander and Landreth 1996).[11] This changed dramatically as a result of the outstanding performance of the economy under government planning during WWII and the success of the new model of big-government capitalism that underpinned the "Golden Age" of post-WWII capitalism that ended in the 1970s. What turned out to be a one-generation phase in the historical trajectory of modern capitalism was interpreted by most economists to be the permanent state of modern capitalism. The near-universal acceptance of the IS/LM model as the sole legacy of Keynes's work helped put his radical economic theory and his support of Liberal Socialism into the dustbin of history.

The IS/LM model cleansed Keynes's work of many of its most serious criticisms of the nature of capitalism, including both capitalism's potential for secular stagnation and its destructive disequilibrium processes, including wage and price deflation, and the "insane" behavior of lightly regulated financial markets. When the profession accepted and propagated the view that the IS/LM model incorporated all of Keynes's important contributions in *The General Theory*, the reasons for his persistent commitment to Liberal Socialism got lost in translation.

## Notes

1 This is not to say that no Mainstream Keynesian economist has ever written a paper about unstable points of crisis in financial markets, and the few that did usually dealt with crises triggered by endogenous shocks. However, before the outbreak of the recent global financial crisis in 2008, such papers were rare indeed, and the theory of efficient financial markets ruled the roost in mainstream financial economics. Moreover, much of the analysis of the recent financial crisis also relied heavily on exogenous shocks and not on endogenously generated instability. Hyman Minsky's interpretation of Keynes's theory of financial markets, which is adopted by many Post Keynesians, does deal with the theory of endogenous sources of financial instability.

2 Hicks explained this property of Keynes's model via an "analogy" with the Walrasian static short-term multi-market equilibrium model. This is interesting because the Walrasian general equilibrium model exists in real time only when in a general equilibrium state. Trading outside general equilibrium is not permitted. When the economy does not have a market-clearing price vector, no real or calendar time passes as the "auctioneer" searches for the equilibrium price vector, so the system is always in general equilibrium in actual time. If trading at a non-equilibrium price vector were to take place, the distribution of wealth would change, causing the general equilibrium position to change. An analogous argument can be made about changes in expectations (and confidence and balance sheets) in out-of-equilibrium positions caused by the conflict between plans and outcomes. They will shift both curves.

3 Nothing in the model changes qualitatively if we assume that the money supply is moderately responsive to changes in the interest rate.

4 Hicks's critique of the LM curve does not apply to the IS curve. If firms know the future states of the economy with certainty, they will be more – not

290  The General Theory

　　less – likely to buy capital goods when the expected profit rate exceeds the long-term interest rate.
5   It does not take as long for a precipitous decline in security prices to destroy confidence in the expectation of continuation of a long-term market boom as it does to create optimistic expectations of a real-sector boom in the midst of a long depression.
6   This is an assumption in IS/LM models. In reality, it does not have to be valid in periods of either rapid expansion or rapid contraction where expectations and confidence are in a state of flux.
7   Keep in mind that $Y_{LR}^{EX}{}_t$ is a proxy for the mec or expected rate of profit on capital investment.
8   Note that a fully specified dynamic mathematical model could incorporate neoclassical risk if the expectation- and confidence-generating functions were assumed to be stochastic. But the model could not incorporate Keynesian uncertainty because the equations of the model could be used to calculate probability distributions of future outcomes that agents could use to make optimal choices.
9   The same logic can be applied to the impact of real-sector distress on the willingness of banks to make loans.
10  In a model with short-, medium-, and long-term interest rates, short-term rates would increase least because they are least affected by potential capital loss. They can be sold at par before much time passes.
11  For a defense of this assertion, see Colander and Landreth (1996).

# 20 Keynes's radical policy views in *The General Theory*

At a quick first reading, *The General Theory* appears to be primarily about economic theory, not about concrete policy proposals. Indeed, the preface opens with the following statement:

> This book is chiefly addressed to my fellow economists. I hope it will be intelligible to others. But its main purpose is to deal with difficult questions of theory, and only in the second place with the applications of this theory to practice.
>
> (CW 7, p. xxi)

Nevertheless, the "second place" policy discussion turns out to be quite important. This is not surprising because the main purpose of the book was to help create a consensus in support of Keynes's new macro theory among economists in the academy, government, business, finance, and main political parties, plus economically literate non-economists. He was especially focused on younger economists who were not yet committed to the then-current orthodoxy. Keynes's hope was that this consensus would lead to support for his radical policies, which are stated repeatedly in the book. In my opinion, the purpose of the new macroeconomic theory unveiled in the book was to provide an impregnable defense of these long-held policy positions.

Keynes believed *The General Theory* to be a revolutionary book. As he wrote to George Bernard Shaw in 1935:

> To understand *my* state of mind, however, you have to know that I believe myself to be writing a book on economic theory which will largely revolutionise – not, I suppose, at once but in the course of the next ten years – the way the world thinks about economic problems.
>
> (CW 13, p. 492, emphasis in original)

This represented something of a shift in Keynes's political strategy. He had previously relied on tireless proselytizing through speeches, newspaper articles, radio broadcasts, work with various government bodies, efforts to gain more political power for the Liberal Party, attempts to create alliances between Liberals and the Labour Party, and so forth. This strategy shift is made clear in a letter he wrote to Sir Arthur Salter in July 1935. Salter had asked Keynes if would be willing to add his signature to those of a group of luminaries whose support for Keynes's radical policies was laid out in a book titled *The Next Five Years*. In his reply, Keynes said:

> I think [the book] is excellently done and I am naturally in sympathy with nearly all of it. I recognize its origins in a good many cases in previous publications with which I was concerned. I think the practical proposals nearly all excellent and a government or party which adopted this volume as its programme would have my enthusiastic support.
>
> (CW 21, pp. 354–355)

But he refused to sign the document because "my own state of mind at this moment, whatever it may have been three or four years ago is materially different from that of the compilers." At "this moment," Keynes was fully engaged in finishing *The General Theory*, which was published the following year.

> My own belief today is that neither the real remedy nor the power of persuading people to adopt it will come except from a more fundamental diagnosis of the underlying situations and a wide-spread understanding of this diagnosis and conviction of its correctness … [W]hilst I thought that the proposal and the sort of ideas which your book contains was my job two years ago, and I daresay it was, I now consider my job is rather different.
>
> (CW 19, pp. 354–355)

Keynes's contemporary British audience was quite familiar with his writings, speeches, and newspaper articles on public investment and national planning. They knew he was a "Liberal Socialist" who had campaigned tirelessly for the adoption of democratic planning in Britain. For his British audience, Keynes did not have to endlessly repeat his radical policies in the book.

What follows is an examination of some of the main policy positions Keynes presented in *The General Theory* more or less in the order they appear in the book. It should not come as a surprise to the reader to discover that the foundation of his policy agenda in the book is reliance on increased public and semi-public investment, low interest rates (supported by capital controls), a drastic reduction in income and wealth inequality, and the elimination of the casino financial markets that helped generate highly volatile capital investment, blew up the global financial system, and contributed to the stagnation of the era. His goal was to have the state-guided rate of capital accumulation rise fast enough and for long enough to create a rapid growth of AD sufficient to achieve and sustain full employment.

What may be a surprise to the reader is the fact that while his radical policies appear all over *The General Theory*, only a handful of economists trained after WWII associate these policies with Keynes. The purpose of this chapter is to provide convincing evidence to support the claim that *The General Theory* repeatedly explains Keynes's radical policy views.

Chapter 10 on "The Marginal Propensity to Consume" is focused on the impact of increased public investment on unemployment; there is no reference to the multiplier on private investment. All students of economics learn that there is a multiplied effect of all exogenous sources of spending, whether public or private, on equilibrium output. But chapter 10 is devoted almost in its entirety to a demonstration that an increment in "public investment" or in "public works" will have a magnified or multiplied effect on equilibrium income and therefore on equilibrium employment. The goal of the chapter is obviously to demonstrate that public investment is a powerful policy tool. As we have seen, Keynes used the concept of the multiplier on public investment repeatedly in his efforts in the 1930s to generate support for his policies. Chapter 10 contains his most detailed defense of this position. Relying on data collected by Simon Kuznets for the USA, which he considered to be the best data available, Keynes estimated the value of the multiplier in the USA to be about 2.5. This meant that an increase in public investment in the USA would have a very strong impact on employment.

Keynes also stressed that the value of the mpc is cyclically variable and therefore so is the value of the multiplier. When the economy is depressed, the multiplier will be much higher than it is when unemployment is low because families will try to sustain their traditional or normal living standards as best they can. This will cause the mpc to be well above its average value in slumps. "The marginal propensity to consume is not constant for all levels of employment, and it is probable that there will be, as a rule, a tendency for it to diminish as employment increases" (CW 7, p. 120). He said that 2.5 is "a figure quite plausible for the boom, but ... improbably low for the slump" (CW 7, p. 128). Public investment will thus have the largest multiplier just when the most powerful demand stimulus is needed. On the other hand, changes in public investment will not subject the economy to excessive instability once full employment is achieved because the mpc and the multiplier will be at their lowest values in this situation.

In chapter 12, Keynes argued that "insane" casino financial markets were a major cause of investment volatility, which logically implies that they reinforce the tendency toward secularly stagnant investment because they make investment risker at all values of the mec. Excessive liquidity in financial markets in combination with fundamental uncertainty contributed to high-amplitude business cycles and were a major cause of the Great Depression. In this chapter, Keynes discussed three possible policies to reduce or eliminate the deleterious impact of excessive financial market volatility on the capital investment decision and thus on income and employment.

First, Keynes argued that the threat posed by financial market instability was so serious that he considered supporting policies *designed to eliminate the connection between private financial markets and capital investment altogether.*

> The spectacle of modern investment markets has sometimes moved me towards the conclusion that to make the purchase of an investment permanent and indissoluble, like marriage, except by reason of death or other grave causes, might be a useful remedy for contemporary evils ... For this would force the investor to direct his mind to the long-term prospects and to these only.
> (CW 7, p. 160)

The fact that this proposal would entail serious costs as long as capital investment spending depended on stock and bond prices would have to be weighed against its substantial benefits. This constituted a "dilemma."

> The liquidity of investment markets often facilitates, though it sometimes impedes the course of new investments. For the fact that each individual investor flatters himself that his commitment is "liquid" (though this cannot be true of all investors collectively) calms his nerves and makes him much more willing to run a risk. If individual purchases of [financial] investments were rendered illiquid, this might seriously impede new [capital] investment, so long as *alternative ways* in which to hold his savings are available to the individual. This is the dilemma.
> (CW 7, p. 160, emphasis in original)

He argued that as long as investors have the option of holding their wealth in the form of safe financial assets like cash, Treasury bills, or short-term savings accounts – "money" for short – that are immune from substantial nominal loss of capital value. "[T]he alternative of purchasing risky capital assets cannot be rendered sufficiently attractive ... except by organizing markets wherein these assets can be easily realised for money" (CW 7, pp. 161–162).

Thus:

> the only radical cure for the crises of confidence which afflict the economic life of the modern world would be to allow the individual no choice between consuming his income and ordering the production of the specific capital asset which, even though it be on precarious

evidence, impressed him as the most promising investment available to him.

(CW 7, p. 161)

This would at least "avoid the disastrous, cumulative and far-reaching repercussions of its being open to him, when thus assailed by doubts, to spend his income on neither one nor the other" by hoarding his income in the form of money (CW 7, p. 161). When investors are "assailed by doubts," the price of stocks will collapse and the long-term interest rate will spike, causing a fall in AD, income, and employment. The fact that Keynes even considered such a radical policy prescription reflected the depth of his concern with casino capitalism in the USA and elsewhere.

Second, Keynes proposed the imposition of a substantial financial transactions tax – now often called a Keynes tax, a Tobin tax, or a Robin Hood tax – that would respond to the dilemma described above by substantially reducing but not totally eliminating the liquidity of financial markets. Keynes observed that the instability of prices on the London Stock Exchange was of a lesser magnitude than it was on Wall Street. In his view, British financial markets were not dominated by speculative gambling. Speculation in London was, in comparison with speculation on Wall Street, "inaccessible and very expensive" due to the:

> high brokerage charges and the heavy transfer tax ... The introduction of a substantial Government transfer tax on all transactions might prove the most serviceable reform available with a view to mitigating the present predominance of speculation over enterprise in the United States.

(CW 7, p. 160)

Since Keynes believed that, given fundamental uncertainty, excessive liquidity made modern capitalist economies dangerously unstable, the transfer tax would have to be *very large* indeed to eliminate most of the volatility in financial markets.

Third, in the last paragraph of chapter 12, Keynes presented his preferred policy solution to both excessive instability and secular stagnation problems. It is a radical solution that reflected his long-held belief that this problem was so deeply rooted in modern capitalism that no normal set of market regulations would be capable of resolving it. In the last section of the chapter, Keynes repeated a statement he had made in his address to the Liberal Party Summer School in 1927, in BIF, and elsewhere: the stock of capital already under public control or guidance was already exceeding large.

> [T]here is a growing class of investments entered upon, or at the risk of, public authorities, which are frankly influenced in making the

> investment by a general presumption of there being prospective social advantages from the investment, whatever its commercial yield may prove to be within a wide range, and without seeking to be satisfied that the mathematical expectation of the yield is at least equal to the current interest rate, – though the rate of interest which the public authority has to pay may still play a decisive part in determining the scale of investment it can afford.
>
> (CW 7, pp. 164–165)

What was needed was a long-term plan by the state to increase this stock at a rate adequate to attain and sustain full employment – a goal that could not be achieved unless the interest rate could be forced to decline by enough to allow accelerated investment spending to cause the mec to fall toward zero. Though the stock of publicly controlled capital was already quite large, Keynes argued that it needed to grow even larger to achieve full employment. In the final paragraph of the chapter, he proposed that the government take "an ever greater responsibility for directly organising investment."

> I expect to see the State, which is in a position to calculate the marginal efficiency of capital-goods on long views and on the basis of the general social advantage, taking an ever greater responsibility *for directly organising investment*; since it seems likely that the fluctuations in the marginal efficiency of different types of capital … will be too great to be offset by any practicable changes in the rate of interest.
>
> (CW 7, p. 164, emphasis added)

This is the exit message for one of the most famous chapters in *The General Theory*. It is hard to understand how the profession missed it.

As we have seen, chapter 16 was a defense of Keynes's thesis that, in the absence of strong counter-tendencies, the profit rate on new investment and the expected profit rate will fall as the capital stock increases over time. He argued that the mec had in fact fallen substantially in the boom of the late 1920s. In chapter 17, Keynes explained that there are institutional as well as behavioral and psychological reasons (related to "liquidity preference") as to why the interest rate has a high lower bound under the current regime and argued that the mec had been too low relative to the long-term interest rate in the UK in the interwar years and in the USA after 1929 to permit a level of capital investment spending high enough to sustain full employment. Under then-current policy regimes, Keynes said in chapter 16, both the USA and the UK would continue to suffer from chronically high unemployment. However: "This disturbing conclusion depends, of course, on the assumption that the propensity to consume and the rate of investment are not deliberately controlled in the social interest but are mainly left to the influence of laissez-faire" (CW 7, p. 219). His proposed policy regime would solve the problem.

Keynes was optimistic that if the state could sustain investment at a level that achieved full employment, the rate of profit on capital investment would approach zero "within a single generation." Of course, this would require that monetary policy and strict capital controls would "ensure that the rate of interest is consistent with the rate of investment which corresponds to full employment" (CW 7, p. 220). Forcing the capital stock to grow rapidly over time through public investment while forcing the interest rate to decline as rapidly as the mec could only be accomplished by a government with unprecedented peacetime power to control economic activity.

> Let us assume ... that State action enters in as a balancing factor to provide that the growth of capital equipment shall be such as to approach saturation point at a rate which does not put a disproportionate burden on the standard of life of the present generation. On such assumptions I should guess that a properly run community equipped with modern technical resources, of which the population is not increasing rapidly, ought to be able to bring down the marginal efficiency of capital in equilibrium approximately to zero *within a single generation*.
> (CW 7, p. 220, emphasis added)

Keynes continued this line of argument, stressing the necessity of a very low interest rate eventually approaching zero in order for his policies to achieve their goals. This would require, he said, the nationalization of the Bank of England. The Board of National Investment was to have control over the majority of long-lived, large-scale capital investments concentrated in areas such as infrastructure, transportation, and public utilities, and it was to have strong influence over spending on residential and business construction. These capital investments are highly interest-elastic. As the interest rate falls, the potential volume of public investments and private investments such as housing that can be undertaken by the Board becomes much larger.

Since, under Keynes's plan, the interest rate would be at or near zero within a generation or so, this would signal the death of the rentier class – "the rentier would disappear" (CW 7, p. 221). This comment foreshadowed his support in chapter 24 for "the euthanasia of the rentier, and, consequently, the euthanasia of the cumulative oppressive power of the capitalist" (CW 7, p. 376).

Keynes fully understood that his policy regime constituted a direct attack on the existence of the economic and politically powerful rentier class. The rentier class and the institutions that supported it knew this as well.

> If I am right in supposing it be comparatively easy to make capital-goods so abundant that the marginal efficiency of capital is zero,

this may be the most sensible way of gradually getting rid of many of the objectionable features of capitalism. For a little reflection will show what enormous social changes would result from a gradual disappearance of a rate of return on accumulated wealth.

(CW 7, p. 221)

In chapter 22, Keynes returned to his chapter 12 attack on casino capitalism, arguing that modern financial markets were a major cause of cyclical instability and had the potential to generate severe depressions when major economic downturns occurred in conditions of high financial fragility. As in chapter 12, Keynes insisted that capital investment was too important to the economy and society to be left in the hands of volatile, destructive and excessively liquid financial markets. He also argued that central bank manipulation of interest rates alone cannot solve the problem. There are two reasons for this, he said. One is that while the mec can fall to very low levels in a serious cyclical downturn (in part because excess capacity is very high) and in the long run due to secular stagnation, the long-term interest "never falls below a conventional level" (CW 7, p. 325).[1] Keynes believed that under then-present institutional arrangements, the long-term interest rate could not fall below 2.5–3.0 percent. Of course, when Britain was on the gold standard, the rate of interest could not be allowed to fall below rates available to investors in other countries (CW 7, p. 339).

The other reason is that a monetary policy strategy of changing interest rates frequently in an attempt to offset volatile market fluctuations cannot work; such economic volatility "cannot be sufficiently offset by corresponding fluctuations in the rate of interest" (CW 7, p. 320).[2] Indeed, a strategy of changing the interest rate in response to every shift in the mec would make central bank policy itself a major creator of uncertainty and would therefore lower the average value of the risk-adjusted or confidence-adjusted mec.

> Thus, with markets organized and influenced as they are at present, the market estimation of the marginal efficiency of capital may suffer such enormously wide fluctuations that it cannot be sufficiently offset by corresponding fluctuations in the rate of interest ... In conditions of laissez-faire the avoidance of wide fluctuations in employment may, therefore, prove impossible without a far-reaching change in the psychology of investment markets such as there is no reason to expect. *I conclude that the duty of ordering the current value of investment cannot safely be left in private hands.*
>
> (CW 7, p. 320, emphasis added)

He used the late 1920s boom in the USA to demonstrate his point. By 1929, "New investment during the previous five years had been, indeed, on so enormous a scale in the aggregate that the prospective yield of further additions was, coolly considered, falling rapidly." Therefore, to generate enough investment to sustain full employment, the Fed would have had to lower interest rates to "an unprecedentedly low level" (CW 7, p. 323). But such low interest rates would have pushed the financial-market boom into an even greater frenzy and caused leverage and financial fragility in the system to rise even higher than the great heights actually achieved in late 1929, worsening the subsequent crisis. "A rate of interest high enough to overcome the speculative excitement [in financial markets] would have checked, at the same time, every kind of reasonable new [capital] investment" (CW 7, p. 323). To resolve this problem would require "a socially controlled rate of investment" (CW 7, p. 325).

Keynes also repeated here his standard argument that the policy of increasing public investment should be accompanied "by redistributing incomes or otherwise, to stimulate the propensity to consume." This could be accomplished not only by much more progressive income tax rates, but also, as we will see in chapter 24 of *The General Theory*, much higher estate or "death" taxes (CW 7, p. 372).

His ideal strategy was to give priority to increasing public investment for a generation or so while moderately increasing the mpc through the progressive redistribution of income and wealth. When investment was no longer scarce, a fall in AD below full-employment AS should be met by a rising mpc.

Keynes strongly believed that there was a great unmet need for public and private investment that could not be satisfied in less than a generation.[3]

> I am myself impressed by the great social advantages of increasing the stock of capital until it ceases to be scarce. But this is a practical judgment, not a theoretical imperative. However, I should readily concede that the wisest course is to advance on both fronts at once. Whilst aiming at a socially controlled rate of investment with a view to a progressive decline in the marginal efficiency of capital, I should support at the same time all sorts of policies for increasing the propensity to consume. There is room, therefore, for both policies to operate together.
>
> (CW 7, p. 325)

In chapter 23, when discussing state economic policy under nineteenth-century laissez-faire, Keynes noted that, unlike modern capitalism, this was "a society where there is no question of direct investment under the aegis of public authority" (CW 7, p. 335). Further along in the chapter, while lamenting the fact that under current conditions policies of free trade and free capital mobility policy were likely to promote war rather than peace, he stated his own belief in public control of investment and in the capital controls required to be able to set the "autonomous" interest rate at a very low level.

> It is the policy of an *autonomous rate of interest, unimpeded by international preoccupations*, and of a national investment programme directed to an optimum level of domestic employment which is twice blessed in the sense that it helps ourselves and our neighbors at the same time.
> (CW 7, p. 349, emphasis added)

Capital controls are obviously a necessary condition for the achievement of an "autonomous interest rate, unimpeded by international preoccupations." Earlier in the book, Keynes explained why capital controls were necessary to get the interest rate to near zero.

> [T]he long-term interest rate may [hit a lower bound] when once it has fallen to a level which, on the basis of past experience and present expectations of future monetary policy is considered "unsafe" by representative opinion. For example, in a country linked to an international gold standard, a rate of interest lower than prevails elsewhere will be viewed with a justifiable lack of confidence; yet a domestic rate of interest dragged up to a parity with the *highest* rate (highest after allowing for risk) prevailing in any country belonging to the international system may be much higher than is consistent with full employment.
> (CW 7, p. 203, emphasis in original)

Now consider the problem faced by Britain in 1936 after it had moved off the gold standard and its fixed exchange rate system. Under Keynes's proposed policy revolution, most large-scale investment would be controlled by the state and used to accumulate capital so rapidly the mec would approach zero. For this policy to be successful, a nationalized central bank would have to be willing to push the interest toward zero. This would lead, as Keynes stressed in chapter 24, to the elimination of the rentier class. The inequality of wealth and income would also decline dramatically under Liberal Socialism. If such a program were perceived as likely to be enacted, a massive and prolonged flight of capital would take place that might be large enough to cause a collapse of financial markets and private investment along with a serious deflation. Keynes's policy revolution therefore could not possibly succeed without capital controls.

The most important discussion of the new role of the state took place in chapter 24, the final chapter in the book, titled "Concluding Notes on the Social Philosophy towards Which the General Theory Might Lead." Here, he argued for a "comprehensive socialisation of investment" (CW 7, p. 378). There is a widespread belief that Keynes's support in chapter 24 for the socialization of investment was just an isolated, last-minute whim unconnected to and unsupported by the core of the book or, for that matter,

Keynes's other writings. For example, a macro textbook written by two distinguished progressive American economists, Sandy Darity and Jamie Galbraith, states: "There is no evidence to suggest that Keynes promoted his proposal for socializing investment, and it only surfaces briefly in the latter pages of *The General Theory*" (Darity and Galbraith 1994, p. 53). As we have seen, this interpretation is profoundly mistaken. *Indeed, in a 1932 draft of the final chapter of the book, Keynes titled this chapter "Socialism"* (O'Donnell 1999, p. 161).

The chapter begins with a reminder that the theory constructed in the book disarms the traditional argument that a very unequal distribution of income and wealth is necessary to generate the high savings rate required for high rates of investment and economic growth. Since, in general – except at full employment – increases in inequality lower the propensity to consume, they also lower AD, equilibrium income, employment, and the total amount saved and invested. Thus, significantly less inequality of income and wealth than at present is needed to generate sustained full employment and is preferable on grounds of social justice as well.

"The outstanding faults of the economic society in which we live are its failure to provide for full employment and its arbitrary and inequitable distribution of wealth and income" (CW 7, p. 372). Keynes applauded the significant increase in the taxes paid by the wealthy "through income tax and surtax and death duties – especially in Great Britain" since the turn of the century. But additional efforts in these directions have been limited by a combination of secular stagnation and the mistaken classical belief, based on the discredited Say's Law, that high savings cause high investment, or:

> by the belief that the growth of capital depends upon the strength of the motive towards individual savings and that for a large proportion of this growth we are dependent on the savings of the rich out of their superfluity ... But it may considerably modify [this belief to understand that] up to the point where full employment prevails, the growth of capital depends not at all on a low propensity to consume, but is, on the contrary, held back by it; and only in conditions of full employment is a low propensity to consume conducive to the growth of capital ... [M]easures for the redistribution of incomes in a way likely to raise the propensity to consume may prove positively favourable to the growth of capital ... In contemporary conditions the growth of wealth, so far from being dependent on the abstinence of the rich, as is commonly supposed, is more likely to be impeded by it. One of the chief social justifications of great inequality of wealth is therefore removed.
>
> (CW 7, p. 373)

There is justification for a modest degree of income inequality, Keynes argued, but this "does not apply equally to inequality of inheritances": very high inheritance taxes are justified on both economic and social justice grounds (CW 7, p. 374). He went on to explain that the distribution of income could be much more progressive without impeding necessary risk-taking or entrepreneurial activities. These would be forthcoming even if their potential rewards were reduced significantly from their current level once everyone adjusted to them. "Much lower stakes [income incentives] will serve the purpose equally well, as soon as the players get used to them" (CW 7, p. 374).

Finally, since, except in conditions of full employment, higher saving is caused or created by higher investment and not, as in classical theory, the other way around, there is no justification for the traditional support by economists of high-interest rate policies because they believed they would maximize total savings. This "has a bearing on the future inequalities of wealth" because rentier income accrued primarily to the richest families in the Britain of his time (CW 7, p. 375). Since high investment is facilitated by a secularly low "autonomous" interest rate (made possible through capital controls), in the world Keynes envisions, interest rates will be cut to a minimum. "Thus it is to our best advantage to reduce the rate of interest to that point relatively to the schedule of the marginal efficiency of capital at which there is full employment" (CW 7, p. 375).

But since the profit rate will approach zero as full employment is sustained over time, the interest rate required to maintain full employment will also have to fall toward zero. The rate of public investment required to achieve and sustain full employment over the long run could only be financed if the rate of interest could be reduced to a "very low figure" (CW 7, p. 375). When the interest rate nears zero at the capital saturation point, the income flow to rentiers would be reduced to a trickle.

Keynes tells us that the policies required to sustain full employment:

> would mean the euthanasia of the rentier, and, consequently, *the euthanasia of the cumulative oppressive power of the capitalist to exploit the scarcity value of capital* ... I see, therefore, the rentier aspect of capitalism as a transitional phase which will disappear when it has done its work. And with the disappearance of its rentier aspect much else in it besides will suffer a sea-change. It will be, moreover, a great advantage of the order of events which I am advocating, that the euthanasia of the rentier, of the functionless investor, ... will need no revolution. Thus we might aim in practice ... at an increase in the volume of capital until it ceases to be scarce, so that the functionless investor will no longer receive a bonus; and at a scheme of direct taxation which allows the intelligence and determination and executive skill of the entrepreneur ... to be harnessed to service of the community on reasonable terms of reward.
>
> (CW 7, p. 376, emphasis added)[4]

Thus, a fall in the interest rate toward zero would not only reduce inequality and facilitate full employment – it would also eliminate an "oppressive" and economically and politically powerful rentier class whose interests were championed not only by their representatives in Parliament, but also by the largest financial institutions and the Bank of England itself. Since the key demand of the rentier class was high interest rates, the economic power of rentiers would have to be eliminated if Keynes's policy agenda was to have any hope of success.

Keynes understood that sustained full employment brought about by a high level of public investment would permanently eliminate Marx's "reserve army" of unemployed and thereby permanently empower workers in their economic and political conflicts with capital. It would simultaneously eliminate the pressure on governments that builds up during depressions and serious recessions to adopt capital-friendly policies in the hope that these policies would tease out more investment and more jobs in the midst of high unemployment. Finally, strict capital controls would be needed to achieve the low interest rates required to eliminate the scarcity of real capital. In the absence of capital controls, the rentier class could force interest rates up to the higher levels available in other countries through capital flight. Without capital controls, capital flight would also be triggered whenever rentiers became dissatisfied with or nervous about the general tenor of government economic policy. It is not an exaggeration to suggest that sustained full employment achieved through high rates of public investment accompanied by the euthanasia of the rentier, radically progressive tax reform, and capital controls would constitute a revolution of sorts in Britain's class relations.

The conventional wisdom is that Keynes wrote *The General Theory* to "save capitalism." Clearly, this is either false or "capitalism" must be redefined to apply to any economic system in which markets, monetary incentives, and freedom of consumer choice are allowed to exist in some form, even if most important economic decisions are determined collectively via democratic political processes before people get to choose in the marketplace. If we use the traditional definition of capitalism, it was clearly Keynes's goal in writing *The General Theory* to replace capitalism with a form of democratic socialism.

A central impediment to the achievement of Keynes's policy objectives was that almost all conservatives and many liberal readers were likely to be very nervous about the program because the powers to be removed from the control of capitalist firms and rentiers and vested in the state were, by the standards of 1930s Britain or, for that matter, current-day America, enormous. He listed some key state responsibilities.

> The State will have to exercise a guiding influence on the propensity to consume partly through its scheme of taxation, partly by fixing

> the rate of interest, and partly, perhaps, in other ways. Furthermore, it seems unlikely that the influence of banking policy on the rate of interest will be sufficient by itself to determine an optimum rate of investment. I conceive, therefore, that a somewhat *comprehensive socialisation of investment* will prove the only means of securing an approximation to full employment; though this need not exclude all manner of compromises and of devices by which public authority will co-operate with private initiative … If the State is able to determine the aggregate amount of resources devoted to augmenting the instruments *and the basic rewards of those who own them*, it will have accomplished all that is necessary. Moreover, the necessary measure of socialisation can be introduced gradually and without a break in the general traditions of society.
>
> (CW 7, p. 378, emphasis added)

We have seen that Keynes thought that the state should use a combination of progressive income taxes, very high inheritance taxes, and historically low interest rates to substantially reduce inequality and, after a time, actually eliminate the powerful rentier class. Keynes's contemporary readers in Britain also knew he was on the public record in favor of the idea that it is the responsibility of the state to manage trade and to control the flow of financial capital across its borders. Here, he added control of the propensity to consume (and, therefore, of the national savings rate), *the rate of profit on capital* ("the basic rewards" to the owners of real capital), and the "somewhat comprehensive socialisation of investment" – which we know was the centerpiece of AD management. The socialization of investment would also allow the state to strongly influence the allocation of capital investment among competing public and private demands. The capital class understood that the combination of all of these policies would constitute a radical transformation of Britain's political economy. This is why most of its members vigorously opposed his policies.

At this point in the chapter, one can begin to detect a hint of political sugarcoating by Keynes to make his policies seem less threatening to the status quo then they in fact were. He states: "In some other respects the foregoing theory is moderately conservative in its implications" because some economic decisions will still be made through decentralized markets. "For whilst it indicates the vital importance of establishing certain central controls in matters which are now left in the main to individual initiative, there are wide fields of activity which are unaffected" (CW 7, pp. 377–378).

> But if our central controls succeed in establishing an aggregate volume of output corresponding to full employment as nearly as is practicable, the classical theory comes into its own again from this point onward. If we suppose the volume of output to be given … by forces outside the classical scheme of thought, then there is no objection to be

raised against the classical manner in which private self-interest will determine what is to be produced, in what proportions the factors of production will be combined to produce it, and how the value of the product will be distributed between them.

(CW 7, pp. 378–379)

This statement either assumes that a much more progressive distribution of income and wealth has already been achieved or it is inconsistent with other sections of the chapter. If markets are allowed to determine "how the value of the product will be distributed between" the factors of production, then it cannot also be true that the state will determine "the basic rate of reward those who own" the means of production (CW 7, p. 378). He had also previously stressed the existence of serious problems associated with the nature of competition in industries with large economies of scale and with the process of downsizing industries with chronic excess capacity that are not mentioned here.

Keynes acknowledged that the existing system suffers from "errors of foresight; but these would not be avoided by centralizing decisions" (CW 7, p. 379). While literally true, the statement is misleading because he believed that the existing system was subject to huge instability and, in that sense, to huge "errors of foresight." Since Keynes also believed that reliance on state-guided public investment was capable of achieving a reasonably close approximation to sustained full employment with relatively moderate cyclical movements, he clearly believed that his preferred economic model would involve much smaller "errors of foresight."

Having presented a long list of the powerful economic functions to be undertaken by the state, he tried to calm his readers' nerves with the following assurance:

> But beyond this no obvious case is made out for a system of [Soviet-style] State Socialism which would embrace most of the economic life of the community. It is not the ownership of the instruments of production which is important for the State to assume.
>
> (CW 7, p. 378)

Keynes was, of course, correct to insist that his "middle way" represented a less radical departure from the status quo than the detailed physical planning of production and distribution under state ownership of all important means of production, which was the stated ultimate objective of the Labour Party. And he insisted, as he had done in "National Self-Sufficiency," that his radical policy proposals had to be achieved through democratic processes.

Keynes ended the substantive part of the chapter with a three-pronged appeal for his readers' sympathy and support reminiscent of the closing arguments in his 1933 essay "National Self-Sufficiency." First, he repeated the argument that his system incorporates some of the most important advantages of individualism. His wording reflects both his own values and his understanding of the brutality involved in some of the more extreme contemporary experiments in national planning.

> Let us stop for a moment to remind ourselves what these advantages are. They are partly advantages of efficiency – the advantages of decentralisation and of the play of self-interest. The advantage to efficiency of the decentralisation of decisions and of individual responsibility is even greater, perhaps, that the nineteenth century supposed; and the reaction against the appeal to self-interest has perhaps gone too far. But, above all, individualism, if it can be purged of its defects and its abuses, is the best safeguard of personal liberty in the sense that, compared with any other system, it greatly widens the field for the exercise of personal choice. It is also the best safeguard of the variety of life ... the loss of which is the greatest of all the losses of the homogeneous or totalitarian state. For this variety preserves the traditions which embody the most secure and successful choices of former generations; it colours the present with the diversification of its fancy; and, being the handmaiden of experiment as well as of tradition and of fancy, it is the most powerful instrument to better the future.
> 
> (CW 7, p. 380)

Second, Keynes expressed his belief that a hoped-for international system of planned economies would greatly reduce the likelihood of future wars. As he so forcefully argued in "National Self-Sufficiency," continuance of the status quo promised only stagnation and war.

> But if nations can learn to provide themselves with full employment by their domestic policy (and, we must add, if they can also attain equilibrium in the trend of their population), there need be no important economic forces calculated to set the interest of one country against that of its neighbours. There would still be room for the international division of labour and for international lending in appropriate conditions. But ... [i]nternational trade would cease to be what it is [in the 1930s], namely, a desperate expedient to maintain employment at home by forcing sales on foreign markets and restricting purchases, which, if successful, will merely shift the problem of unemployment to the neighbour which is worsted in the struggle, but a willing and unimpeded exchange of goods and services in conditions of mutual advantage.
>
> (CW 7, p. 382)

His last argument is certainly the most powerful. It is an old standard for Keynes. Either Keynes's middle-way planning – radical though it is – will be accepted by Britain's economic and political elite or Britain will ultimately end up with a working-class revolution, totalitarian planning, or both. When he says "the world will not much longer tolerate" present-day capitalism, he clearly means that the working class will not much longer tolerate it. As has been stressed, the interwar years were an era of political and armed revolutions. Referring to his policy program as a whole, Keynes argues:

> I defend it ... both as the only practicable means of avoiding the destruction of existing economic forms *in their entirety* and as the condition of the successful functioning of individual initiative ... The authoritarian state systems of to-day seem to solve the problem of unemployment at the expense of efficiency and freedom. It is certain that the world [i.e. the working class] *will not much longer tolerate* the unemployment which, apart from brief intervals of excitement, is associated – and, in my opinion, *inevitably associated* – with present-day capitalistic individualism. But it may be possible by a right analysis of the problem to cure the disease whilst preserving efficiency and freedom.
> (CW 7, p. 381, emphasis added)

When Keynes argued that there would be terrible consequences unless his model of Liberal Socialism was adopted in Britain and elsewhere, he was deadly serious.

Toward the end of chapter 24, Keynes raised an important question concerning the ultimate determinant of government economic policy in a capitalist society. He asked whether "vested interests," by which he means capitalist class interests, or "ideas," theories about the how the economy works, posed the greatest impediment to the implementation of his proposed new policy regime. In the often-cited exit lines of the book, Keynes argued that, in the long run, ideas are more powerful that class interests.

> [The] ideas of economists and political philosophers, both when they are right and when they are wrong, are more powerful than is commonly understood. Indeed, the world is ruled by little else. Practical men, who believe themselves to be quite exempt from any intellectual influences, are usually the slaves of some defunct economist. Madmen in authority, who hear voices in the air, are distilling their frenzy from some academic scribbler of a few years back. I am sure the power of vested interests is vastly exaggerated compared with the gradual encroachment of ideas ... But, soon or late, it is ideas, not vested interests, which are dangerous, for good or evil.
> (CW 7, pp. 383–384)

He made a similar argument in a November 1934 radio lecture.

> The strength of the self-adjusting [classical] school depends on its having behind it almost the whole body of organized economic

thinking and doctrine of the last hundred years. This is a formidable power. It is the product of acute minds and has persuaded and convinced the great majority of the intelligent and disinterested persons who have studied it. It has vast prestige and a more far-reaching influence than is obvious. For it lies behind the education and habitual modes of thought, not only of economists, but of bankers and businessmen and civil servants and politicians or all parties.

(CW 12, p. 488)

It seems to me that *in these comments* Keynes incorrectly assumed that there is no relation between dominant ideas and material or class interests. Marx would appear to be far more persuasive on this issue. He too believed that ideas could be a powerful political force, but he also argued that there was an important, though not a mechanistic, relation between dominant ideas and class interests in every stable historical era. In *The German Ideology*, he wrote:

The ideas of the ruling class are in every epoch the ruling ideas, i.e. the class which is the ruling material force of society, is at the same time its ruling intellectual force. The class which has the means of material production at its disposal, has control at the same time over the means of mental production, so that thereby, generally speaking, the ideas of those who lack the means of mental production are subject to it. The ruling ideas are nothing more than the ideal expression of the dominant material relationships, the dominant material relationships grasped as ideas.

(Marx 1932, p. 64)

But Keynes's position here is also at odds with arguments he made elsewhere in *The General Theory*. We repeat his comments so the reader can compare them with the previous quotations. Individualism and laissez-faire "could not ... have secured their lasting hold over the conduct of public affairs, if it had not been for their conformity with the needs and wishes of the business world of the day" (CW 7, p. 286). In chapter 3 of *The General Theory*, in explaining how Ricardian economics "conquered England as completely as the Holy Inquisition conquered Spain," Keynes wrote that the fact that it "afforded a measure of justification to the free activities of the individual capitalist, attracted to it the support of the dominant social force behind authority" (CW 7, pp. 32–33). This would appear to be compatible with Marx's answer to the question of whether ideas or class interests are more influential in the determination of the economic role of the state in capitalism.

The consistency and clarity with which Keynes presented and defended his radical, pro-democratic socialist theory and policies in *The General Theory* once again raises a question I posed earlier. How is it possible that one of the most important and influential books in the history of economic thought, written by one of the most important and influential economists who ever lived, came to be so profoundly misunderstood by the economics profession?

## Notes

1 "During the downward phase, when both fixed capital and stocks of material are for the time being redundant ... the schedule of the marginal efficiency of capital may be so low that it can scarcely be corrected, so as to secure a satisfactory rate of new investment, by any practicable reduction in the rate of interest" (CW 7, p. 319–320).
2 See also page 164, where Keynes said that fluctuations in the market estimation of the mec "will be too great to be offset by any practicable changes in the rate of interest."
3 BIF (Liberal Industrial Inquiry 1928) contained an extensive catalog of important large-scale capital investment projects.
4 Note that Keynes foresees the euthanasia of the "functionless" investor and not of everyone who works in financial services. Some financial "entrepreneurs" provide "intelligence and determination and executive skill," but their services "could be obtained much cheaper than at present" (CW 7, p. 376–377).

# Part III
# State planning, public investment, and Liberal Socialism after *The General Theory*

# 21 From *The General Theory* until Britain entered WWII: 1936–1939

By 1936, the political situation in Europe had deteriorated badly. Hitler had occupied the Rhineland and the Spanish Civil War had broken out. The British economic upturn of the mid-1930s slowed, coming almost to a halt in 1936–1937. Average real working class income declined between 1934 and 1937, though the rate of unemployment continued to fall (Aldcroft 1986, p. 33). However, in 1936, Britain announced a large five-year defense buildup, which was bound to have a significant impact on output and employment.[1] Indeed, by April 1939, Keynes would declare that, due to war spending, "the problem of abnormal unemployment will cease to exist during the financial year 1939–40," and that "Government priorities, an acute shortage of skilled labour, trade union restrictions, the task of shifting workers to the districts where demand is greatest, the curtailment of unessential services – all the problems of the last War – are round the corner" (CW 21, pp. 509, 511). Thus, all of Keynes's statements after 1936 must be interpreted in light of his understanding of the likely economic effects of this huge military buildup.

In January 1937, Keynes published a series of articles in *The Times* on controlling the business cycle. Keynes acknowledged that the extreme instability of private investment, emphasized in *The General Theory*, might make adequate control of the business cycle challenging, even if given a relatively smooth path of public investment. He argued that acceleration or deceleration of public investment could be used as a countercyclical tool to balance fluctuations in private investment. He stressed that under no circumstances should monetary policy be used to raise interest rates to slow an overheated boom, an argument also found in chapter 22 of *The General Theory*.

> We must avoid it, therefore, as we would hell-fire ... For if we allow the rate of interest to be affected, we can not easily reverse the trend. A low enough long-term rate of interest cannot be achieved if we allow it to be believed that better terms will be obtainable from time to time by those who keep their resources liquid. The long-term rate of interest must be kept *continuously* as near as possible to what we

believe to be the long-term optimum. It is not suitable as a short-period weapon.

(CW 21, p. 389, emphasis in original)[2]

Rather, to slow an overexuberant boom, the authorities might temporarily raise taxes (an approach he would later reject), let in a greater volume of imports, and postpone the starting date of suitable public investment projects. Keynes also argued that the chief task at the moment is not to "avoid the perils of a somewhat hypothetical boom," but to ensure that the current moderate upturn does not fall back into a slump at some point in time. And he reiterated a theme from *The General Theory*: after investment has contributed all it can to growth, the state should use its powers of taxation to progressively redistribute income and, in so doing, raise the propensity to consume.

The concluding section of the articles ("Planning Investment") is most interesting. Keynes stressed yet again the importance of creating an institutional structure that can support the new role of investment planning.

> The capital requirements of home industry and manufacture cannot possibly absorb more than a fraction of what this country, with its present social structure and distribution of wealth, chooses to save in years of general prosperity; while the amount of our net foreign investment is limited by our exports and our trade balance. *Building and public transport and public utilities lie half-way between private and public control.*[3] They need, therefore, the combined stimulus of public policy and a low rate of interest. But a wise public policy to promote investment needs, as I have said, long preparation. *Now is the time to appoint a board of public investment to prepare sound schemes against the time that they are needed.* If we wait until the crisis is upon us we shall, of course, be too late. We ought to set up immediately an authority whose business it is not to launch anything at present, but to make sure that detailed plans are prepared. The railway companies, the port and river authorities, the water, gas, and electricity undertakings, above all, perhaps, the London County Council and the other great Corporations with congested population, should be asked to investigate what projects could be usefully undertaken if capital were available at certain rates of interest – 3.5 per cent, 3 per cent, 2.5 per cent, 2 per cent. The question of the general advisability of the schemes and their order of preference should be examined next. What is required at once are acts of imagination by our administrators, engineers, and architects, to be followed by financial criticism, sifting, and more detailed designing; so that some large and useful projects, at least, can be launched at a few months' notice ...
>
> In special cases subsidies may be justified, *but in general it is the long-term rate of interest which should come down to the figure which the*

*marginal project can earn ... If we know what rate of interest is required to make profitable a flow of new projects at the proper pace, we have the power to make that rate prevail [assuming strict capital controls].* A low rate of interest can only be harmful and liable to cause an inflation if it so low as to stimulate a flow of new projects more than enough to absorb our available resources ... Is there the slightest chance of a constructive or a forethoughtful policy in contemporary England? Is it conceivable that the Government should do anything in time? Why shouldn't they?

(CW 21, pp. 394–395, emphasis added)

Keynes lays out here a sophisticated view of macro planning. It presumes capital controls and managed trade. It proposes that public investment – not monetary policy – be used to moderate the instability inherent in the capitalist investment process. For the long term, it envisions a national investment board of technical and financial experts who will initiate investment projects as well as facilitate their initiation by others, creating a prioritized portfolio of projects available for implementation so as to set an optimum average level of national income. The potential scope of such projects is vast. The Treasury and the Bank of England should set interest rates with the sole objective of facilitating the board's efforts to match investment with full-employment savings. Unusually low long-term interest rates may be required because the high-investment policy will generate a declining mec, but they will be possible to achieve because of capital controls and the prohibition against raising short-term rates to control the cycle. The board will subsidize projects if and when this is necessary to fulfill the plan, but, in general, it is expected that there will be no deficit in the capital budget of the state.

In March 1937, Keynes evaluated the likely economic impact of the government's plan to borrow £80 million a year to finance a military buildup. His comments stress the need for an improved set of institutions to facilitate state economic planning. He estimates that this spending increase might raise national income by perhaps 4.5 percent at a time when the insured unemployment rate was "as high as 12.5 per cent." He did not think this spending would cause inflation provided, consistent with his general support for industrial policy, that "measures to ensure that all possible orders are placed in the Special Areas [of high unemployment] where surplus resources are available" are taken (CW 21, p. 407). However, for the short term, there might be "some congestion" because capital spending was still on the rise. Therefore:

It is essential to set up at the centre an organisation which has the duty to think about these things, to collect information and to advise as to policy. Such a suggestion is, I know, unpopular. There is nothing a Government hates more than to be well-informed; for it makes the process of arriving at decisions much more complicated and difficult. But, at this juncture, it is a sacrifice which in the public interest they ought to make. It is easy to employ 80 to 90 per cent of the national resources without taking much thought as to how to fit things in. For there is a margin to play with, almost all round. But to employ 95 to 100 per cent of the national resources is a different task altogether. It cannot be done without care and management.

(CW 21, p. 409)

*In May 1937, Keynes suffered a severe heart attack* that slowed down his work pace considerably in subsequent months and affected him on and off for the rest of his life (see Skidelsky, 2002, for the details). But, as we shall see, Keynes's slowed pace was still faster than almost anyone else on the planet.

By early 1938, the USA had sunk back into severe recession, largely as the result of more restrictive fiscal policy, and the British recovery had faltered. Keynes wrote a personal letter to President Roosevelt imploring him to undertake a more aggressive policy of public investment to restart the US economy and, in the process, help other nations with their own recoveries. The problem in the USA, according to Keynes, was that the policy required to restore prosperity – a persistent large-scale increase in public investment – had never before been implemented. The banking system had been repaired and credit was now cheap, but, as he stressed in *The General Theory*, this is a necessary but not sufficient condition for recovery. "An increased [credit] supply will not by itself generate an adequate demand [for capital goods]" (CW 21, p. 435).

Note in the quote to follow Keynes's habitually pragmatic approach to the question of nationalization. The traditional view that Keynes was ideologically opposed to the nationalization of industry is not true. His clear preference here is for public ownership of the American public utility and railroad industries. Note as well his message to Roosevelt: either nationalize these industries so that you can directly raise their levels of investment or stop subjecting them to legal hassles and the threat of nationalization, both of which almost guarantee low rates of capital investment. Finally, Keynes stressed his approval of the New Deal's support of labor unions and of minimum wages and hours legislation; *he consistently supported legislation designed to protect and empower unions*. He focused as always on the centrality of public and semi-public investment – in housing, utilities, and transport. His preferred policies for the USA are consistent with the ones he had designed for Britain.

> Now one had hoped that the needed ... factors would be organised in time. It was obvious what these were – namely increased investment in durable goods such as housing, public utilities and transport ... Can your Administration escape criticism for the failure of these

factors to mature? ... Housing is by far the best aid to recovery ... In this country we partly depended for years on direct subsidies. There are few more proper objects for such than working-class houses. If a direct subsidy is required to get a move on, ... it should be given without delay or hesitation ... Next utilities ... Is it not for you to decide either to make real peace [with the privately-owned utilities] or to be much more drastic the other way? Personally, I think there is a great deal to be said for the ownership of all utilities by publicly owned boards. But if opinion is not yet ripe for this, what is the object of chasing the utilities round the lot every other week? If I was in your place, I should buy out the utilities at fair prices ... But elsewhere I would make peace on liberal terms, guaranteeing fair earnings on new investments and a fair basis of evaluation in the event of the public taking them over ... Finally, the railroads ... Whether hereafter they are publicly owned or remain in private hands, it is a matter of national importance that they be made solvent. *Nationalise them if the time is ripe.* If not, take pity on the overwhelming problems of current managements ... I am afraid I am going beyond my province. But the upshot is this. A convincing policy, whatever its details may be, for promoting large-scale investment under the above heads is an urgent necessity. Those things take time. Far too much precious time has passed ... Forgive the candor of these remarks. They come from an enthusiastic well-wisher of you and your policies. *I accept the view that durable investment must come increasingly under state direction ... I regard the growth of collective bargaining as essential. I approve minimum wage and hours regulation.* But I am terrified lest progressive causes in all the democratic countries should suffer injury, because you have taken too lightly the risk to their prestige which would result from a failure measured in terms of immediate prosperity.

(CW 21, pp. 436–438, emphasis added)

He repeated the core of this message in his response to Roosevelt's reply.

[F]urther experience since I wrote you seems to show that you are treading a very dangerous middle path. You must either give more encouragement to business or take over more of their functions yourself. If public opinion is not ready for the latter, then it is necessary to wait until public opinion is educated. Your present policies seem to presume that you possess more power than you actually have.

(CW 21, p. 440)

At about the same time, in an address to life insurance executives, Keynes stressed that effective government planning was not a threat to economic and political "freedom," but rather the only way to preserve it. As he argued in the final chapter of *The General Theory*, the effective choices facing the UK were depression, war, and totalitarianism or democratic socialism with state economic planning.

> For the difficulty of avoiding disastrous depression in the modern world can scarcely be exaggerated ... A great deal is at stake. We are engaged in defending the freedom of economic life in circumstances which are far from favourable. We have to show that a free system can be made to work. To favour what is known as planning and management does not mean a falling away from the principles of liberty which could formerly be embodied in a simpler system. On the contrary, we have learnt that freedom of economic life is more bound up that we previously knew with deeper freedoms – freedom of person, of thought, and of faith.
>
> (CW 21, p. 446)[4]

In September 1938, Keynes wrote an article reviewing a report evaluating technical change and the rapid rise in labor productivity over the past ten years. He was quite impressed with the data, but worried that the maldistribution of productivity growth across industries contributed to structural unemployment. He also concluded that there was a greater margin for growth in the economy than was generally assumed, even with the rise in military spending. And he worried again about whether Britain could hope to successfully compete with the planned German economy unless she adopted her own democratic variant of planning.

> This helps to explain what may otherwise perplex us in the German economy. If British industry could be fully occupied at modern standards of efficiency, the additional output beyond what was sufficing for our needs a few years ago would be enough to provide a prodigious volume of resources available for purposes of peace – or defence ... We are still allowing a great volume of potential wealth to evaporate ... How can we hope to keep pace with a form of government [in Germany] which has devised a means of producing and maintaining full employment? This is the critical task before us, if we are to maintain the supremacy of our own notions of what civilization should mean.
>
> (CW 21, pp. 481–482)

In a supplementary note to this piece, Keynes argued that the combination of rapidly rising labor productivity and sluggish final demand was creating a situation in which the depreciation reserves of industry were more than enough to finance their new investment needs. In *The General Theory*, he had warned about the disastrous consequences of this condition for long-term growth. Under these conditions:

it becomes increasingly improbable that anything approaching full employment can be maintained without normal loan expenditure by the Government on one ticket or another. At any rate, it is certain that in the last quarter century such a state of affairs has never existed, apart from very brief periods in abnormal conditions, in any industrial country in the world, except perhaps in the United States in 1928. The problem thus presented is the outstanding problem of today, and cannot be solved by turning a blind eye to it.

(CW 21, p. 483)

Its solution, he adds, will require managed trade – the creation of "new and necessary machinery for linking up exports with imports, so as to make sure that those from whom we buy spend a reasonable proportion of the proceeds in corresponding purchases from us" (CW 21, p. 483).

In terms of the evolution of Keynes's thinking about policy and planning, early 1939 marks the end of an era. From here on, war spending and the war itself will substantially alter the economic and political context within which Keynes must struggle. In April 1939, he wrote:

The Chancellor of the Exchequer should frame his Budget on the assumption that the problem of abnormal unemployment will cease to exist during the financial year 1939–40, and that all plans and special provisions for dealing with this problem should be dropped forthwith as being a waste of time and money.

(CW 21, p. 509)

Keynes estimated that loan expenditure for the coming year would be on the order of £200 million greater than the previous year. With a multiplier of about two, this would raise national income by 8 percent and increase employment by well over 1 million. And there were immediate plans to add 200,000 young men to the military (CW 21, p. 532).

Government priorities, an acute shortage of skilled labour, trade union restrictions, the task of shifting workers to the districts where demand is greatest, the curtailment of unessential services – all the problems of the last War – are round the corner.

(CW 21, p. 511)[5]

But the restoration of full (and even overfull) employment due to war did not change his belief that the era of laissez-faire ended with WWI and that Britain would have to move, once the current war crisis ended, to an entirely new economic role for the state as the fulcrum of a democratically planned economy.

The war effort and postwar economic planning would now occupy all of Keynes's work time. He was largely responsible for creating Britain's system of war finance, for preparing Britain's proposals for a new postwar international system and defending them against increasingly devastating attacks by the bullying Americans, and for negotiating with the Americans over the terms of the reconstruction loan – a Herculean undertaking for anyone, much less someone with a serious heart condition. *At the same time, he was also the person most responsible for planning Britain's postwar economy.* He did so in a way that was completely consistent with the trajectory of his thinking through the 1920s and 1930s. As the war unfolded, he became increasingly convinced that postwar state planning for full employment as well as a more comprehensive social welfare system in Britain were inevitable; political reality would demand it. The relevant questions for Keynes, then, became not whether state planning would be created, but what its form and content should be and how to get the state to adopt his preferred policies.

The inevitability of postwar full-employment planning, which the war period cemented in his mind, seemed clear to Keynes before the war effort was even underway. He believed it would be politically impossible for any party to try to take Britain back to its nineteenth-century economic model.

> [T]he grand experiment has begun. If it works, if expenditure on armaments really does cure unemployment, I predict that we shall never go all the way to the old state of affairs. If we can cure unemployment for the wasted purposes of armaments, we can cure it for the productive purposes of peace. Good may come out of evil. We may learn a trick or two which will come in useful when the day of peace comes, as in the fullness of time it must.
>
> (CW 21, p. 532)

He continued in this vein.

> The armament programme will bring abnormal unemployment to an end. Some day, and the sooner the better, we hope to stop the existing abomination and return to the ways of peace. Is that to mean a return to abnormal unemployment? It will go hard with the fabric of society if it does. To avoid this outcome, it will be necessary for productive investment, public and private, out of borrowed money to continue at a rate at least as high as this year's programme.
>
> (CW 21, p. 546)

This theme is also reflected in his correspondence with his sister Margaret in June 1939. She was on a Royal Commission studying the feasibility of a public board responsible for the location of industry. Keynes reminded her that he had not written anything recently on the subject of a National Investment Board, that his "first proposals on this were not published in my own name," but included in the report of the Liberal

Industrial Enquiry (1928), and that he had "got something similar somewhere into the report of the Macmillan Committee" (CW 21, p. 590). He then suggested that at war's end, whichever party was in power would be likely to create some form of National Investment Board.

> My own feeling is that, when we are ready for reforms again, opinion will be found to have hardened a good deal in this direction. *Any government except an ultra-Conservative one might be expected to make a beginning towards introducing it.* I am interested that you are meeting with the argument that it is not possible to find work of a useful and public character to employ any very large number of men. This used to be the argument of Neville Chamberlain and the Government in the last slump. But most people, I had thought, had quite given it up. It is a wholly untenable position. It is some time since anyone had the face to use it in public ... Anyhow, *I should say that practically all reforming minds are in favour of making some move in the direction of the establishment of a National Investment Board* ... If a National Investment Board were to be set up, it would be most advisable that it should work in close collaboration with a Board for the location of industry. But the functions of the former body would go ... very far beyond those of the latter.
> 
> (CW 21, pp. 590–591, emphasis added)

In January 1939, *The New Statesman* published an important "conversation" between Keynes and the editor Kingsley Martin. The topic was "Democracy and Efficiency." The main points stressed by Keynes were the urgent need for ambitious central planning in the new era and the compatibility of such planning with democracy and liberal values. He again called his preferred new system "Liberal Socialism."

Martin opens with this statement: "You have held that private capitalism is an out-of-date institution incapable of meeting the requirements of the twentieth century." Keynes responds: "I agree entirely" (CW 21, p. 492). He continued:

> In contemporary conditions we need, if we are to enjoy prosperity and profits, so much more central planning than we have at present that the reform of the economic system needs as much urgent attention if we have war as if we avoid it. The intensification of the trade cycle and the *increasingly chronic character of unemployment* have shown that *private capitalism was already in its decline as a means of solving the economic problem.* But the breakdown of international good faith and the constant threats to peace are making it still more obvious that, *quite apart from war, we have to move a long distance along that very road which actual war would make it imperative for us to take* ... But it is not the threat which the necessary [planning] measures might offer to personal liberty and

democratic institutions which stands in the way of what wants doing to make us prosperous within and safe without. Any such threat is so remote from the first and the next and the next things that want doing, that it is not now, and is a long way from being, a practical issue.

(CW 21, p. 492, emphasis added)[6]

Since Keynes was quite familiar with the extreme degree of planning that war entails from his experience in government during WWI, his view that we had to go "a long way along that very road" even if war did not occur is quite telling.

Martin then asks: what is preventing the country from satisfying the "desperately obvious" need for planning? Keynes responds that, first, the public is lukewarm "towards the particular amalgam of private capitalism and state socialism which is the only practicable recipe for present conditions" (CW 21, p. 492). Second, the needed reforms are "not in tune with the inherited slogans" of any of the major political parties.

Keynes next stresses the importance of maintaining a significant role for private property and private enterprise in a new system of planning because of their "profound connection" to personal and political liberty. But he immediately adds the caveat that he does not defend the "fact that the lawyers of the eighteenth century perniciously twisted this into the sanctity of vested interests and large fortunes" Martin agrees.

> I know of no more extraordinary confusion than that which identifies the right to own the fruits of one's own labour in pre-industrial society with the right of Mr Rockefeller or the Duke of Westminster to own the labour and control the conditions of life of thousands of other people. Surely the monopoly ownership of our day is one of the great enemies of liberty. But I agree that the right of personal property is inseparable from the conception of liberty, and that this confusion between personal property, which no intelligent Socialist has ever wished to take away from anyone, and property in the sense of the right to play the money market, and employ, sack or pay what wages one likes, has had very serious results.
>
> (CW 21, pp. 493–494)

Keynes then takes up the question of the lack of sympathy for his views in the parties. The problem is not that there are no sympathizers within each party; there are in fact many liberals (with a lower-case "l") in all three. But their views lack "organised expression." "There is no one in politics today worth sixpence outside the ranks of liberals except the post-war generation of intellectual Communists under thirty five. Them, too, I like and respect" (CW 21, pp. 494–495).[7]

Martin suggests that the political situation is hopeless unless liberals and "amateur" Communists can work together, which is why he finds the anti-communism of the Labour Party so disturbing: "they seem intent rather on fighting their own left than on providing an alternative to the capitalist governments they are supposed to be opposing" (CW 21, p. 496). Keynes agrees.

> Yes; the attitude of the official Labour Party towards all this strikes me as one of the silliest things in the history of British politics ... I sympathise with Mr Bevin in fighting shy of contact with the professional Communists, regarding their body as a Trojan horse and their overtures in doubtful faith. But I should risk contact all the same, so as not to lose touch with the splendid material of the young amateur Communists. For with them in their ultimate maturity lies the future.
> (CW 21, pp. 495–496)[8]

Keynes then moves on to another major obstacle to the radical changes needed in the economic role of government – the Civil Service. This is extremely important to Keynes because of his belief that the details of planning must be conducted primarily by "expert" civil servants, not politicians.

> [T]he present heads of our Civil Service were brought up in, and for their part still adhere to, the *laissez-faire* tradition. For constructive planning the civil servants are, of course, much more important than Ministers; little that is worth doing can be done without their assistance and good will. There has been nothing finer in its way than our nineteenth-century school of Treasury officials. Nothing better has ever been devised, if our object is to limit the functions of government to the least possible and to make sure that expenditure, whether on social or economic or military or general administrative purposes, is the smallest and most economical that public opinion will put up with. But if that is not our object, then nothing can be worse. The Civil Service is ruled today by the Treasury school, trained by tradition and experience and native skill to every form of intelligent obstruction. And there is another reason for the heads of the services being what they are. We have experienced in the ... years since the War two occasions of terrific retrenchment and axing of constructive themes. This has ... inevitably led to the survival and promotion of those to whom negative measures are natural and sympathetic ... I am afraid that they are becoming a heavy handicap in our struggle with the totalitarian states and in making us safe from them.
> (CW 21, pp. 496–497)

Finally, Martin observes that totalitarian states have been able to use central planning to fully utilize their national economic capacity, but unfortunately this success is directed toward war and "has wiped out liberty, decency and indeed almost everything that makes life worth living." As a result, "we in Britain are doomed unless we can make the essential changes quickly and without these unnecessary and appalling sacrifices" (CW 21, pp. 499–500). "Yes. That is the truth," Keynes replies. But he adds that there is no need to be concerned about such losses in Britain, at least not for a long time to come. "I say that we are so far from such a situation that the risk does not now exist" (CW 21, p. 500). He concludes his remarks with a call for *"liberal socialism"* in Britain.

> The question is whether we are prepared to move out of the nineteenth-century laissez-faire state into an era of *liberal socialism*, by which I mean a system where we can act as an organised community for common purposes and to promote economic and social justice, whilst respecting and protecting the individual – his freedom of choice, his faith, his mind and its expression, his enterprise and his property.
> 
> (CW 21, p. 500, emphasis added)

## Notes

1 In February 1937, the Government announced it would borrow £500 million over five years for military purposes.
2 See also CW 21 (pp. 549, 565).
3 Keynes frequently referred to the importance of "semi-public" investment projects. Here, he refers to investment in buildings (both residential and non-residential), public transport, and public utilities as examples of semi-public investment. Some of this is semi-public because it is under the control of public corporations.
4 In an article in *The Economic Journal* in September 1938 (calling for state control of the storage of important commodities in order to minimize the fluctuations in their prices and supplies), Keynes observed, not for the last time, that the state will spend its way to full employment in war but not in peace. "If only we could tackle the problems of peace with the same energy and whole-heartedness as we tackle those of war! Defence is old – established as a proper object for the state, whereas economic well-being is still a *parvenu* ... Nevertheless, we are at this moment allowing war expenditure for defence to help solve our problem of unemployment as a by-product of such spending, whereas if disarmament had prevailed we might have allowed a serious recession to have developed by now before introducing loan expenditure on a comparable scale for the productive works of peace" (CW 21, p. 463).
5 Still, in June 1939, Keynes believed that "there is room for a very substantial increase of the national income, say, by something between 5 and 10 per cent" (CW 21, p. 548).
6 Keynes's reference to "the increasingly chronic character of unemployment" implies that he continued to be concerned about secular stagnation even as the war buildup was underway.

7 He continued: "Perhaps in their feelings and instincts they are the nearest thing we now have to the typical nervous nonconformist English gentlemen who went to the Crusades, made the Reformation, fought the Great Rebellion, won us our civil and religious liberties and humanised the working classes last century" (CW 21, p. 495).
8 See Durbin (1985) for a detailed discussion of the relation between Keynes and important elements of the Labour Party and "young amateur Communists," who he strongly influenced in this period.

# 22 Keynes and government postwar economic planning for "Liberal Socialism" during the war: 1939–1945

Britain entered WWII on September 3, 1939. Though Keynes had no important title in Britain's wartime economic administration, he was by far the most influential individual in the country in the determination of: its wartime domestic and international financial policy; its strategy and tactics in the long-drawn-out and ultimately failed negotiations with the USA over the postwar international financial system[1]; its economic planning for the war; and, more importantly for my purposes in this book, its postwar economic planning.

There are two main objectives in this chapter. The first is to demonstrate that in all his work on postwar economic planning in this period he continued to argue in favor of the same socialist transformation of Britain's political economy he had supported since the mid-1920s. I will show that neither his theory of capitalism nor his radical policy positions were meant to apply only to the conditions of the Great Depression, to be discarded when the economy recovered. The second objective is to demonstrate that during the war Keynes became the most powerful figure in the government's internal debate about postwar economic planning and used his influence with considerable success to move the government toward his radical views. It is one thing for an economist to create a theory critical of capitalism and use this theory to support policy proposals designed to generate radical change. Many economists have done that. It is quite another thing to actually convince government policy-makers at the highest level to support much of the radical change proposed.

We will comment only in passing about Keynes's important work on financing the war and his central role in the negotiations between Britain and America in the construction of the postwar international financial system.

For the first two years of the war, Keynes spent most of his time working out an efficient and fair system to pay for the war. His short book explaining his plans to the public – *How to Pay for the War* – was published in February 1940.

Keynes put the social functions of the [1941] budget centre stage ... The purpose of the wartime budget was not to divert resources to the government – that would have happened anyway – but to do so with justice and efficiency. "The importance of a war budget," Keynes wrote, "is social; to prevent the social evils of inflation now and later [and] to do this in a way which satisfies the popular sense of social justice."

(Skidelsky 2002, p. 89)

In October 1941, the government set up an interdepartmental Committee on Post-War Internal Economic Problems, which included the Treasury and the Economic Section of the War Cabinet, charged with identifying prospective major economic problems of the postwar era, analyzing them, and recommending solutions to the appropriate ministers. According to Skidelsky, Keynes eventually became the most influential member of this crucial Committee involved in the debates on postwar economic planning.

The emergence of an economic secretariat at the heart of government happened by necessity rather than design. The planning system needed technicians not administrators. Following the change in government in 1940, the Central Economic Information Service ... was greatly enlarged to serve the new super committees; in January 1941 it was split into an Economic Section and a Central Statistical Office, both based in the War Cabinet Offices, the former under the direct control of the Lord President of the Council ... [T]he Economic Section had between nine and twelve economists, the Central Statistical Office another seven or eight. Together they formed the statistical "brain" of the centrally planned war economy ... Keynes called it "the nucleus of that economic general staff which we have long talked about."[2] ... Once the planning system was set up and running, members of the Economic Section like James Meade were left free to think about post-war problems.

Keynes served as the main bridge between the Treasury and the economists recruited into the Economic Section, the Central Statistical Office and the Ministries. These were his professional colleagues, many of them former students for whom he was the natural leader and ally. Keynes himself was suggested as first head of the CSO, in December 1940, but refused, preferring to remain footloose in the Treasury. The Economic Section was immediately seen as a dangerous rival by the Treasury, which tried to curtail its scope and functions. Keynes played an important role in arranging a *modus vivendi*, and he and Lionel Robbins, director of the Economic Section from September 1941 to November 1945, "worked together in great harmony," despite their pre-war quarrels. Keynes was happy with these fluid arrangements.

(Skidelsky 2002, pp. 139–140)

In April 1942, Keynes gave a radio address as part of a BBC series on postwar planning that reflected his general state of mind on the economics and politics of this issue. Though the address was supposed to focus on the financial aspects of planning, most of the talk was devoted to general issues related to state planning after the war.

Keynes first comments on the critical difference in public expectations about the retention of the wartime economic controls into the postwar era between the First and Second World Wars.

> In 1919 public opinion and political opinion were determined to get back to 1914 by scrapping at the first possible moment many of the controls which were making the technical task [of war planning] easier. I do not notice today the same enthusiasm to get back to 1939. I hope and believe that this time public opinion will give the technicians a fair chance by letting them retain so long as they think necessary many of the controls over the financial machinery which we are finding useful, and indeed, essential.
> (CW 27, p. 266)

For Keynes, the first priority was to meet the minimum daily needs of the country and to rebuild the export industry. Reconstruction through public investment required production/income beyond these two necessities. A major theme is that the potential for reconstruction and renewal through planning is enormous, though care must be taken to avoid haste and inefficiency.

> To make sure of good employment we must have ready an ample programme of re-stocking and of development over a wide field, industrial, engineering, transport and agriculture – not merely building. Having prepared our blue-prints, covering the whole field of our requirements and not building alone – and these can be as ambitious and glorious as the minds of our engineers and architects and social planners can conceive – those in charge must then concentrate on the vital task of central management, the *pace* at which the programme is put into operation, neither so slow as to cause unemployment nor so rapid as to cause inflation ... It is extremely difficult to predict accurately in advance the scale and pace on which [building and construction plans] can be carried out. In the long run almost anything is possible. Therefore do not be afraid of large and bold schemes. Let our plans be big, significant, but not hasty.
> (CW 27, p. 268, emphasis in original)[3]

The key to an efficient economic plan is consistency: for example, the building industry cannot be made to grow or shrink in a short period of time. It is therefore essential that there be a believable commitment to a long-term plan. The firm expectation of sustained full employment is crucial to the success of all parts of the plan. "For if the building industry is to expand in an orderly fashion, it must have some assurance of continuing employment for the larger labour force" (CW 27, p. 268).

Keynes then makes some crude guesses about the likely initial level of construction spending in the immediate postwar period.

> Now these are very large sums. Continued, year by year, over a period of ten years or more, they are enormous. We could double in twenty years all the buildings there are now in the whole country. We can do almost anything we like, *given time*. We must not force the pace – that is necessary warning. In good time we can do it all. But we must work to a long-term programme.
> (CW 27, p. 269, emphasis in original)

This statement helps explain why Keynes argued in several places in *The General Theory* that under state control of most large-scale capital accumulation the capital stock could be increased to such a degree in one or two generations that capital would cease to be scarce and the profit rate could be driven to zero. He foresaw a great expansion of the nation's capital stock – for example, doubling the number of buildings in the country – under the guidance of a powerful Board of National Investment as a practical and politically achievable goal.

It was not just the provision of the basic necessities of daily life that could be achieved through successful planning. Properly designed and implemented, state planning can enormously enrich social, cultural, and public life *in Britain* as well. Indeed, it can be used to create a "New Jerusalem" in Britain. This is quite important to Keynes.

> I should like to see that the war memorials of this tragic struggle take the shape of an enrichment of the civic life of every great centre of population. Why should we not set aside, let us say, £50 million a year for the next twenty years to add in every substantial city of the realm the dignity of an ancient university or a European capital to our local schools and their surroundings, to our local government and its offices, and above all perhaps, to provide a local centre of refreshment and entertainment with an ample theatre, a concert hall, a dance hall, a gallery, a British restaurant, canteens, cafes and so forth. Assuredly we can afford this and much more. Anything we can actually *do* we can afford. Once done, it is *there*. Nothing can take it from us ... Yet these must be only the trimmings on the more solid, urgent and necessary outgoings on housing the people, on reconstructing industry and transport and on re-planning the environment of our daily life. Not only shall we come to possess these excellent things. With a big programme carried out at a regulated pace we can hope to keep

employment good for many years to come. We shall, in fact, have built our New Jerusalem out of the labour which in our former vain folly we were keeping unused and unhappy in enforced idleness.

(CW 27, p. 270, emphasis in original)

Keynes's memoranda and letters about postwar economic planning through 1943 are of the greatest possible significance to anyone interested in the policy views of the mature Keynes. By 1944, his attention would be focused almost exclusively on British–American negotiations over the shape of the postwar international financial system and the size and character of the American loan. Thus, it is primarily to the 1943 writings – especially those related to the government's evolving "White Paper on [Postwar] Employment Policy" – we must turn in order to understand Keynes's role in postwar economic planning.

One of the key roles played by Keynes in these discussions was to serve as a counterweight to the pessimism of some of the representatives of the Treasury on the Committee on Post-War Internal Economic Problems about the economic prospects of postwar Britain, including his old friend and current enemy Hubert Henderson, who wrote a pessimistic memorandum on the subject.[4] The Treasury foresaw a few years of inflationary boom after the war ended followed by a downturn and sluggish growth – just as was the case after WWI – as well as a slow rate of technical progress. All of Keynes's interventions assumed fairly rapid technical progress and an average rate of unemployment after the war of between 3 and 5 percent as the result of effective planning. "I do not at all share the pessimism" in Henderson's memo, Keynes asserted. "I think the memorandum greatly under-estimates the consequences of full employment and of the improvement in technical production, which will not cease to take place but will in some directions have been even accelerated during the war period" (CW 27, p. 272). This debate affected all others; it obviously made an enormous difference to the potential generosity of social welfare policy; for example, whether the economy would be in a slump or running at full capacity after the war.[5] The paper coauthored by Keynes and Richard Stone[6] titled "National Income and Expenditure After the War" (CW 27, pp. 280–298) formed the centerpiece of the debate.

One of the strongest of Keynes's arguments in support of his working assumption of an unemployment rate of 5 percent or less was his continued insistence that *the postwar public would not politically tolerate anything higher.* He believed that the high unemployment rates of the interwar years would no longer be politically feasible after the war once the public had experienced the effectiveness of wartime planning and had irrefutable evidence that the state could maintain full employment through planning if it had the will to do so. Put somewhat differently, the working class that had sacrificed and died for king and country in the war would not meekly accept economic stagnation and penury thereafter. He forcefully reminded the reader of this political fact of life.

> But it is quite a misunderstanding to suppose that the 5 per cent [figure I have been assuming] is a prophesy of what will happen if nothing is done and pre-war methods, generally speaking, are continued. Mr Stone and I chose as our basic assumption [5 percent unemployment] chiefly on the ground that it seemed to us that this was about the highest that the public would stand in post-war conditions without demanding something very drastic to be done about it, coupled with the fact that it did not seem to us impracticable to take drastic steps which would bring down the figure to this total. If one was to put in, as Sir H. Henderson suggests, a figure approaching 2 million men normally out of work after the war [or 12.5 percent unemployed], I should have expected the rejoinder that we were wasting our time in assuming a situation which could not possibly happen.
> (CW 27, p. 299)

Keynes reinforced this position in a memo.

> I consider [5 percent] rather on the pessimistic side. It certainly does not assume a continuance of the pre-war situation ... That is to say, we are assuming a reasonable government policy in the face of the actual circumstances and the change which will have taken place in public opinion in the light of war experience as to the practical possibilities of keeping unemployment at a reasonable figure ... I am afraid I am quite impenitent after having read the comments up to date about our assumptions being too optimistic. Indeed, further reflection is leading me, if anything, rather in the other direction.
> (CW 27, pp. 303–304)[7]

Some of Keynes's early 1940s comments on postwar economic policy were stimulated by a debate kicked off by the radical reorganization and expansion of Britain's social welfare system proposed by William Beveridge, a plan that eventuated in the modern British welfare state. In 1945, the Labour Party won the general election and implemented many of Beveridge's proposals, creating comprehensive unemployment compensation, national health care, and a substantial welfare system.

Keynes and Beveridge had a very lengthy exchange of letters about his plan – 61 pages of volume 27 of the CW are given over to this exchange. Keynes tried to help Beveridge get serious government consideration for his proposals by suggesting cost reductions while also arguing against the pessimistic Treasury view that postwar economic conditions would not be prosperous enough to afford some reasonable variant of the program. Keynes wrote to Beveridge in his initial letter (of March 17, 1942) that, though he had concerns about particular elements of the program and about its cost, he was "in a state of wild enthusiasm for your general scheme" (CW 27, p. 204). He also told Beveridge in October 1942 that the final draft was "a grand document" (CW 27, p. 205).

Indeed, Keynes devoted the draft of his upcoming maiden speech before the House of Lords on February 24, 1943, to his enthusiastic support of the Beveridge Report. The draft argued that the Beveridge proposals were unlikely to create substantial budgetary problems, even in the long run. Against criticism by the Treasury Department and others that postwar Britain could not afford to finance such an ambitious set of social programs given the uncertainty of economic conditions when the war ended, Keynes argued that the funds generated by the Plan would more than cover its costs, provided that the postwar economy was not allowed to fall back into depression.

> I am ... at a loss to know how it is proposed to save money from the budget by *not* having the Beveridge Plan ... It is, therefore, precisely because I am deeply concerned about the Budget position in the early years after the war that I welcome the Beveridge proposals.
> (CW 27, p. 258, emphasis in original)

The Plan was surely fiscally sound in the early decades, Keynes argued, because it would collect contributions from a large number of current workers and initially make payments to a small number of current pensioners.

Keynes's optimism about the affordability of the Plan over the longer run was largely based on his belief that substantial parts of his desired economic policies, including a high rate of growth in the capital stock under state planning, would be adopted and that technological progress would be rapid. "We could increase output in both industry and in agriculture by at least 50 per cent compared with 1938 merely by putting to work modern methods and techniques that already exist" while sustaining full employment (CW 27, p. 259). The Plan would be soundly funded even "with merely normal technical progress such as we experienced for many years" (CW 27, p. 259).

Keynes ended his draft by issuing a general call to defeat the pessimists who opposed Beveridge's comprehensive social welfare reform out of fear that it would be too expensive. The only thing that could make it too expensive would be a refusal to follow Keynes along the path to radical progressive change. It was Keynes's version of Roosevelt's famous "the only thing we have to fear is fear itself" first inaugural address.

> The future will be what we choose to make it. If we approach it with cringing and timidity, we shall get what we deserve. If we march on with confidence and vigour the facts will respond. It would be a

monstrous thing to reserve all our courage and powers of will for War and then, crowned with victory, to approach the Peace as a bunch of bankrupt defeatists ... The real problems of the future are first of all the maintenance of peace, of international co-operation and amity, and beyond that the profound moral and social problems of how to organise material abundance to yield up the fruits of a good life. These are the heroic tasks of the future. But there is nothing, my Lords, in what we are discussing today which needs frighten a mouse.

(CW 27, pp. 260–261)

However, the day before Keynes was to deliver this speech, he wrote a letter to his mother telling her that he had decided against speaking in support of the Beveridge Plan because of vigorous opposition from the government, especially from his long-time nemesis, the Treasury. On the surface, it appears to be shocking that he would undercut the Beveridge Plan for which he had such genuine enthusiasm in order to avoid offending his traditional enemies at the Treasury. We know that Keynes was normally quite comfortable speaking unpalatable truth to power.

Do not be disappointed when you see no speech from me in the papers on Thursday. Great pressure has been put on me not to speak ... They [at the Treasury] have all got themselves into a hideous mess over this [Beveridge] Report, and it has become a very sore political mess. They think, perhaps truly, that, if I make a candid statement of the position, it will not rebound to their advantage ... [and] *my general relations with the Treasury might become somewhat embarrassed.* I am not convinced by all this. I think a few honest words generally do more good than harm; all the same, I have given way and agreed not to speak ... *I value too highly my present relations with everyone in the Treasury to want to run the risk or disobliging them.*

(CW 27, p. 256, emphasis added)

I have already hinted at the explanation for this seeming inexplicable act of political cowardice. To understand it, we first need to explain why Keynes made peace with the Treasury during the war and, indeed, became surprisingly protective of its institutional interests. The reason he did this was simple: he eventually became the dominant figure in the Treasury during the war. In the immortal words of Pogo: "We have met the enemy and he is us."[8]

Keynes retained his anomalous position at the Treasury from August 1940 till he died in 1946. He was enormously influential. This influence was based on personal authority rather than official position. Officially he remained an unpaid, part-time advisor to the Chancellor of the Exchequer. He was "in the Treasury but not of it." Despite this, he "was the Treasury," according to one of his colleagues, who cited in support of this contention the "masterly war-time Budgets, the conception of Bretton Woods, and the gradual domination of overseas financial policy." ... Keynes's eye ranged over the whole field of economic policy, lighting on whatever interested him ... As often as not it was a memorandum from Keynes which clarified the intellectual and technical issues involved in some proposal, and thus nerved the Treasury's "administrators" to back it. *If Keynes chose to get fully engaged in something, his influence tended to be decisive, in the sense that policy was made with the framework of Keynes's analysis of the problem.* This was as true in big matters as in small.

(Skidelsky 2002, pp. 135–136, emphasis added)

In his narrower, and subordinate, sphere, *Keynes rivaled Churchill.* He was, in fact, the Churchill of war finance and post-war financial planning. His achievement was the more remarkable in that he held no official position ... In a Presidential (or dictatorial) system he probably would have been Minister of Finance. *In the British system he was for many purposes, de facto Chancellor of the Exchequer [or head of the Treasury].* Sometimes he was regarded as such by the Americans, and sometimes as President of the Board of Trade as well.

(Skidelsky 2002, p. xvi, emphasis added)

Schumpeter put the matter more concisely in his 1946 survey of Keynes's contributions to economic theory and policy in the *American Economic Review*. "Everyone knows that during the war he entered the Treasury again (1940) and that his influence grew, along with Churchill, until nobody thought of challenging it" (Schumpeter 1946, p. 518).

The speech in support of Beveridge was to be delivered in early 1943, just as Keynes was guiding the Treasury toward a postwar planning process whose institutions and policies would be devoted to the pursuit of his socialist agenda. This goal was far too important to him to risk undercutting it by offending those at the Treasury who were not in full support of the Beveridge Plan.

James Meade, an avid admirer of Keynes who was attached to the Economic Section of the War Cabinet Secretariat, was an extremely important contributor to the debates over postwar economic planning. Skidelsky described Meade as follows:

Meade, a future Nobel Prize winner, was the most powerful economic thinker in the [Economics] Section, as well as its main visionary. Early in the war, he was chiefly involved, with Richard Stone at the Central Statistical Office, in setting up the system of national income accounts [inspired by and based on the categories of Keynes's macro model]. Later he concentrated on post-war employment and commercial policy. Meade was a liberal socialist ... Meade worshipped Keynes without being overawed by him. Keynes greatly respected Meade's analytical powers – at meetings of officials he would sometimes call on Meade to expound "Keynesian" theory – but was skeptical of his utopianism, and, as we shall see, gave only limited support for stabilizing demand by varying national insurance contributions [he thought the main emphasis should be on managing investment] and was much less of a free trader than Meade was.

(Skidelsky 2002, p. 149)[9]

Keynes's correspondence with Meade on postwar policy and planning provides important information about Keynes's ideas on this critical issue. We begin with Meade's proposal that automatic variations in the contributions to the social insurance fund be used as part of countercyclical fiscal policy after the war. In May 1942, while focused on the Beveridge Report, Keynes wrote to Meade saying that while he found Meade's plan interesting, he thought there were rather tight limits on the extent to which one can stabilize consumption in the face of downturns caused by reductions in investment demand. "One can prevent perhaps an aggravation of the falling off of effective demand by stabilising consumption," he wrote, "but that is the best one can hope for" (CW 27, pp. 206–207). On the other hand, he wrote more optimistically about Meade's proposal to Sir Richard Hopkins, Permanent Secretary to the Treasury.

> Mr Meade will be putting forward a proposal, which I think deserves consideration, namely, that the amount of contribution from employers and employed to the Social Security Fund should vary in amount according to the state of employment, rising when unemployment falls below a critical figure and falling when it rises above it.
> 
> (CW 27, p. 278)

Since, under the Beveridge Plan, contributions for social security could be made to fluctuate between £400 million and zero per year, "there is a fairly large sum to play with, quite free from the objections to interfering with the normal tax system for such a purpose" (CW 27, p. 278).

In this memorandum, Keynes also reiterated his belief that *fluctuations in public investment should be the main tool of countercyclical policy*. He consistently took this position.

> I should aim at having a surplus on the ordinary Budget, which would be transferred to the capital Budget, thus gradually replacing dead-weight debt by productive or semi-productive debt on the lines which the Government of India have successfully pursued for many years. But this would not involve repayment of debt, since I should expect for a long time to come that the government debt

or government-guaranteed debt would be continually increasing in grand total.

It is probable that the amount of such surplus would fluctuate from year to year for the usual causes. But I should not aim at attempting to compensate for cyclical fluctuations by means of the ordinary Budget. I should leave this duty to the capital Budget.

(CW 27, pp. 277–278)

Correspondence with Meade over his proposal in September 1942 again showed restrained enthusiasm. One problem was that Meade was using a long-run assumption in a short-term argument according to Keynes, by asserting that the reduction in employers' contributions in the presumably short-term downturn would lead them either to increase jobs (due to increased profit margins) or to substantially cut prices. These are "likely not to happen at all precisely because the reduction in question is by hypothesis temporary." He suggested that Meade limit the proposal to employees' contributions, where there might be more bang per buck. Still, he agreed, it was an "important and interesting contribution to a vital problem" (CW 27, p. 311).

Keynes then wrote a memo defending the Meade proposal against its Treasury critics. The memo opens with a reference to "the great potentialities of the Meade proposals." It then notes Meade's assumption that virtually everyone now believes that the state should and will take responsibility for the maintenance of full employment through AD management at war's end.

> [Meade] was assuming that measures of increased general purchasing power as a cure for unemployment were now widely approved, both by experts and the general public, and he was considering the best technique for injecting purchasing power, assuming one wishes to do so.
>
> (CW 27, p. 311)

Keynes next discussed the merits of Meade's proposal, which suggested that social insurance contributions should drop by about 1 percent of national income for every 2 percent rise in the rate of unemployment above its target level. "The multiplier is generally taken as being, in this country, a trifle above 3," but Keynes assumes a value of 2 for purposes of analysis. Given this assumption, he argues that the mechanism might function effectively.[10] But, he warns:

> neither Meade nor anyone else has suggested that his proposal is in fact adequate *by itself* to maintain a constancy of employment. But he can argue, I think, that its quantitative effect is highly significant relative to the evil it attacks.
>
> (CW 27, p. 312, emphasis in original)

In January 1943, James Meade wrote Keynes a fascinating letter in which he tried to get Keynes to take the lead in the internal government debate over postwar employment policy in a rather public way. It was a flattering letter, with an offer that, if Keynes accepted the writer's premises, would seem awfully hard for him to refuse. It essentially asked Keynes to write the definitive government report on postwar domestic economic planning, make the report public, and call it the "Keynes Report."

> The great public support which the Beveridge Report has received has suggested to me that there ought really to be a similar publication on the subject of post-war employment. The enthusiastic public reception of the social security proposals shows that there is an exceedingly strong feeling in the country about post-war internal reconstruction and that people are in such a mood as they have never been before for the reception of imaginative ideas for social reform ... People do not realise that the Government is giving any serious attention to [the prevention of large-scale postwar unemployment] and it would be my guess that a really imaginative approach to this problem would now have such a reception as permanently to influence the course of post-war policy ... A *public* investigation and report on this topic should not be very politically controversial, but would put new heart into the public and would probably ensure once and for all that a sensible government policy in this field would in fact have to be adopted by any post-war government ... It may be that there are better methods of getting these ideas across, but it occurs to me, to be quite frank, that what we really require is a Keynes Report to follow up the Beveridge Report.
> (CW 27, pp. 314–315, emphasis added)

Keynes wrote a surprisingly brief (thirteen-line), surprisingly negative reply to this seemingly attractive proposition. Keynes was rarely bashful about taking the lead on key policy issues. His proposals on war finance, for example, were referred to as the "Keynes Plan." He said that three key differences between postwar social welfare and postwar employment policies informed his negative response. First, policy planning cannot be concretized and neatly packaged into the precise form required for legislation, and no new legislation is necessary to get the job done: "Post-war unemployment is far less a question of a really concrete plan and would involve little, if any, definite legislation" (CW 27, p. 315). Second, the operation of employment planning will depend on the nature of the new international financial institutions, the size of the US loan, and the state of British exports: "it is very much more mixed up with external policy" (CW 27, p. 315) about which no hard expectations could be formed with confidence. Third, several government bodies are already working on the problem and progress is being made:

> Above all, all sorts of aspects of it are already being worked out by different Departments and by various Hurst Committees. It seems to me impossible to have a new commission working alongside all the present activities. Moreover, it is much too soon to decide that those activities are not being quite well and fruitfully conducted.
>
> (CW 27, p. 315)

I think what Keynes meant was: first, that the most important thing was to solidify the government's ironclad commitment to sustained full employment as the cornerstone of postwar economic policy and public and semi-public investment as the main policy tool to achieve it; and second, to outline the basic structures of economic planning without yet concretizing them. It was not necessary at this point, he believed, to prepare a fully detailed, time-specific plan. It is also quite likely that Keynes did not want his work at the Treasury on economic planning, which he believed was going extremely well at this point in time, to be disrupted by an announcement that there was a new grand "Keynes Plan" for employment planning in the works.

Work on postwar employment planning moved ahead. James Meade contributed a paper on the maintenance of full employment to the interdepartmental Committee on Reconstruction Priorities that would become the focus of debate and conflict about postwar economic policy. For that reason, we explore Keynes's role in this debate at some length.

Meade wrote Keynes a letter in April 1943 expressing concern with Keynes's insistence that the budget be divided into a current and a capital budget, with the former kept strictly in balance. Meade's paper supported Keynes's insistence that the state should rely on changes in the level of total capital investment spending regulated by public capital investment to prevent any serious fluctuations in national income around the full-employment target. But Meade was concerned that the level of total investment could not always be altered "fully and promptly" enough to do the job. "We argue in our paper that one should try to control investment in such a way as to prevent violent fluctuations in national income, but we suggest that this may not alone be successful" because the government may not be able to fine-tune total investment spending to the degree required (CW 27, p. 317). In this case, tax cuts to stimulate consumption might be needed. His plan for countercyclical social insurance contributions would help, especially because they were "an instantaneous automatic stabiliser" and therefore required no change in the tax laws (CW 27, p. 318). Moreover, the state must consider situations in which it foresees a future slump in demand coming and needs to cut taxes in anticipation of it. But this requires the freedom to run intentional budget deficits. Meade wrote:

> [W]e must be free to plan taxation (and so the deficit of the current budget) ahead. I conclude, therefore, that we want both a potent

"instantaneous automatic stabiliser" such as the social security scheme and freedom to plan ahead year by year for a deficit or a surplus in the current budget; and I fear that the latter freedom would be prejudiced by a division of the budget.

(CW 27, p. 318)

The main point made in Keynes's response is that fluctuations in investment, not consumption, should be the centerpiece *even of countercyclical policy*. If there is need for a cyclical stimulus to AD, new investment projects from the portfolio of potential investment projects prepared by the Board of National Investment should be undertaken sooner and/or ongoing projects should be accelerated. There are two reasons why this is the case, Keynes said. First, since people have customary standards of living that they will not alter substantially in the face of temporary changes in income, a countercyclical policy that relies primarily on shifting tax burdens onto consumers will not work.

People have established standards of life. Nothing will upset them more than to be subject to pressure constantly to vary them up and down. A remission of taxation on which people could only rely for an indefinitely short period might have very limited effects in stimulating their consumption. And, if it was successful, it would be extraordinarily difficult from the political angle to reimpose the taxation again when employment improved.

(CW 27, p. 319)

In the late 1960s, macroeconomists rediscovered the insight that income tax cuts understood by their recipients to be temporary would not have a significant impact on consumption. Many criticized Keynes for bequeathing the profession a simplistic and misleading theory of consumption on which to base countercyclical policy. This is but one example of a number of instances in which Keynes's views were first severely distorted and then oversimplified by his followers, after which he was criticized for being naively simplistic. The two chapters on consumption theory in *The General Theory* demonstrate quite clearly that Keynes anticipated almost all of the subsequent so-called revisions to his version of consumption theory.

To the extent that changes in personal tax rates were to be used for this purpose, Keynes preferred the automatic stabilizer property of Meade's social insurance scheme to discretionary changes in income tax rates. Not only is Meade's plan automatic, but it puts purchasing power into the hands of the working class, who are most likely to respond with some alteration of spending. Income tax cuts involve "a huge time lag" between policy change and consumer response and "short-run changes are most inconvenient" politically (CW 27, p. 319).

Second, there are several positive reasons to rely primarily on raising public investment to sustain employment in the face of declining demand. The state already has the power to alter public investment. And recessions provide an opportunity to accelerate the pace of capital accumulation, which is desirable for reasons independent of its ability to raise AD: "it is better for all of us that periods of deficiency expenditure should be made the occasion of capital development until our economy is much more saturated with capital goods than it is at present" (CW 27, p. 320).

Finally, public investment is less likely than income tax cuts to raise budget deficits. It had been Keynes's consistent position that the lion's share of investment projects he envisioned would have positive gross, if not net, expected present value, and therefore involve at most very modest direct budgetary subsidies that would likely be more than compensated for over time by the tax revenue increases, user fees, and unemployment compensation reductions they induce. Tax cuts are:

> a much more violent version of deficit budgeting. Capital expenditure would, at least partially, if not wholly, pay for itself ... Moreover, the very reason that capital expenditure is capable of paying for itself makes it much better budgetwise and does not involve the progressive increase of budgetary difficulties, which deficit budgeting for the sake of consumption may bring about or, at any rate, would be accused of bringing about.
>
> (CW 27, p. 320)

In May 1943, Meade circulated the final version of his memorandum on postwar employment policy. This was the all-important "White Paper" on this crucial subject. The memorandum led to intense debate at the Treasury. Hubert Henderson, Keynes's persistent antagonist, responded with a pessimistic evaluation of Meade's memorandum. Keynes wrote a critique of the Henderson analysis entitled "The Long-Term Problem of Full Employment."

*Keynes's response is of the greatest importance because it shows that he never abandoned his belief in his version of the secular stagnation thesis or in the necessity for the government to rely on public and semi-public investment to generate and sustain full employment in the postwar period until the rate of profit on investment was driven to zero.* Since he would shortly be devoting almost all of his time to the UK–US negotiations over the shape of the postwar international financial order, this might be considered his last major input to postwar domestic economic planning.

Keynes begins by explaining that the institutions and social and behavioral practices prevalent at war's end would determine the level of savings generated at full employment. He called this the "indicated" level of savings. The main task of employment policy was to see that investment equaled the indicated full-employment savings level. There were likely to be "three phases" of the unfolding of the postwar era. The immediate postwar phase was likely to see a boom fueled by pent-up demand, with an excess of investment over indicated savings "in the absence of rationing and other controls" (CW 27, p. 321). This was phase 1.

Phase 2 would be the period:

> when the urgently necessary investment is no longer greater than the indicated level of savings in conditions of freedom, but it is still capable of being adjusted to the indicated level by deliberately encouraging or expediting less urgent, but nevertheless useful, investment.
>
> (CW 27, p. 321)

Phase 3 would begin when the point Keynes here calls "capital saturation" was achieved, when all potentially productive capital investments had already been made: "when investment demand is so far saturated that it cannot be brought up to the indicated level of savings without embarking upon wasteful and unnecessary enterprises" because the profit rate on new investment would, at this point, be zero (CW 27, p. 321).[11] When the economy enters phase 3, Keynes argued, fiscal policy should begin to shift its emphasis from public investment to tax cuts designed to progressively redistribute income, both for the sake of social justice and to raise the propensity to consume.

Keynes's memorandum conclusively demonstrates that, seven years after the publication of *The General Theory* and only three years before his death, he continued to defend both the tendency of the rate of profit to fall in a context of rapid capital accumulation and the "socialist" economic policies developed in that book and elsewhere to deal with this problem. Moreover, he had by now maneuvered himself into a position where he could defend this theory and these policies to the most important officials and senior staff in the Treasury and the Economic Section of the War Cabinet, the two most important government agencies involved in postwar economic planning.

In the first phase, demand will have to be restrained by controls on all kinds of investments, by consumption rationing "and the like." Guiding the economy through this will be a "ticklish business," he admits: it "will require a sensitive touch and the method of trial and error operating through small changes." This phase might last five years – "it is anybody's guess" (CW 27, p. 322).

The second phase is the crucial period for Keynes. His vision for planning in this period is quite clear, extremely ambitious, and consistent with all of his thinking in the previous two decades. *His "two-thirds or three-quarters" estimate of the share of public and semi-public investment in total investment is consistent with the estimates he made in the late 1920s.*

Sooner or later it should be possible to abandon both types of controls [on private consumption and investment] entirely (apart from controls on foreign lending). We then enter the second phase which is the main point of emphasis in the paper of the Economic Section. *If two-thirds or three-quarters of total investment is carried out or can be influenced by public or semi-public bodies, a long-term programme of a stable character should be capable of reducing the potential range of fluctuation to much narrower limits than formerly,* when a smaller volume of investment was under public control and when even this part tended to follow, rather than correct, fluctuations of investment in the strictly private sector of the economy ... The main task should be to prevent large fluctuations by a stable long-term programme. If this is successful it should not be too difficult to offset small fluctuations by expediting or retarding some items in the long-term [investment] programme.

(CW 27, p. 322, emphasis added)

Keynes goes on to acknowledge that the size of the purely public investment spending (as distinct from semi-public investment) that will be required to balance total savings and maintain full employment is difficult to accurately predict, but in any case, it will be quite large – perhaps as much as 20 percent of net national income.

It will depend on the social habits and propensities of a community with a distribution of taxed income significantly different from any of which we have experience, on the nature of the tax system and on the practices and conventions of business. But perhaps one can say that it is unlikely to be less than 7.5 per cent or more than 20 per cent of the net national income, except under new influences, deliberate or accidental, which are not yet in sight.

(CW 27, p. 323)

Keynes states that the secular trend of public investment in phase 2 should be set so as to maintain full employment, which, as he has made abundantly clear, refers to a measured unemployment rate of at most 5 percent and no less than 3 percent. Of course, uncontrolled and even unforeseeable shifts in private segments of AD will, from time to time, generate disequilibrium problems. But he is also clear, again, that deliberate fluctuations in the pace of public investment must bear the primary burden of countercyclical policy.

Emphasis should be placed primarily on measures to maintain a steady level of employment and thus to prevent fluctuation. If a large fluctuation is allowed to occur, it will be difficult to find adequate offsetting measures of sufficiently quick action. This can only be done through flexible methods by means of trial and error on the basis of

experience which has still to be gained. If the authorities know quite clearly what they are trying to do and are given sufficient powers, reasonable success in the performance of the tasks should not be too difficult. I doubt if much is to be hoped from proposals to offset unforeseen short-period fluctuations in investment by stimulating short-period changes in consumption. But I see very great attractions and practical advantage in Mr Meade's proposal for varying social security contributions according to the state of employment.
(CW 27, pp. 323–324)

Keynes is surprisingly optimistic about how long it will take to achieve the "golden age" of capital saturation. Whereas in *The General Theory* he speculated that it might take at least a "generation," here he suggests that it could be as soon as "five or ten years" (CW 27, p. 323). On the other hand, by way of balance, a few months later, he estimates it will take "twenty years of large-scale investment" (CW 27, p. 350). In any case, once we reach the third phase, in which the scarcity of capital has been virtually eliminated by massive public and semi-public investment:

It becomes necessary to encourage wise consumption and discourage saving, – and to absorb some part of the unwanted surplus by increased leisure, more holidays (which are a wonderfully good way of getting rid of money) and shorter hours. Various means will be open to us with the onset of this *golden age*. The object will be slowly to change social practices and habits so as to reduce the indicated level of saving. Eventually depreciation funds should be almost sufficient to provide all the gross investment that is required.
(CW 27, p. 323, emphasis added)

This paper clearly demonstrates that Keynes believed that his theory of secular stagnation as developed in *The General Theory* would continue to apply to the postwar economy, as it did in the Great Depression, and that his radical interwar policy scheme would be required to maintain full employment in the post-WWII era.

Keynes concluded this particular intervention by associating himself with certain general perspectives expressed in Henderson's paper. He approvingly quotes Henderson as follows:

Opponents of Socialism are on strong ground when they argue that the State would be unlikely in practice to run complicated industries more efficiently that they are run at present. Socialists are on strong ground when they argue that reliance on supply and demand, and the forces of market competition, as the mainspring of our economic system, produces most unsatisfactory results. Might we not conceivably find a *modus vivendi* for the next decade or so in an arrangement under which the State would fill the vacant post of entrepreneur-in-chief, while not interfering with the ownership or management of particular businesses, or rather only doing so on the merits of the case and not at the behest of dogma?[12]

(CW 27, p. 324)

Sir Wilfred Eady, the controller of finance, wrote Keynes a note in May 1943 in which he agreed to the circulation of Keynes's critique of Henderson to cabinet ministers. But, Eady added, Keynes's ideas are "a voyage in the stratosphere for most of us ... You will find your official colleagues obtuse, bat-eyed and obstinate on much of this!" (CW 27, p. 325). Keynes's answer suggests that he was not amused by Eady's comments.[13] Keynes said that he believed that his ambitious hopes for the impact of *The General Theory* on the thinking of younger economists had been realized. "There is scarcely an undergraduate of the modern generation from which these truths are hidden."

> Very sorry, but it does seem to me quite essential that all of you should become accustomed to the stratosphere – if that really is what it is! For, if the argument which I have tried to bring into the open in my paper is not understood by those responsible, they are understanding nothing whatever ... And, after all, it is very easily understood! There is scarcely an undergraduate of the modern generation from which these truths are hidden. And once they have been digested and have entered into the apparatus of the mind, it is possible for most people to move fairly safely over a terrain otherwise most dangerous.
>
> (CW 27, pp. 325–326)

Keynes sent his memorandum on Henderson's paper along to Meade, with an accompanying letter evaluating Meade's employment paper. He criticized Meade's short-run focus, noting again his own stress on the use of public investment to influence the long-term trajectory of the economy. He repeats here his insistence in his memorandum that the key to postwar prosperity was that the "the bulk of investment" must be "under public or semipublic control," with the growth rate of capital accumulation selected to sustain full employment over time. Moreover, by ensuring a relatively steady rate of public and semi-public capital accumulation, the state could provide a kind of center of gravity for the rate of economic growth that would drastically reduce private corporations' sense of uncertainty, thereby making private investment larger and more stable as well.

> (1) I think you lay too much stress on cure and too little on prevention. It is quite true that a fluctuating volume of public works at short notice is a clumsy form of cure and not likely to be completely

successful. On the other hand, *if the bulk of investment is under public or semi-public control and we go in for a stable long-term programme, serious fluctuations are enormously less likely to occur.* I feel, therefore, that you do a little less than justice to investment under public auspices by emphasising the deficiencies of this method in the short period, *whilst underestimating their efficiency for preventative purposes and as a means of avoiding the sharp fluctuations which, once they have occurred, it is so difficult to offset.*

(2) I have much less confidence than you have in off-setting proposals which aim at short-period changes in consumption. I agree with Henderson that one has to pay great attention to securing the right long-period trend in the propensity to consume. But the amount one can do in the short period is likely to be meagre.

(CW 27, p. 326, emphasis added)

Keynes concluded the letter with a puzzling comment that there was no reason for the government to immediately begin work on the design and implementation of the structures of state investment planning. This seems quite strange given the ambitious goals he had set for government planning and the obvious necessity for institutional innovation and strategic planning if his hopes were to have any chance of fulfillment at war's end – not to mention Keynes's own statements about the need to create new planning institutions. Moreover, some set of fairly elaborate government economic controls would have to be used in phase 1 to guide the economy, and decisions would thus have to be made about the relation of these controls to the phase 2 planning apparatus.

It did not seem to me that Henderson's document was really inconsistent with yours. It was largely concerned with a more distant period. Both of you are getting a little too academic for the purposes of the Ministers. The only matters about which it is necessary that they should take immediate decisions relate to the first phase, whereas you, as it seems to me, are largely concerned with the second phase, and Henderson with the third phase.

(CW 27, p. 327)

James Meade believed there was a fundamental problem in Keynes's position. In early June of 1943, he and Keynes exchanged two quite important letters concerning Meade's belief that the government had to begin to make decisions *now* about the institutions and practices that would constitute the phase 2 postwar economic system (CW 27, pp. 326–327). Meade's letters outline in some detail the important tasks that the government had to confront at the moment in order to be in a position at war's end to successfully plan the postwar economy. *Their significance lies in the fact that, at the end of this discussion, Keynes expressed complete agreement with Meade on the key issues regarding phase 2 economic planning.* This is why I quote Meade at such unusual length.

The first letter implored Keynes to prod the government to begin at once to create the institutions and policies that would be needed in the crucial phase 2 for a number of reasons. Among these are the fact that, having taken numerous decisions about how to manage the immediate postwar years, ministers need to tie these into the transition to the crucial phase 2, as well as the fact that the public will demand to have mechanisms put in place right away that ensure the maintenance of full employment in the new economic regime.

> I confess, however, that I cannot so readily assent to your suggestion that Ministers need not at the moment take decisions relating to anything later than the first post-war period in which supplies will be scarce and effective demand will be high. There are a number of reasons for taking the opposite view:
>
> (i) If it is possible (even if it were not probable) that we shall, after two years of peace, be back where we were in the 1930s, Ministers should by the end, say, of the first year of peace have taken more or less final decisions on the broad lines on which they intend to deal with the situation. In view of all the complex problems they will have to deal with in the post-war period and of the hectic political situation in which they will have to operate, it is certainly not too soon for them to start work on this subject now in the calm of war.
>
> (ii) Much work has already been done and many decisions by Ministers have already been taken on the immediate post-war problems ... Having taken general decisions on the first stage, and having started detailed work on that stage, they are being asked now to prepare to take general preliminary decisions on a stage only a little further on.
>
> (iii) What we plan to do in the immediate post-war transitional period should be related to our longer aims. There is a grave danger that Whitehall will plan to deal with these immediate transitional problems as if the problems were completely separate from the subsequent problems [of phase 2]. For example, Civil Servants always treat the problems of "physical reconstruction" and of "public works policy" as if they existed in separate universes. In your note you properly show that, fundamentally, the same analysis applies to the three periods which you analyse; and the same should be true to a certain degree in our administrative mechanisms for dealing with them. In fact, some of the immediate post-war mechanisms ... can be used to stabilise and stimulate as well as restrain, and it might be wise to turn these into more or less permanent features of the economy from the start. Is

it, for example, really political wisdom to suppose that we shall have any chance of success if we put off discussing the scheme for variations in social security contributions until the close of the transitional period ... when the willingness on the part of politicians to consider radical change will have passed? This is the surest way to assure that we shall get no such scheme.

(iv) The public are, I am told, more concerned about employment prospects after the war than about any other post-war issue. As the prospects of victory become clearer, this public interest will become more and more marked. Already Beveridge has set up his bureau to deal with the problem. He will probably get the answer wrong; but if his is the only answer in the field, and if the Government has not its own answer ready (and an answer which does not refer merely to good projects for employment for a year or so after the war) there will be another first-class political row.

(v) Finally, I feel it would be truly tragic if this opportunity were lost. The policy which is advocated is one which is in the interests of all political parties; it is one for the success of which intellectual enlightenment rather than a change of heart is required and we have at the moment the unique opportunity of all political parties in a government which is seriously willing to consider social innovations. The opportunity is unlikely to recur. Perhaps you would allow me to add the personal note that, in these matters of a full employment policy, I have always regarded you as the guiding intellect and the moving force; and I believe that in this I am typical of the younger generation of economists.

(CW 27, pp. 327–329)

Keynes's response to this letter from Meade was surprisingly brief. He claims to not understand precisely what it is that Meade wants him to pressure the ministers to do. He tells Meade:

I should find it easier to say whether I agree with you that there are further decisions which Ministers ought to take in the near future if you would tell me what the decisions are which you think they ought to take. You will have noticed that in my paper I deliberately excepted your social security contributions proposal from deferment. I agree with you that it deserves early consideration. But I am not clear what else there is, which does not depend on the actual progress of events for it to be ripe for ministerial decision at this stage.

(CW 21, pp. 329–330)

Meade responded to Keynes's letter with one of his own the very next day, listing critical issues on planning the postwar economy about which "Ministers might fruitfully take decisions in the near future."

Meade presented Keynes with an ambitious ministerial agenda for his consideration.

> There are decisions which should be taken now on the control of investment. It should be realised that the forward planning, control and timing of public investment is important both in the immediate transitional period, in order to restrain and spread out the demands for physical reconstruction, and also in the longer period for the stimulation of such investment. For example, it might be decided, in principle, that public authorities should prepare and revise annually a five-year plan for their future capital works, and this should be reviewed periodically by a central body for the purpose of the timing of expenditure. Certain inducements might be considered to persuade local authorities to keep in step with such a plan, e.g., by varying the rate of state grants for different types of works, according to the period in which they were undertaken. Here surely is a field of action and of administration, which is equally relevant to the immediate war period of restraint and to the subsequent period of stimulation. The danger is that if Civil Servants and Ministers concentrate exclusively on *ad hoc* mechanisms of restraint immediately after the war, they will fail to have built their controls in a way which will also be useful for stimulation later on ...
>
> I am pretty sure that the same principle might be applied in perhaps a lesser degree to the control of private investment. Various measures will be used immediately after the war for its restraint. Which of these measures of control will, and which will not, be useful after to stimulate private investment? The question should be considered now, since it should influence the way in which the controls are constituted in the immediate post-war transitional period ...
>
> We have suggested in our paper ... that it may be worthwhile controlling the terms of hire-purchase finance [i.e. purchase of goods on an installment plan] in such a way as to impede such purchases when restraint is needed and to ease them when stimulation is required. Here again is a mechanism which ... could subsequently be readily used to stimulate buying ...
>
> There are broad issues on which Ministerial decisions should be sought for the purpose of dealing with "structural" unemployment ... Labour movement must be regarded as a continuing [postwar] need, and decisions should be take now to perpetuate, and, in certain cases, to develop so much of the Ministry of Labour machinery as is considered desirable. Here, in my view, is an outstanding case of the need for considering the long-term problem when decisions are being taken on the maintenance of controls for the transitional period ...
>
> The same is true of the location of industry. The problem of bringing work to the men (as a supplement to bringing men to the work) should be regarded as a continuing one ...

The above are examples of important economic issues on the long-run aspects of which discussions and decisions should be started now ... [As] I mentioned in my earlier letter ... many of these things will require considerable legislative or administrative changes and that these changes may be politically possible now or immediately after the war, and impossible later on.

The overriding argument, in fact, for taking decisions now, in my opinion, is yet another political consideration. The public are demanding plans for post-war employment policy; and if the Government have not fairly soon reached preliminary decisions on the matter (extending well beyond the immediate post-war transition) there will be another political explosion.

May I end by an argumentum ad hominem? In the international sphere you have advocated an International Clearing Union. In the immediate post-war years the principles of such a Union could not be fully applied ... The Clearing Union scheme is, in essence, a longer-term measure for more normal times. Why, in this case, did Ministers need to take these decisions of long-term principle before they considered all the detailed hugger mugger of the process of adjustment? The answer, in my view, is clear: it was in order that they might see where they were going before they started to go there. Is this not true of internal policy as well?

(CW 27, pp. 330–332)

The letter called for detailed legislative, administrative, and policy changes to implement Keynes's central vision of long-run postwar planning for sustained full employment. The changes proposed need to be integrated with those mechanisms that will be used to reconvert the economy from a wartime footing to normalcy. Public investment policy is, of course, the key, but administration and planning must also be prepared for guiding private investment through a kind of indicative planning, for creating a system of state-guided credit allocation, and for creating industrial policies to deal with labor mobility and the location of new industry to help reduce structural unemployment. The political environment is now ideal for organizing to achieve government approval for a radical reconstitution of the economic role of the state, Meade argues. The public will demand it and all parties will support some variant of it. Failure to do so might trigger a political explosion. Finally, the scope and detail of these plans should be similar to those contained in Keynes's superbly ambitious International Clearing Union, which contained a detailed plan for a postwar international financial system radically different from the old gold standard. All of these phase 2 policy institutions and plans need to be created now.

In his letter responding to Meade, *Keynes expressed complete agreement with Meade's position.* The misunderstanding arose, according to Keynes, because he could not see that any of the key proposals in Meade's and Henderson's memoranda required *immediate* ministerial attention. Of course, he agrees, such attention *is required* by those constructing the blueprints for the implementation of state economic planning that ministers will have to approve. This is the institutional infrastructure Keynes needed in order to construct his postwar Liberal Socialist economy in Britain.

> Substantially there is nothing with which I disagree in the list given in your letter of June 3rd of the main points on which Ministers might take early decisions. Indeed, the first page and a half of your letter seems to me to give much more suitable material for a brief memorandum for Ministers that the documents actually in their hands. When I said there was nothing on which Ministers could take early decisions, I did not mean to rule out these various important matters. My point – not clearly expressed – was that it did not seem to me that any matters arose either out of yours or out of Henderson's memorandum which led up to decisions which ought to be taken now ... These points have the great advantage of bringing the issues back to practical matters and away from a debate [between Meade and Henderson], which seemed to me was getting academic and might be endless.
> (CW 27, pp. 332–333)

The Treasury was working on a response to the Economic Section memorandum by Meade in the summer of 1943. Keynes wrote a lengthy critique of a draft reply by Sir Wilfred Eady. Keynes again insists that the primary tool of postwar state economic planning was to be variations in public and semi-public investment. This was the tool that would guide the long-run equilibrium path of the economy so as to achieve sustained full employment. To accomplish this task: "two-thirds or three quarters of total investment [must be] under public or semi-public" control.

> The capital budget will be a necessary ingredient in this exposition of the prospects of investment under all heads. If, as may be the case, something like two-thirds or three quarters of total investment will be under public or semi-public auspices, the amount of capital expenditures contemplated by the authorities will be the essential balancing factor ... It has nothing whatever to do with deficit financing.
> (CW 27, p. 352)

Countercyclical policy is a decidedly secondary though not unimportant concern, and even here changes in the volume of public investment were to be the first line of defense. Moreover, current account deficits were to be avoided if possible.

Quite apart from this is the proposal that if, for one reason or another, the volume of planned investment fails to produce equilibrium, the lack of balance would be met by unbalancing one way or another the current Budget. Admittedly this would be a last resort, only to come into play if the machinery of capital budgeting had broken down. Thus the capital budgeting is a method of maintaining equilibrium; the deficit budgeting is a means of attempting to cure [short-term] disequilibrium if and when it arises ... Personally I like Meade's social security proposal. It is not open to many of the objections of other forms of deficit finance. Indeed, it can be defended on the ground that it will actually promote stability of the social security fund itself. It is arguable, that is to say, that in periods of increasing unemployment the fund will actually make up a significant part of what it loses through reduced contributions through having to pay out less unemployment relief than would otherwise be the case. About other forms of deficit financing I am inclined to lie low because I am sure that, if serious unemployment does develop, deficit financing is absolutely certain to happen, and I should like to keep free to object hereafter to the more objectionable forms of it ... So very decidedly I should ... not lead the critics to think that the Chancellor is confusing the fundamental idea of a capital budget with the particular, *rather desperate expedient of deficit financing*.

(CW 27, pp. 352–354, emphasis added)

Keynes next agrees that it is appropriate to focus on structural unemployment, but he warns Eady against the Treasury's tendency to overstress structural unemployment relative to unemployment caused by a deficiency of "effective demand."

But I wonder if the Chancellor of the Exchequer appreciates into what deep water the adoption of the more pessimistic expectation on this heading leads him. The optimistic view on this, and also on some other matters, which I am charged with maintaining is by no means intended as a prophecy of what is certain to happen. I regard it much more as the only hypothesis on which the kind of economic future which the Chancellor and probably most other people in the Treasury envisage as desirable really has a chance. It might turn out to be true that anything at all closely resembling free enterprise is incapable of dealing with the problem of structural unemployment. If so, I feel sure that free enterprise will go by the board to the necessary extent. I have not abandoned the view that something like free enterprise can be made to work. I think we ought to have a good try at it. And that try ought to be based on the assumption that the underlying conditions are not such as to make it impossible ... I fancy he will find himself open to some rather unexpected rejoinders if he takes

> a defeatist line about the possibility of free enterprise dealing satisfactorily with the outstanding problem of the age ... Would it not be much better to end up with a recommendation for the preparation of detailed proposals how to handle structural unemployment in a free enterprise environment?
>
> (CW 27, pp. 354–355)

On the other hand, as he stressed in chapter 24 of *The General Theory*, if the state can sustain full employment through public and semi-public investment (supported by capital controls, managed trade, and various industrial policies), much of the rest of the economy can be organized through free enterprise. Of course, as he continued to emphasize, only a third to a quarter of the large-scale capital investment in the economy will be under the control of private-sector bodies.

Keynes concludes by suggesting a more positive and activist tone for the memorandum, with investment planning used as the primary tool to manage AD and various industrial policies focused on curing structural unemployment.

> The Chancellor could then conclude by saying that the problem really seems to divide itself into two main headings. The first is the means of ensuring stability in the long-term investment programme coupled with proposals for adjusting its tempo to unforeseen changes[14] ... The second aspect is the problem of structural unemployment. This comprises the question of the location of industry and inducements of private enterprise to come here rather than go there. It also involves the mobility of labour with particular reference to social security. Finally it is particularly concerned with the question of our new industries, where we start with a fairly free hand as to location. *Pari passu*, therefore, with the study of the investment programme should be a study of structural unemployment under the above headings.
>
> (CW 27, p. 357)

In yet another letter to Eady in July 1943, Keynes commented on an Economic Section paper on "the maintenance of investment" (CW 27, p. 359). He clearly sees this as a secular problem. He again refers to the policy switch point at capital saturation, at which a progressive redistribution of wealth must be undertaken.

> [S]ooner or later, we shall be faced, if not with saturation of investment, at any rate with increased difficulty in finding satisfactory outlets for new investment. It is very difficult to predict when this will come about. When it does come about, we shall then have to start

on very important social changes, aimed at the discouragement of savings and a redistribution of the national wealth and a tax system which encourages consumption and discourages saving.
(CW 27, p. 360)

By late 1943, Keynes's work on British–American negotiations concerning the postwar international financial order had begun to monopolize his time, though he did keep "a protective eye on the Meade scheme" (CW 27, p. 364). When he returned from a trip to America in early 1944, he wrote a critical evaluation of the Steering Committee's report of January 1944 on "Post-War Employment Policy." His order of points, which I follow, reflects the structure of the Steering Committee document. He begins by supporting "the possibility of directly influencing the pace of private investment" through a kind of indicative planning. "Something might be done," he suggests, "if the major, private firms were brought to regard it as their duty to pay attention to the indications of the official barometer" (CW 27, p. 365).

The next point is crucial and harkens back to his correspondence with Meade over the need to create more effective planning institutions. The report points out the inadequacy of present government procedures for approving investment projects and refers to "the delays to [public] investment caused by the present complicated parliamentary procedure." Improved administration of investment planning is essential. "This is very important. Should not there be a specific recommendation for the improvement of the existing expensive and out-of-date machinery of the private bill?" (CW 21, p. 365).

The longest section of Keynes's note is devoted to exposing the fallacy embodied in the report that full-employment planning entails substantial budget deficits. "Exactly the opposite is the truth." The notion that the maintenance of full employment must:

> unstabilise the national budget, is surely topsy-turvy. It would be a *failure* to adopt a remedy for severe cyclical unemployment which might have that effect. There appears to be no glimmer of recognition that measures to stabilise the national income are *ipso facto* measures to stabilise the national budget. The additional charges falling on the budget in years of bad unemployment are, in fact, almost negligible; whilst the effect on the revenue of maintaining the national income should be obvious. The Committee give the impression that, whilst the measures they propose to avoid unemployment are necessary and advisable, a price has to be paid for them in the shape of budgetary deficits and perhaps a weakening in international confidence in our position. Exactly the opposite is the truth. It would be a failure to take such measures which would inevitably unstabilise the budget and weaken confidence.
> (CW 27, p. 366, emphasis in original)

Keynes sees two key reasons why the Committee report is marred by this error. First, in spite of the fact that *The General Theory* was published more than seven years prior, "there is no hint of the operation of what economists call 'the multiplier', that is to say the effect of injecting additional demand into the system in increasing national income by at least double its own amount" (CW 27, pp. 365–366). Second, the report fails to incorporate into its analysis of the postwar budget the revenues to be generated by the investment projects that are the core of employment policy. This point is absolutely essential for understanding Keynes's argument that postwar employment policy will not involve secular budget deficits. Public investment projects such as housing, roadbuilding, public utilities, and so forth will produce enough direct tax revenue over their lifetimes that they ultimately will require *at most* modest subsidies; and these subsidies will be smaller than the induced or indirect taxes that will flow from the rise in national income created by the multiplied effects of the new investment. Keynes uses a hypothetical example to make these two points crystal clear.

> Suppose for example that additional investment of £100 increases the total national income and output by £200 (which is probably an under-statement), and that the additional investment will not have a genuine permanent value in excess of £80 (which, one may hope, will also be an understatement). It follows that the net result to the nation's production, strictly valued, will not be a loss of £20 (as some once argued) but a gain of £180. It follows that, if the increment of [tax] revenue exceeds one ninth of the increment of national income (which it certainly does), the transaction taken as a whole positively benefits the Exchequer there and then. The additional taxes, collected as a result of the induced investment in that very year in which it takes place, should be more than enough to write off the excess of the investment's cost over its true value. How slow dies the inbred fallacy that it is an act of financial imprudence to put men to work!
>
> (CW 27, p. 367)

Thus, Keynes criticizes the Committee not for its concern over large-scale budget deficits – "By all means emphasise the importance of maintaining budget equilibrium" – but for associating large secular budget deficits with the public investment program. Let an analysis of the policy's effect on the budget "be represented as an important argument in [its] favour … as it most truly is, and not as an argument against [it]" (CW 27, p. 367).

Keynes then discussed the importance of a detailed capital budget to the planning process.

> A capital budget, in the sense in which I understand it, means a regular survey and analysis of the relationship between sources of savings

and different types of investment and a balance sheet showing how they have been brought into equality for the past year, and a forecast of the same for the year to come. If aggregate demand gave signs of being deficient, the analysis would indicate a deflationary gap exactly corresponding to the inflationary gap which we have so often discussed during the war. This survey and balance sheet might well be presented on the occasion of the regular Budget Statement and form a part of the Budget White Paper. It would give an annual opportunity for examining whether the state of demand during the ensuing year looked like being adequate to maintain employment and national income at the desirable level and for the Government to explain to Parliament what steps it had in view to remedy a prospective disequilibrium in either direction. Such a procedure as this might give greatly increased confidence to the public that the maintenance of employment and national income was now an avowed and deliberate aim of financial and economic policy.

(CW 27, p. 369)

The note contains yet another urgent plea by Keynes for the government to dramatically upgrade its collection, analysis, and dissemination of economic statistics so as to make efficient investment planning feasible. For example, he wants the Board of Inland Revenue to have a statistical staff "on the scale of the statistical staff of the Bank of England." Once that enlarged staff was in place, extraordinary improvements in fiscal policy and in general administration, as well as in the information, analysis, and forecasting needed to plan investment effectively, would become possible.

With the Ministry of Labour handling labour statistics on the lines proposed, the Board of Trade conducting a continuous census of production, ... the Inland Revenue digesting and analysing the vast body of information which passes through its files, and the Bank of England continuing its running analysis of our external position, the new era of the "Joy through Statistics' (I do not write ironically) can begin.

(CW 27, p. 371)

Theoretical economic analysis has now reached a point where it is fit to be applied. Its application only awaits the collection of the detailed facts which the economist, unlike the scientist, cannot collect in a laboratory by private enterprise. The authors of the Report would, I think, have written with more confidence about their plans for the future and in a spirit of more buoyant hope if they had fully appreciated what knowledge is capable of doing in making the future different from the past as soon as we decide to furnish the social sciences with *data* comparable to the *data* of the other sciences ... [Until this is done], no one can quantify his recommendations or say except in the most general terms what ought to be done, and [when such data are available], it will all be obvious and as clear as the daylight with no room left for argument.

(CW 27, p. 371–372, emphasis in original)

In this 1944 document, Keynes put great faith in the historic importance of Britain's project of constructing an effective and democratic state planning process to maintain full employment, one that could eliminate the gross inefficiency of laissez-faire yet avoid the severe problems he believed were inevitably associated with totalitarian planning. He hopes it

will be the role of this country to develop a middle way of economic life which will preserve the liberty, the initiative and (what we are so rich in) the idiosyncrasy of the individual in a framework serving the public good and seeking equality of contentment among all.

(CW 27, p. 369)

The official government "White Paper on Employment Policy" was drafted in March and April 1944. It was designed to be the most important document in determining the character of Britain's postwar economic policy regime, which helps explain why there was so much conflict associated with it. Keynes was ill during this period and generally engrossed in British–American negotiations over the postwar international financial system. As a result, he had little direct input into the White Paper. But Hubert Henderson sent Keynes a copy of a memorandum he wrote condemning the White Paper. Keynes circulated his response to Henderson's views.

Henderson believed Britain's postwar export situation would be bleak, a fact that the White Paper failed to sufficiently consider in its recommendation for a full-employment policy. Keynes agreed that the export picture was not good, but he drew different conclusions than Henderson. He argued that Britain would have to manage trade; in particular, imports would have to be restricted. But import restrictions would be good for the effort to raise domestic employment. Henderson also believed it would be good for Britain's access to international credit "if we allow large-scale unemployment." Keynes thought this to be a "plain delusion ... It will improve our external credit if we are seen tackling the problem of internal unemployment vigorously, and just to stand aside will have the opposite effect" (CW 27, p. 374).

Keynes's trump card against Henderson's position was the fear of domestic unrest in the face of a postwar depression. Remember that the necessity to raise unemployment at home to improve the balance of trade was the Achilles' heel of the gold standard. Keynes warned again here that, as he had put it in the exit chapter of *The General Theory*, "the world will not much longer tolerate the unemployment which is ... inevitably associated with capitalist individualism" (CW 27, p. 381).

> Finally, Sir H. Henderson does not appear to expect, or does not at any rate attach any importance to, the social and political consequences of deliberately using domestic unemployment as a remedy for external disequilibrium. Even if this policy had its advantages, it is surely obviously out of the question and *might mean the downfall of our present system of democratic government.*
> (CW 27, p. 374, emphasis added)

The White Paper was distributed in May 1944. Keynes sent the Chancellor of the Exchequer suggestions for his consideration in preparing his speech to the House of Commons in defense of it. Much of the material is quite familiar. Keynes repeats his prohibition against the use of high interest rates to restrain the boom. And he stresses the fact that a full-employment policy centered on public investment will help avoid budget deficits, not create them. "A forward employment policy is therefore entirely compatible with budgetary equilibrium; and not only so, but it is in fact the best way of ensuring budgetary equilibrium" (CW 27, p. 377).

A key focus is on the possible criticism that the White Paper, while putting the government behind the principles of postwar planning, does not specify its unemployment target or the precise policies required to achieve it. Keynes agrees that the "illustrative" figures presented are on the cautious side. (After all, he had been a persistent internal critic of the timidity of the White Paper.) But his main point is that the specifics of planning – the blueprints – cannot be constructed until *after* the government approves the general lines of the policies proposed. *Obtaining the commitment of the government and the public to sustained full employment as the main policy goal and to public investment as the main policy tool, along with a commitment to the broad outline of the proposed policy process, is the most important thing for Keynes.* Once this commitment was firm, the experts and technicians inside and outside the government could finally get on with the creation of the administrative, legislative, and strategic infrastructure needed to make his vision a reality.

> All that the Government is attempting to lay down at this stage is the general line and purpose of policy, the basic assumptions on which it proposes to accept as correct. The quantitative and detailed working out can only be done satisfactorily over a period of time. It would be quite premature to attempt something of that sort now and any attempt that might be made would almost certainly be proved inaccurate by events. As soon, however, as the general policy has been laid down, then it will be the duty of the various Departments

and all other authorities concerned, to work out the details, with far greater particularity than has been done, or could be done, up to this point. The object of the White Paper is to choose the pattern of our future policy. This must not be confused with the technical working out of the very extensive blue prints, which will be needed to implement this policy, when it has been approved by Parliament. To the preparation of these blue prints, those concerned will of course proceed, as soon as the general line has been laid down and approved by Parliament.

(CW 27, pp. 378–379)

Keynes expressed the same position about the White Paper more concisely in a letter to Austin Robinson in June 1944.

[I]t is better to have something, even if it is wrong in detail, because I believe the Civil Service has infinite power of making things work out if it is clear it intends to work it. My own feeling is that the first sentence [committing the government to the maintenance of full employment] is more valuable than the whole of the rest.

(Moggridge 1992, p. 709)

Keynes had been appointed to the National Debt Enquiry committee, which was to advise the government on postwar monetary policy in general and on the problem of the postwar interest burden of the national debt in particular. In March and April 1945, Keynes made several presentations to the Enquiry concerning postwar monetary policy and other subjects. His main messages in these presentations was that, with the existence of exchange and import controls, capital controls, and the removal of interest rates from countercyclical policy, the monetary authorities can achieve whatever rates of interest they desire. "The monetary authorities can have any rate of interest they want" (CW 27, p. 390). He argued that low interest rates were desirable because they both helped sustain investment spending and minimized the interest burden on the Treasury. He proposed a 0.5 percent Treasury bill rate and 1.5 and 2 percent rates on five- and ten-year Treasury bonds, respectively.[15]

In June 1945, less than a year before his death, Keynes presented a memorandum to the National Enquiry on "The Concept of a Capital Budget," devoted primarily to the mechanics of state investment planning. In it, Keynes distinguished between an Exchequer (Treasury) Capital Budget, a Public Capital Budget, and a National Investment Budget. The first referred to the costs and revenues associated with longer-term projects under the direct control of the central government.[16] A more inclusive Public Capital Budget is needed, to be financed by sources of investible funds similar to those that were to be used to support the ambitious investment agenda of the National Investment Board in BIF (CW 27, pp. 407–408).

It has been the practice of this country hitherto to entrust most capital expenditure of a public character to Local Authorities or Public Boards. I am not aware of any intention to change this. If so, the significance of the Exchequer Budget will be incomplete if taken in isolation, and it should be regarded rather as an item required in building up the Public Capital Budget, which should also comprise the capital expenditure of all bodies, boards, authorities and institutions which are scheduled as belonging to the public, as distinct from the private, sector of the national economy.

(CW 27, p. 408)[17]

The primary burden of maintaining full employment continued to be placed on public capital investment. The major policy planning tool is to be the annual National Investment Budget derived from the longer-term investment plans of the Exchequer Budget. The Investment Budget will project total investment spending – including expected private-sector investment and those public investment projects previously approved – for the coming period. If total national investment spending for the coming period appears to be too small to sustain full employment, the Treasury will be the body responsible for accelerating public investment – and vice versa.

It is an integral part of the Government's full employment policy, as I understand it, that some authority will exist (*the Treasury I hope*) charged with the duty of examining and reporting on the state of the Public Capital Budget as a whole, not merely after the event but also prospectively. *At one time I had conceived that this should be the task of a semi-independent statutory authority to be called the National Investment Board.* But with modern developments of policy, decisions on such matters have become so much a part of the Government's economic programme as a whole that they should not be dissociated from the Chancellor of the Exchequer as the responsible Minister and his official Department. Nevertheless, in this event the Treasury will have to be as self-conscious and publicly explicit as a National Investment Board would have been.

(CW 27, p. 408, emphasis added)

Since Keynes had become the dominant force at Treasury with respect to postwar economic planning (and much else), he was in effect proposing to cede the power to control total investment spending in pursuit of sustained full employment to himself and his friends, allies, and acolytes.

Let us sum up Keynes's proposals for postwar economic planning in Britain in the year of 1945. *They represent the institutional concretization of his vision of Liberal Socialism constructed over the interwar period, defended in* The

General Theory, *and considered for adoption at the highest levels of the wartime government*. The core agenda of BIF, published in 1928, and indeed of all of Keynes's important interwar policy positions, remained intact in 1945. *The policy perspective developed at the Treasury under Keynes's influence has little in common with the understanding of Keynes's policy views by today's "Keynesian" economists.*

The main institutional change in the 1940s from Keynes's interwar views is that the functions previously to be vested in an independent National Board of Investment were now to be ceded to the Treasury. The main function of the Treasury in this regard would be to try to ensure that total national investment, public and private, would remain equal to what Keynes called the "indicated" or full-employment level of national savings, thereby ensuring sustained full employment. It would accomplish its goal through its control of the approximately 70 percent of total investment represented by public and semi-public investment. In the critical phase 2, the mandate to the Treasury was to increase total investment spending rapidly enough to drive the profit rate down toward zero over a few decades. Given the high propensity to save, this was the only way to keep investment equal to the indicated level of national savings.

The central bank was to be nationalized (which it was in 1946), and its main objective was to keep the long-term interest rate below the rate of profit on new capital investment. Since, in Keynes's view, the rate of profit would fall toward zero due to the rapid growth of the capital stock, rentier capitalism would eventually be eliminated, just as Keynes hoped it would be in the last chapter of *The General Theory*. Of course, the interest rate could not be driven toward zero without effective capital controls.[18] As noted, even under the final, weakened form of the Bretton Woods Agreement, all countries were permitted to adopt strict capital controls.[19] The Bank of England was willing to follow a low-interest rate policy during the war and immediately thereafter because it made it easier for the government to pay interest on its expanding debt.

The Treasury was also empowered to raise or lower the pace of public and semi-public investment in order to moderate the amplitude of business cycles around the full-employment trend. This was to be the major tool for cycle control, though a minor role was reserved for automatic fiscal stabilizers such as Meade's scheme for automatically adjusting the rate of contributions to the national pension fund. If successful, state control of investment spending would create a form of indicative planning for private investment substantially reducing investing firms' sense of uncertainty.

There were to be no planned deficits in the government's current account, but the all-important capital budget could run short-term deficits when necessary. However, the portfolio of investment projects to be supported by the Treasury would be expected to pay for themselves over the long run.[20]

Once the stock of capital was no longer scarce, the main tool to be used to sustain AD at a level consistent with full employment was to be more progressive income and wealth taxes that would raise society's propensity to consume and reduce inequality.

Finally, the ability of the government to sustain high investment and a full-employment economy over the longer run was to be supported by capital controls, tightly managed trade, and the panoply of industrial policies discussed in this book.

The proposed postwar economic system Keynes put before the key ministries from 1943 through 1945 clearly constituted an economic revolution against traditional British capitalism in support of democratic or Liberal Socialism. As argued earlier, it was a revolution in class power as well. The planned decline in the interest rate would eventually lead to the "euthanasia" of Britain's powerful rentier class, while the nationalization of the Bank of England and the shift in the status of the Treasury from an enemy of Keynes's policies to an ally would further weaken rentier political power. Meanwhile, sustained full employment would empower labor in its multidimensional struggles with capital. There would be no significant "reserve army" of unemployed to weaken labor's bargaining power, and the new welfare state would dramatically increase labor's "fallback" position in its negotiations with capital. Capital controls would eliminate the ability of the capitalist class to force labor and the government to acquiesce to their policy demands under the threat of capital flight. *This is the true Keynesian revolution in economic theory and policy that Keynes put before the British government during WWII.*

In June 1944, on his way to the USA for the Bretton Woods negotiations, Keynes read Hayek's *The Road to Serfdom*. When he arrived, he wrote Hayek a letter about his reaction to the book. This letter again demonstrates his hostility toward totalitarian planning, as well as his belief that Hayek's unplanned capitalism would be catastrophic.[21] Keynes argued that while the totalitarian planned economies had demonstrated the economic superiority of planning, technical progress would permit both prosperity and individual liberty even in a less economically efficient democratic planning process. He stressed his belief in the centrality of the "moral values" of the planners and the community in determining the social and political outcomes of planning. It will be safe to grant substantial economic power to state planners, he argued, if both the planners and the community that democratically control them hold liberal rather than authoritarian values. Since this interchange is between the most prestigious economists associated with the opposing sides of this great historical clash of ideas, I quote Keynes at length.

> In my opinion it is a grand book ... Morally and philosophically I find myself in agreement with virtually the whole of it ... It seems to me ... that the Communist doctrine is so desperately out-of-date, at least

in its application to U.S.A. and Western Europe. They ask us to concentrate on economic conditions more exclusively than in any earlier period in the world's history precisely at the moment when by their own showing technical achievement is making this sacrifice unnecessary. This preoccupation with the economic problem is brought to its most intense at a phase in our evolution when it is becoming ever less necessary. The line of argument you yourself take depends on the very doubtful assumption that planning is not more efficient. Quite likely from the purely economic point of view it is efficient. That is why I say that it would be more in line with your general argument to point out that even if the extreme planners can claim their technique to be more efficient, nevertheless technical advancement even in a less planned community is so considerable that we do not today require the superfluous sacrifice of liberties which they themselves would have to admit have some value ... I come finally to what is my only serious criticism of the book. You admit here and there that it is a question of knowing where to draw the line [between plan and market]. You agree that the line has to be drawn somewhere, and the logical extreme is not possible. But you give us no guidance whatever as to where to draw it. In this sense you are shirking the practical issue. It is true that you and I would probably draw it in different places. I should guess that according to my ideas you greatly underestimate the practicability of the middle course. But as soon as you admit that the extreme is not possible, and that a line has to be drawn, you are, on your own argument, done for, since you are trying to persuade us that as soon as one moves an inch in the planned direction you are necessarily launched on the slippery path which will lead you in due course over the precipice. I should therefore conclude your theme rather differently. I should say that what we want is not no planning, or even less planning, indeed I should say that we almost certainly want more planning. But the planning should take place in a community in which as many people as possible, both leaders and followers, wholly share your own moral position. Moderate planning will be safe if those carrying it out are rightly oriented in their own minds and hearts to the moral issue. This is in fact already true of some of them. But the curse is that there is also an important section who could almost be said to want planning not in order to enjoy its fruits but because morally they hold ideas exactly the opposite of yours, and wish to serve not God but the devil. Reading the *New Statesman & Nation* one sometimes feels that those who write there, while they cannot safely oppose moderate planning, are really hoping in their hearts that it will not succeed; and so prejudice more violent action. They fear that if moderate measures are sufficiently successful, this will allow a reaction in what you think the right and they think the wrong direction ... What we need therefore, in my opinion, is not a change in our economic programmes, which could lead in practice to disillusion with your philosophy; but perhaps even the contrary, namely an enlargement of them. Your greatest danger ahead is the probable practical failure of the application of your philosophy in the U.S. in a fairly extreme form. No, what we need is the restoration of right moral thinking – a return to proper moral values in our social philosophy. If only you could turn your crusade in that direction you would not look or feel quite so much like Don Quixote. I accuse you of perhaps confusing a little bit the moral and the material issues. Dangerous acts can be done safely in a community which thinks and feels rightly, which would be the way to hell if they were executed by those who think and feel wrongly.

(CW 27, pp. 385–388)

Keynes died on April 21, 1946.

## Notes

1 See Crotty (1983) for a defense of the proposition that Keynes was so disappointed in the outcome of these negotiations that he seriously considered speaking in favor of rejection in the debate in Parliament over the Bretton Woods arrangements.
2 Keynes's use of the term "economic general staff" here presumably refers to the proposal of an economic general staff in the Liberal Industrial Inquiry (1928).
3 Keynes stressed the need for central coordination. "The problem of pace can be determined rightly only in the light of the competing programmes in all other directions" (CW 27, p. 268).
4 According to Skidelsky: "Henderson was the biggest thorn in Keynes's side throughout the war" (2002, p. 148).
5 Keynes hammered home the same basic point in a June 1943 piece estimating likely postwar income and employment. He criticized a report that forecast average postwar unemployment to be 1,200,000, or 7.5 percent of the workforce. Note again his complete confidence that there would be a near-universal, effective political demand after the war that the unemployment rate be maintained at or near full employment. "[E]ven 1,200,000 is a pessimistic assumption in the light of the greater knowledge and experience of these problems and, above all, of the greater will to grapple with them and to regard their solution as one of our primary responsibilities, which exists in all quarters. We cannot, on this view, regard the unemployment problem as substantially solved so long as the *average* figure is greater than 800,000, namely 5 per cent of the wage-earning population, or rest content without resort to drastic changes of policy so long as it exceeds 1 million" (CW 27, p. 335, emphasis in original).
6 Stone won the Noble Prize in Economics in 1984.
7 The 5 percent figure, he argued, includes reasonable estimates of the virtually unemployable, seasonal factors, men moving between jobs, and "misfits of trade or locality due to lack of mobility." "It compares with ... less than 1 per cent ... unemployed at the present time" (CW 27, p. 305).

8. *Pogo* was the title of a popular comic strip in the USA. This sentence was used in support of the first "Earth Day," a celebration dedicated to protecting the environment.
9. Skidelsky seems to me to be consistently reluctant to acknowledge Keynes's persistent commitment to Liberal Socialism.
10. Of course, the impact of a change in employees' income on AD will depend on the short-run propensity to consume, which is, as Keynes stressed in *The General Theory*, quite variable over the cycle.
11. Keynes's analysis appears to neglect the effect of technical change on the profit rate of new investment projects. This is confusing because, as we know, he had stressed the rapidity of technical progress in the recent past and extrapolated it into the intermediate future. On the other hand, we also know that Keynes believed that private industrial investment, where much of the technical change was taking place, was dominated quantitatively by public and semi-public investment. Perhaps he thought that the rate of technical change was much more modest in these public sectors.
12. In addition to expressing Keynes's view on nationalization quite well, this statement is reminiscent of one he made in the *Treatise on Money* in 1930: "But the choice may conceivably lie between assuming the burden of a prospective loss, allowing the slump to continue, and socialistic action by which some official body steps into the shoes which the feet of the entrepreneurs are too cold to occupy" (CW 6, p. 335).
13. Skidelsky said that Keynes "never established the same rapport with Sir Wilfrid Eady, the new controller of finance" in 1943 as he had with his predecessor. "Keynes once said to him, after some argument, 'If I had taken you very young, I might have taught you the elements of economics' … Because, however, [Eady] lacked authority, he could annoy Keynes but not thwart him … At the end, only Richard ('Otto') Clarke, another outsider, could stand up to Keynes in the Treasury. But he was a much younger man and, like everyone else, in awe of him. Keynes was left as a solitary mountain towering over the foothills" (Skidelsky 2002, pp. 147–148).
14. Keynes stressed again that "long-term stability of employment may largely depend on having a stable long-term investment programme." Thus, we shall "have to have a periodic survey of investment prospects of which the capital budget may be an important ingredient; and, if we can find ways of retarding or accelerating the long-term programme to offset unforeseen short-term fluctuations, so much the better" (CW 27, p. 356).
15. Keynes made several other arguments worth noting. One referred to the asymmetric effect of the interest rate on investment spending. "Experience shows, however, that whilst a high rate of interest is capable of having a dominating effect on inducement to invest, it becomes relatively unimportant at low levels compared with the [profit rate] expectations affecting the inducement" (CW 27, p. 390).
16. Keynes argued that monetary profit or loss should not be a major criterion for the selection of investment projects: "With a full employment policy, we should not be biased as between two useful projects because one will bring in a direct cash return and the other a social or indirect cash return" (CW 27, p. 407).
17. Keynes stressed that the Public Capital Budget would not "facilitate deficit spending" (CW 27, p. 406).

18 We know from the ferocity of Keynes's attack on "insane" unregulated or lightly regulated national and international "casino" financial markets in the 1930s that he was in favor of tightly regulated national financial markets supported by strict capital controls in the post-WWII period. However, I have not found any specific sources to support this hypothesis with respect to national financial markets during the war years. In the case of the UK, which, of course, was his main concern, this may well be because, as I demonstrated earlier, he did not believe that the UK financial markets were insane casinos. His main complaints were about the government's policy commitment to a strong pound and high interest rates and its facilitation of overseas at the expense of domestic investment. The USA, on the other hand, was the home of the insane casino gambling that triggered the global financial and economic crisis in the 1930s. However, in response to the financial market collapse in the USA in the early 1930s, the government dramatically increased its regulation of financial institutions and markets in order to remove their sources of volatility and fragility. And, of course, government control of financial markets in the USA during the war was especially tight, as it was in the UK. By the 1940s, Keynes presumably assumed that casino capitalism in the USA was dead and buried, which it was, more or less, in the first two decades after the war, after which insane casino financial markets returned.

19 In the proposals for a postwar international financial regime Keynes worked out with Harry Dexter White, the chief US negotiator, capital controls were mandatory. Indeed, countries that received illegal capital transfers were obligated to return the funds to the country of origin. Even under the final agreement imposed on Britain by its dominant and dominating partner, all nations had the right to maintain strict capital controls. Moreover, in a letter to Kalecki in 1944, Keynes stressed the centrality of managed trade to postwar employment planning. "If, as is alleged, I said that the International Monetary Plan 'would ensure the conditions necessary to maintain full employment at home irrespective of conditions abroad', I must have been out of my mind" (CW 27, pp. 382–383).

20 The nationalization of major industries, such as those that took place under the Labour government after the war, was not inconsistent with Keynes's plans. As mentioned above, he supported nationalization when it made economic sense. But he also believed that the government already had control or influence over such a large percentage of capital investment that there was no need in principal to support further nationalization. He argued that proposed nationalizations should be decided on their merit on a case-by-case basis.

21 Though Keynes and Hayek disagreed on many things, they both believed that fundamental uncertainty was an inherent characteristic of the nature of agent economic choice.

# 23 Thoughts on the relevance of Keynes's work to solving today's economic problems

## The society–economy nexus, methodology, theory, and policy

In this book, I have attempted to describe the arc of Keynes's thinking on economic, social, and political developments in Britain and elsewhere from WWI through his death in 1946 and to defend the proposition that he wanted to replace capitalism with Liberal Socialism. My interpretation of Keynes's views on these issues clashes rather dramatically with the standard interpretation held by what I have referred to as Mainstream Keynesianism, the semiofficial view of Keynes's legacy in theory and policy in the post-WWII era, especially, but not exclusively, in the USA. In this concluding chapter, I offer some thoughts on four aspects of Keynes's political economy that might help in the search for solutions to the serious economic problems that confront us in the current era.

### Keynes's "vision" of the appropriate relation between economy and society

In standard economic theory, we formally (in general equilibrium models) or informally (in partial equilibrium models assumed to be embedded in general equilibrium systems) assume we are representing a marketplace in which non-cooperating, isolated individuals and firms come together to buy and sell goods and services. The distribution of wealth among agents is exogenous, unexplained within the confines of the theory. Price signals in the market guide the allocation of economic resources and the distribution of income among economic agents. Much of the history of economic thought has been devoted to demonstrating that an idealized model of a free-market economy generates outcomes that optimize a social welfare function.

The vision of society embedded in standard mainstream models of market economies is thus one in which individuals have no connection with one another except through what Marx referred to as a "cash nexus." Everyone looks out only for themselves, while the market system determines economic and social outcomes. It is reasonable to assume that the "winners" in such an economy – those with the greatest wealth – would have a disproportionate influence on the character of the society in which it was embedded and would be capable of transmitting this power intergenerationally. The economy–society nexus would thus tend to be dominated by the character of the "free-market" capitalist economy. Of course, most governments and other non-market institutions in real-world capitalist economies interfere in market activities in many ways, but they generally do not do so in ways that knowingly threaten the economic, political, and ideological dominance of the capitalist system. Countries committed to strong forms of social democracy are an exception to the rule.

As I noted in several places in this book, the assumption set required to generate Pareto-optimal general equilibrium describes an absurdly unrealistic economy that could not possibly exist in the real world. What, then, was the purpose of devoting so much professional economic talent to the creation of such a theory? Keynes believed the answer to this question was largely ideological: orthodox theory supported the domination of capitalism and capitalists over society.

> That it could explain much social injustice and apparent cruelty as an inevitable incident in the scheme of progress, and the attempt to change such things as likely on the whole to do more harm than good, commended it to authority. That it afforded a measure of justification to the free activities of the individual capitalist, attracted to it the support of the dominant social forces behind authority.
> (CW 7, pp. 32–33)

There is an alternative way to structure the relation between economy and society: let society dominate the society–economy nexus. Start from assumptions about what kind of society the citizens of a country would like to have, as determined through effective democratic processes, and then ask what kinds of economic institutions and policies would be consistent with and supportive of the reproduction of the values and priorities of the "good society" or of "economic and social justice." For example, in their teachings about the relation between capitalism and society and community in papal encyclicals, the Catholic Church has always been deeply suspicious of the compatibility of capitalism with Christian commitments to social and economic justice "All economic institutions must support the bonds of community and solidarity that are essential to the dignity of persons. Wherever our economic arrangements fail to conform to the demands of human dignity lived in community, they must be rejected" (National Conference of Catholic Bishops 1986, p. 15). In the post-WWII era, a number of countries have attempted to institutionalize the dominance of society over economy. The social democratic Nordic countries are prime examples. But as the global neoliberal regime strengthened in recent decades, its incentives and constraints have weakened societal control over the economy, even in these nations.

The reading I have done by and about Keynes in the process of working on this book has led me to the conclusion that in the troubled interwar period Keynes clarified his ideas about what constituted a "good society"; came to believe that British capitalism was inconsistent with the requirements of a "good society"; rejected the then-current capitalist domination of economy over society; and eventually developed a new Liberal Socialist model of political economy in which societal values and imperatives expressed through democratic processes regulated and constrained capitalist markets more than the other way around. Liberal Socialism was Keynes's particular version of social democracy. I would argue that the dominance of society over capitalism in Keynes's vision of Liberal Socialism was greater than in the postwar social democracies of Europe, especially as we moved from the Golden Age to the global neoliberal regime.

Keynes's new model of political economy has been discussed at length throughout this book. The core economic objectives are clear: sustained full employment and job security for everyone who wishes to work; a rapid decline in the inequality of the distribution of income and wealth; the "euthanasia of the rentier, and, consequently, the euthanasia of the cumulative oppressive power of the capitalist to exploit the scarcity value of capital" (CW 7, p. 376); rapidly rising income per capita; and the creation of a comprehensive and generous social welfare system. As stressed throughout this book, to be sustainable, Liberal Socialism would require strict capital controls, managed trade, and various industrial policies.

The major policy tool required to accomplish this transition from laissez-faire capitalism to Liberal Socialism, as Keynes stressed in 1942, was societal control over two-thirds to three-quarters of all large-scale capital investment. Private capitalists operating in private markets would no longer determine the basic trajectory and character of the economy and society over the long run. That would be done primarily by state economic planners and executives in public corporations under the general guidance of the democratic process operating through a Board of National Investment or, later, through the Treasury. Criteria for project selection were not limited to the expected rates of monetary return. They included quality-of-life issues such as contributions to arts, culture, and education, priorities for working-class housing, and environmental concerns.

I stress the importance of the society–economy nexus here in part because, over the decades since WWII, and especially since the early 1980s, capitalism has evolved into a globally integrated neoliberal regime in which the dictates of capitalist markets and the interests of the rich and politically powerful increasingly dominate both the economy and society almost everywhere. In my opinion, the world is in desperate need of a peaceful revolution in which progressive democratic political processes empower society to take control of economic systems and transform them in the spirit of Keynes's Liberal Socialism, though not necessarily in its particular institutions and policies.[1]

## Keynes on the methodology needed to study capitalist economies

We discussed key differences between Keynes's methodology and the positivism of mainstream theory in Chapter 12 of this book. The overwhelming majority of mainstream economists accept Milton Friedman's dictum that the realism and completeness of the assumption set used to construct a theory has no bearing on the truth content of hypotheses derived from these assumptions. The only legitimate test of a theory, he argued, is the consistency of its derived hypotheses with relevant empirical data. However, the Duhem–Quine thesis in the philosophy of science correctly asserts that is not possible to adequately test the empirical validity of hypotheses derived from a theory based on the theory alone. Assumptions from outside the theory must be added to the theory to make it empirically testable. Consider econometric tests of the investment demand function of the neoclassical firm. This requires, among other things, specifying the firm's *expectations* of the profit flows to be generated by the new capital goods over their expected lifetime. This information is not provided by neoclassical theory; rather, it must be added to the theory by specifying a separate theory of expectation formation. Therefore, the empirical tests may be passed even if the theory is wrong because its errors are compensated for by errors in the expectation-formation assumption, and the tests may fail to support the theory even if it is correct because of compensating errors in the expectation-formation assumption.

Keynes, to the contrary, insisted that you cannot build a realistic theory of capitalism based on a crudely unrealistic and/or significantly incomplete assumption set. The realism and completeness of the assumption set matters. In the one-page opening chapter of *The General Theory*, Keynes sought to differentiate his general theory of capitalism from what he saw as the special case embedded in classical theory. The assumption set of classical theory, he said, is "applicable to a special case only and not to the general case, the situation which it assumes being a limiting point of the possible positions of equilibrium" (CW 7, p. 3). In the last chapter of the book, Keynes made a fundamental attack on classical methodology.

> Our criticism of the accepted classical theory of economics has consisted not so much in finding logical flaws in its analysis as in pointing out that its tacit assumptions are seldom or never satisfied, with the result that it cannot solve the problems of the actual world.
> (CW 7, p. 378)

I believe that it is of the utmost importance that the economics profession reject positivism and adopt Keynes's belief that you must build economic theory on a realistic and reasonably complete assumption set.

Consider one rather extreme example of this problem. During the period from the early 1980s to the global financial crisis starting in 2008, mainstream financial economists relied on the "efficient financial market" hypothesis to construct theories of modern financial markets.[2] Efficient financial market theory was built on a stunningly unrealistic assumption set that posited, among other things, that investors had "rational" or correct expectations of the stationary probability distributions that determine future states of the economy. They therefore knew the probability distributions of the cash flows associated with all securities. Investors could thus never be fooled into taking more risk than they wanted to take: they could organize their investment portfolios according to their true risk–return characteristics.[3] This theory, in which nothing can go wrong in financial markets, infected the dominant theories of the macroeconomy. The fact that the economics profession gave the theory its imprimatur made it easier for government legislators to support the process of radical financial market deregulation that took place in the era and also reinforced the widespread belief among investors that the emerging financial boom of the era might never end, which helped sustain the boom and worsen the bust. Almost all mainstream economists celebrated the wonders of global financial markets just as they were about to collapse after 2007. Some economists who adopted Keynes's approach to the theory of financial markets made popular by Hyman Minsky understood that a financial crisis had become quite likely in the mid-2000s.[4] The realism of assumptions matters.

There is a methodological corollary to the insistence that the realism of the assumption set affects the truth content of derived hypotheses that I stressed in Chapter 12. In the historical record, there is no such thing as a generic capitalism – there are only historically, institutionally, and behaviorally unique social formations within which private property and market processes play different roles. Keynes attacked classical theory because its assumption set did not incorporate the actual "facts" of then-current British capitalism, but rather was selected in order to demonstrate that laissez-faire capitalism created the best of all possible worlds. This led to the conclusion that the full-employment equilibrium was the only possible equilibrium position of the economy and that disequilibrium dynamics would always adjust wages, prices, and interest rates in a manner that ensured that this equilibrium position was stable. Incorporation of the institutional and behavioral "facts" specific to time and place that determine the actual behavior of wages and the price of goods and financial assets led Keynes to the conclusion that while nineteenth-century British capitalism may have been "glorious," interwar British capitalism was destructive and could not be reformed. It needed to be replaced by Liberal

Socialism. The message Keynes bequeaths to us here is that economists should build theories that incorporate the distinct character or the institutional and behavioral "facts" of the economies they study and not rely solely on abstract-level models of generic capitalism.

## Economists need to restore key aspects of Keynes's theory that were left out of Mainstream Keynesian theory

Mainstream Keynesian theory does incorporate some of Keynes's most important contributions to macro theory. In particular, it demonstrates that a capitalist economy has many possible states of short-run equilibrium other than full-employment equilibrium, that underemployment equilibriums can be stable or persistent, that the AD (or total spending) function is a crucial determinant of the equilibrium levels of income and employment, that changes in investment spending affect equilibrium income via a "multiplier" that depends on the mpc (and therefore on the distribution of income and wealth), and that the government can influence the equilibrium levels of income and employment in the short run through monetary and fiscal policy. This constituted a transformation in macro theory and policy that eventually replaced classical theory and discredited its laissez-faire macro policies after WWII. Mainstream Keynesianism thus made a significant contribution to the creation of the Golden Age of capitalism that lasted from WWII into the 1970s, though there were many other powerful secular economic trends that also contributed to the prosperity of this era.

Unfortunately, as we have seen, many of the most important innovations in Keynes's theory emphasized in this book were never incorporated into Mainstream Keynesian theory. One can only speculate on the reasons why they were not, but certainly that the Golden Age was a period of widely shared prosperity in many countries was one factor, and the fact that Keynes's radical theory and policy threatened the economic and political dominance of capitalism may have been another. The early postwar period of Trumanism and McCarthyism in the USA was one of extreme hostility to all socialist ideas, labeling them "un-American." I will briefly review some of Keynes's most important contributions to economic theory that were lost in the Modern Keynesian translation of Keynes and should be resurrected.

First, contrary to conventional wisdom, neither *The General Theory* nor, for that matter, the bulk of Keynes's work in the interwar period is devoted exclusively to the theory of the short run. I have argued that Keynes believed that modern capitalism was an economic system that tended toward long-term stagnation in the absence of historically contingent factors such as high population growth, war, or system-transforming technical change. He became convinced early in this era that the model of global capitalism that dominated in the "glorious" nineteenth century was permanently broken and could not be restored after WWI. This is the main theme of *The Economic Consequences of the Peace*, which is discussed in Chapter 2. Chapters 13 and 14 of this book document his emphasis on the theoretical possibility of secular stagnation and explain why he believed that Britain and much of the world would remain stagnant unless currently unforeseeable new sources of long-term growth emerged. WWII and its aftermath led to the end of that particular episode of stagnation.

Keynes's focus on the possibility of long eras of stagnation disappeared from economists' understanding of Keynesian economics after the war. His theory was replaced by Mainstream Keynesian theory, a theory focused on the short and intermediate runs. It promised a perpetual Golden Age under appropriate macro policy and seemed to deliver on that promise for a generation or so. The disastrous economic and political aftereffects of the recent global financial and economic crisis, a crisis that was neither predicted nor explained by Mainstream Keynesian theorists, showed this theory to be fundamentally flawed and led to a renewed interest in the possibility of secular stagnation in modern capitalism by some respected Mainstream Keynesian economists. Long-term stagnation remains an important area of study and neither Keynes nor those Modern Keynesians interested in stagnation theory have had the last word on the subject.

Second, there are two major system-changing innovations in Keynes's macro theory. The first is the model of high unemployment equilibrium caused by inadequate AD – the model taught in university courses on Keynesian economics. The second is Keynes's assumption of fundamental or radical uncertainty, which, as we have seen, transformed not only the theory of agent choice, but also the theory of the ontology and epistemology of the agent.

Keynes had the courage to accept an obvious and important "fact" that almost all other economists reject – that the probability distributions that describe future states of the economy are unknowable in the present and are affected by the choices agents make in the present in ignorance of the future. Radical uncertainty changed the behavioral equations inserted into Keynes's AD-driven macroeconomic model and therefore changed the basic characteristics of the model, a model derisively labeled "chapter 12 Keynesianism" by many mainstream economists. Keynes's agents do not have the complete and correct information about future economic states needed to make assuredly optimal decisions. They therefore have to conjure up expectations through behavioral and conventional heuristics, then decide how much "confidence" to place in the truth content of these expectations before they can determine the choices they should make in the marketplace. Keynes was thus one of the earliest creators of behavioral theory in economics. He used his more radical form of behavioral theory to overthrow received theory rather than make moderate adjustments to it as today's behavioral theorists claim to do.

Keynes argued that expectations are typically formed through extrapolation from past trends, that confidence in expectations reflects the accuracy of expectations in the recent past, and that when expectations thus formed suddenly become substantially inaccurate, confidence in the truth content of expectations evaporates and agents can suddenly become extremely risk averse. The radical change that the assumption of fundamental uncertainty imparts to the theory of financial markets is self-evident, as is the stark contrast between "efficient" financial market theory and Keynes's theory of the "insane" financial gambling casino.

Keynes's macro theory, which combines his theory of agent choice based on radical uncertainty with his theory of the semiautonomous behavior of AD, has a number of major implications for improving the current state of macro theory.

First, it generates a theory of an economic system that is incessantly changing and evolving due to *endogenous* processes. It does not have to be exogenously "shocked" to move.

Second, unlike neoclassical theories of general equilibrium, Keynes's capitalism has no demonstrably optimality properties; sometimes it works well (see again the "glorious" nineteenth century, which worked very well for Britain's ruling elites) and sometimes it creates depression and mass unemployment. It all depends on the institutional and behavioral "facts" specific to time and place.

Third, Keynes's theory can explain *why* capitalist economies experience bouts of extreme instability such as the boom–crash experience in the USA in the late 1920s and early 1930s or the global economic and financial crisis that began in 2008. This can be seen most clearly in chapters 11–15 and 22 of *The General Theory*, which deal with financial markets, capital investment, and business cycles. Keynes's theory of endogenously generated instability, which has a key role in financial markets, was popularized by Hyman Minsky. Any economic theory that claims to explain the long-term behavior of capitalist economies must be able to explain not just ordinary business cycles, but also why such economies experience both vigorous expansions and severe economic downturns and depressions from time to time. Mainstream Keynesian theory cannot do this.

Fourth, Keynes insisted that, in order to have useful economic theories of actually existing capitalist economies, we must study the "facts" about how disequilibrium dynamics function under various institutional and historical conditions. Recall that about 40 percent of *The General Theory* is devoted to an analysis of disequilibrium dynamics. Mainstream Keynesian theory typically just assumes that disequilibrium processes are stabilizing. Keynes argued that under certain conditions disequilibrium dynamics can be destructive; they can magnify rather than cushion negative "shocks" to AD. In Chapters 15–18 of this book, we presented Keynes's explanation of the circumstances under which wage and price deflation triggered by a negative demand shock can increase rather than minimize the size of the ultimate downturn and of why the shock might trigger rising interest rates and falling stock prices that aggravate the downturn. This is another major contribution to macro theory by Keynes that is not reflected in Modern Keynesian theory.

## Relevance of Keynes's radical policy positions for today's economies

The entry thesis for this chapter was that Keynes believed that our economic system must be constructed so as to conform to the requirements of society's commitment to economic and social justice rather than the other way around. Of course, the economic resources required to support government commitments to providing economic and social justice are obviously constrained by the economy's ability to generate income. But for Keynes, economic and social justice is the objective and the ability of the economy to generate income the constraint. Keynes believed that replacing laissez-faire capitalism with Liberal Socialism would dramatically loosen that constraint.

Keynes's simple macro model of capitalism asserts that the equilibrium level of income is equal to the level of investment (as determined by the expected profit rate minus the interest rate) times the inverse of the mpc – or the "multiplier." Keynes's long-run theory stressed capitalism's tendency toward secular stagnation brought on by inadequate capital investment (caused by a falling rate of profit), a relatively high interest rate, and a low investment multiplier due to excessive inequality in the context of financial market instability. This simple macro model can also be used to construct an outline of Keynes's vision of Liberal Socialism. We have to add to the model: state planning and/or guidance of most large-scale investment projects; monetary policy designed to drive the risk-adjusted interest rate toward zero; and a sharp decline in the inequality of the distribution of income and wealth through progressive taxation that would increase the value of the mpc and thus of the investment "multiplier." The long-term trajectory of the economy under Liberal Socialism would therefore be heavily influenced by societal preferences under an economic system designed to generate sustained full employment, substantial income growth, and a more egalitarian society.

In the last chapter, we saw that Keynes was the central figure in the creation of the British government's plans for the reconstruction of the economy after WWII ended, plans that would build institutions and policies that embodied Keynes's vision of Liberal Socialism. We earlier quoted Schumpeter: "Everyone knows that during the war [Keynes] entered the Treasury again (1940) and that his influence grew, along with Churchill, until nobody thought of challenging it" (Schumpeter 1946, p. 518). Chapter 22 of this book laid out in detail Keynes's three-stage plan designed to achieve sustained full employment primarily through state planning of two-thirds to three-quarters of large-scale capital expenditures, a plan that was supported at the highest levels of government. Adoption of his plan would mean that the future trajectory of the economy would be primarily determined by societal preferences expressed through a democratic political process and only secondarily by the capitalist market system. State-guided investment policy was to be accompanied by a generous social welfare system, highly progressive taxes, a low interest rate monetary policy (implemented by a nationalized Bank of England), strict capital controls, managed trade, and non-casino financial markets. We also saw that there was reason to expect that some variant of his radical view of the future organization of the British economy would be implemented even if the Conservative Party remained in power when the war ended. Keynes's economic revolution was not just a utopian dream; *it had become a politically feasible project.*

How times have changed! Social democracy is in retreat almost everywhere. Authoritarian oligarchies are on the rise in many nominally democratic countries, including in the USA, and the globally integrated neoliberal system institutionally empowers rich investors and multinational corporations to punish any country that does not play by their preferred rules of the game. This means that control over the economy is passing from democratic processes that at least had the potential to help society control the economy through the political process to economic policy regimes that serve the interests of giant corporations and the rich. The evidence of this is everywhere. Within-country tax structures have become more regressive, income and wealth inequality have skyrocketed in most countries, social welfare systems are under extreme duress, and most labor movements are in a state of collapse. Not only are large-scale non-defense capital investment projects overwhelmingly controlled by private-sector capitalist firms rather than the state, there has also been a huge increase in recent decades in the privatization of previously large-scale public utilities of all sorts, often under crony capitalist arrangements.

Of course, the fact that Keynes's preferred system of Liberal Socialism is not politically viable in the current era does not mean that Keynes has nothing to teach us about economic policy in today's world. On the contrary, as I have argued throughout this book, many important aspects of his scathing critique of laissez-faire capitalism are applicable to today's capitalist economies. I offer four examples of Keynes-inspired policy interventions that could improve economic performance in the future. Even taken together they would not constitute a radical transformation of the economic system. At least three of them were widely used in the West after WWII. However, none of them are likely to be adopted unless society can manage to sharply reduce the political influence of its giant corporations and oligarchs.

First, as we argued above, we need more realistic theories of the performance of capitalist economies over the long run to serve as a policy guide for long-run economic planning. In both *The General Theory* and in much of his other writings throughout the interwar years, Keynes argued that, left to its own devices, a modern capitalist economy has a tendency to stagnate over the long run, though it can also achieve spurts of rapid growth from time to time. The central cause of this problem in Keynes's view was inadequate large-scale capital investment. This led to his conclusion that public and semi-public bodies should control the lion's share of such investment projects, which they did in Britain at the time. In the last chapter, we outlined his concrete proposals for state planning of most long-term large-scale capital investment projects. The objective was to create and prioritize a portfolio of economically and socially attractive investment projects large enough to defeat secular stagnation by persistently closing the gap between private investment and the investment level required to keep AD equal to full-employment AS. The composition of this investment was to be influenced by both the social and economic priorities of society.

The policy lesson for the current era would be that government and other publicly oriented institutions should attempt to take responsibility for a larger share of total national investment spending and, in particular, should *coordinate* their annual capital investment expenditures in order both to sustain full employment and to achieve key social objectives *over the long run*. For example, it is widely understood that there is a need for much greater investment in infrastructure, in public utilities, in clean energy, in education, and so forth in the USA and elsewhere. The American Society of Civil Engineers in 2017 estimated that the amount of investment needed to repair and modernize US infrastructure over the next ten years is on the order of $4.5 trillion, almost all of which will be funded by public authorities. If this infrastructural investment was planned and *coordinated* to achieve sustained full employment and other economic and social objectives, we might consider this to be a weak variant of Keynes's plan for a Board of National Investment. This would even be helpful in the intermediate run. If the USA had taken a coordinated approach to the determination of public and semi-public investment spending in the recession years from 2008 to 2015, it could have borrowed long term at extremely low real interest rates and increased investment by enough to substantially weaken the long recession of that period.

Second, Keynes taught us that highly liquid, loosely regulated, globally integrated, excessively large, and non-transparent financial systems are, in his words, insane gambling casinos that can accelerate and sustain financial booms and economic expansions, but also create devastating financial- and real-sector crises. We have been living with a modern insane gambling casino for several decades.

The central policy implication of mainstream financial market theory is that governments should use a light touch in its regulation of financial markets. This consensus view of the economics profession lent support to the government's disastrous radical deregulation of US financial markets that began in the early 1980s and culminated in the global financial and economic crisis that broke out in 2008. This crisis is inexplicable within mainstream financial theory but is perfectly consistent with the Keynes–Minsky theory of financial markets.

The central policy implications of Keynes–Minsky theory are that financial markets need to be much smaller, less complex, more transparent, less globally integrated, and more tightly regulated, and that financial firms have to be much smaller (eliminating "too big to fail" status), much less leveraged, much more transparent, barred from gambling activities with depositors' money, and forced to focus primarily on providing safe assets for depositors and financing productive investment activity. It would not take a political revolution to implement important pieces of this policy agenda. The economics profession could help in this task if it would end its allegiance to "efficient" financial market theory and adopt Keynes–Minsky theory.

Third, Keynes argued that high levels of income and wealth inequality not only violate norms of social justice, they also substantially reduce the mpc and thus lower the investment "multiplier." This leads to lower levels of income and employment. As we have seen, he considered this to be a major cause of the secular stagnation of the interwar years. Keynes also understood that high inequality led to bloated and unstable financial markets and excessive political power of those at the top of the income and wealth distributions. For all of these reasons, he made a large reduction in income and wealth inequality a major policy objective. Reversing the huge rise in within-country inequality in most countries in the last few decades would sharply increase global AD and substantially reduce global unemployment. It should become a major policy objective of political movements everywhere.

Fourth, Keynes was vigorously opposed to having Britain so deeply embedded in an integrated global economic and financial system that it could not control its own economic future. Recall his tirade against excessive global integration in his 1933 essay "National Self-Sufficiency," which we discussed in Chapter 11 of this book: "let goods be homespun whenever it is reasonably and conveniently possible; and, above all, let finance be primarily national" (CW 21, pp. 235–37). The most urgent task facing Britain, he said, was to create a "transition towards greater national self-sufficiency and a planned domestic economy" (CW 21, p. 245). The planned investment regime at the heart of Liberal Socialism could not be achieved and sustained unless Britain adopted strict capital controls – to prevent capital from fleeing the country when British interest rates fell below rates offered elsewhere – and imposed managed trade, so that high domestic growth did not lead to chronic trade deficits. The extreme degree of global economic and financial integration under today's neoliberal order makes it extraordinarily difficult for any country to experiment with major institutional and structural changes in its political economy that are opposed by large corporations and wealthy elites. Capital controls and managed trade are necessary but hardly sufficient conditions for societies to substantially increase their control over their own national economic outcomes in today's neoliberal global capitalism.

## Notes

1 There are obviously many possible forms of democratically guided socialism.
2 The efficient financial market hypothesis states that all information relevant to security pricing is known to all participants in the market. Expectations of the future cash flows associated with all securities are correct or "rational." It must be incorporated into a theory (such as the Capital Asset Pricing Model) that explains how this information is used to determine security prices. Since this is an equilibrium model in which all agents have the same information, there is no trading in the model.
3 See chapter 1 in Crotty (2017) for a more complete listing of the unrealistic assumptions used to build the theory.
4 See chapter 4 in Crotty (2017), which is based on a paper first presented in late 2006.

# References

Aldcroft, D.H. (1986). *The British Economy: Volume 1: The Years of Turmoil 1920–1951*. New York: Columbia University Press.
Beckert, S. (2015). *Empire of Cotton: A Global History*. New York: Vintage.
Board of Governors of the Federal Reserve System (1943). *Banking and Monetary Statistics, 1914–1941*. Available at http://fraser.stlouisfed.org/title/38 (accessed January 15, 2018).
Camerer, C.F. and Lowenstein, G. (2004). Behavioral Economics: Past, Present, and Future. In: Camerer, C.F., Lowenstein, G., and Rabin, M. (eds.). *Advances in Behavioral Economics*. Princeton: Princeton University Press, pp. 1–61.
Carlstrom, C.T. and Fuerst, T.S. (2001). *Perils of Price Deflation: An Analysis of the Great Depression*. Cleveland: Federal Reserve Bank of Cleveland.
Chandler, A.D. (1990). *Scale and Scope: The Dynamics of Industrial Capitalism*. Cambridge, MA: Harvard University Press.
Colander, D. and Landreth, H. (1996). *The Coming of Keynesianism to America*. Brookfield: Edward Elgar.
Crotty, J. (1983). On Keynes and Capital Flight. *Journal of Economic Literature*, 21(1), pp. 59–65.
Crotty, J. (1990). Owner–Manager Conflict and Financial Theories of Investment Stability: A Critical Assessment of Keynes, Tobin, and Minsky. *Journal of Post Keynesian Economics*, 12(4), pp. 519–542.
Crotty, J. (1994). Are Keynesian Uncertainty and Macrotheory Compatible? In: Dymski, G. and Pollin, R. (eds.). *New Perspectives in Monetary Macroeconomics: Explorations in the Tradition of Hyman P. Minsky*. Ann Arbor: University of Michigan Press, pp. 105–142.
Crotty, J. (2005). The Neoliberal Paradox: The Impact of Destructive Product Market Competition and "Modern" Financial Markets on Nonfinancial Corporation Performance in the Neoliberal Era. In: Epstein, G.A. (ed.). *Financialization in the World Economy*. Cheltenham and Northampton, MA: Edward Elgar.
Crotty, J. (2013). The Realism of Assumptions Does Matter. In: Epstein, G.A. and Wolfson, M.H. (eds.). *The Handbook of the Political Economy of Financial Crises*. New York: Oxford University Press, pp. 133–158.
Crotty, J. (2017). *Capitalism, Macroeconomics and Reality: Understanding Globalization, Financialization, Competition, and Crises*. Cheltenham and Northampton, MA: Edward Elgar.
Darity Jr, W.A. and Galbraith, J.K. (1994). *Macroeconomics*. Boston: Houghton Mifflin Company.

## References

Durbin, E.F. (1985). *New Jerusalems: The Labour Party and the Economics of Democratic Socialism*. London: Routledge/Thoemms Press.

Eichengreen, B. (2004). The British Economy between the Wars. In: Floud, R. and Johnson, P. (eds.). *The Cambridge Economic History of Modern Britain*. Cambridge: Cambridge University Press, pp. 314–343.

Fazzari, S.M. (1985). Keynes, Harrod, and the Rational Expectations Revolution. *Journal of Post Keynesian Economics*, 8(1), pp. 66–80.

Federal Reserve Bank of Cleveland (1998). Interest Rates in the 1920s. *Economic Trends*, No. 98-02. Available at: www.clevelandfed.org/newsroom-and-events/publications/economic-trends/economic-trends-archives/1998-economic-trends/et-19980201-interest-rates-in-the-1920s.aspx (accessed February 20, 2019).

Findlay, M.E. and Williams, E.E. (2008). Financial Economics at 50: An Oxymoronic Tautology. *Journal of Post Keynesian Economics*, 31(2), pp. 213–226.

Garside, W.R. (1990). *British Unemployment 1919–1939: A Study in Public Policy*. Cambridge: Cambridge University Press.

Gordon, R. (2016). *The Rise and Fall of American Growth: The US Standard of Living since the Civil War*. Princeton: Princeton University Press.

Harrod, R.F. (1951). *The Life of John Maynard Keynes*. New York: W.W. Norton and Company.

Hicks, J.R. (1937). Mr. Keynes and the "Classics": A Suggested Interpretation. *Econometrica*, 5(2), pp. 147–159.

Hicks, J.R. (1980). IS-LM: An Explanation. *Journal of Post Keynesian Economics*, 3(2), pp. 139–154.

Hobsbawm, E.J. (1969). *Industry and Empire*. Middlesex: Penguin Books.

Kalecki, M. (1943). Political Aspects of Full Employment. *The Political Quarterly*, 14(4), pp. 322–330.

Keynes, J.M. (1920). *Economic Consequences of the Peace*. New York: Harcourt, Brace, and Howe.

Keynes J.M. (1937). The General Theory of Employment. *The Quarterly Journal of Economics*, 51(2), pp. 209–223.

Keynes, J.M. (1971–1989). *The Collected Writings of John Maynard Keynes* (Vol. 4, *A Tract on Monetary Reform*). Johnson, E. and Moggridge, D. (eds.). Cambridge: Cambridge University Press for the Royal Economic Society.

Keynes, J.M. (1971–1989). *The Collected Writings of John Maynard Keynes* (Vol. 5, *A Treatise on Money: The Pure Theory of Money*). Johnson, E. and Moggridge, D. (eds.). Cambridge: Cambridge University Press for the Royal Economic Society.

Keynes, J.M. (1971–1989). *The Collected Writings of John Maynard Keynes* (Vol. 6, *A Treatise on Money: The Applied Theory of Money*). Johnson, E. and Moggridge, D. (eds.). Cambridge: Cambridge University Press for the Royal Economic Society.

Keynes, J.M. (1971–1989). *The Collected Writings of John Maynard Keynes* (Vol. 7, *The General Theory of Employment, Interest and Money*). Johnson, E. and Moggridge, D. (eds.). Cambridge: Cambridge University Press for the Royal Economic Society.

Keynes, J.M. (1971–1989). *The Collected Writings of John Maynard Keynes* (Vol. 9, *Essays in Persuasion*). Johnson, E. and Moggridge, D. (eds.). Cambridge: Cambridge University Press for the Royal Economic Society.

Keynes, J.M. (1971–1989). *The Collected Writings of John Maynard Keynes* (Vol. 12, *Economic Articles and Correspondences: Investment and Editorial*). Johnson, E. and

Moggridge, D. (eds.). Cambridge: Cambridge University Press for the Royal Economic Society.

Keynes, J.M. (1971–1989). *The Collected Writings of John Maynard Keynes* (Vol. 13, *The General Theory and After: Part I, Preparation*). Johnson, E. and Moggridge, D. (eds.). Cambridge: Cambridge University Press for the Royal Economic Society.

Keynes, J.M. (1971–1989). *The Collected Writings of John Maynard Keynes* (Vol. 14, *The General Theory and After: Part II, Defense and Development*). Johnson, E. and Moggridge, D. (eds.). Cambridge: Cambridge University Press for the Royal Economic Society.

Keynes, J.M. (1971–1989). *The Collected Writings of John Maynard Keynes* (Vol. 19-I, *Activities 1922–1929: The Return to Gold and Industrial Policy Part I*). Johnson, E. and Moggridge, D. (eds.). Cambridge: Cambridge University Press for the Royal Economic Society.

Keynes, J.M. (1971–1989). *The Collected Writings of John Maynard Keynes* (Vol. 19-II, *Activities 1922–1929: The Return to Gold and Industrial Policy Part II*). Johnson, E. and Moggridge, D. (eds.). Cambridge: Cambridge University Press for the Royal Economic Society.

Keynes, J.M. (1971–1989). *The Collected Writings of John Maynard Keynes* (Vol. 20, Activities 1929–1931: *Rethinking Employment and Unemployment Policies*). Johnson, E. and Moggridge, D. (eds.). Cambridge: Cambridge University Press for the Royal Economic Society.

Keynes, J.M. (1971–1989). *The Collected Writings of John Maynard Keynes* (Vol. 21, *Activities 1931–1939: World Crises and Policies in Britain and America*). Johnson, E. and Moggridge, D. (eds.). Cambridge: Cambridge University Press for the Royal Economic Society.

Keynes, J.M. (1971–1989). *The Collected Writings of John Maynard Keynes* (Vol. 27, *Activities 1940–1946: Shaping the Post-War World: Employment and Commodities*). Johnson, E. and Moggridge, D. (eds.). Cambridge: Cambridge University Press for the Royal Economic Society.

Keynes, J.M. (1971–1989). *The Collected Writings of John Maynard Keynes* (Vol. 29, *The General Theory and After: A Supplement*). Johnson, E. and Moggridge, D. (eds.). Cambridge: Cambridge University Press for the Royal Economic Society.

Lawson, T. (1988). Probability and Uncertainty in Economic Analysis. *Journal of Post Keynesian Economics*, 11(1), pp. 38–65.

Liberal Industrial Inquiry (1928). *Britain's Industrial Future*. London: E. Benn Ltd.

Lucas, R. (1981). *Studies in Business-Cycle Theories*. Cambridge, MA: MIT Press.

Marx, K. (1932). *The German Ideology*. Moscow: Marx-Engels Institute (Original work published 1846.)

Marx, K. (1967). *Capital, Volume III: The Process of Capitalist Production as a Whole*. Engels, F.E. (ed.). New York: International Publishers Co., Inc. (Original work published 1894.)

Minsky, H.P. (1975). *John Maynard Keynes*. New York: Columbia University Press.

Mitchell, B.R. and Deane, P. (1962). *Abstract of British Historical Statistics*. Cambridge: Cambridge University Press.

Moggridge, D.E. (1992). *Maynard Keynes: An Economist's Biography*. London and New York: Routledge.

Moody's (2018). *Moody's Seasoned Baa Corporate Bond Yield*. Retrieved from FRED, Federal Reserve Bank of St. Louis. Available at https://fred.stlouisfed.org/series/BAA (accessed January 15, 2018).

National Conference of Catholic Bishops (1986). *Economic Justice for All: Pastoral Letter on Catholic Social Teaching and the U.S. Economy*. Available at www.usccb.org/upload/economic_justice_for_all.pdf (accessed January 15, 2018).

O'Donnell, R. (1999). Keynes's Socialism: Conception, Strategy and Espousal. In: Sardoni, C. and Kriesler, P. (eds.). *Keynes, Post Keynesianism and Political Economy: Essays in Honour of Geoff Harcourt, Volume III*. New York: Routledge, pp. 149–175.

Piketty, T. (2014). *Capital in the 21st Century*. Cambridge, MA: Harvard University Press.

Pollard, S. (1983). *The Development of the British Economy: 1914–1980*. Baltimore: Edward Arnold.

Rabin, M. (2002). A Perspective on Psychology and Economics. *European Economic Review*, 46(4–5), pp. 657–685.

Schumpeter, J.A. (1942). *Capitalism, Socialism and Democracy*. New York: Harper & Brothers.

Schumpeter, J.A. (1946). John Maynard Keynes 1883–1946. *The American Economic Review*, 36(4), pp. 495–518.

Shackle, G.L.S. (1972). *Epistemics & Economics: A Critique of Economic Doctrines*. Cambridge: Cambridge University Press.

Skidelsky, R. (1992). *John Maynard Keynes. Volume II: The Economist as Saviour, 1920–1937*. London: Macmillan.

Skidelsky, R. (2002). *John Maynard Keynes: Fighting for Britain, 1937–1946* (Vol. 3). New York: Penguin Group.

United States Bureau of Labor Statistics (2018). *Consumer Price Index for All Urban Consumers: All Items*. Retrieved from FRED, Federal Reserve Bank of St. Louis. Available at https://fred.stlouisfed.org/series/CPIAUCNS (accessed January 15, 2018).

United States Bureau of the Census (1975). *Historical Statistics of the United States from Colonial Times to 1970, Part 1*. Washington, DC: US Department of Commerce, Bureau of the Census.

# Index

References to notes are given as the page reference followed by the letter "n" and the note number.

"abnormal" times 143, 247, 252, 271–272, 280
abstraction 72, 82
AD (aggregate demand) 10, 13, 14, 46, 166, 178, 210, 223, 304, 372; and deflation 210, 213, 215; falling with AS, in destabilizing bond markets 224–226; Modern Keynesian IS/LM and AD/AS analysis 272–276; and multiplier concept 50–51; negative shock to 14, 222, 223, 257; *Tract on Monetary Reform* 39
agent choice theory 13, 168, 231, 240; rational agent choice, classical/neoclassical theories 258–259
aggregate demand (AD) *see* AD (aggregate demand)
aggregate supply (AS) *see* AS (aggregate supply)
Aldcroft, D.H. 58, 61n6
"Am I A Liberal?" 80, 82n1
*American Economic Review* 5
applied models 165–166, 168, 169
AS (aggregate supply) 11; disequilibrium processes in the bond market 222, 223; falling with AD, in destabilizing bond markets 224–226; Modern Keynesian IS/LM and AD/AS analysis 272–276
assets: capital 95, 96, 100, 128–129, 184, 266, 284; collateral 217; durable 189; financial 13, 14, 137, 139, 144, 200n9, 235, 294, 370, 377; "insane" financial markets of the 1920s/1930s, US 139, 141, 145; interest-bearing 236, 237n7; liquid 28, 193–194, 217, 226, 294; real 193–199, 256, 284; risky 142, 194, 232; secular stagnation 180, 182, 184, 194
autarky 155

Bagehot, W. 186–187
balance of trade surpluses 9
balance sheets 142
Baldwin, S. 61n9
bank failures 141
Bank of England 9, 38, 59, 92, 118, 302, 315; nationalization of 297, 361, 375
bankruptcy: of classical/neoclassical theories of rational agent choice 258–259; indebted firms 91; of the less efficient 72
"Bastard Keynesianism" 70; *see also* Mainstream Keynesian theory
"bear" market 136, 137, 265
Beckert, S. 170n5
Beveridge, W. 21n13, 101, 106, 331, 347; Beveridge Plan 332–335; Beveridge Report 337
Bevin, E. 116, 120
Board of National Investment 6, 129, 198, 320, 329, 339, 368; capital accumulation, regulation 96, 99, 102–104, 106, 109
bonds 14, 28, 54, 169; Dead-weight Debt, National Investment Bonds 105; disequilibrium processes in bond market 221–238; interest rates 222, 223, 225, 226–232; Keynes's theory of potentially destabilizing bond markets 224–232; liquidity preference theory 229, 231, 233–234,

384  *Index*

236, 237n12, 280; Mainstream Keynesian theory 169; prices 12–14, 229; and stock markets 221, 237n6; temporary excess demand for 12–13; and uncertainty 221, 226–232
booms: boom and bust 168, 233; construction industry 148; financial *see* financial/stock market booms; housing 102; railway 52, 57
Brand, Robert 97, 102
Bretton Woods arrangements 363n1
Britain: Bank of England 9, 38, 59, 92, 118, 302, 315; coal industry *see* coal industry, Britain; cotton industry 82n2, 89, 90, 92, 167, 170n5, 212; deflation *see* deflation; disequilibrium, deflationary 64–69; economy seen as rigid and inflexible 150n2; export industries 48, 55, 59, 63, 85, 89, 99, 181, 337, 356; financial panic of 1930s, not involved in 144; interwar period, economic problems in 98, 116, 119, 121, 123, 169–170; investment stagnation, interwar period 27; Labour Party *see* Labour Party, Britain; Liberal Party *see* Liberal Party, Britain; "New Jerusalem," creating 104, 329, 330; nineteenth-century vs interwar capitalism 164; population growth, fall in 147; postwar social welfare system 21n13, 331; pre-WWI dominance in international trade, evaporation of 33n4; public corporations *see* public corporations; railways 52; rentier class 9, 10, 42, 43, 62n17, 78, 297; ruling elites 373; social welfare system 21n13, 331; stagnation suffered by 52; Trade Facilities Act 61n8, 105, 114n4; unemployment rates 138; "way of life" 80; working classes 1, 33n2, 68
*Britain's Industrial Future* (BIF), Liberal Party manifesto 4, 82, 84, 93, 95–135, 138, 295, 309n3; Book 2 100, 104, 107; Book 4 100, 104; Chapter VI, Section 2 102; macro dimensions of policy proposals 100; radical policies of Keynes, attempts to gain support for 116–135; *see also* Liberal Party, Britain
British Union of Fascists 122
brokerage charges 169, 295

brokers' loans 233, 238n15, 255, 286
bubbles 14, 146; bond market, disequilibrium processes 233–234; expectations, long-term 255, 257, 260; financial 162, 288; speculative bubble of 1919–1920 93n2
Building Societies 102
"bull" market 136, 137, 265
business cycle theory 148, 168, 233, 264–268, 294; intermediate-run model of 15, 165, 269

Camerer, C.F. 259
capital 90, 153; amounts 101–103; composition 175; development 110, 131; flight of 54, 153, 156; marginal efficiency of *see* marginal efficiency of capital; marginal product of 200n3, 208n1, 219n7; movement of 2, 61n9, 63, 157; physical 248; products 183; rate of profit on 8, 9, 62n13, 179–180, 183, 200n3, 270, 287, 297, 304; regulation of 87; resources 100; scarcity value 9, 180; stocks of 176, 180, 181, 183; zero rate 297
capital accumulation 26, 40, 44, 176, 207, 340; domestic 102, 118; foreign 102; and full employment 78; long-term 52, 78; process 53, 125; public investment and state planning 53, 56, 60, 62n13; public/semi-public 152, 344; real 90; regulation of 95–115
capital assets: business cycle theory 266; capital accumulation, regulation 95, 96, 100; IS/LM model 284; radical policy views of Keynes 128–129; secular stagnation 184; *see also* assets; capital accumulation; capital controls; capital expenditure/investment; capital saturation; capitalism
capital controls 8–9, 10, 114, 118, 300; and relevance of Keynes's work for modern economic problems 377–378; support for 153–154
capital expenditure/investment 6–7, 42, 58, 100, 121, 250; endogenously generated movement 286; instability of long-term expectations determining 247–257; large-scale 309n3, 376; rate of profit on *see* rate of profit; and relevance of

Keynes's work for modern economic problems 375, 376; state planning, in Liberal Socialism 2, 3, 6, 8, 48–62; *see also* capitalism; investment; Liberal Socialism; public investment; state, the
capital, flights of 54
capital saturation 8, 20n4
capitalism 2, 368; of the 1920s 155–156; big-government 289; British 368; capitalist economies, required research methodology 369–371; crises tendencies of modern capitalism 192–199; and endogenously generated movement 285–286; free-market 218, 367; and full employment 217–218; "glorious nineteenth century" 163, 167; Golden Age of modern capitalism 19, 191, 200n8, 289, 371; Great Depression 155; Keynes's opposition to 1–21, 30, 45, 155–156; laissez-faire *see* laissez-faire policies; low unemployment under 8; managed 108; mass movements against 17; methodology required to study capitalist economies 369–391; modern, crisis tendencies 142; nineteenth-century vs interwar Britain 164; replacement with Liberal Socialism, Keynes's hopes for 2, 3–4, 11, 16, 276, 288, 368; slow long-term growth 26–27; structural dysfunctions 8; *Tract on Monetary Reform* 39; traditional definition 11, 302; *see also* capital; capital accumulation; capital assets; capital controls; capital expenditure/investment; capital saturation
capital-safety preference *see* liquidity preference theory
Carlstrom, C.T. 219n3
cartels 89, 90, 93
casino analogy *see* "insane gambling casino" financial markets, US
Catholic Church 367
central planning 126
Chandler, A. 250
Churchill, W. 4, 5, 57
Civil Works Administration program 133
classical economic theory: agent choice theory 13, 168, 258–259; competition concept 72–74; as conventional wisdom 189; equilibrium 11, 163; "glorious nineteenth century" 163, 167; ideological function 164; interest rates 221, 222; Keynes on *see* classical economic theory, Keynes's opposition to; Mainstream Keynesian theory compared 14–15; methodology and ideology 169; and Modern Keynesianism 11–17; New Classical theory 20n12; out-of-equilibrium dynamic processes assumed 14, 162, 223; positivist methodology 71, 82n3; roots 163, 164; *see also* Mainstream Keynesian theory
classical economic theory, Keynes's opposition to 1, 5, 45, 64, 71; disequilibrium processes in the bond market 221–238; methodology and ideology 161–171; and Modern Keynesianism 11–17; Say's Law 11; secular stagnation thesis 202; wage and price deflation 12, 209–220
coal industry, Britain: capital accumulation, regulation 107; deflation 212, 218; gold standard, return to (1925) 66–68; lockout (1926) 218; new economic role of the state 84, 87–89, 92; public investment and state planning 56, 58; stagnation/secular stagnation 172
collateral assets 217
*Collected Writings of John Maynard Keynes* (CW) 1, 116; Volume 19 84; Volume 20 116
Committee of Economists 121
Committee on Finance and Industry 116
Committee on Industry and Trade 64–65, 69n1
Committee on National Debt and Taxation 57
Committee on Post-War Internal Economic Problems 327, 330
Commons, J.R. 81
comparative static analysis 162, 170n2, 183, 194; exercises 209, 216; and exogenous shocks 281–285; legitimacy 276–281; *see also* economics; static models
competition theory 72–74, 84, 114n6; destructive competition 90, 92, 172, 173, 212, 219n6; "free" competition 85, 113; perfect competition 71, 93,

211–212; *see also* cartels; monopolies; oligopolies
"Concluding Notes on the Social Philosophy towards Which the General Theory Might Lead" 300–301
confidence: evaporation of expectations in 1930s 247–257; expectations, role in truth content 230, 245–247, 258, 269; loss of in "insane" financial markets 143
Conservative Party, Britain 96, 114
consumption spending *see* household spending, low
corporatism 76
cotton industry 56, 82n2, 84, 92, 107; Britain 82n2, 89, 90, 167, 170n5, 212; global 189
Cotton Yarn Association, Britain 89, 92
countercyclical macroeconomic policy 17, 18, 169–170, 339, 350
Crotty, J. 2–3, 93n3, 158n3, 170n1, 250, 263n9, 363n1, 378n3, 378n4
crowding-out thesis 120, 276

Darity, S. 301
Darwinian theory 72, 74
debt: Committee on National Debt and Taxation 57; National Debt 105; productive/unproductive 57; public 51; war 34, 58, 62n16, 139
deflation: and AD theory 210, 213, 215; in Britain 149; dangers of according to Keynes 12, 15, 30, 33n7, 34, 36–37, 39, 43–44, 64, 65, 139–140, 210; disequilibrium/ destructive disequilibrium 64, 140, 165; and exports 98; financial fragility thesis 145, 210, 216, 219; gold standard, return to (1925) 64, 65; high unemployment 235, 271; and inflation 33n7; inflation–deflation cycle 43, 44, 45; interest rates, deflation-adjusted 139, 142; Keynes's theory vs classical and Mainstream Keynesian theory 165; marginal product of labor (MPL) 210, 212, 213, 219n2, 219n7, 220n13; post World War I 34, 35–36; and poverty 43–44; radical policy views of Keynes 132; secular stagnation 197; *see also* inflation; price deflation; wage deflation

democratic socialism 11, 124, 190, 303, 318, 378n1
depression, cumulative 173
disequilibrium/destructive disequilibrium 37, 74, 269; bond market, disequilibrium processes *see* bonds; deflation 64, 140, 165; instability 188; Keynes's theory vs classical and Mainstream Keynesian theory 14, 162, 165; problems in Britain 64–69; sources 264; stock market 221, 237n6; wage and price deflation 15–16, 47n12, 64, 67, 138, 269, 271, 289; *see also* equilibrium
"Does Unemployment Need a Drastic Remedy?" 48, 70, 109
dollar, and pound 59
"A Drastic Remedy for Unemployment" (1924) 54
DSGE (dynamic stochastic general equilibrium) models 171n8
durable assets 189

Eady, W. 344, 350
Economic Advisory Council 121
"The Economic Consequences of Mr. Churchill" 33n5, 50, 59, 62n14, 63
*The Economic Consequences of the Peace* 20, 25, 31, 32, 34, 40, 109, 185, 372; Chapter 2 166; methodology and ideology 166, 167
*The Economic Journal* 15, 145, 324n4
Economic Section, War Cabinet 327, 334, 341, 342, 350, 352
economics: applied models 165–166, 168, 169; capitalist economies, required research methodology 369–371; classical economic theory *see* classical economic theory; classical economic theory, Keynes's opposition to; economic policy agenda in Liberal Socialism 6–11; government postwar economic planning for Liberal Socialism 4, 326–365; laissez-faire *see* laissez-faire policies; long-run economic outlook for Europe 8; neoclassical theories 258–259; new economic role of the state 84–94; proper economic role of the state 70–83; relevance of Keynes's work for modern problems 366–378; and society, Keynes's "vision" of appropriate relation between 366–369; static models

see comparative static analysis, static models; see also macroeconomics
economy–society nexus 367
Eichengreen, B. 27
elites see ruling elites
employment, full see full employment
"The End of Laissez-Faire" 70, 79
endogenous balance sheets 269, 270, 276
Engineering, Metal and Shipbuilding Unions 49
equilibrium: classical economic theory 11, 163; under-employment equilibriums 161; endogenous disruption 162; fixed-equilibrium model 137; full employment 13, 14, 117, 222, 257, 370; general see general equilibrium; high-employment long-run 192; high-unemployment long-run equilibrium see stagnation/secular stagnation; market-clearing 117; out-of-equilibrium processes 14, 162, 223, 274; short-term high unemployment 15, 269; stability 12, 15, 188, 209; temporary 49; Walrasian general equilibrium model 20n8, 82n5, 224, 289n2; see also disequilibrium/destructive disequilibrium
*Essays in Persuasion* 70, 93
evolution of Keynes's ideas, writings on: from 1919 to early 1920s 25–47; Liberal Socialism (1931–1932) 124–134; National Self-Sufficiency (1933) 2–3, 4, 46n4, 138, 152–158; new economic role of the state (1927–1928) 84–94; prior to World War II (1936–1939) 313–325; proper economic role of the state (1925–1926) 70–83; public investment and state planning (1924) 48–62; relevance of Keynes's work to current economic problems 366–378; return to gold (1925) 63–69; stagnation/secular stagnation (1937) 201–208; in World War II (1939–1945) 326–365; see also writings
exchange rates: fixed (gold standard) 29, 300; flexible 37–38, 44, 45; fluctuations 46n3, 55, 58; and gold standard 29, 45, 68, 300; stable 26, 195
exogenous shocks: bond market, disequilibrium processes 224–225; endogenously generated movement 15, 285–287; reliance on comparative statics to analyze 284–285; stability and comparative statics 281–284
expectations/expectation formation: agent choice theory 231; confidence, role in truth content of 230, 245–247, 258, 269; conventional expectations formation 41, 221, 286; instability 42, 247–257; long-term 239, 247–257; profit rate, expected 40, 175, 178, 186, 187, 223–224, 235, 247, 252, 264, 270, 277, 282, 290n4, 290n7, 296, 374; radical uncertainty and long-term expectation formation 241–245; rational expectations model 195, 208; security-price, endogeneity 137; short-to intermediate-term 194–195; see also mec (marginal efficiency of capital)
exports/export industries 319, 328; British 48, 55, 59, 63, 85, 89, 99, 181, 337, 356; and deflation 98; depression/shrinking of traditional sectors 48, 50, 57, 63, 65, 85, 89, 99, 100; export-oriented firms 61n8; growth/stimulation 9, 145, 328; markets 37, 57, 173; new equilibrium 93; permanent erosion of traditional export markets 57; public investment and state planning 48, 50, 54, 55, 57–58; and return to gold standard 58, 63, 64; role of the state 71; staple industries 71, 74; traditional sectors 36, 48, 50, 56, 57, 60n2, 63, 65, 84, 85, 89, 99, 100; unemployment 66, 99; wage cuts 218

Fazzari, S. 280
Federation of Master Cotton Spinners, Britain 89
financial assets 13, 14, 200n9, 235, 294; "insane" financial markets of the 1920s/1930s, US 137, 139, 144; relevance of Keynes's work for modern problems 370, 377; see also assets; capital assets
financial fragility thesis 28, 39, 365n18; bond market, disequilibrium processes 233, 236; business cycle theory 168; deflation 145, 210, 216, 219; endogenous creation 260; *The General Theory* (Chapter 12) 240, 255, 256, 260; "insane

gambling casino" financial markets, US 139, 145; methodology and ideology 168; radical policy views 132, 298, 299; stagnation/secular stagnation 172, 176
financial markets: casino analogy *see* "insane gambling casino" financial markets, US; collapse of in the United States (from 1929) 12, 116, 136–139, 141, 169, 234, 264, 269, 365n18; efficiency 370, 378n2; financial market cycles theory 136–137; volatility 136, 137, 269, 294, 295, 298, 365n18; *see also* financial fragility thesis; financial/stock market booms
financial/stock market booms 139, 171n8, 172, 232, 299, 370, 376; IS/LM model 286, 288, 290n5; in the United States (late 1920s) 136, 138, 187, 260, 264, 267, 278, 298
free trade 153, 158
Friedman, M. 82n3, 163
Fuerst, T.S. 219n3
full employment: achieving 50; aggregate demand (AD) 11; and capital accumulation 78; and capitalism 217–218; defining 49, 60n3; equilibrium 13, 14, 117, 222, 257, 370; institutions used to regulate capital accumulation in pursuit of 95–115; and Liberal Socialism 2; "Long-Term Problem of Full Employment" 340; permanent 10; and public investment 302; radical policy program designed to achieve 3; required policies 302; savings levels 340–341; and war 17, 324n4

Galbraith, J. 301
Galton Lecture (1937) 8, 28, 202, 242, 270
Garside, W.R. 60
Geddes, E. 61n10
Geddes Axe 54, 61n10
general equilibrium 164; dynamic stochastic models 171n8; exogenous shock to AD 210; high-employment long-run equilibrium 192; Pareto-optimal 367; Walrasian model 20n8, 82n5, 224, 289n2; *see also* equilibrium
General Strike (May, 1926) 88, 214, 218
*General Theory of Employment, Interest and Money (The General Theory)*: Chapter 2 12, 36, 148, 185, 192, 269; Chapter 3 176, 192; Chapter 5 192; Chapter 7 170n4; Chapter 8 170n4, 177; Chapter 10 277, 284, 293; Chapter 11 220n11, 240; Chapter 12 136, 143, 146, 192, 216, 221, 230, 239–263, 271, 278, 279, 293–294, 298; Chapter 13 136, 192, 271, 286; Chapter 14 12, 192, 221; Chapter 15 136, 192, 199, 271, 286; Chapter 16 8, 179, 270, 296; Chapter 17 175, 183, 192–199, 270, 296; Chapter 19 12, 36, 148, 162, 170n2, 184–185, 192, 269, 279; Chapter 22 136, 168, 187, 192, 233, 264–267, 268n1, 269–271, 279, 313–314; Chapter 23 187; Chapter 24 206, 300, 352; concrete historical facts 172–174; contradictions in 308; crises tendencies of modern capitalism (Chapter 17) 192–199; determination of "general" 165–170; exogenous shocks 281–285; expectations, long-term 239–263; five models 15–16, 269, 272–276; IS/LM interpretation *see* IS/LM model; Keynes's support of Liberal Socialism in 6, 170; Keynes's views on 266, 291; and Mainstream Keynesian Theory 5; objectives 1–2, 190; opening page 71; priority of stagnation/secular stagnation in 174–190; purpose of writing 1–2, 302; radical policy views in 291–309, 374–378; stability properties and legitimacy of comparative static macro-policy analysis 276–281; stagnation/secular stagnation 138; *see also* Liberal Socialism
global depression 93n1
global financial crisis (1930s) 138, 139, 144
global financial crisis (2008) 13, 15, 18, 191
gold standard, return to (1925) 8, 29, 33n5, 62n14, 62n16, 63–69, 170n6; critique by Keynes 33n5; and mining industry 67–68; at prewar par 35–37, 57–59, 63, 64, 66, 67, 69, 70, 74, 80, 88, 98, 173, 218; run-up to 62n14
Gordon, R. 19, 191
government funding 51
Great Depression 1, 9, 30, 155, 191, 212–213, 264, 269, 294, 326; prior to 288–289

Hansen, A. 8, 192
Harrod, R.F. 96, 152
Hayek, F.A. 361, 365n21
Henderson, H. 122, 134n3, 141, 330, 340, 344, 350, 356, 357, 363n4
Hicks, J.R. 20n5, 32–33, 237n10; critique of LM curve 279, 289n4; IS/LM model created by 14, 165, 273, 274, 275
high unemployment 17; deflation 218, 235, 271; with stable equilibrium 12, 15, 269; sustained, long-term model *see* stagnation/secular stagnation; *see also* IS/LM model; "Keynesian Cross"; unemployment
Hilton, J. 112
Hitler, A. 153, 313
Hobsbawm, E. 5–6, 30–31, 167
Hopkins, R. 335
household spending, low 167–168, 183
housing 147
*How to Pay for the War* (Keynes) 326
Hume, David 188
hypotheses: truth content 163; validity and assumption set 162–165

imports 9, 66, 89; capital accumulation, regulation 110, 117; immediate prewar period 314, 319; radical policy views, obtaining support for 120, 130; restricting 145, 173, 356; during World War II 356, 358
"The Inducement to Invest" 239
Industrial Inquiry, Liberal Party (1928) 95–97, 115n8, 309n3; Executive Committee 96; postwar economic planning 320–321, 363n2
industrial policy 50, 187, 315; capital accumulation, regulation 98, 107; new economic role the state 84, 89
Industrial Revolution 30–31
industry rationalization movement 89, 113, 114
inflation 41, 43–45; and deflation 33n7; high 200n11; inflation–deflation cycle 43, 44, 45; and interest rates 226; moderate 200n11; and postwar economic planning 315, 327, 328, 330, 355; redistribution of wealth 30; war-generated 28–30, 34
"insane gambling casino" financial markets, US 15, 18, 136–146, 365n18, 373; bond market, disequilibrium processes 226, 231, 234; capital investment,

long-term expectations 247; construction industry 147–148; and economic stagnation 146–149; innovation, lack of 147; investment volatility 293–294; methodology and ideology 168, 169; and Schumpeter 273; and secular stagnation 172, 176, 191, 253; short-term speculation 240; stock markets 221, 253; volatility 136, 137; *see also* United States
instability: disequilibrium/destructive disequilibrium 188; endogenously generated movement 15, 165, 270, 285–287; extreme, short-run quasi-model of periods of 15, 269, 271; interest rates 226–232; and long-term expectations 247–257; substantial price 41; wage and price deflation, rapid 12
institutions: appropriate institutional forms, in a democracy 75; regulation of capital accumulation 95–115
interest elasticity of consumption 225
interest rates: autonomous 300; bonds 54, 222, 223, 225, 226–232; classical economic theory 221, 222; deflation-adjusted 139, 142; determination of 228; falling 8, 9, 11; high 59, 118; and inflation 226; instability 226–232; liquidity preference 220n11, 233–234; in London 58; long-term 8, 9, 118, 142, 158n2, 167, 181–182, 241; low *see* low interest rates; moderate 27; negative shocks to AD 14; nominal and real long-term 13; and return to gold standard 36; rising 38, 234; risk-adjusted long-term 8, 9, 158n2; volatility 192, 231; zero 302
International Clearing Union 349
International Monetary Fund (IMF) 9
interwar period 2, 16, 27, 29, 60, 71, 377; Britain's economic problems 98, 116, 119, 121, 123, 169–170; "facts" 167; secular stagnation of *see* stagnation/secular stagnation; writings of 1936 to 1939 313–325
investment: capital *see* capital expenditure/investment; domestic demand 56–57; investment-savings, liquidity-money model *see* IS/LM model; irreversibility 90, 92; low rates of expenditure on 27, 69n2, 167, 207, 316, 374; low spending

on 204–205; public *see* public investment; volatility 248, 256, 263n3, 293
irreversibility: investment 90, 92; labor 92, 99
IS curve 277, 278
IS/LM model 16–17, 165; adopted by Modern Keynesians 16; compatibility with *General Theory* models 269–270; creation by John Hicks 14, 165, 273, 274, 275; falling interest rates 14; Keynes's five models and Modern Keynesian IS/LM and AD/AS analysis 15–16, 269, 272–276; and multiplier concept 270, 281; short-run nature of 15, 16, 32–33, 269; stability 274, 276–281; underemployment equilibriums 161

*Journal of Economic Literature* 2

Kalecki, M. 10, 365n19
"Keynes effect" 217
Keynes, J.M.: advisor to Lloyd George 25; chief representative of British Treasury Department 25; commitment to socialism 4, 52–53, 125; comparison with Churchill 4; death (1946) 25, 30; influence of 1; "Keynes Plan" 337, 338; negotiations with the US 8–9; opposition to capitalism 1–21, 30, 45, 155–156; "vision" of 1919 31, 32; visit to the US 138, 149; writings *see General Theory of Employment, Interest and Money* (*The General Theory*)
"Keynesian Cross" 161, 165, 269
Keynesian revolution, real 50, 70, 361
Keynes–Minsky model 233, 240, 377
Krugman, P. 19, 191, 270
Kuznets, S. 293

labor: full employment 96; irreversibility 92, 99; labor movement/transfer 68, 98–99; labor–management–state relations 87–88; markets *see* labor markets; redundant 100; unemployment 104; *see also* full employment; high unemployment; unemployment
labor markets 11, 57, 64, 210, 213, 219n4; labor market policy 49, 87
labor unions 49, 60n2, 214, 316

Labour Party, Britain 6, 53, 62n15, 80, 86, 292, 323; Annual Conference 128; "doctrinaire State Socialism" 77, 101, 125
laissez-faire policies 1, 2, 5, 7–8, 17, 81, 108, 163, 188, 299, 319; proper economic role of the state 72–75; public investment and state planning 55, 61n11
Lancashire cotton 89, 90
laws of motion 239
Lenin, V. 29–30
Leninism 83n9
Liberal Industrial Inquiry (1928) 95–97, 115n8, 309n3, 320–321, 363n2
Liberal Party, Britain 80–81, 97, 292; Industrial Inquiry (1928) *see* Liberal Industrial Inquiry (1928); and Keynes 84–85, 87, 115n7; Liberal Industrial Committee 87; "Liberalism and Industry" speech to (1927) 84–85; *The Nation and Athenaeum* 48, 122, 134n3; *Orange Book* 110; Summer School 134n3, 295; trusts and combinations, attitudes to 86–87; "Yellow Book" *see Britain's Industrial Future* (BIF), Liberal Party manifesto
Liberal Socialism 1–21, 33, 82, 198, 207, 324, 350, 374; anti-capitalist dimensions 9; economic policy agenda 6–11; essays from 1931 to 1932 124–134; government postwar economic planning for 4, 326–365; and inequality 300; investment planning, by state 2, 3, 6, 8, 48–62; Keynes's support for in *The General Theory* 170; Labour Party policies contrasted 6; and Mainstream Keynesian Theory 17–20; origins of Keynes's ideas 4; pursuit of full employment under 95–115; radical policy views of Keynes 300, 307; replacement of capitalism with, Keynes's hopes for 2, 3–4, 11, 16, 276, 288, 368; Soviet Union polices contrasted 6; sustained prosperity resulting from, belief in 16; and US postwar political economy 18; *see also* socialism
"Liberalism and Labour" (1926) 80, 86
liquid assets 28, 193–194, 217, 226, 294
liquid stock market, "dilemma" created by 260–262

liquidity preference theory: and behavior of US interest rates in the late 1920s/early 1930s 233–234, 236; bond market, disequilibrium processes 229, 231, 233–234, 236, 237n12, 280; and endogenously generated movement 286; impact on interest rates 220n11; "insane gambling casino" financial markets, US 136, 137, 142; radical policy views of Keynes 296; secular stagnation 184, 186, 194
liquidity premium 193, 194, 199
liquidity trap 198
Lloyd George, D. 25, 60, 82, 87, 88, 95, 96, 104
LM curve 217, 266; bond market, disequilibrium processes 228, 238n13; critique by Hicks 279, 289n4; and IS/LM model 273–276, 279, 281, 282, 283; vertical 276
Local Loans Fund 105, 114n3
"Long-Term Problem of Full Employment" 340
low interest rates 6, 375; bond market, disequilibrium processes 228; business cycle theory 267; capital accumulation, regulation 102, 105; immediate prewar period 313, 314, 315; "insane gambling casino" financial markets, US 142; IS/LM model, compatibility of Keynes's theories with 275; methodology and ideology 170; and radical policy views of Keynes 130, 132, 292, 297, 302, 303, 309n1; self-sufficiency 156; stagnation/secular stagnation 198, 200n4, 207; during World War II 358, 360; *see also* interest rates
Lowenstein, G. 259
Lucas, R. 213, 259

MacDonald, R. 48, 149
Macmillan, H. 114, 130
Macmillan Committee 119, 162; Report 158n1
macro planning 315
macroeconomics 84, 171n8, 291, 339; countercyclical policy 17, 18, 169–170; macroeconomic stimulus 49, 98–99; outcomes 40, 203; policy 17, 100; public investment and state planning 49, 50; relevance of Keynes's work for modern problems 370, 372; stagnation/secular stagnation 205, 208n2; *see also* economics
macro-policy analysis, comparative static 276–281
Mainstream Keynesian theory 11, 12, 371; agent choice theory omitted 13; classical economic theory compared 14–15; growth models 17; and Keynes's theory 12; and Liberal Socialism 17–20; methodology and ideology 169; need for restoring key omitted aspects 371–374; out-of-equilibrium dynamic processes assumed 14, 162; policy perspective 5; positivism 71, 82n3, 163, 169; and relevance of Keynes's work for modern economic problems 372, 373; *see also* classical economic theory; Modern Keynesian theory
managed capitalism 108
managed trade 9
marginal cost 93, 211, 212
marginal efficiency of capital *see* mec (marginal efficiency of capital)
marginal product of labor (MPL) *see* MPL (marginal product of labor)
marginal propensity to consume *see* mpc (marginal propensity to consume)
marginal propensity to save (mps) 177, 270
Martin, K. 321, 322, 323–324
Marx, K. 10, 26, 81, 174, 212, 219n6, 268n2, 366
Meade, J. 327, 334–340, 343–351, 353
"The Means to Prosperity" 131
mec (marginal efficiency of capital) 7, 9; behaviorally determined variables 220n11; business cycle theory 267; Chapter 12 of *The General Theory* 240, 244–246, 256, 257, 262n3; collapsing 266, 283; confidence-adjusted 298; declining 138, 179, 180, 182–183, 200n3, 208n1, 219n7, 268n1, 299, 309; and deflation 216, 220n11; expectations, long-term 251, 262n3; falling 167, 175–176, 179, 180, 183, 196, 199, 315; formal definition 262n3; high 185; and long-term interest rates 181–182, 241; low 181, 183, 186; methodology and ideology 166; secular stagnation

173, 175–177, 179, 180, 185–187, 193, 195, 201; zero-rated 300; *see also* capital; mpc (marginal propensity to consume); mps (marginal propensity to save)
mercantilism 187–188
methodology and ideology 72; assumption set 71, 162–165; classical economic theory, Keynes's opposition to 161–171; realism and completeness of assumption set 162–165; required to study capitalist economies 369–391; validity of derived hypotheses 162–165
micro theory *see* agent choice theory
mining industry 67–68
Minsky, H. 14, 28, 39, 142, 168, 194, 200n8, 287, 289, 370, 373; Keynes–Minsky model 233, 240, 377
Modern Keynesian theory 16, 17, 163, 262n3, 284; and classical economic theory 11–17; IS/LM and AD/AS analysis 272–276
Moggridge, D.E. 83n7, 96, 97, 116, 123
monetary policy 35–38, 45, 58, 313, 358; expansionary 48, 53, 190; fluctuations 238n19; objectives 38; optimal 53; postwar 358; radical policy views 297, 298, 300; relevance of Keynes's work for modern problems 374, 375; tightening 267
"money": defining 235–236, 237n7; "money illusion" 12, 215; risk-free 262
money wages 12, 36–37, 43, 47n12, 64, 199; cutting, falling or reducing 67, 68; and deflation 64, 211, 212, 214–216, 218; gold standard, return to (1925) 64, 67, 68; *see also* nominal wages; real wages; wage deflation
monopolies 56, 322; capital accumulation, regulation 101, 107; and combination 73, 113; economic role of the state 74, 83n7, 84; natural 61n7; private 112; *see also* oligopolies
morbid psychology 142, 143
Mosley, O. 60; Manifesto 122–123
mpc (marginal propensity to consume) 20n4, 170n4, 216; declining 175, 176, 199, 283, 377; high 293; increasing 204, 299, 374; low 168, 175, 186; methodology and ideology 166; and multiplier concept 186, 204, 293,
371, 374, 377; stagnation/secular stagnation 173, 175, 176, 177, 186; variable 293; *see also* mec (marginal efficiency of capital); mps (marginal propensity to save); multiplier, investment
MPL (marginal product of labor) 210, 212, 213, 219n2, 219n7, 220n13
mps (marginal propensity to save) 177, 270; *see also* mec (marginal efficiency of capital); mpc (marginal propensity to consume)
Muir, Ramsey 96
multiplier, investment 20n4, 61n5, 110, 319; and AD theory 50–51; formalization of 131; IS/LM model 270, 281; low value 168; methodology and ideology 168; and mpc 186, 204, 293, 371, 374, 377; postwar economic planning 336, 354; public investment 293; radical policy views of Keynes 117, 121, 133, 135n5, 293; stagnation/secular stagnation 175, 177, 181, 183, 185, 186, 204, 207
Mussolini, B. 153

Napoleonic Wars 28, 40
*The Nation* 53, 54, 56
*The Nation and Athenaeum* 48, 122, 134n3
National Debt 105
"National Income and Expenditure After the War" (Keynes and Stone) 330
National Investment Board *see* Board of National Investment, proposed
"National Self-Sufficiency" 2–3, 4, 46n4, 138, 152–158, 377; radical policy views of Keynes 305, 306
nationalization 9, 76, 316, 317, 365n20; of Bank of England 297, 361, 375
natural monopolies 61n7
negative shocks 14, 222, 223, 257
neoclassical theories 90, 163, 173, 200n3; agent choice theory 13, 168, 258–259; *see also* classical economic theory; classical economic theory, Keynes's opposition to
neoliberalism, Keynes's opposition to 19
New Deal, US 17, 316
New School for Social Research, New York 139–140

*New Statesman, The* 2
nominal wages 11–12, 36, 55, 215, 217; in the United States 148, 211; *see also* real wages; wage deflation
"Notes on Mercantilism, Etc," 187

O'Donnell, R., "Keynes's Socialism" 3–4
old order, dissolution 25–26, 33
oligarchies 375
oligopolies: capital accumulation, regulation 101, 107, 108; economic role of the state 73, 74, 84, 86–87; public investment and state planning 56; *see also* monopolies
orthodox theory 11, 53, 72–74, 208n2, 291, 367; *see also* classical economic theory; classical economic theory, Keynes's opposition to
out-of-equilibrium processes 14, 162, 223; IS/LM model 274, 276; *see also* disequilibrium/destructive disequilibrium; equilibrium

Paris Peace Conference (1919) 25
Parliamentary Companies 102–103
perfect competition 71, 93, 211–212
Piketty, T. 33n6, 200n5
planning: investment 2, 3, 6, 8, 48–62; postwar economic planning 326–365
*The Political Quarterly* 124
Pollard, S. 20n1, 59, 110–113; *The Development of the British Economy* 110
positivism 71, 82n3, 163, 169
postwar economic planning 4, 18, 326–365; construction spending 329; income and employment 330–331, 363n5; Keynes's proposals in 1945 359–360; long-term 329; public investment 328; reconstruction 328; Steering Committee "Post-War Employment Policy" report (1944) 353, 354; War Cabinet, Economic Section 327, 334, 341, 342, 350, 352; "White Paper on Employment Policy" (1944) 356
pound: overvalued 29, 59, 64, 170n6; parity with dollar 59; rise in value of 65, 66
Prescott, E. 213
price deflation 12, 15–16, 64, 197; from 1919 to early 1920s 45, 47n12; asset price 12; disequilibrium/destructive disequilibrium 15–16, 36, 64, 67, 138, 269, 271, 289; effects 209–220; falling bond prices 14; "insane gambling casino" financial markets, US 138; low prices 35, 91; methodology and ideology 162, 165; rapid 12; and unemployment/high unemployment 215, 235, 271
prices: bonds 12–14, 229; deflation *see* price deflation; financial assets 14; market liquidity and price volatility 170n7; price-adjusted wage 12; rise in 14; security 137, 138, 254–255, 290n5; substantial instability 41; unexpected changes 42; volatility 143, 170n7, 194, 226
principle of effective demand 176
production–employment cycle 43
profit rates 296
profitability 52, 63, 175, 179, 185, 207, 251, 287, 321
profits: constraints on 56; expected flows 262n3, 263n3; future/prospective 11, 26, 245, 248, 256, 274, 277; immediate 249; long-term expectations 247, 252; non-profit organizations 20, 77, 95; normal 91–93; private motive 77, 101, 102, 108, 179; for-profit industries 96; rates of *see* rate of profit; subsidies 88; windfall 41
"Properties of Interest and Money" 183
prosperity, cumulative 50, 52, 54, 173
"The Public and the Private Concern" (1927) 95
public concerns 102, 105–106, 107
public corporations 6, 111–112, 128, 324n3, 368; capital accumulation, regulation 107, 110–114, 114n5; proper economic role of the state 75–77
public debt 51
public investment: and aggregate demand (AD) 10; debt-financed 149; defense of effectiveness 209–210; expenditure 118; and full employment 302; large-scale 56–58, 132; Liberal Socialism 2, 3, 6, 8, 48–62; multiplier 293; postwar economic planning 328, 360; preferred economic policy of Keynes 182–183; secular trend 342;

394  *Index*

semi-public 6, 8, 129, 324n3, 360; size 129; state control/planning 48–62, 99
public utilities 76, 130, 204, 226, 297; capital accumulation, regulation 103, 111; and immediate prewar period 314, 324n3; "insane gambling casino" financial markets and secular stagnation, US 142, 146; and public investment 6, 53, 61n7; and relevance of Keynes's work for modern problems 375, 376
public works 3, 51, 55, 61n6, 293, 344, 346
Public Works Administration program 133

Quantity Theory of Money 223, 227
*Quarterly Journal of Economics* (QJE) 136, 229, 266, 278, 286; "insane" financial markets of the 1920s/1930s, US 241–243, 245; Keynes's defense of *The General Theory* (1937) 266; long-term expectations 242, 243; secular stagnation 192, 198

radical policy views of Keynes 3, 44–45; efforts to gain support for 116–135; financial fragility thesis 132, 298, 299; in *The General Theory* 291–310; and low interest rates 130, 132, 292, 297, 302, 303, 309n1; monetary policy 297, 298, 300; and multiplier concept 117, 121, 133, 135n5, 293; "National Self-Sufficiency" lecture (1933) 152; relevance for current economies 374–378
radical uncertainty 13, 15, 372; and long-term expectation formation 241–245
rate of profit 69n2, 175, 177–182, 185, 186, 221; actual 187, 264, 265, 278; on capital/capital accumulation 8, 9, 62n13, 118, 167, 172, 179–180, 183, 200n3, 270, 287, 297, 304; decline in 167, 183, 188, 202, 265, 266, 268n1, 270, 282, 341, 360, 374; expected 40, 175, 178, 186, 187, 223–224, 235, 264, 270, 277, 282, 290n4, 290n7, 296, 374; high 167; investments 27, 52, 53, 56, 57, 119, 179, 189, 201, 239, 240, 253, 286, 297, 341, 360, 364n11, 369; low, on capital 8, 118, 172; rise in 264, 286, 336; zero 180–182, 187,

237n2, 297, 302, 329, 340, 360; *see also* profitability; profits
rational agent choice, classical/neoclassical theories 13, 168, 258–259
real assets 193–199, 256, 284
real money supply, rising 217
real wages 12, 47n12, 69, 229n10; deflation 212, 215; fall in 13, 20n8, 36, 55, 64, 148, 210–214, 218, 219n2, 219n8, 220n17, 222; high 154; rising 212, 219n7; *see also* money wages; nominal wages; wage deflation
"regime of money contract" 139, 140
rentier class 9, 10, 42, 43, 78, 297; "euthanasia of the rentier" 62n17
Ricardo, D. 164, 308
Robbins, L. 122
Robin Hood tax 295
Robinson, A. 358
Robinson, J. 70, 245
Roosevelt, F.D. 17, 133, 316, 317, 332–333
ruling elites 29, 33n6, 63, 74, 373
Russia *see* Soviet Union

Sargent, T. 213
Say's Law 11, 46n8, 215, 219n6, 223, 224, 301
Schumpeter, J. 4–5, 16, 31–32, 82n4, 91, 114n6; creative destruction 219n6; and "insane gambling casino" financial markets, US 136, 145; and models in *The General Theory* compared with IS/LM model 272, 273; pre-analytic vision 164, 273
Second World War *see* World War II
secular stagnation *see* stagnation/secular stagnation
security prices 138, 254–255, 290; security-price volatility theory 137
semi-autonomy 75
semi-public investment projects 6, 8, 129, 324n3, 360
Shaw, G.B. 291
Shocks *see* exogenous shocks; negative shocks
Sidney Ball Lecture, Oxford (1924) 70
sinking funds 51, 105, 177
Skidelsky, R. 36–39, 44–45, 48, 58, 79, 97, 327, 334–335, 363n4, 364n9, 364n13
slump, financial 147
social class 69, 307; working classes 1, 33n2, 68, 313

social welfare system 21n13, 331
socialism 2, 5, 18, 19, 38; in Britain 123; democratic 11, 124, 190, 303, 318, 378n1; goal of 4, 125; Keynes's commitment to 4, 52–53, 125; practical 123; State socialism 60, 77, 101, 322; "true socialism of the future" 52–53, 130; *see also* Liberal Socialism; State socialism
Society for Socialist Inquiry 124
Soviet Union 6, 157–158, 191; Five-Year Plan 126, 128; Soviet-style planning 38, 62n15, 103, 125, 127
Spanish Civil War 313
specialization, international 155
speculation 37, 42, 46n3, 97, 146, 150n3, 257; in Britain 295; defining 256; in the late 1920s and 1930s 248; short-term 240; speculative bubble of 1919–1920 93n2; in the United States 255, 295
stability: equilibrium 12, 15, 188, 209; exchange rates 26, 195; exogenous shocks and comparative statics 281–284; in *The General Theory* 276–281; in IS/LM model 274, 276–281; and legitimacy of comparative static macro-policy analysis 276–281; long-term, of employment 364n14; long-term expectations and instability 247–257; stable equilibrium with high unemployment 12, 15, 269; *see also* instability
stagnation/secular stagnation 15–17, 26, 31, 138, 172–208, 324n6; evaluating accuracy of Keynesian theory 190–192; Galton Lecture (1937) 8, 28, 202, 242, 270; Keynes's views on 8, 138, 166, 201–208; link with casino financial markets 172, 176, 191, 253; long-term 16, 20, 25, 147, 166, 186, 188, 190, 270, 272, 276, 371, 372; low interest rates 198, 200n4, 207; mec (marginal efficiency of capital) 173, 175–177, 179, 180, 187, 201; methodology and ideology 165, 171n9; model in *The General Theory* 270; and multiplier concept 175, 177, 181, 183, 185, 186, 204, 207; priority of in *The General Theory* 172–200; in United States 146–149
"The State and Industry" 125

State socialism 60, 101, 322; Labour Party 77, 101, 103, 125
state, the: institutions used to regulate capital accumulation 95–115; investment planning, in Liberal Socialism 2, 3, 6, 8, 48–62; new economic role 84–94; peacetime economic role, postwar increase 18; proper economic role 70–83; semi-autonomy within 75
static models 198, 199, 270, 272, 275; comparative static analysis 162, 170n2, 183, 194, 209, 216, 276–285; exercises, comparative static analysis 209, 216; exogenous shocks and comparative statics 281–285; legitimacy of comparative static macro-policy analysis 276–281
sterling *see* pound
stock markets: bond market, disequilibrium processes 221, 237n6; as "gambling casinos" 221, 253; liquid stock market, "dilemma" created by 260–262; volatile price movements 252
Stone, R. 330
structural unemployment 49, 50, 54, 348
subsidies 88, 314
Summers, L. 19, 170n8, 191, 270
"Sundry Observations on the Nature of Capital" 179–180

takeovers 250
tariffs 89, 120, 154
taxation policies 6, 10, 17, 20n4, 41–42, 117, 190, 237n1, 354; cutting tax 338–340; "death" tax 299, 302; direct tax 302; economic role of the state 96; and full employment 109; gold standard, return to (1925) 68–69; income tax 299, 301, 342, 361; indirect 354; inheritance tax 302; personal tax rates 339; progressive 10, 190, 303, 374, 375; raising tax 131, 301, 314, 339, 340; rates of tax 299, 339; substantial financial transactions 295; surtax 301; tax system 335, 342, 353; transfer tax 295; wealth tax 29, 36, 361
time series data 204–205
Tobin, J. 250
Tobin tax 295

Tobin's q theory of investment 262, 263n6
totalitarianism 128, 318
*Tract on Monetary Reform* 30, 35, 37, 39–46, 59, 61n4, 91, 210, 218
Trade Facilities Act, Britain 61n8, 105, 114n4
trade unions 49, 60n2, 214, 316
transaction costs, low 193, 232, 248, 261, 262
*Treatise on Money* 136–137, 154, 237n6, 364n12
*Treatise on Probability* 73
Treaty of Versailles 25, 154
Trump, D. 19

uncertainty: and bonds 221, 226–232; fundamental 73, 240, 243, 258–259; and interest rate instability 226–232; radical *see* radical uncertainty
unemployment 8, 60n2, 104; chronic nature 324n6; export industries 66, 99; of 5 percent or less 330–331; high-unemployment long-run equilibrium *see* stagnation/secular stagnation; low 8, 17, 49, 267, 293; rates of 18, 130, 138, 150n1, 330–331; "reserve army" of unemployed workers, elimination of 10, 174, 212; stable equilibrium with high unemployment 12, 15; structural 49, 50, 54, 348; in the United States 17, 149; wage and price deflation 12
United Kingdom *see* Britain
United States: armed forces 17; boom of late 1920s 136, 138, 187, 260, 264, 267, 278, 298; business cycle theory 168; capitalism in 1; collapse of stock market and subsequent crisis (from 1929) 12, 116, 136–139, 141, 169, 234, 264, 269, 288, 365n18; economic stagnation in 146–149, 177–178; financial structure 140; "insane gambling casinos," financial markets seen as *see* "insane gambling casino" financial markets, US; interest rates and liquidity preference theory (late 1920s/early 1930s) 233–234; Keynes's preferred policies for 316–317; Keynes's visit to 138, 149; managerial firm 250; McCarthyism 371; negotiations with Keynes 8–9; New Deal 17, 316; New School for Social Research,

New York 139–140; nominal wages in 148, 211; population growth, fall in 147; postwar political economy 18; security prices 138; stock market 221; Trumanism 371; unemployment rates 17, 149

volatility 171n8, 240, 256, 271; financial markets 136, 137, 269, 294, 295, 298, 365n18; "insane gambling casino" financial markets, US 136, 137; interest rates 192, 231; investment 248, 256, 263n3, 293; prices 143, 170n7, 194, 226

wage deflation 11–12, 16, 140, 165, 209–220; cuts 218; disequilibrium/destructive disequilibrium 15–16, 36, 47n12, 64, 67, 269, 271, 289; raising AS 15; rapid 12; real wages 13, 20n8, 36, 55, 64, 148, 210–214, 218, 219n2, 219n8, 220n17, 222; and unemployment/high unemployment 215, 235, 271
wages *see* money wages; nominal wages; real wages; wage deflation
"Wall Street" 246
Walrasian general equilibrium model 20n8, 82n5, 224, 289n2
War Cabinet, Economic Section 327, 334, 341, 342, 350, 352
war debt/finance 34, 58, 62n16, 139, 320
White, H.D. 8–9, 365n19
"White Paper on Employment Policy" (1944) 356
working classes 1, 33n2, 68, 313
World Economic Conference 152
World War II: and full employment 17, 324n4; Keynes's writings prior to 313–325; postwar economic planning during (1939–1945) 326–365; postwar economic structure 18; war debt/finance 34, 58, 62n16
writings: "Am I A Liberal?" 80, 82n1, 212; *Collected Writings of John Maynard Kaynes* (CW) 1, 84, 116; "Concluding Notes on the Social Philosophy towards Which the General Theory Might Lead" 300–301; "Does Unemployment Need a Drastic Remedy?" 48, 70, 109; "A Drastic Remedy for

Unemployment" 54; "The Economic Consequences of Mr. Churchill" 33n5, 50, 59, 62n14, 63; *The Economic Consequences of the Peace* 20, 25, 31, 32, 34, 40, 109, 166, 167, 185, 372; *Essays in Persuasion* 70, 93; *General Theory of Employment, Interest and Money (The General Theory) see General Theory of Employment, Interest and Money (The General Theory)*; *How to Pay for the War* 326; "The Inducement to Invest" 239; "Liberalism and Industry" 84–85; "Liberalism and Labour" 80, 86; "Long-Term Problem of Full Employment" 340; "The Means to Prosperity" 131; "National Income and Expenditure After the War" (Keynes and Stone) 330; "National Self-Sufficiency" 2–3, 4, 46n4, 152–158, 305, 306, 377; "Notes on Mercantilism, Etc" (*The General Theory*) 187; "Properties of Interest and Money" (*The General Theory)* 183; "Sundry Observations on the Nature of Capital" (*The General Theory*) 179–180; *Tract on Monetary Reform* 30, 35, 37, 39–46, 59, 61n4, 91, 218; *Treatise on Money* 136–137, 154, 237n6, 364n12; *Treatise on Probability* 73; *see also* evolution of Keynes's ideas, writings on